WHAT
YOUR
BIRTHDAY
REVEALS
ABOUT
YOU

WHAT
YOUR
BIRTHDAY
REVEALS
ABOUT
YOU

366 Days of Astonishingly Accurate
Revelations about Your Future, Your Secrets,
and Your Strengths

PHYLLIS VEGA

CASTLE BOOKS

This edition published in 2007 by

Castle Books ®

A division of Book Sales, Inc.
276 Fifth Ave., Suite 206
New York, NY 10001

This edition published by arrangement with and permission of

Quayside Publishing Group

33 Commercial Street
Gloucester, MA 01930

Text © 2005 by Phyllis Vega

First published in the USA in 2005 by Fair Winds Press,
a member of Quayside Publishing Group,
33 Commercial Street, Gloucester, MA 01930

Library of Congress Cataloging-in-Publication Data available

Book design by Laura H. Couallier, Laura Herrmann Design
Cover illustrations by Mark Hannon

ISBN-13: 978-0-7858-2238-7
ISBN-10: 0-7858-2238-0

Printed in the United States of America

"There was a star danced, and under that I was born."

— William Shakespeare, *Much Ado About Nothing*

Dedication

To my daughters Debra and Sharon,
granddaughter Yesenia, and grandson Alexis

And in loving remembrance of Beth Cunningham
December 31, 1950 – April 13, 2004

Table of Contents

PART THREE: The 366 Birthdays of the Year 61

How to Use This Book

> "A thing born of a moment has
> all the qualities of that moment."
>
> — Carl Jung

Your birthday is more than just the day of the year you were born. Each day in the yearly cycle emits distinct vibrations and contains its own unique characteristics. The influence of your day of birth is one of the dynamics that distinguishes you from other people. It's a defining factor in who you are and who you hope to become.

What Your Birthday Reveals about You is an easy-to-use handbook that explores the particular forces at work on the day you were born. It is user friendly, so you won't have to do any tedious calculations. Your birth date (or someone else's) is the only key you need to unlock the secrets of your own or another individual's true potential.

This book is a lively, up-to-date guide to self-awareness and an appreciation of your place in the cosmic scheme of things. It provides fresh insight into character, personality, temperament, relationships, and prospects for success. *What Your Birthday Reveals about You* draws on the symbolism of astrology, numerology, mythology, tarot, and historical events to give you a better understanding of your own inclinations and capabilities, as well as those of your significant other, friends, relatives, and associates.

The book is divided into three sections. Part One, The Twelve Signs of the Zodiac, includes introductory information about the Sun signs and a description of each solar type. The twelve astrological profiles are divided into three sub-headings: The Myth (a tale from mythology that conveys the symbolic meaning of the zodiacal sign), Character and

Personality, and Relationships. Part Two, The Nine Basic Numbers, provides a brief introduction to the single-digit (root) number derived from your birth date, as well as a numerological profile for each of the nine root numbers. Part Three, The 366 Birthdays of the Year, gives a comprehensive reading for each birth date, including a brief list of observances and noteworthy birthdays associated with that day. Each birthday profile contains a plethora of information to help the person born on that day maximize his or her natural abilities in ways that are truly challenging and meaningful.

I hope you enjoy discovering what your birthday reveals about you!

Phyllis Vega

Part One

*The Twelve Signs
of the Zodiac*

I n this section of *What Your Birthday Reveals about You,* I'll present each of the twelve signs of the zodiac and discuss them in detail. But before we start, there are a few things with which you should become more familiar: the signs themselves, of course, as well as how the signs are grouped into three Qualities and four Elements and what these Qualities and Elements represent.

Born on the Cusp?

The dates given in the Sun Sign Chart (on the following page) are only an approximation, because the Sun does not enter each of the signs on the same day or at the same time every year. If you were born on a cusp (a day when the Sun changes signs), you will need to determine which sign the Sun was in at the time you were born.

As long as you know your time of birth, you can get an accurate horoscope chart. There are several Internet sites, such as AstroDienst (www.astro.com), where you may obtain a free copy of your chart. Or, for a nominal fee, you can order a copy of your natal chart from the professional chart makers at Astro Communications Services in San Diego, California, 800-888-9983.

If you were born on a cusp day and don't know your exact birth time, you may never know for sure which sign is the correct one. In this case, you should read the interpretation for the adjacent Sun sign as well as the one for your birthday to see which one is a better fit.

Sun Sign Chart

ARIES

(Cardinal, Fire),
March 21–April 19

TAURUS

(Fixed, Earth),
April 20–May 20

GEMINI

(Mutable, Air),
May 21–June 20

CANCER

(Cardinal, Water),
June 21–July 22

LEO

(Fixed, Fire),
July 23–August 22

VIRGO

(Mutable, Earth),
August 23–September 22

LIBRA

(Cardinal, Air),
September 23–October 22

SCORPIO

(Fixed, Water),
October 23–November 21

SAGITTARIUS

(Mutable, Fire),
November 22–December 21

CAPRICORN

(Cardinal, Earth),
December 22–January 20

AQUARIUS

(Fixed, Air),
January 21–February 18

PISCES

(Mutable, Water),
February 19–March 20

The Sign Groupings in Astrology

The signs of the zodiac are divided up in a number of different ways. The principal divisions are the three *Qualities* (the Triplicities), which represent types of activities, and the four *Elements* (the Quadruplicities), which represent tendencies of temperament. The Qualities are Cardinal, Fixed, and Mutable, and the Elements are Fire, Earth, Air, and Water.

THE QUALITIES

Cardinal: Aries, Cancer, Libra, Capricorn

Cardinal signs initiate action (then often lose interest). They tend to be active, independent, social, and outgoing.

Fixed: Taurus, Leo, Scorpio, Aquarius

Fixed signs stabilize and preserve what has been started. They tend to be constant, reliable, and determined, but also stubborn, inflexible, and resistant to change.

Mutable: Gemini, Virgo, Sagittarius, Pisces

Mutable signs diffuse and pass on what has been started and stabilized. They tend to be flexible, resourceful, adaptable, and quick to learn, but they are also changeable and easily swayed away from their purpose.

THE ELEMENTS

Fire: Aries, Leo, Sagittarius

Fire signs are active, energetic, courageous, idealistic, self-sufficient, and dynamic. Their initiative, vision, and need to be in charge push them toward positions of leadership.

Earth: Taurus, Virgo, Capricorn

Earth signs are practical, definite, cautious, pragmatic, and good at managing people and things. Their need for stability and security keeps them down to earth and focused on the material world.

Air: Gemini, Libra, Aquarius

Air signs are intellectual, communicative, social, and articulate. Their need to acquire, understand, communicate, and compare information prompts them to use, share, and apply what they know.

Water: Cancer, Scorpio, Pisces

Water signs are sensitive, emotional, intuitive, romantic, and fruitful. Their need to feel rather than think makes them psychic, creative, fluid, and changeable.

Aries
The Pioneer

♈

Planetary Ruler: **Mars**
Symbol: **The Ram**
Color: **Red**
Metal: **Iron**
Gemstone: **Diamond**

Character and Personality

Ariens are the pioneers and initiators of the zodiac. Your astrological symbol is the ram, and you're as high-spirited and assertive as a young ram. Aries likes winning and wants to be *first* in everything. Aries natives live for excitement and adventure, so patience is definitely not one of your virtues.

Like the ram, you're quick to anger, yet you are just as quick to forgive and forget. Your enthusiasm sometimes gets the better of you, and you're often accused of running roughshod over other people's feelings and ideas. Fueled by adrenaline and the energy of fire, you prefer taking the initiative instead of waiting around for something to happen. When life gets too quiet, you get antsy and begin searching for ways to stir things up.

Relationships

Nothing is hidden in the Aries personality—what people see is what they get. In love and friendship, you are direct in your approach and honest in your responses. When you see somebody who interests you, you pull out all the stops and go after that person. Although your fragile ego is easily wounded by rejection, you don't hold grudges. You may pitch a fit if someone hurts your feelings, but once you've finished screaming and hollering, you'll shrug off your disappointment and forget all about it.

Rams are not loners, yet despite your natural sociability, you resent having restrictions placed on your personal freedom. You have a generous, caring nature, yet you patently refuse to compromise either your independence or your ideals. You're ardent, loving, passionate, and extremely loyal to those you love, but you can be rash and impulsive when the spirit moves you. If a relationship or job becomes intolerably boring, dull, or routine, you're capable of leaving without so much as a backward glance.

The Myth

Athena, patroness of Athens, is the Greek goddess of wisdom, military victory, and handicrafts. She's the daughter of Zeus (the Roman Jupiter) and his first wife Metis, the Titaness who presides over reason and knowledge. According to one of the most popular stories of Athena's birth, when Zeus found out that Metis was pregnant, he visited the oracle at Delphi, who prophesied that Metis' child would dethrone him. The king of the gods did not take this prediction lightly, because that was exactly what he had done to his father and what his father had done to his grandfather.

Determined not to lose his throne, Zeus playfully challenged Metis to a game of shape changing. When Metis changed into a fly, Zeus opened his mouth and swallowed her. Zeus obviously thought that would be the end of the matter. However, things did not go according to plan, and swallowing Metis did nothing to stop her baby from being born.

Day and night, Metis hammered away inside Zeus's head, fashioning a helmet. The constant hammering gave Zeus unbearable headaches. One day, while resting, he developed the worst headache of all. It was so bad that he told the god Hephaestus (Vulcan) to crack his skull open with an ax. When Hephaestus did as he was commanded, Athena popped out fully grown and wearing battle armor that included the brilliant helmet. Since Metis had not actually given birth to Athena, Zeus got to keep his throne, and his beautiful, gray-eyed daughter became her father's favorite.

Taurus
The Collector

Planetary Ruler: **Venus**
Symbol: **The Bull**
Color: **Green**
Metal: **Copper**
Gemstone: **Emerald**

Character and Personality

Taurus is the most grounded of the twelve zodiac signs. Abstract ideas hold little fascination for you; your focus is on security and the practical necessities of life. Unlike Aries, who is drawn by love of the game and the desire to win, you are a lot more interested in the game's rewards. Reliability is your trademark, and your determination, stability, and quiet strength tend to inspire trust in others. You view broken promises and betrayals of any type as threats to your security, and you don't take kindly to disappointment.

Bulls are typically stubborn and impervious to change. You prefer doing things at your own pace and rarely welcome innovations not of your own making. Comfort is your main concern. You like being surrounded by pleasing, soothing things and people. Above all, you enjoy the sensual pleasures. Especially fine food, drink, art, music, and a happy home and harmonious love life.

Relationships

Most Taureans are deeply passionate, yet somewhat shy and reserved. Most of what you feel takes place beneath the surface, and your approach to love and romance is decidedly more passive than aggressive. You'd much rather sit back and wait for others to come to you, and they usually do.

When you do decide to take the bull by the horns and make the first move, you're subtle in your approach. You may be the consummate romantic, but you'll think long and hard before making a serious, long-term commitment. However, once you do commit, you expect to maintain the status quo and find it really difficult to let go. You'd rather hang on to a worn-out love affair than deal with the discomfort of ending it and starting over with someone new.

The Myth

King Minos, who attained the Cretan throne with the aid of the sea god Poseidon (Neptune), aspired to mastery of the Mediterranean and, once again, appealed to the god for assistance. After preparing for a sacrifice to Poseidon, Minos prayed for a bull to emerge from the sea. The obliging Olympian god sent a beautiful snow-white bull, which Minos was to sacrifice in return for Poseidon's help. However, when the king saw the magical bull, he decided to keep it and add it to his own herd. Minos reneged on his obligation to Posideon and sacrificed a lesser bull in its place.

The angry god decided to teach the ungrateful king a lesson and asked Aphrodite (Venus), goddess of love, to devise a punishment. Aphrodite caused Minos' queen, Pasifae, to be filled with a great lust for the beautiful bull. Pasifae commissioned the palace's craftsman, Daedalus, to make a wooden bull in which she could disguise herself and mate with the animal. Thus the queen copulated with the bull, was impregnated by it, and gave birth to the Minotaur, a monster with the head of a bull and the body of a man.

When Minos found out about the Minotaur, whose hunger could only be satisfied by human flesh, he ordered the repentant Daedalus to build a suitable cage where the Minotaur could be kept without possibility of escape. Daedalus devised the Labyrinth, an enormous maze, and placed the Minotaur at the center. There the confined beast remained, fed on youths and maidens sent as tribute by the king's vassals, until it was slain by the Greek hero Theseus.

Gemini
The Communicator

♊

Planetary Ruler: **Mercury**
Symbol: **The Twins**
Color: **Yellow**
Metal: **Mercury**
Gemstone: **Agate**

Character and Personality

The typical Gemini native is clever, quick-witted, and often hysterically funny. A great communicator, you can talk your way into or out of anything. Like Hermes (Mercury), the mythological messenger of the gods, twins are swift-moving free spirits. You spend your time rushing from place to place, spreading the latest news and checking into whatever looks most interesting or unusual. You love exchanging thoughts and ideas and rarely pass up a chance to join in a spirited discussion. When life gets too quiet, you may deliberately stir things up in an attempt to make something exciting happen.

You're interested in practically everything but not inclined to delve deeply into any one topic. There's just too much to do, to talk about, and to learn for you to take the time to probe the depths of a single thing. Your attention is quickly caught, and you follow wherever it leads. However, you're easily distracted and likely to go off on a tangent at the drop of a hat. Because you spread yourself so thin, you may garner a reputation for being rather superficial.

Relationships

As the member of a dual sign, you want to be free, but you don't want to be alone. You're prepared to sacrifice some of your freedom in exchange for an enduring relationship. Love is important to you, but friendship and companionship are equally important. Although you thoroughly enjoy romantic encounters, in your mind they will never replace scintillating conversation. Intelligence and humor are more likely to attract and hold your attention than beauty or style.

Twins live mainly in the mind. Emotional displays scare you, and you're uncomfortable dealing with feelings (yours or anyone else's). When you commit to someone, you like to know that you're cared about and appreciated, but you don't want your partner to make a big deal about it.

The Myth

Many of the Gemini myths revolve around sets of twins representing the sign's opposing possibilities. In Greek mythology, there's Zethus and Amphion, the sons of Zeus (Jupiter) and Antiope, queen of Thebes. When the twin boys were born as a result of Antiope's rape by Zeus, her uncle Lycus forced her to expose them on Mount Cithaeron. The boys were saved from certain death by shepherds and raised without any knowledge of their royal origin. Hermes (Mercury) gave Amphion a lyre and taught him to play it, while his brother Zethus hunted and tended the flocks. When they grew up, the twins rescued their mother from the usurper Lycus and assumed their rightful heritage.

Gemini duality can be seen quite clearly in the Celtic tale of the twins Nisien (peaceful) and Efnisien (hostile) as told in the Welsh epic The Mabinogion. Half brothers to the god Bran, Efnisien and Nisien are described as the Bringer of Strife and the Bringer of Peace, respectively. Nisien had great compassion and was the only one who could understand and control his twin, for whom he died to protect during the war with Ireland. An easily insulted troublemaker, Efnisien actually brought on the war by disfiguring King Malthowch's horses, an act of spite Efnisien committed because he was not consulted when Bran promised his sister Branwen in marriage to the Irish king. Yet Efnisien could also be heroic, as he was when he gave his own life to save Bran and the Welsh invaders.

Cancer
The Nurturer

Planetary Ruler: **The Moon**
Symbol: **The Crab**
Color: **Silver**
Metal: **Silver**
Gemstone: **Moonstone**

Character and Personality

The fluctuating moods of Cancer's natives are related to the phases of its ruler, the mysterious, ever-changing Moon. Consequently, you're very sensitive, and when you're feelings are hurt, you'll retreat into your crab's shell and refuse to come out. Closely attuned to your own emotions and those of others, you pick up on what people are feeling. When you become aware of someone's pain, you'll instinctively reach out in an attempt to nurture the sufferer.

As the sign of motherhood, hearth, and home, Cancer relates to family, domesticity, and security. If you're anything like most members of this sign, you're a confirmed homebody, and your own residence may be the only place where you feel totally safe. However, the Moon bestows both a predilection and a fondness for travel, and you may travel a great deal, especially for business.

Cancer belongs to the world of reality as well as the realm of dreams and the unconscious. Cancer is a water sign (imagination), but it is also a cardinal sign (action). Crabs are naturally hard workers, and your shrewdness with money is legendary. Your unremitting search for security extends outward from your home to your workplace, and you're likely to be extremely successful in both venues.

Relationships

In intimate relationships you are an imaginative sweetheart who likes to kiss and cuddle. However, Cancer is a sign of contradictions, and crabs can be difficult to get to know. Although you're romantic and sentimental, you don't give your heart away easily. You'd rather keep your feelings hidden until you're certain they are reciprocated.

When you do find the love and affection you crave, you immediately begin worrying about losing it. Driven by insecurity, your imagination has a way of running away with itself, and you can become extremely jealous and possessive.

The Myth

The Greek demigod Heracles (Hercules) was the son of Zeus (Jupiter) and the mortal woman Alcmene. He was named "glory of Hera" for Zeus's wife, the queen of the Olympian gods. But Hera hated her namesake and sent two serpents to kill the infant in his cradle; Heracles strangled both with his bare hands. Hera would not be deterred, however, and continued to make trouble for Heracles. At one point she caused him to lose his mind, and, in a fit of temporary insanity, he killed his own wife and children. When he awakened from his confused state, the great hero was understandably shocked and upset. He prayed to Apollo, and the god's oracle told Heracles that he must atone for his crime by showing obedience to the Greek king, Eurystheus.

Eurystheus sent Heracles on a journey, during which the hero was to complete twelve nearly impossible labors. If he succeeded, his place among the gods would be assured. The second of the twelve tasks called for the destruction of the Lernean hydra, a monster that was terrorizing the countryside. The hydra was a venomous, nine-headed serpent that had been specifically reared by Hera to fight Heracles.

Heracles traveled to Lerna to hunt the hydra. During the fight, all the animals favored the Greek hero. But, just when Heracles seemed to be gaining the advantage, a giant crab sent by Hera emerged from a cave and managed to get a claw-hold on his foot. Because of this distraction, Heracles nearly lost the battle. Eventually Heracles succeeded in crushing the life from the crab and then went on to defeat the hydra. Nevertheless, Hera was so impressed with the crab's loyalty and courage that she placed its image in the night sky as the constellation Cancer.

Leo
The Ruler

♌

Planetary Ruler: **The Sun**
Symbol: **The Lion**
Color: **Gold**
Metal: **Gold**
Gemstone: **Ruby**

Character and Personality

The Sun-ruled personality is difficult to miss because Leos love dramatizing their experiences. You lions are enthusiastic and ambitious and thrive on excitement and adulation. Never one to shy away from the limelight, you can be found wherever the action is the thickest. Even the most timid pussycat types are actors at heart. Your role is a noble one. You despise anything that's mean or petty. Lions thrive on approval and appreciation. Fame and recognition are infinitely more important to you than money or power.

You feel entitled to the best life has to offer, and you willingly share what you have with others. You'll open your heart and your wallet to anyone in need. As a take-charge kind of person, your self-assurance and sunny optimism inspire confidence in others. However, patience is not your strong suit, and you need to learn to discipline your fiery approach to things. You actually enjoy helping other people manage their lives, but if you're not careful, you can end up trying to run them.

Relationships

Leo's relationships tend to be larger than life. The fifth zodiacal sign is the sign of love and romance, and you won't find many loners born under it. If you're a typical lion, you are in love with the drama that surrounds a romantic relationship.

You are an idealist, and your expectations are so high that you are often disappointed. However, you never stay down in the dumps for long. Your need to always be in love with someone spurs you on in your search for the ideal lover. Once committed, you are ardent, generous, and loyal, and you expect total loyalty in return. Anyone who hurts your pride or undermines your dignity will hear the lion roar.

The Myth

Many of the ancient heroic myths, like the twelve labors of Heracles (Hercules) and the journey of Jason and the Argonauts, are built around the twelve-month passage of the Sun through the zodiacal signs. The ancient Sumerian Epic of Gilgamesh *is another calendar-theme solar myth. The twelve tablets of the Gilgamesh cycle tell of the many feats of the legendary hero/king and are a mirror of the Sun's journey throughout the year.*

Overconfidence, pride, and arrogance have brought about the downfall of more than one would-be solar hero. In Greek mythology, when Clymene told her son Phaethon that his father was Helios, god of the Sun, the boy went to Helios and requested a boon that would remove the stain of his illegitimacy. The god, as a sign of his favor, promised to grant his son's dearest wish. Phaethon asked for permission to drive the chariot of the Sun through the heavens. Bound by his oath, Helios had to allow the boy make the attempt. Too young and inexperienced to successfully drive the chariot across the sky, Phaethon was unable to control the horses. As a result, the Sun came too near the earth and scorched it. To prevent further damage, Zeus (Jupiter) was forced to slay the unfortunate boy with a thunderbolt.

A similar fate came about when Daedalus, master builder and architect of King Minos of Crete, fell from favor and was imprisoned along with his son, Icarus. In an effort to escape, Daedalus fashioned wings of wax and feathers for himself and Icarus and strapped them on. After warning his son not to fly near the Sun lest the wings melt, they took off. Although Daedalus made it safely to Sicily, the exuberant boy ignored his father's warning and flew toward the Sun. As a result, his wings melted and he fell into the sea and drowned.

Virgo
The Organizer

♍

Planetary Ruler: **Mercury**
Symbol: **The Virgin**
Color: **Dark Blue**
Metal: **Nickel**
Gemstone: **Sapphire**

Character and Personality

No sign pays more attention to order and detail than Virgo. Your greatest asset is your logical, inquisitive mind, which makes you a natural critic and something of a perfectionist. The sixth sign is about service, and you can always be counted on to help out in a pinch. You actually enjoy analyzing problems that others find tedious. You'll prod and probe the depths of a situation until you come up with the answers you seek. You're methodical, conscientious, practical, and reliable. However, you are so detail oriented that you can get bogged down in the minutiae of a situation and lose sight of the bigger picture.

Like Gemini natives, who share Mercury's rule, Virgos are excellent communicators. Also, like your Gemini counterpart, you are a restless bundle of nervous energy, constantly on the lookout for things that need doing or situations that need improving. Worry, however, is your number one bugaboo. Members of your sign are unusually health conscious and fastidious about hygiene and cleanliness. You tend to take good care of yourself and may look years younger than your real age. You are acutely aware of the connection between what people eat and how they feel. Despite your predisposition to proper exercise and nutrition, you may suffer from tremendous anxiety with regard to your health.

Relationships

Virgos make loyal, dependable mates who truly care about their loved ones. While you crave love and affection, you also fear rejection and are hesitant about risking your heart. Your critical nature makes it difficult for you to let your hair down. You are likely to get caught up in over-analyzing your romantic relationship instead of just relaxing and enjoying it. You need to learn how to set your mental judgments aside and respond on a purely physical or emotional level. Every once in a while you should try turning off the incessant mental chatter and just live in the moment and celebrate its joys.

The Myth

Virgo is usually depicted as a winged woman holding a palm branch in one hand and an ear of corn or sheath of wheat in the other. The palm symbolizes the passage of time through the year, and the grain relates to the harvest season.

As the only female figure in the zodiac, Virgo has been associated with the goddesses of many cultures. Such diverse deities as Ishtar, Innana, Dike, Ceres, Demeter, Astrea, Erigone, Isis, Tyche, Fortuna, and even the Virgin Mary have at one time or another been put forth as Virgo's celestial representative.

One of the lesser-known Olympian goddesses who is sometimes linked to this sign is Hestia, the Greek goddess of hearth and home. Although she was one of the daughters of the Titans Rhea and Cronos, her duties to the consecrated hearth kept her from mingling with the other gods. On her oath, she remained a maiden and was wedded only to the sacred fire.

Hestia's hearth could be found in the center of every temple honoring the other Greek gods and goddesses. In appreciation of Hestia, attending worshippers often left small gifts of food and drink near the fire. Hestia's hearth could also be found in every home, where, by tradition, it was tended by the maiden daughters of the household.

Hestia's diligence as the goddess of hearth and home is an apt symbol for Virgo's willingness to attend to practical matters and be of service to the community. In people's homes, Hestia signified family unity; at the ever-burning public hearth, known as the prytaneion, she was called Prytantis. It was there that the first fruits, oil, wine, and cows of the harvest were sacrificed to her.

Libra
The Mediator

Planetary Ruler: **Venus**
Symbol: **The Scales**
Color: **Indigo**
Metal: **Bronze**
Gemstone: **Opal**

Character and Personality

Like your sign's symbol, the scales of justice, you are evenhanded and impartial. Libra is about peace and harmony, and more than the other signs, you're inclined to diplomacy and refinement. You abhor conflict and strife and will bend over backwards to avoid controversy. Inherently a team player, you prefer collaboration and cooperation to living or working alone. Venus, your ruling planet, bestows a love of beauty, music, and art. Libra's airy quality imparts a sharp intellect and an attraction to literature, mathematics, and the sciences.

Libra is also a cardinal sign, and its natives are ambitious. Although you're amiable and agreeable, you are no pushover. In fact, your sign is sometimes referred to as "the iron fist in the velvet glove." The typical depiction of Venus-ruled individuals as gentle doves of peace is misleading. Scales are not always in perfect balance—they dip back and forth. Like the scales, you have your ups and downs. And when you are down, you can be as bad-tempered and difficult as any Aries.

Relationships

You think in pairs and may not feel complete without a partner. A true romantic, you thoroughly enjoy the "dance of love." In fact, many of the Venus-ruled actually prefer the courtly rituals of romance to the unbridled passion of earthy sexual encounters. In a committed union, you are a model mate with a knack for doing the right thing at the right time. No other lover knows how to make his or her object of affection feel more adored.

Unfortunately, you can fall *out* of love almost as easily as you fall *in* love. As the member of an air sign, you respond more readily to ideas or ideals than to feelings. When your mate no longer fits your idealized version of a lover, the romance quickly fades.

The Myth

Libra is the only sign of the zodiac symbolized by an inanimate object—the scales. In the northern hemisphere, the constellation appears when the days and nights are equal, signifying balance. The early Greeks did not recognize Libra as the scales. Credit for identifying Libra in this manner is usually given to the Romans, who included this symbol in the Julian calendar. On coins, Julius Caesar was often represented with scales, signifying his authority and sense of justice. Both Julius and his nephew Augustus Caesar were associated with this constellation.

There is an earlier correlation of Libra with the scales that connects both the sign and the symbol to the Babylonian myth of the last judgment and the weighing of the souls. The ancient Hebrews also viewed this group of stars as a balance and called it Moznayim, or scale-beam. In Hawaiian mythology, Libra is called Mahoe Hope and is depicted as the god Hokeo balancing the gourds of truth.

The scales also figure prominently in the mythology of ancient Egypt, where they play a large part in the story of the soul's passage from this life to the next. Anubis, the jackal-headed god, and his brother Apu-at watched over the two roads that led to the underworld. Anubis used the scales to weigh the souls of those who had died and to judge the value of what they had done on earth. The judgment ceremony took place in the Hall of Double Justice, in front of Egypt's gods and goddesses. Anubis weighed the dead person's heart on one side of the scale, balancing it against a feather representing truth. The trial was presided over by Osiris, ruler of the underworld, and the ibis-headed god Thoth, who recorded the results. If the deceased was found worthy, he was admitted to eternal life. If not, his heart was fed to a beast called the Devourer.

Scorpio
The Regenerator

♏

Planetary Ruler: **Pluto**
Symbol: **The Scorpion**
Color: **Dark Red**
Metal: **Steel**
Gemstone: **Topaz**

Character and Personality

Ruled by Pluto, the planet that represents transformation and death, Scorpio is the astrological sign of rebirth and regeneration. Your view of the world is filtered through your emotions. Consequently, other people's ideas have less impact on you than your own gut feelings. You inhabit a black-and-white universe of fixed opinions, and it's virtually impossible to get you to change your mind once it's made up. Your curiosity is immeasurable, and you're constantly probing and prodding the depths to see what lies beneath the surface. Although you prefer to play your own cards close to the chest, you're a great one for ferreting out other people's secrets.

You're highly motivated, strong-willed, and determined. It is always a mistake to count you out, because no matter what the situation, you refuse to give up on your desires. Long after everyone else has abandoned a project, the tenacious scorpion inside you holds on and continues to fight. As a result, you often accomplish things that other people consider impossible.

Relationships

In love and romance, few can resist the power of your magnetic person-ality and captivating sensuality. You may not set out to be mysterious, yet you can be very difficult to get to know and even harder to understand.

You make a loyal and ardent, but demanding, partner. While there is nothing you won't do for the person who has won your heart and your trust, you can nevertheless be stubborn about getting your own way. In your love life, as in everything else, you are rarely spontaneous. All of your moves are well thought out and carefully planned in advance. You know what you want, you're not afraid to go after it, and you won't rest until you get it.

The Myth

The best known of the Scorpio myths portrays the scorpion as the creature that killed Orion the Hunter. In one version of the story, the giant Orion threatened to use his hunting skills to exterminate all the wild beasts in the world. This angered the Moon goddess Artemis (Diana), who, although a huntress herself, was the divine game warden and guardian of pregnant animals and their young. She appealed for help from the Earth's goddess Gaia, who sent a giant scorpion to sting Orion to death.

When Zeus found out what had happened, he placed the hunter and the scorpion in the heavens as the constellations Orion and Scorpio. However, he set them far apart from each other so that Orion would be eternally out of danger. Supposedly this explains why, when Scorpio is rising, chasing after Orion, the hunter is already starting to disappear behind the western horizon.

One of the more provocative tales regarding the scorpion comes from Aesop's Fables: One day a scorpion is walking along a riverbank, trying to find a way to get to the other side. He spies a frog preparing to leap into the river and swim across. The scorpion walks up to the frog and asks to be taken along. The frog, knowing the reputation of scorpions, asks, "If I help you across the river, will you promise not to sting me?" The scorpion quickly replies, "Of course I won't sting you, because if I did, we would both drown." So the frog, satisfied with the answer, tells the scorpion to climb up on his back. Halfway across the river, the scorpion stings the frog, and the dying frog croaks, "Why ever did you do that? Now we shall both die." The scorpion replies, "Because it's my nature."

Sagittarius
The Traveler

Planetary Ruler: **Jupiter**
Symbol: **The Archer**
Color: **Light Blue**
Metal: **Tin**
Gemstone: **Turquoise**

Character and Personality

Archers are the wanderers and truth-seekers of the zodiac. You are inherently exuberant and enthusiastic and have an inquiring mind that is captivated by the world and everything in it. Knowledge and independence are the hallmarks of your existence. With your restless nature and passion for variety and change, you need a lot of freedom to pursue your many interests. You particularly enjoy traveling, visiting exotic places, and meeting new people. You're equally at home in the outdoors, on the open road, or in a classroom. You view life as an ongoing search for knowledge and experience and as an engaging adventure in which the journey itself is more important than the destination.

You have a wide-ranging mentality equipped with intelligence, foresight, and intuition. Your forte is taking action and initiating things. Although your intentions may be grand, you are better at starting projects than finishing them. You'll sometimes lose interest before a job is completed and begin looking around for something fresher and more exciting. The Jupiter-ruled are gamblers and risk takers by nature. Overconfidence can become a problem, especially if you over-extend yourself financially. However, you are lucky and resourceful, and when you fall, you usually manage to get right back up on your feet.

Relationships

Typically, archers love to party, and they enjoy a very active social life. You are outgoing, playful, and flirtatious, and no one is more adept than you at working a crowd. In intimate relationships you make a charming, sexy lover who is affectionate, straightforward, and sincere. An idealist, you truly believe that each new love is going to last forever. However, you love your freedom and independence more than anything or anyone. You certainly mean to be faithful, but archers are hunters, and if you find someone more appealing, you may suddenly take off in pursuit of your new interest.

The Myth

Zeus, omnipotent ruler of the Greek pantheon, was virtually identical to the mighty and powerful deity known to the Romans as Jupiter or Jove, who rules the sign of Sagittarius. The ancient Greeks looked upon Zeus as a father figure and revered him as the bringer of victory, preserver of order and justice, and protector of both gods and men.

Zeus's father Cronus (Saturn) had learned, however, that one of his children was destined to dethrone him, so he swallowed each of them as soon as they were born. When his wife Rhea gave birth to Zeus, she substituted a stone wrapped in swaddling cloth for Cronus to swallow. When Zeus grew up, he liberated his siblings by causing Cronus to vomit and spit them out. Then he led his brothers and sisters in a fight to wrest control from their father. Once they'd deposed Cronus and the other Titans, Zeus imprisoned most of Titans in Tartarus. Then he appointed himself supreme authority on Earth and ruler of the family of Olympian gods and goddesses.

If Zeus (Jupiter) represents the exuberant, adventurous, freewheeling, self-indulgent side of Sagittarius, Chiron symbolizes the philosophical teacher and healer. Chiron was a centaur, a being represented as half man and half horse. He learned to overcome the animal instincts of his dual nature in order to mentor a generation of Greek heroes. Chiron himself was a pupil of the twin gods Apollo and Artemis (Diana). He was renowned for his skill in hunting, medicine, music, and the art of pro-phecy and was revered for his exceptional goodness and wisdom. He tutored Heracles (Hercules), Achilles, Jason, Asclepius, and Actaeon. He also founded the Chironium, a healing temple on Mt. Pellius, where he instructed his students and helped them fulfill their highest potential.

Capricorn
The Worker

♑

Planetary Ruler: **Saturn**
Symbol: **The Goat**
Color: **Dark Brown**
Metal: **Lead**
Gemstone: **Garnet**

Character and Personality

In nature, goats are creatures that can survive under the most difficult conditions. They are sure-footed on steep mountainsides, will eat anything, and can tolerate practically any weather. In some ways the human goat is a lot like his or her animal counterpart. Industrious, efficient, and disciplined, you Capricorns are determined climbers and naturally hard workers. Your outstanding characteristics are ambition, determination, resiliency, and the persistence to overcome just about any setback. You win because you refuse to quit, and when you are knocked down, you bounce right back up again.

You rarely sit around and wait for things to come to you. You decide what it is you want, and then you go after it. Moreover, you are willing to wait as long as it takes, and you will do whatever is necessary to reach your goal (as long as it's not unlawful or morally wrong). In fact, many goats have five-year, ten-year, and twenty-year plans for the future always in place. A born executive, you are most comfortable when you are the one who is in charge. Capricorn feels naked and insecure without a strong financial base, which probably accounts for the goat's reputation as a materialist.

Relationships

Within yourself, you're extremely passionate and longing for affection, but you have difficulty expressing your true feelings. With career and family responsibilities dominating your time, you sometimes experience a deep sense of loneliness.

Actually, no other member of the zodiacal family is as much in need of love as the seemingly cool Saturn-ruled goat. Capricorns are extremely sensual, and the sign ranks as one of the more physically passionate in the zodiac. When you let yourself go, you make an ardent, caring, affectionate lover. Once committed, you're in for the long haul, and no one is a more dependable or responsible partner than you.

The Myth

The Greeks related Capricorn to Amalthea, the goat-nymph who served as the baby nurse to Zeus (Jupiter) after Zeus's mother Rhea hid the infant god on the island of Crete to save him from the wrath of his father Cronus (Saturn). Amalthea, half goat and half nymph, was sister to the half-goat, half-human god Pan, who is also associated with Capricorn.

Amalthea fed the baby Zeus on her magical nanny-goat's milk. When Zeus grew up, he broke off one of her horns and turned it into the cornucopia, or horn of plenty. Since the goat-nymph was able to produce milk rich enough to feed a young god, Zeus he believed that the cornucopia made from her horn could provide magical nourishment for all the children of the Earth. As a reward for her nurturing and devotion, Zeus placed his one-horned nanny in the heavens as the constellation Capricorn.

Earlier in history, the sign Capricorn was associated with an older zodiacal creature, the goat-fish of the ancient Babylonians. The god Ea was one of the major deities of the old Babylonian pantheon. He was depicted as half man, half fish, or as a man cloaked in a cape of fish skin with a fish head over his head and with the bottom of his cloak trailing in the form of a fishtail. He ruled over wisdom and the water beneath the Earth. He kept the Tigris and Euphrates rivers flowing, thus making it possible for life to exist on the land. It is said that he rose out of the water during the day in order to teach wisdom and the arts of civilization to the ancient Sumerians and that he returned to the river's depths at night.

Aquarius
The Innovator

♒

Planetary Ruler: **Uranus**
Symbol: **The Water Bearer**
Color: **Electric Blue**
Metal: **Aluminum**
Gemstone: **Amethyst**

Character and Personality

Aquarians are individualists who hate conformity and resent any authority other than their own. As an Aquarian, your most outstanding characteristics are idealism, progressive ideas, and humanitarian principles. As a member of an air sign, you're more at home in the realm of ideas than feelings. Emotions frighten you, and at times you can come off as a really cool customer. Nevertheless, you truly care about people and will lie awake nights worrying about the future of mankind.

More than anything, you need a mission in life, and you often dream of reaching out to help the world solve its problems. However, you see things from a different perspective than the natives of other signs, and you tend to come up with original solutions that other people consider odd or eccentric.

A trend spotter, you are a prophet of progress and innovation. You're always a little ahead of everyone else when it comes to accepting new ideas and technology. Although you're open-minded, Aquarius is fixed sign, and once your mind is made up, you can be quite stubborn and inflexible. And while some members of your sign are eccentric by nature, others actively cultivate eccentricity as a lifestyle. You love to shock and may go to considerable lengths to get a rise out of people.

Relationships

Aquarius is a sign of paradoxes, and no two water bearers are alike. Some want casual attachments without commitment, whereas others prefer a lasting partnership. Your initial reaction to people is usually more cerebral than physical. It's difficult for anyone to arouse your interest without some type of mind-to-mind contact. Even in your most intimate associations, your deepest need is for a relationship that satisfies you on a mental level. Romantically, you may be something of a slow starter, but once you get going, you make a passionate, imaginative, considerate lover.

The Myth

Zeus (Jupiter) assigned to Prometheus and his brother Epimetheus the task of populating the Earth. Epimetheus immediately began creating all the animals, giving them wonderful gifts of strength, courage, cunning, and speed. Meanwhile, Prometheus shaped man out of earth and water. When Prometheus finished, he discovered that his brother had already handed out all the best gifts to the animals. There was nothing left for men, who were supposed to be superior to the animals.

Prometheus asked Zeus to give his mortals some of the sacred fire to put them on an even keel with the animals. With fire, they could make weapons and tools to defend themselves and cultivate the Earth. Zeus refused, stating that fire belonged to the gods alone. He thought men would become arrogant if they possessed this divine blessing.

Prometheus felt that Zeus's attitude was unfair, so he rebelled and stole some of the fire from Zeus's hearth and gave it to man anyway. Zeus was enraged, but once the gift was made, it could not be taken back. The father of the gods took vengeance on Prometheus by chaining him to a rock. Prometheus hung from his chains and suffered, but he did not recant nor submit to the will of the tyrannical god.

In a further act of revenge, Zeus sent a beautiful woman named Pandora to Epimetheus, who took her gladly, despite his brother's warning not to accept anything from Zeus. Knowing that curiosity would get the best of her, the gods provided Pandora with a box and instructed her never to open it. Unable to resist, she unlatched the forbidden box and inadvertently released all the evils that afflict the human race. By the time Pandora managed to slam the lid closed, only hope remained to comfort humanity.

Pisces
The Dreamer

♓

Planetary Ruler: **Neptune**
Symbol: **The Fish**
Color: **Sea Green**
Metal: **Platinum**
Gemstone: **Aquamarine**

Character and Personality

Since Pisces is a water sign and mainly emphasizes feelings, its natives relate to the world through their emotions. Your sign's symbol, a pair of fish swimming in opposite directions, emphasizes the duality of your nature. Some Pisceans are shy and quiet, and even those who aren't tend to be elusive, refusing to show their real selves to the world at large. The aura of mystery surrounding you comes from a deep-seated need to protect your cherished dreams and secrets from those who may not understand them.

The pair of fish represents consciousness and unconsciousness, reality and illusion, sleeping and waking. Although some people may write you off as an impractical dreamer, your qualifications for worldly success are grossly underestimated. Your vivid imagination and inherent flexibility allow you to comprehend the entire range of human behavior. Like a chameleon, you adapt readily to changing surroundings and rapidly shifting circumstances. As a result, you're able to fit in anywhere and get along with all different kinds of people.

Relationships

Fish are innately kind and compassionate. The acts of caring and giving are second nature to you. However, your own feelings are easily hurt by the slightest misguided comment, and you require constant encouragement to keep from feeling insecure. You consider love a basic necessity; without it, you feel empty and incomplete. When you fall in love, you fall hook, line, and sinker. However, fear of rejection makes you skittish and reluctant to make the first move.

Although Pisces natives are not normally aggressive in romantic situations, they are beguiling and seductive. Love has a way of finding you. The telepathic signals you send out are unmistakable, and the object of your interest and affection rarely has trouble interpreting the message.

The Myth

The quintessential Pisces myth is that of the journey of Odysseus (Ulysses) as recounted by Homer in The Odyssey. *Having spent ten years fighting in the Trojan War, Odysseus was battle weary and longing for home and the company of his faithful wife Penelope and young son Telemachus. However, the goddess Athena (Minerva) was furious at the way the Greek captains had mistreated Priam's daughter, the prophetess Cassandra. When Troy was being sacked, Cassandra was in Athena's temple and under the goddess's protection. Nevertheless, one of the Greek commanders tore her from the altar and dragged her out of the sanctuary. When no Greek protested this sacrilege, Athena vowed revenge on them all. She appealed to Poseidon (Neptune) to "give the Greeks a bitter homecoming."*

When the victorious Greek captains put out to sea, the sea god sent a fearful tempest that destroyed many of their ships and blew others off course. Odysseus didn't die, but Poseidon pitched him and his men into uncharted waters. They were cast up onto many beaches where they encountered various mythological creatures, both good and evil. Their long journey home was one of amazing discovery, alternating with nightmarish periods of great confusion.

Although Odysseus was gone for a total of twenty years, Penelope never lost faith that one day her beloved husband would return to her. She sent Telemachus to seek news of Odysseus in the courts of the other kings who had made it home from the Trojan expedition. While on his search, Telemachus received counsel from Athena, who advised him to go home. Then Athena presented herself to Odysseus. She forgave him and helped him return to Ithaca, where he and Telemachus foiled a plot by one of Penelope's suitors to kill Telemachus, marry the queen, and assume Odysseus' rightful place on the throne.

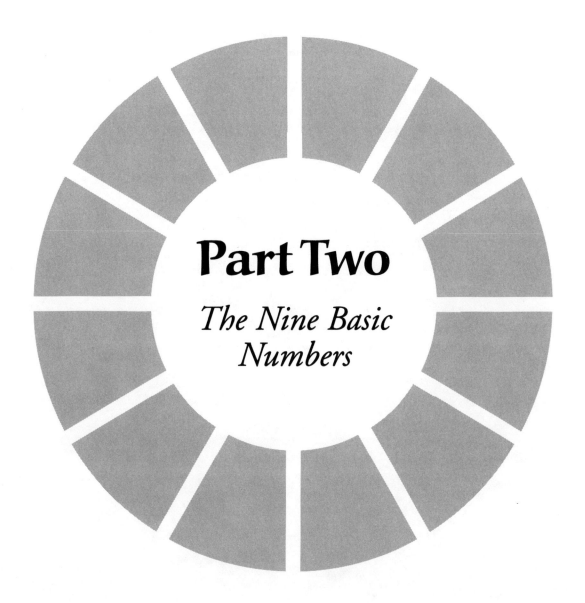

Part Two

The Nine Basic Numbers

N umbers play a key role in astrological computations—days, months, years, and even hours, minutes and seconds. The most widely used of the modern numerological systems is that of the Greek mathematician Pythagoras, who said, "All things can be expressed in numerical terms, because all things are ultimately reduced to numbers."

Pythagoras saw numbers as the basis of all art, science, and music. He and his followers also believed that by contemplating numbers, they would discover the spiritual key that leads to the divine. In this part of *What Your Birthday Reveals about You*, I'll show you what numbers can tell you about yourself and your loved ones.

Root Numbers

There are nine basic or root numbers (see chart on following page), and one of these is associated with you and your birthday, as you'll see in the pages that follow. Here's how to calculate your root number.

The sum of any compound number, when reduced to a single digit, is its basic or root number. The root number for your birthday is the day of the month on which you were born, reduced to a single digit. If your birthday is on the twenty-eighth day of any month, you simply add the two digits together: $2 + 8 = 10$. If necessary, you reduce the result further until you arrive at a single digit: $1 + 0 = 1$. Therefore, the root digit for the twenty-eighth day of any month is one.

Birth-Date Numbers

In addition to the meaning the root number has for every birth date, each of the numbers or dates from one to thirty-one also possesses its own individual vibration. These vibrations provide the subtle differences that distinguish a particular number, or birth date, from others that have the same root.

Both the root number and the actual date of your birth reveal something about you and your potential.

Root Number Chart

NUMBER **1** Born on the 1st, 10th, 19th, or 28th of any month	**NUMBER** **2** Born on the 2nd, 11th, 20th, or 29th of any month	**NUMBER** **3** Born on the 3rd, 12th, 21st, or 30th of any month
NUMBER **4** Born on the 4th, 13th, 22nd, or 31st of any month	**NUMBER** **5** Born on the 5th, 14th, or 23rd of any month	**NUMBER** **6** Born on the 6th, 15th, or 24th of any month
NUMBER **7** Born on the 7th, 16th, or 25th of any month	**NUMBER** **8** Born on the 8th, 17th, or 26th of any month	**NUMBER** **9** Born on the 9th, 18th, or 27th of any month

1 Number One

Individuality

Born on the 1st, 10th, 19th or 28th of any month

One is the number of beginnings, individuality, and independence. Ones are the forthright leaders, pioneers, and fearless adventurers of society. Your dynamic, self-reliant personality prompts you to assume a leading role in all your endeavors. Full of initiative, you're driven by your ideals and convictions. Personal inspiration is the key to your motivation. You express yourself through your own originality and creativity.

You also have great mental foresight and the ability to think for yourself. Ones don't respond well to authority or the advice of others. You particularly resent it when your plans and beliefs are questioned. If you come up against strong opposition, you'll either fight for your ideas or stubbornly resist all attempts to get you to change them.

You like winning, and your naturally competitive temperament encourages you to take risks that others generally prefer to avoid. Your basic nature is active, forceful, and aggressive. Finesse is not your forte. You overcome obstacles by meeting them head on and barreling your way through them. Although you can be exact about details, you're much better at starting projects than finishing them. If you become really bored, you may suddenly drop what you're doing and move on to something new.

Number Two
Duality

Born on the 2nd, 11th, 20th, or 29th of any month

Two is the number of duality, cooperation, and diplomacy. Twos are the partners and peacemakers of a society. Your sociable, courteous nature brings balance and harmony to all your interactions. You think in pairs and actually prefer sharing authority and responsibility to going it alone. Companionship is your top priority, and union your ultimate goal. Your forte is the ability to compromise and bring opposing forces together. Tact and a decided knack for smoothing ruffled feathers are the primary tools in your diplomatic arsenal.

Your highly flexible, adaptable nature helps you deal with all types of people and situations. A good listener and persuasive talker, you are also astute at working behind the scenes. Your success as a mediator stems from your ability to gently manipulate conflicting parties and win them over to your point of view. When thwarted or blocked in your efforts, you'll mix a bit of cunning with your charm to help turn things around.

The "urge to merge" is the main motivation underlying this number's vibration. You want beauty and order in your life, and you especially enjoy creating a pleasant atmosphere for yourself and your loved ones. Twos are romantic, faithful, and affectionate, and you expect fidelity, love, and devotion in return. Because you dislike disagreements, you're usually the first to make up after an argument.

3 Number Three

Exuberance

Born on the 3rd, 12th, 21st, or 30th of any month

Three is the number of self-expression, enthusiasm, optimism, and sociability. Threes are the friendly, the witty, and the charmers of society. You are a born entertainer with a cheerful, easygoing manner and a gift for gab that endears you to all kinds of people.

Three is also the number of good fortune. Some threes are so lucky they seem to be under the protection of a guardian angel. Even your difficulties usually have a way of working out for the best.

Despite your light-hearted approach to life, there is nothing superficial about your desire to succeed. Threes are inherently ambitious and hard working. A genuine distaste for occupying subordinate positions fuels your climb to the top.

Threes are generally multi-talented and sometimes have difficulty choosing among various career options. Naturally artistic and creative, you have a knack for synthesizing and communicating your knowledge and ideas. Cleverness, versatility, and quick thinking make it easy for you to outwit the competition. However, a tendency to spread yourself too thin by scattering your energies in a number of different directions may hamper your success.

In your personal life, you are devoted to friends and family. A generous, warm, and loving person, you enjoy interacting with people in social gatherings and intimate one-on-one situations.

Number Four

Stability

Born on the 4th, 13th, 22nd, or 31st of any month

Fours are the workers and builders of society. Your strength lies in knowing the best way to get a project up and running and keep it functioning properly. Your vitality, sense of purpose, and will power keep you going long after others have run out of steam. Loyal to employers and fair to employees, you make an excellent boss or manager. Driven by ambition and the desire to succeed, there is virtually nothing you can't do once you put your mind to it.

Most number four individuals possess technical or mechanical abilities, are hard workers, and enjoy seeing the practical results of their labors. The need for security and stability motivates them to build strong structures and institutions. This means that if your root number is four, you're particularly good at adapting the ideas of more visionary people and putting them to practical use. Your approach to most things is precise and systematic. Your outlook is traditional and you dislike upsetting changes; you find fulfillment in dependable, routine endeavors.

Fours love their homes and families and are unusually faithful and devoted to their mates. As a four, you're totally trustworthy and dependable and may be relied upon to follow through on your promises. Fours generally spend less time having fun than other people, and when overworked, they can suffer bouts of depression. If you allow yourself to get stuck in a negative mindset, you may become repressed or repressive.

5 Number Five
Freedom

Born on the 5th, 14th, or 23rd of any month

Someone who is a five is a freewheeling adventurer who adapts readily to any situation. Yours is an inquiring mind with a deep-seated need know why things are the way they are. You have a genial personality, are a good mixer, and make friends easily. Because of your characteristic sociability, you rarely feel down or depressed. Fives are generally lucky and able to bounce back from any difficulty. Your knack for coping with the unexpected gives you the confidence to try new things that are unusual and exciting.

Fives are generally able to juggle career, hobbies, and personal relationships with amazing ease. You are particularly adept at networking and communicating. You like exchanging ideas with as many different types of people as possible. Your easygoing style is extremely witty and entertaining, but your clever quips sometimes have a hurtful edge to them. Freedom and change are the touchstones of your existence, and a potent combination of wanderlust and nervous energy keeps you in perpetual motion.

Fives are sensual and sexy, naturally loving, and affectionate, but you're also likely to jump in and out of romantic relationships. Although you rarely admit to being fickle, there is a decided fear of intimacy in your basic makeup. If you settle down, you're likely to choose someone who shares many of your interests and is a friend as well as a lover.

Number Six

Harmony

6

Born on the 6th, 15th, or 24th of any month

The individual whose root number is six is self-expressive, creative, imaginative, artistic, and musical. You strive for peace and harmony and are happiest when life runs smoothly, with a minimum of stress and discord. Essentially an idealist, you're the original Good Samaritan. You refuse to give up on people and have helped many a grateful friend stave off disaster. However, your concern for people can be taken too far, and sixes are sometimes accused of meddling in the affairs of others.

Sixes like to entertain and will spend lavishly for parties and other social affairs. You love your home and derive great joy from being surrounded by beautiful objects. Six is considered a fortunate number, and those under its vibration tend to attract money and property. Nevertheless, people and pleasure are more important to you than material possessions.

Sixes tend to be charming and attractive, with magnetic personalities that draw others to them. Love is important to you, but your ideas about relationships are overly romantic and sentimental. You don't like being alone, and without a loving, intimate relationship in your life, you may feel incomplete. However, given your emotional vulnerability, you're as likely to fall in love with a romantic ideal as with a real person.

7 Number Seven
Wisdom

Born on the 7th, 16th or 25th of any month

The typical number seven is a truth-seeking intellectual with a decided knack for sizing up any situation in the blink of an eye. You have a deep reservoir of wisdom, a vivid imagination, and possibly clairvoyant or psychic abilities. Your insight and intuition work hand in hand with your analytical mind to tie data together. Musical, poetic, and artistic ability is quite common among those with this vibration, and you could be skilled in handicrafts, writing, dancing, or painting. Other people may regard you as a genuine mystery, because your somewhat solitary nature is much given to private contemplation.

Seven is a spiritual number, and you could be deeply religious or interested in various aspects of mysticism and the occult. Although some sevens are drawn to traditional religions, others prefer alternative spiritual movements. Occasionally sevens create religions of their own based on their unorthodox mystical beliefs. If your root number is seven, you are extremely curious and willing to experiment outside the mainstream when it suits your purpose.

Intimate relationships, however, can be difficult for you. You function best in an individual capacity where you are the authority in your own realm. Because you breathe the rarefied air of a visionary, you may feel misunderstood and unappreciated. You need to find a partner who understands your moodiness and desire for periods of solitude. You're actually happiest on your own or with someone who's tuned in to your wavelength.

Number Eight

Authority

8

Born on the 8th, 17th, or 26th of any month

Eight represents power and authority in the material world. It is the number of leadership, business acumen, tenacity, and hard work. You possess sound business judgment, marked executive ability, and a knack for commanding the respect and cooperation of others. Inherently industrious, patient, and persevering, you don't expect opportunity to be handed to you on a silver platter. Consequently, most of your rewards in life stem from accomplishments achieved through your own efforts.

Since many number eights are wealthy and powerful, the vibration is often misunderstood or misinterpreted as greed or ruthlessness. Actually, most eights must work extremely hard to get to the top, and their paths to success are often strewn with difficulties. Eights are so dedicated that they are generally viewed as workaholics. As a manager, you expect the best from your staff, yet you wouldn't dream of asking them to do anything you're not willing to do yourself.

Despite their tough outer shells, eights often experience deep feelings of loneliness. You may demand constant reassurances from your loved ones, but what you're really seeking is proof of their love. You're not the easiest person to live with, but once you've satisfied your need for emotional security and acceptance, you make a loyal, devoted partner or parent. Still, you have difficulty expressing your true feelings, and at times you appear rather cold and distant.

9

Number Nine

Compassion

Born on the 9th, 18th, or 27th of any month

Nine is the number of universal receptivity and heightened awareness. There's an aura of prophetic wisdom about you. You possess an extremely perceptive mind with intuitive powers bordering on the psychic. The touchstones of your existence are humanitarianism and compassion, and you have a tremendous capacity for tolerance and spiritual achievement. You understand the human condition, and in your work with others you are and selfless and courageous.

Nines are born fighters, and you're not afraid of anything or anyone. You refuse to tolerate injustice and can usually be found in the forefront of any battle against discrimination and inequity. However, you are also impatient and impulsive and often forget to think before you speak. Sometimes you get so carried away with impractical plans and ideas that your potential for doing good becomes lost in aimless dreaming. When you allow your heart to completely rule you head, you can become so overly sympathetic to the plight of the less fortunate that you are willing to give away everything you own.

You are sincerely devoted to those you love, and you're prepared to sacrifice everything for them. As romantic as you are compassionate, you tend to fall passionately in love with an ideal. When the reality doesn't live up to your expectations, you may be deeply disappointed and anxious to move on to another "ideal mate."

Part Three

The 366 Birthdays
of the Year

January Birthdays

January 1

♑ Capricorn, 1

Those born on this day are ambitious, high-achieving, powerful executive types with an overwhelming desire to win. Determination and the need to be first drive your climb up the ladder of success. You view life as a series of challenges to be met and overcome. Your standards are high, and you refuse to compromise on principle. You expect the best from yourself and others and have little patience with laziness or incompetence. You probably don't think about becoming famous. You just do what you do best and let the chips fall where they may. Still, there's no denying your ability to stand out from the crowd.

Capricorn's caution doesn't prevent you from taking a gamble when the odds appear to be in your favor. Whether in business, sports, politics, or the arts, your fearless enthusiasm and innovative ideas place you on the cutting edge of your profession. When you're feeling insecure, restless, or impatient on the inside, you refuse to let it show on the outside. When necessary, you'll hide your anxieties rather than allow them to hold you back.

Although you may appear cool on the surface, at heart you're a passionate and caring secret romantic. Family means a lot to you, and you are extremely loyal and dependable. You like taking charge, however, and can be so demanding that relatives may find you rather difficult to live with.

On This Day:

Celebrations on the Kalends, or first day, of January include New Year's Day and the festival of the two-faced Roman Janus, god of gates, door-ways, journeys, and new beginnings. This day is sacred to the Greek gods Zeus and Hera and to the Roman Jupiter and Juno; it is a day of offerings to the Roman Fortuna, goddess of fortune and fertility, and is sacred to the red-haired Irish goddess of war, The Morrigan.

Born Today: Maurice Bejart (choreographer); Xavier Cugat (band leader); E. M. Forster (writer); Barry Goldwater (U.S. senator); Hank Greenberg (baseball player); J. Edgar Hoover (FBI director); Carol Landis (actress); Don Novello (comedian); J. D. Salinger (writer); Ousmane Sembene (director); Alfred Stieglitz (photographer)

January 2

♑ Capricorn, 2

The individual born on January 2 is ambitious and determined, with a competitive nature that's been tempered by the spirit of cooperation. Although you're more relaxed than some Capricorns, you are just as willing to work hard for what you want. You want to make it to the top, but not necessarily alone. You enjoy joint enterprises and interacting with a partner or group. You sense other people's needs and desires, and when a mediator is called for, you're often the one they turn to.

Those born on this date are lovers of art and music and know how to put their creativity to practical use. Consequently, your strong intellect is more concrete than abstract. Learning for its own sake holds little appeal for you. You'd rather channel your ideas toward a specific goal. Totally devoted to the principles of law and order, you place a high value on fairness and justice for everyone. In business, you make an outstanding executive who's popular with associates, co-workers, and clients.

You're gracious and sociable, and relating comes naturally to you. You may not feel whole without the companionship of a mate or partner. However, it usually takes more than love and romance to hold your interest. What you really need is someone who shares your goals and your strong sense of purpose.

On This Day:

In Egypt, the performance of a religious ceremony known as the Advent of Isis from Phoenicia occurs on this day, as does the celebration of the nativity of the goddess Inanna, Sumerian Queen of Heaven and Earth. The Perihelion of the Earth also takes place every year on this date and occurs when the planet Earth reaches the point in its orbit closest to the Sun.

Born Today: Isaac Asimov (writer); Jim Bakker (Pentecostal TV evangelist); William J. Crowe (U.S. admiral); Taye Digs (actor); Jose Ferran (dancer); Cuba Gooding, Jr. (actor); Sally Rand (astronaut); Saint Therese de Lisieux, "The Little Flower" (mystic); Renata Tebaldi (opera singer); Christy Turlington (supermodel); Peter Young (artist)

January 3

♑ Capricorn, 3

Those born on this day have vibrant, outgoing personalities that make them extremely popular with their many friends and associates. Although you are as hard working and responsible as any goat, you're also fun loving and sociable. The serious side of your Capricorn nature is lightened by your youthful effervescence and great sense of humor. You are full of enthusiasm and original ideas, but your interest in attempting new things can cause you to spread yourself too thin.

People with birthdays on January 3 possess wonderful imaginations and a flair for the dramatic often found in those who work in the media or the arts. You are naturally artistic, and your star quality and love for the limelight are equaled only by your desire for material success. Your fluency with language and ease of self-expression guarantees that you're never at a loss for words. You are very dependable and determined but nevertheless refuse to let personal responsibilities or career aspirations keep you from having a good time.

You lead an active lifestyle fueled by nervous energy. You need to learn how to relax or you'll risk burning yourself out. In personal relationships, you want a partner who gives you considerable freedom of movement, yet you expect a strong commitment and total loyalty and devotion from your significant other in return.

On This Day:

In Norse tradition, this day marks the rite of Charming of the Plow to petition Odin and Frigg to make the land fertile, as well as the annual fertility ceremony known as the Deer Dances, which are performed by the Pueblo Indians. In ancient Greece, a festival called Lenaia was celebrated on this date to honor Dionysus, the god of wine and fertility.

Born Today: Victor Borge (comic pianist); Dabney Coleman (actor); Marion Davies (actress); Mel Gibson (actor); Bobby Hull (hockey player); Sergio Leone (director); George Martin (music arranger/producer); Ray Milland (actor); Pola Negri (actress); Victoria Principal (actress); John Sturges (director); J. R. R. Tolkien (writer/scholar)

January 4

VS Capricorn, 4

People with birthdays on this day are society's patient, determined builders and its extremely ambitious, conscientious, goal-oriented workaholics. While you may have big ideas, however, you value stability and safety over glamour and adventure. It's not at all surprising that a serious Capricorn number four would crave success or feel compelled to put business before pleasure. What is surprising is your delicious, offbeat sense of humor that can astonish people who don't know you well. Moreover, your dry, quick wit has a way of surfacing at unexpected moments and sending everyone around you into fits of hysterical laughter.

There are no quitters born on this day. In fact, you're known for your ability to hang in and see things through to the end. Moreover, you won't balk or run off at the first sign of trouble, and those who depend on you know that you'll always be around when needed. Still, you can be very demanding, and you expect a great deal from associates and loved ones alike. Nevertheless, beneath your sober façade lurks a protective, caring person who feels duty bound to do whatever is necessary to assist family or friends who are in trouble.

You need to be loved, but you are cautious regarding emotions and would rather hold back than appear vulnerable. When you're able to trust someone enough to let down your guard, you make a sensual, loving, and faithful partner.

On This Day:

In Korea, the annual Sacrifice to the Seven Stars is performed at midnight. To encourage good fortune and divine blessings, water and white wine are offered to the god who rules the constellation Ursa Major. In East Anglia, this date was dedicated to Saint Genevieve of Paris. In Elizabethan England, this day was set aside for weather forecasting.

Born Today: Luis Braille (creator of reading/writing system for the blind); Dyan Cannon (actress); Jacob Grimm (writer); Sterling Holloway (actor); Sir Isaac Newton (mathematician); Julia Ormond (actress); Floyd Patterson (boxer); Carlos Saura (director); Don Shula (football coach); Jesse White (actor); Jane Wyman (actress)

January 5

♑ Capricorn, 5

The typical person born on this date is a maverick dressed in conventional clothing. As such, you are a far-sighted reformer on the inside, but you're more comfortable implementing your innovative ideas in an established framework. Even so, you don't allow your concern for the welfare of others to interfere with your personal goals. As a free-spirited adventurer with the goat's practicality and persistence, you're quite capable of garnering success and acclaim in both materialistic and altruistic endeavors.

You're enormously persuasive and pragmatic enough to make your mark as an entrepreneur in business, the media, or the arts. You're particularly suited to professions related to sales, promotion, publishing, or travel. Your passion for roaming is tempered by the level-headedness of your Capricorn Sun. Nevertheless, you resent sacrificing fun for work and may be tempted to overextend yourself physically. If you burn the candle at both ends, even your seemingly boundless energy will eventually run out.

In an intimate relationship you're passionate and loving, but you require a considerable amount of personal freedom. You are loyal and have strong feelings regarding family and community. Nevertheless, you don't respond well to the demands of an overbearing partner. You're more likely to remain committed to someone who understands your overachieving personality and your need for time to pursue your various outside interests.

On This Day:

In England, Twelfth Night and Wassail Eve herald the end of Christmas. In some parts of Italy, the crone goddess Befana is said to distribute sweets to good children and lumps of coal to bad ones. Her festival is celebrated with songs, music, horns, and noisemakers. The loud sounds drive away evil and mark the passage of winter.

Born Today: Alvin Ailey (choreographer); Edith Custer (publisher); Robert Duvall (actor); Umberto Eco (writer); Marilyn Manson (rock star); Pamela Sue Martin (actress); Jim Otto (football player); Zebulon M. Pike (U.S. Army officer/explorer); George Reeves (actor); W. D. Snodgrass (poet); Paramahansa Yogananda (spiritual teacher)

January 6

VS Capricorn, 6

Toughness and tenderness combine in the January 6th individual to produce a paradoxical nature that is outwardly pragmatic, yet inwardly compassionate and idealistic. A practical visionary, you tend to express your humanitarianism through conscientious devotion to duty. Ambitious and tenacious on the one hand, you are innately spiritual and philosophical on the other. You have a great love for art and poetry and may be artistically talented yourself. However, you prefer putting your creative abilities to use producing things that are functional as well as beautiful.

You're basically peace loving and will go out of your way to avoid a disagreement. But your amiability should not be confused with weakness. You have a strong need for recognition and appreciation and hate being taken for granted. However, your inner defense system springs into action when you are feeling hurt or insecure. If things don't go your way, you will conceal your disappointment in order to keep up appearances.

You're considerably more emotional than most goats, and a loving relationship is truly important to you. In an intimate union, you're a caring, responsive lover and a practical, dependable partner. Your domestic side craves a home and a family. The intensity of your desire to create a happy, secure haven, however, can cause you to appear overbearing and bossy and may make those closest to you feel claustrophobic.

On This Day:

Three Kings Day, commemorating the visit of the Three Wise Men to Bethlehem, is observed in many parts of the world with gifts and feasting. This date was also Twelfth Night in old Europe, when the ashes of the Yule log and other debris of the Yule feast were cleared away. In ancient Greece, it was the celebration day of the Epiphany of Kore/Persephone.

Born Today: Rowan Atkinson (actor); Kahlil Gibran (writer); Joan of Arc (mystic); Lou Harris (pollster); Johannes Kepler (astronomer/astrologer); John C. Lilly (psychiatrist/writer); Tom Mix (actor); Carl Sandburg (writer); Heinrich Schliemann (archaeologist); Alan Watts (philosopher/writer); Loretta Young (actress)

January 7

♑ Capricorn, 7

Those with birthdays on this day are sociable and friendly enough to garner people's respect and admiration without sacrificing their own privacy or independence. As one of these Capricorns, you have a sensitivity and apparent vulnerability that endears you to others. Yours is a highly spiritual nature that resonates with the suffering and injustices in the world. Mentally, you're both logical and intuitive, an unusual combination that produces the odd dichotomy of a scientific mind with an artistic temperament.

Your idiosyncratic approach to things and the occasional tendency to isolate yourself can cause you to feel lonely or cut off from the world around you. It's not that you don't enjoy company; it's just that you've always followed your own path. You know what you want to do, and you refuse to be sidetracked by extraneous circumstances. Inherently clever and intuitive, you're shrewd about people and understand human foibles. Many of those born on January 7 have psychic skills and mystical or occult interests. If this applies to you, you should take the time to develop these areas.

Sometimes you comprehend more about what everyone else is feeling than you do about your own emotions. You yearn for love and intimacy, yet remain aloof unless you feel totally secure with the other person. You'll put off commitment until you're certain that the relationship is right, but when you make a promise, you stick with it.

On This Day:

The ancient Egyptian goddess Sekhmet, the lion-headed goddess who sustained the spirits of the dead, was honored on this day. In England, January 7 was Saint Distaff's Day, when work began again after Christmas. Not a real saint's day, it was instead a tongue-in-cheek commemoration of women's return to their household chores.

Born Today: Charles Addams (cartoonist); Saint Bernadette of Lourdes (religious visionary); Sandra Bernhard (comedian); William Peter Blatty (writer); Nicholas Cage (actor); Katie Couric (TV news show host); Oscar Dominguez (artist); Gerald Durrell (naturalist); Carolyn Bessette Kennedy (model); Terry Moore (actress); Nicholas Zabaleta (musician)

January 8

♑ Capricorn, 8

The individual whose birthday is January 8 is competitive, competent, and goal-oriented. There are no lazy people born under this vibration, and most are ambitious, overachieving workaholics. It's not surprising, then, that you crave success. Power, authority, and material security make you feel safe and secure in an uncertain world. More than anything, however, you aspire to great accomplishment. For you, it's all about the work. You want to make your mark in the world and be remembered for what you've done.

Once you've started something, you'll hang on and see it through to the end. You refuse to quit, and if you're knocked down, you bounce right back up. Although you tend to vacillate between self-assurance and self-doubt, overall you have faith in your own capabilities. With an excellent head on your shoulders, you reason things out carefully and plan all your moves with care and exactitude. Your organizational and executive skills give you a decided edge in business or the professions. As a boss or manager, you're fair, but you expect a lot and can be extremely demanding.

Your deepest need is to love and be loved, but you are cautious with regard to relationships and would rather hold back then appear vulnerable. You'll only let down your guard if you feel secure enough to trust the other person. If and when this happens, you make a sensual, loving, dependable partner.

On This Day:

The New Year of the Druids is a day sacred to the Roman Justita (Themis), the goddess who carries the scales of justice and personifies law and order. In Rome, Justita was thought to be present at all social gatherings and oath-swearing ceremonies. In Greek Macedonia, this was Midwife's Day, dedicated to Eleithyia, the goddess of birth.

Born Today: Shirley Bassey (singer); David Bowie (rock star); Wilkie Collins (writer); Jose Ferrer (actor); Bill Graham (rock impresario); Yvette Mimieux (actress); Stephen Hawking (physicist); Charles Osgood (TV journalist); Elvis Presley (singer); Soupy Sales (comedian); Larry Storch (comedian); Sander Vanocur (TV journalist)

January 9
♑ Capricorn, 9

Idealism, compassion, and benevolence are associated with this birthday. If you're born on this day, you possess an intuitive understanding of the human condition that prompts you to try to make the world a better place. Moreover, you have specific ideas regarding how it should be done. You are ambitious, with a good head for business, excellent organizing skills, and a decided knack for making money. Your capabilities are wide-ranging, and you function best in a position of authority. Your strong sense of obligation to society is complimented by your personal aspirations for success. Even as you implement plans for accomplishing your personal goals, you feel compelled to help people in need.

You're considerably more intuitive and receptive to outside influences than other Capricorns. Although your demeanor may give the impression of great forcefulness, there are actually two distinct sides to your character. Your confident exterior masks an inner nature subject to numerous doubts and insecurities. When you get the contradictory sides of your nature to work together, you are the consummate practical idealist.

In intimate situations, you are tenderhearted and something of a romantic. You're very loyal and devoted, and you have a humorous, whimsical side that makes you fun to be with. Although you tend to be rather less serious than the typical Capricorn, you are as dependable and protective as any goat.

On This Day:

On this day, the Ancient Roman festival of Jana and Janus, the Romans paid homage to Jana, whose name means "luminous sky," and to her husband Janus, guardian of the passage-ways. Traditional offerings included wine, incense, and barley. Jana was invoked to shine her light on the new year, and a ram was sacrificed to Janus for his protection.

Born Today: Joan Baez (folksinger); Simone de Beauvior (writer); Rudolf Bing (director of the Metropolitan Opera); Crystal Gayle (singer); Judith Krantz (writer); Fernando Lamas (actor); Gypsy Rose Lee (stripper/TV host); Richard Nixon (U.S. president); Bart Starr (football player); Susannah York (actress); Chic Young (cartoonist)

January 10

The typical individual born on this date possesses an innovative mentality and a practical approach to problem solving. Having this birthday means you are able to foresee future possibilities without losing sight of tried and tested principles. With your strong will and fearless enthusiasm, you're more of a risk taker than the average Capricorn. As a pioneering self-starter, you are more inclined to stand by your own beliefs than to go along with the crowd. Your capabilities are wide-ranging, and with your willingness to work hard, you can succeed in virtually any career area.

People with this birthday don't suffer fools gladly. Nevertheless, you're a master at hiding your personal feelings for at least as long as it takes to cut a deal and get it signed. On the inside, you are restless and impatient and more interested in moving forward with an overall objective than slaving over routine details. You're particularly adept at combining a tycoon's shrewd mentality with the enterprising spirit of an entrepreneur.

In an intimate union, you are a sensual and passionate lover, but you have a private side to your nature that makes its difficult for you to reveal your true feelings. When you do commit to another person, you are loyal and devoted, but a lack of trust can cause you to act in a controlling and possessive manner.

On This Day:

This day is sacred to the ninth century Welsh bard Geraint, the Blue Bard of Wales. Native American Iroquois Indians celebrate the new year on this date with a centuries-old ritual known as the Feast of Dreams. In rural Europe, a plough is paraded through the streets and accompanied by a ritual sweeping with brooms to drive away evil spirits from the village.

Born Today: Pat Benatar (singer); Ray Bolger (dancer); Jim Croce (singer); Ruben Dario (poet); George Foreman (boxer); Paul Henreid (actor); Walter Hill (director); Gisele MacKenzie (singer); Willie McCovey (baseball player); Sal Mineo (actor); Johnnie Ray (singer); Max Roach (drummer); Rod Stewart (singer); Galina Ulanova (dancer)

January 11
♑ Capricorn, 2

There is little that's ordinary or commonplace about the idealistic individuals born on this day. As one of them, you're on a mission to help others by leading them to a better way of life. Outwardly you may be as practical and realistic as any Capricorn, but your soul is that of a mystic. Your essential makeup is an interesting blend of the goat's shrewd determination, a philosophical mind, and an artistic temperament. Consequently, you're less likely to be driven by the desire for power and money that affects other goats. A true humanitarian, you feel a strong obligation to aid people in need.

The January 11th mentality is extremely creative, with a decided flair for turning dreams and ideas into practical realities. You could find yourself drawn to the study of metaphysics, the occult, or other alternative paths of illumination. Your sharp, incisive mind makes it easy for you to assimilate theoretical knowledge, and your psychic-like intuition provides you with empathy for the human condition. As a leader and teacher, you're able to inspire those around you and to stimulate their creative or spiritual potential. Personally, you have a strong, powerful outer will, but you are rather thin-skinned and emotionally fragile within.

Although relating comes naturally to you, you tend to be shy in intimate situations. You're a tenderhearted romantic, but your insecurities may keep you from opening your heart to another person. You do best with a partner who understands or shares your interests.

On This Day:

The first day of Carmentalia, a Roman festival honoring the goddess Carmenta, was celebrated on this date. Carmenta presided over childbirth, and her priestesses, the nymphs of prophecy, cast the fortunes of children at the moment of their birth. In ancient Rome, this day was also sacred to Juturna, a divinity of prophetic waters.

Born Today: Tracey Caulkins (swimmer); Kim Coles (actress); Ben Crenshaw (golfer); Ezra Cornell (businessman); Alexander Hamilton (patriot); William James (psychologist); Naomi Judd (singer); Eve La Galliene (actress/producer); Amanda Peet (actress); Rod Taylor (actor); Grant Tinker (TV producer/media executive)

January 12
♑ Capricorn, 3

The typical individual born on this day is considerably more sociable than the average Capricorn. You have the ability to assimilate knowledge quickly and then use what you've learned to bring others around to your point of view. You're never afraid to speak your mind, and you can be as charming as you are convincing. People often disagree with you, but they'll usually listen to what you have to say. Your mode of expression is forceful, yet sympathetic. When the occasion calls for diplomacy, you're often the one who comes up with a plan that's acceptable all to concerned.

You are sincere and resolute, with a practical view of the world. Your seemingly easygoing outer personality masks a lot of self-doubt and suspicion. On an emotional level, you are changeable and contradictory, and this volatility can be puzzling to those around you. You may be roguishly high-spirited one moment and then shift gears and be the conventional businessperson the next. When you're in a relaxed mood and your satirical wit surfaces, you surprise everyone with your playful conversation.

You are companionable, yet very aware of your need to be in control. In love and romance, you are loyal and affectionate. You benefit from a committed union, but you may get restless if the relationship falls into a rut.

On This Day:

In India, this day marks the Makara-Sankranti celebration of the Hindus with saffron, songs of joy, and ritual river baths. The Roman festival of Compitalia, in honor of household gods called the Lares, falls on this day, which also is sacred to Odin's wife Frigg, the stately Norse sky goddess and queen of the Aesir, who is thought to know the future of humankind.

Born Today: Jeff Bezos (founder and CEO of Amazon.com); Joe Frazier (boxer); Hermann Goring (Nazi founder of the Gestapo); Rush Limbaugh (radio talk show host); Jack London (writer); Louis Ranier (actress); Tex Ritter (actor); John Singer Sargent (artist); Howard Stern (radio talk show host); Swami Vivekananda (spiritual teacher)

January 13

♑ Capricorn, 4

The January 13th person is hard working, cautious, purposeful, and pragmatic. No one is more practical or better at coming to grips with the reality of a situation than you. You take your work very seriously and never shirk your responsibilities. Spontaneity is not your style, and you rarely undertake anything new without careful thought and planning. The keynote of your thinking is structure. Like a good architect, you prepare a solid foundation before you begin building.

You don't seek life's rewards for yourself alone. Those born on this day are conscious of their obligation to society and feel duty bound to help others. If you deem it necessary, you'll set your personal needs aside in favor of the greater good. Despite a tendency to work too hard and play too little, when you do take time out to play, you're extremely witty and fun to be around. However, there's often a dark side to your jokes and clever remarks because, like many goats, you're a master of the art of black humor.

You come off as emotionally cool on the surface, but you're warm and sensitive underneath. You are basically shy, but also very sensual and capable of intense passion. Loyalty and fidelity are everything to you. You may be slow to commit to a love relationship, but when you find the right person, you'll stick around for the long haul.

On This Day:

This is the day of the Norse rite of Midvintersblot, or Midwinter's offering, called Tiugunde Day in Old England. On this date in Druidic Ireland, the Feast of the Brewing took place. In Urnasch, Switzerland, where pre-Julian New Year's Eve continues to be celebrated, the villagers drive away evil spirits on this night with clanging bells.

Born Today: Horatio Alger (writer); Orlando Bloom (actor); Michael Bond (writer); Julia Louis Dreyfus (actress); Ralph Edwards (TV host); George Gurgieff (philosopher); Richard Moll (actor); Charles Nelson Reilly (actor); Robert Stack (actor); Sophie Tucker (singer/entertainer); Gwen Verdon (dancer/singer); Anna May Wong (actress)

January 14

♑ Capricorn, 5

The typical individual whose birthday falls on January 14 is clever, ambitious, communicative, and independent. If you were born on this day, you're as practical and hard working as any goat; however, your idea of what's important goes far beyond material rewards. A deep-seated need for self-expression prompts you to explore your many creative possibilities. You have a sharp mind that picks up information like a magnet and provides you with a solid foundation of knowledge. Humanitarian impulses stimulate your desire to find a way to make a difference in the world. Whatever path you chose in life will be your own path, not one mandated by the rules of society.

As a Capricorn with the root number five, you have a restless nature and an inventive, progressive mentality that requires a variety of new experiences to keep you from getting bored. You are intelligent and observant, with a methodical mind and a fluency with language that assures you are never at a loss for words. Your ability to translate perceptions and ideas into clear images and deliver them with wit and charm makes you an accomplished speaker and writer. With your enthusiasm and breadth of interests, you would be an excellent teacher or mentor.

You are inherently generous and loving with the people you care about. In intimate relationships, you are affectionate and extremely loyal. Although you tend to be somewhat reserved at the outset, once you relax and loosen up, you can turn into quite a playful comedian.

On This Day:

In Southern India, the three-day Pongal festival begins on this date each year to celebrate the rice harvest, to give thanks to the spirits who bring the rainy season, and to honor Surya, the source of infinite knowledge. In Old Europe, this day was known as Saint Hilary's Day for the patron of backward children, who was invoked against snake bites.

Born Today: Jason Bateman (actor); Julian Bond (civil rights leader); LL Cool J (rap star); John Dos Passos (writer); Faye Dunaway (actress); Lawrence Kasdan (director); Joseph Losey (director); Berthe Morisot (artist); Yukio Mishima (writer); Andy Rooney (satirist/TV journalist); Albert Schweitzer (physician/philosopher)

January 15
♑ Capricorn, 6

Harmony, elegance, and tranquility in every area of life are the ultimate goals of people born on January 15. Whenever possible, you surround yourself with pleasant, cooperative people and beautiful things. You have the same burning ambition and desire for success and recognition as the typical workaholic goat, yet you manage to find time to engage in social pleasantries and pursue your cultural interests. Many creative individuals celebrate birthdays on this day, and those who are not artists, writers, or musicians themselves are often enthusiastic patrons of the arts.

You are inherently sympathetic to the needs of others. You place a high value on the principles of fairness and justice, and you always try to do the right thing. You also like doing things properly, and although you're not a perfectionist, you have a gift for organizing the world around you. When you combine the charm and diplomacy of your number six personality with Capricorn's reliability and steadfast determination, you're able to accomplish virtually anything you set your mind to. This birthday often produces an overwhelming sense of mission. Whatever your mission may be, you'll pursue it with tenacity.

In other areas of life you are practical and realistic, but in intimate relationships you're a romantic idealist. You have a demanding, critical nature and may be severely disappointed if the object of your affection doesn't live up to your high standards. However, as long as everything goes well, you make a devoted and faithful lover.

On This Day:

In Ancient Rome, people celebrated the Feast of the Ass, a festival in honor of the animal that was sacred to Vesta, the veiled goddess of the hearth. Traditional offerings of homemade bread and salt cakes were left at Vesta's temple, where her hearth fire burned continually, tended by six virgin priestesses known as the Vestal Virgins.

Born Today: Charo (singer); Lloyd Bridges (actor); Gene Krupa (drummer); Aristotle Onassis (shipping magnate); Martin Luther King, Jr. (civil rights leader); Moliere (playwright); Gamal Abdul Nasser (president of Egypt); Margaret O'Brien (actress); Maria Schell (actress); Edward Teller (nuclear physicist); Mario Van Peebles (actor)

January 16

♑ Capricorn, 7

People born on January 16 can be an enigma to those around them. One reason is that you manage to satisfy Capricorn's desire for material success without losing sight of your innate spirituality. You walk a thin line between the physical world and the inner world of dreams, and you refuse to be totally absorbed by either. Your psychic-like intuition, with its ability to see through situations and people, is close to uncanny. When you let yourself to be guided by your own gut feelings, you rarely make a mistake.

Although you handle the day-to-day pressures of life quite well, you're essentially a gentle soul. You require frequent breaks from the hectic pace to recharge your batteries. It may help to seek out peaceful surroundings where you can be close to nature. You also love children and animals and have a definite knack for getting along with all types of people. Your quick wit, intelligence, and wisdom draw them to you. Because you connect with others on so many levels, people turn to you for and advice and comfort. However, your compassion can overwhelm you, especially if you get too caught up in the problems of friends and family.

You're very idealistic regarding romantic involvement. Naturally kindhearted, loyal, and devoted, you desperately want the security of a close, loving union. Nevertheless, you may have difficulty establishing an equal relationship. Either you're too needy yourself, or you allow the other person to become excessively dependent on you.

On This Day:

In ancient Rome, people celebrated the festival of Concordia, the goddess of harmonious relationships. In Indonesia, the fire-god Betoro Bromo is honored on this date by pilgrims and Buddhist monks who gather at Mount Bromo. At the first stroke of midnight, offerings of flowers and food are cast into the volcano where the god dwells.

Born Today: Aaliyah (singer); Debbie Allen (dancer/choreographer); John Carpenter (director); Dizzy Dean (baseball player); Dian Fossey (naturalist); A. J. Foyt (auto racer); Ethel Merman (singer/actress); Andre Michelin (tire manufacturer); Kate Moss (supermodel); Francisco Scavullo (fashion photographer); Susan Sontag (writer)

January 17

♑ Capricorn, 8

The dynamic individuals born on this day are among the most ambitious and hard-working members of society. Inherently capable and eminently professional, you could serve as a model for success achieved through one's own efforts. Your taste for power and control pushes you toward positions of authority. You like being the person who is in charge and calling the shots. As a no-nonsense pragmatist, you put a high value on material acquisition and expect to be well compensated for your efforts.

Capricorns with the root number eight are typically shrewd and business-minded, and your intellect is deep and profound. You cautiously explore all possibilities before putting your plans into action. Nevertheless, you're considerably more innovative in your thinking than many other goats. Despite your caution and respect for tradition, you hold some progressive ideas with regard to changing social attitudes. You like helping people and seem to gain almost as much satisfaction from working for altruistic goals as material ones.

Your approach to close relationships is careful and conservative. You're not someone who's likely to fall in love at first sight. It can take you quite awhile to decide whether what you're feeling is the real thing. However, once you make a commitment, you are no fair-weather friend. You stand by your promises and can be relied on to stick around no matter what the circumstances.

On This Day:

In Celtic Britain, the annual ritual of Wassailing the Apple Trees was performed on the eve of old Twelfth Night, which falls on this date. Cider was poured over the roots of the trees, and a chant was offered to drive off evil spirits and make the trees fertile. The word "wassail" is from the Middle English for "to be of good health."

Born Today: Muhammad Ali (boxer); Jim Carrey (actor); Benjamin Franklin (statesman/writer/printer); James Earl Jones (actor); Shari Lewis (ventriloquist); Andy Kaufman (TV comic/actor); Maury Povich (TV talk show host); Vidal Sassoon (hairdresser); Konstantin Stanislavski (director/acting theorist); Betty White (actress)

January 18

VS Capricorn, 9

January 18th people know what they want and refuse to be sidetracked by extraneous circumstances. Once you've set your course, nothing stops you from reaching your goal. You have a good head for business and an instinct for making and handling money. However, you need to be emotionally involved in whatever you are doing, or you will lose interest and your energy will stagnate. If you find a career that is significantly challenging, you immerse yourself in it and can easily become a workaholic.

People born under a number nine vibration rarely allow materialism to distract them from their higher purposes. This means you're a fierce fighter for just causes. Since taking charge comes naturally to you, you feel a responsibility to help those who are less assertive or unable to help themselves. You possess a judicial temperament, and your intuitive understanding of what others are feeling borders on the psychic. Despite a tendency to take life seriously, you have a slightly wacky sense of humor and a magnetic personality that attracts attention and admiration.

In intimate relationships you're a sensuous and passionate lover, but you have an intensely private side to your nature that makes it difficult for you to share your deepest feelings. Sometimes you seem cool and uninvolved, yet on other occasions you are warm and caring. Nevertheless, once you decide to commit to someone, you make a loyal, generous, and devoted partner.

On This Day:

The celebration of the Australian Festival of Perth is sacred to the Aborigine mother goddess Nungeena, who restored beauty to the world after the evil spirit Marmoo destroyed it with insects. In China, the kitchen god Zao Jun is honored with prayers, rice cakes, and paper images on this night, which marks the end of the Chinese New Year.

Born Today: John Boorman (director); Kevin Costner (actor/director); Cary Grant (actor); Oliver Hardy (comic actor); Danny Kaye (comic actor); Mark Messier (hockey player); A. A. Milne (writer); Peter Mark Roget (physician/lexicographer/creator of Roget's Thesaurus); Daniel Webster (politician/statesman); Robert Anton Wilson (writer)

January 19

♑ Capricorn, 1

ndividuals with birthdays on this date are innovative visionaries, yet they are practical enough to understand that it takes more than good intentions to turn dreams into realities. A careful, determined planner, you're prepared to work as hard as necessary to bring your ideas to fruition. Although the path is not always smooth, your persistence and refusal to give up virtually ensure your success. You are a seeker trying to bring together worldly matters and patterns of universal truth. You want to use your talents and resources to create something substantial and lasting for humanity.

You are also extremely competitive and ambitious regarding your own career goals. Sharply intelligent and determined, you expect recognition for your personal accomplishments. You like being in a position of authority where you can use your influence to help yourself and others. More spontaneous and versatile than the typical goat, you can accomplish just about anything that allows you to express yourself creatively. Many artists, entertainers, and sports champions were born on January 19.

You are sociable and friendly, yet independent and individualistic. You may be totally involved in the world around you, and yet, on an emotional level, you remain somewhat detached from it. In personal relationships you value loyalty above all else. You can be the truest lover or friend, but only to one who is true to you.

On This Day:

Thorrablottar, or Husband's Day, is celebrated in Iceland on this date. In ancient times, the festival honored the mighty Norse god Thor, the red-bearded lord of lightning bolts and thunder. The Tarbh-Feis, or Bull Prophecy, was also performed on this day by the ancient Druids to seek help from the spirits for the king and the community.

Born Today: Paul Cezanne (artist); Michael Crawford (actor/singer); Stefan Edberg (tennis player); Phil Everly (singer); Tippi Hedren (actress); Patricia Highsmith (writer); Janis Joplin (rock star); Gustav Meyrink (writer); Dolly Parton (singer/actress); Edgar Allan Poe (writer); Junior Seau (football player); Alexander Woolcott (journalist/critic/actor)

January 20

♑ Capricorn, 2

The person born on the Capricorn/Aquarius cusp is a study in paradoxes. To begin with, you're an unconventional thinker who is determined to give form to your theories and ideas, even when they seem strange to others. On the one hand, you are rebellious and driven by the desire to change the world. On the other, you're a hard-working goat with a practical approach to life and the ability to endure whatever comes along.

The number two's vibration gives you a friendly, persuasive manner and a charming way of getting others to see things from your point of view. Your inherently sociable nature makes it easier for you to combine business with pleasure than for most Capricorns, and you make more progress cooperating with others than working alone. You want peace and harmony and can be charming and gracious when you remember that the world doesn't revolve around your personal objectives, no matter how noble they happen to be.

Although relating comes naturally to you, you are romantic in a pragmatic way. Eventually, you may come to resent the time and energy a relationship consumes. Your union is more likely to be successful if it's based on common interests and a shared sense of purpose. At the very least, your significant other needs to understand your ambitious nature and be willing to make allowances for your little eccentricities.

On This Day:

This day is sacred to the Yoruban mother goddess Oya of Nigeria. Oya, the consort of the god Shango, is the guardian deity of the river Niger. Also a goddess of storms and thunder, her sacred animal is the buffalo, and her presence is symbolized by its horns. Oya is depicted as a nine-headed woman representing fertility and femininity.

Born Today: Edwin " Buzz" Aldrin (astronaut); George Burns (comedian); Frederico Fellini (director); DeForest Kelley (actor); Carol Heiss (skater); Josef Hofmann (pianist); David Lynch (director); John Naber (swimmer); Patricia Neal (actress); Susan Rothenberg (artist); Ruth St. Denis (dancer); George Stavropoulos (fashion designer)

January 21

♒ Aquarius, 3

1ndividuals born January 21 are highly communicative original thinkers with dynamic, outgoing personalities. As such, your inventive mind and quick-witted curiosity combine to produce a left brain/right brain mentality capable of understanding science and technology on the one hand and philosophy and religion on the other. Some of the time, you live inside your head and its realm of logical thought. At other times you are motivated by strong feelings of compassion generated by your humanitarian ideals. Your challenge lies in finding a balance point between the two sides of your nature.

You are a consummate performer with a flair for the dramatic, and you enjoy occupying the center of the stage. In company, you're friendly, charming, and sincere. You like being surrounded by friends and associates with whom you can discuss common interests. Despite a well-earned reputation as a visionary with rather eccentric ideas, when you speak, your words have a noticeable effect on people. You're definitely not a loner, but you are extremely independent and resent having restrictions imposed on you by society's code of behavior.

Essentially a charming, sociable people-person, you will strike up a conversation with anyone. However, you often function better in casual relationships than in heavily emotional, romantic ones. You tend to be more comfortable in a companionable partnership that begins as a friendship and develops into an intimate union based on shared goals and ideas.

On This Day:

Saint Agnes' Day, named after the Roman Catholic child martyr who was beheaded in 304 C.E. for refusing to marry, is traditionally a time for divination by fire, casting love spells, and conjuring information about love's path and relationships in the coming year. This day is also sacred to Yngona, a goddess worshiped in ancient Denmark.

Born Today: Cristobal Balenciaga (fashion designer); Robby Benson (actor); Geena Davis (actress); Christian Dior (fashion designer); Placido Domingo (singer); Jill Eikenberry (actress); Richie Havens (singer); Wolfman Jack (disk jockey); Igor Moiseyev (choreographer); Jack Nicklaus (golfer); Telly Savalias (actor); Paul Scofield (actor)

January 22

♒ Aquarius, 4

"Anything goes" is the theme of those whose birthday falls on this day. As one of them, you believe in doing your own thing and letting other people do theirs. You're very talented, and you have the power to accomplish amazing things. Although Aquarius is a fixed sign, the influence of the number four means you are not partial to dull routine. Rather, yours is an adventurous spirit, with a great love for variety and change. Hard working and naturally self-directed, you know what you want to accomplish and patently refuse to be diverted from your objectives.

As an independent, unconventional visionary with a progressive mentality, you don't just break the rules, you destroy them. With your maverick tendencies and innovative ideas, you are a farsighted trendsetter light-years ahead of the rest of the crowd. Your chosen work must satisfy your idealism as well as your ambitions. Honor is your personal touchstone. You do what you believe is right, without a thought to what other people may think of your actions.

In social situations your charismatic personality attracts friends and admirers. However, you project an air of detachment that often belies your deep devotion to those you care about. Intimacy is not your strongest point, because overt displays of emotion make you feel uncomfortable. You want a partner who can provide intellectual stimulation along with love and affection.

On This Day:

This is Saint Vincent's Day. In ancient Greece, this date was dedicated to the Sun god, Apollo. It was believed that for anyone who carried his emblem, good luck, light, and truth would follow. The nine Greek goddesses of inspiration who watch over musicians, poets, and artists are also honored on this day with the celebration of the Festival of the Muses.

Born Today: Andre Marie Ampere (physicist); Sir Francis Bacon (writer/philosopher); Bill Bixby (actor); Linda Blair (actress); George Gordon Lord Byron (poet); Sergei Eisenstein (director); D. W. Griffith (producer/director); John Hurt (actor); Jerome Kern (composer); Diane Lane (actress); Piper Laurie (actress); August Strindberg (playwright)

January 23

♒ Aquarius, 5

People with birthdays that fall on January 23 are unconventional, paradigm-busting idealists. As a true Aquarian rebel with an innovative mentality, your forte is your capacity for modifying established ideas by rethinking them and restating them in entirely new ways. You are sociable, friendly, and compassionate, but your air of emotional detachment makes your humanitarianism seem more universal than personal. Although you identify with all different kinds of people, you do not fit any particular mode. The only group you're likely to feel totally comfortable with is one made up of highly individualistic people like yourself.

Despite your obvious intelligence and sound, theoretical mind, your oddball eccentricities may earn you a reputation as something of a flake. You're witty and quick thinking and have a way with words that makes you a natural storyteller. Curious about everything, you have an extremely low threshold for boredom and dull routine. Most Aquarians are as fascinated with the past as with the future. Consequently, you may have a compelling interest in space age technology and an equally strong fascination for ancient history and archeology.

Personal freedom is very important to you, yet you're eminently loyal and honorable in your treatment of others. In a close union, you tend to be more idealistic than romantic. The partner you're seeking is your soul mate, and the relationship you're hoping for is one based on friendship, companionship, and common interests.

On This Day:

The annual festival known as the Day of Hathor took place on this date. Hathor, meaning "dwelling of Horus," was the patroness of women and mistress of merriment. She was the beloved cow-headed goddess of heaven, beauty, and love. In Egypt, a libation of cow's milk was poured into the River Nile as prayers were recited.

Born Today: Humphrey Bogart (actor); Gary Burton (musician/composer); Caroline (princess of Monaco); Rutger Hauer (actor); Ernie Kovacs (comedian); Edouard Manet (artist); Jeanne Moreau (actress); Chita Rivera (actress); Randolph Scott (actor); Edward Stone (physicist); Tiffani-Amber Thiessen (actress); Hideki Yukawa (nuclear physicist)

January 24

♒ Aquarius, 6

ater bearers born on this day are easygoing, charming, and peaceable as long as no one steps on their toes. As such, you are a friendly, outgoing person with a sensitive, humanitarian nature. Inherently judicious, you believe that most differences can be resolved through discussion and compromise. Despite your amiable personality, you have a serious side to your character. You are hard working, ambitious, and resourceful, with a good head for business and a logical approach to solving problems.

Although you come across as someone who is coolly self-sufficient, you're a committed people-person. Eclectic in your choice of associates, you are fair and equitable with everyone you meet. You have an open mind, and your insight into human nature makes you a good judge of people and their motivations. You are multi-talented and artistically creative, with a keen appreciation for all things beautiful and harmonious.

You enjoy getting together with a group of friends and going out for some fun. But family also means a lot to you, and you're content to stay home and relax in your personal domain. At times you may feel torn between your independent nature and your need to belong. In a love relationship, you are sensitive, generous, and giving—sometimes so much so that you willingly sacrifice your own interests to those of your loved one.

On This Day:

In La Paz, Bolivia, Ekeko, the Aymara Indian god of prosperity, is honored on this date with a fair called the Alacitas. The Blessing of the Candle of the Happy Woman, an annual pagan purification ceremony, is performed in Hungary. The Cornish Tinner's and Seafarer's Day celebration of old "Labor Day" takes place in Cornwall.

Born Today: John Belushi (TV comic/actor); Ernest Borgnine (actor); Neil Diamond (singer); Mark Goodson (TV producer); Nastassja Kinski (actress); Desmond Morris (anthropologist); Robert Motherwell (artist); Mary Lou Retton (gymnast); Oral Roberts (evangelist); Maria Tallchief (dancer); Sharon Tate (actress); Edith Wharton (writer)

January 25

≈≈≈ Aquarius, 7

The January 25th individual is personable and charming, yet difficult to know. As someone born on this date, your nature is a complex blend of Aquarian rational mentality and the dreamy mysticism of the root number seven. This combination unites your fine intellect and vivid imagination. Your contrasting characteristics give you a unique individuality and a mysterious, paradoxical quality. You're as independent and self-sufficient as other water bearers, but you have a very un-Aquarian-like susceptibility to the moods and feelings of other people.

Although there's a scientific side to your mentality, it's heavily influenced by intuitive hunches and flashes of inspiration. You're probably fascinated with the occult. Still, there's a good deal of common sense mixed in with your mysticism, and that can cause you to question your own conclusions. You have great faith in your dreams and in your ability to make them come true. You may appear to be wasting time daydreaming and speculating, but eventually you figure out a way to put your creative notions to good use.

You're more sensual and romantic than most other Aquarians, but also quicker to fall in and out of love. People interest you; potential lovers interest you most of all. But you still have the water bearer's need for space and freedom. Anyone who gets involved with you will soon find out that you're a lot easier to catch than to keep.

On This Day:

Tet, the Vietnamese New Year festival, takes place on this date with traditional feasts, good luck rituals, and offerings to ancient deities. Evil spirits are driven away with whistles, bells, and horns. According to the old runic calendar, Disting, the Feast of Disir, the Norse guardian goddess, took place on this date at the temple in Uppsala, Sweden.

Born Today: Corazon Aquino (Philippine president); Robert Boyle (chemist/physicist); Robert Burns (poet); Youssef Chahaine (director); Mildred Dunnock (actress); Jacqueline du Pre (cellist); Etta James (singer); Alicia Keys (singer); Dinah Manoff (actress); W. Somerset Maugham (writer); Edwin Newman (TV journalist); Virginia Woolf (writer)

January 26

♒ Aquarius, 8

People who celebrate their birthdays on this day possess a magnetic intensity and commanding personality that rarely fails to attract attention. Strength of character and shrewd intelligence provide you with your unique persona. You have the requisite enterprise, stamina, and stability to succeed in any venture. When your aura of supreme self-confidence casts its hypnotic spell, others start believing that you can do no wrong. However, your actions often spark controversy because you're not afraid to strike out in unexplored or unexpected directions.

The diverse aspects of your character form the basis of your realistic humanitarian outlook and eminently practical idealism. You are charismatic, doggedly determined, and a real powerhouse when it comes to getting things done. In business, you're at your best in a position of authority. You always do what you believe to be right, but you like things done your way. Since you are self-directed, with a strong rebellious streak, if you disagree with society's rules, you make up your own. You expect recognition and appreciation for your hard work and accomplishments, but when you don't get it, you'd rather suffer in silence than admit your disappointment.

In a close union, you want affection and understanding, yet you're afraid of overt displays of emotions. You may have some difficulty establishing an intimate relationship, but once you do, your loyalty and devotion outweigh your emotional shortcomings.

On This Day:

On or around this day each year, the Chinese begin their two-week long New Year celebration. On the first day, ancestral spirits are honored and homes are decorated with strips of red paper to attract luck and ward off evil ghosts. Being on one's best behavior brings good fortune, and eating various rice-based dishes gives long life.

Born Today: Anita Baker (singer); Ellen DeGeneres (comic); Jules Feiffer (cartoonist); Wayne Gretzky (hockey player); Anne Jeffreys (actress); Eartha Kitt (singer); Douglas MacArthur (U.S. Army general); Paul Newman (actor); Gene Siskel (film critic); Bob Uecker (baseball player); Roger Vadim (director); Eddie Van Halen (rock star)

January 27

♒ Aquarius, 9

The January 27th character blends the water bearer's philosophical humanitarianism with the number nine's compassionate spirituality. This makes you a born crusader capable of making tremendous sacrifices for a cause you believe in. Once convinced of the value a project, you'll dedicate yourself to promoting it. Your sincerity and talent for demonstrating and illustrating your plans helps win others to your point of view. With your active nature and ability to make things happen, you could leave a profound imprint on your time.

Although you often depend on hunches and intuition, there's usually a good deal of common sense mixed in with your mysticism. As a maverick and nonconformist, you like doing things in your own, inimitable way. Since you are self-motivated, you dislike supervision and generally do your best work alone. However, just doing something with your life is not enough for you. You like helping people fulfill their potential. Your ultimate goal is to contribute something important to the world and to inspire others to do the same.

Naturally curious and sociable, you enjoy the company of a large variety of acquaintances who are as interested as you in exploring and discussing the mysteries of life. However, you find the emotional demands of others restricting and may be close to very few people. In a love relationship, you need a romantic partner who is independent and either shares your interests or is involved in his or her own path.

On This Day:

The Day of Ishtar was celebrated in honor of the Assyrian/Babylonian goddess of love, who was acknowledged as "Light of the World" and goddess of the morning and evening. Ishtar was the divine personification of the planet Venus (the morning and evening star) and the dispenser of the Never-Failing Waters of Life.

Born Today: Lewis Carroll (writer/photographer); Troy Donahue (actor); Bridget Fonda (actress); Samuel Gompers (labor leader); Skitch Henderson (bandleader); William Randolph Hearst (publisher); Jerome Kern (composer); Wolfgang Amadeus Mozart (composer); John Ogdon (pianist); Donna Reed (actress); Ingrid Thulin (actress)

January 28

♒ Aquarius, 1

The self-motivated January 28th individual is not your typical team player and doesn't respond well to other people's rules. Brimming with enthusiasm, you are a hearty adventurer. In addition to tremendous mental and physical energy, you have a resolute attitude and an upbeat, positive outlook. You want the best for everyone, and you're prepared to do something about it. Unlike some water bearers who seem to enjoy watching life from afar, when you're summoned to a cause worth fighting for, you respond by suiting up for battle.

The nonconforming mavericks born on this day live in a way that reflects their personal style and originality. With your inventive mind, progressive ideas, and pioneering spirit, you're a natural born crusader. You're quick to champion any cause or ideal that catches your fancy. In social situations you're friendly, generous, and warm-hearted. However, diplomacy is not your strong point, and when the adrenaline starts pumping, you plunge ahead with little regard for tact or subtlety. You say exactly what you mean, and you expect other people to be as up front as you are.

Despite your self-sufficiency, relationships are vitally important to you. Friendship is almost as necessary to you as love, and your initial attraction to someone is often mental. You're more passionate than most Aquarians, and you prefer a permanent romantic involvement as long as your partner doesn't try to restrict your freedom.

On This Day:

The centuries-old Norse Festival of Fire, known as Up-Helly-Aa, is celebrated in the Shetland Islands on or around this date each year. It derives from the old Yuletide celebration of the triumph of the Sun over the darkness of winter and pays tribute to the old Viking gods and goddesses with the burning of a replica of a Viking ship.

Born Today: Alan Alda (actor/director); Mikhail Baryshnikov (dancer); Henry VII (king of England); Parry O'Brien (shot-putter); Claes Oldenburg (artist); Auguste Piccard (physicist); Jackson Pollack (artist); Arthur Rubinstein (pianist); Sir Henry Morton Stanley (explorer); Bill White (baseball player/National League president); Elijah Wood (actor)

January 29

♒ Aquarius, 2

The challenge of those born on this day is to maintain a balance between the independent spirit of the Aquarian outsider and the number two's desire to be part of a group. This paradoxical aspect of your nature stems from your conflicting beliefs. You are torn between your ideas about the sanctity of individualism and a deep-seated need to belong. Naturally broad-minded and tolerant, you are eclectic in your choice of associates. Your intuitive insight into human nature makes you a good judge of character. Despite your caring, humanitarian outlook, your idealistic solutions to the world's woes are not always practical and tend to work better in theory than in practice.

Talkative, friendly, and socially aware, you have a way of drawing people out and finding out what makes them tick. You believe in cooperation and think most problems are best resolved through discussion and compromise. Basically rational and reasonable, you approach things intellectually rather than emotionally. Your unusual combination of a scientific mind and an artistic temperament comes from the ability to mix and match your creative ideas with your love of beauty and technological insight.

You are more romantic than most Aquarians and more likely to want a partner to share your life. However, once you find your soul mate, you expect an ideal relationship. In love, you are capable of real devotion, but if your significant other should disappoint you in any way, you're also quite capable of leaving without a backward glance.

On This Day:

This is the birthday of Irene, the Greek goddess of peace, who was worshiped in Athens with bloodless sacrifices. In Vietnam, the mystical, centuries-old Parade of the Unicorns takes place each year around this date. Some Indian tribes in Mexico perform the Hukuli Dance to reach altered states, during which they search out peyote for their religious rites.

Born Today: Paddy Chayevsky (playwright/screenwriter); Anton Chekov (writer); W. C. Fields (actor); John Forsythe (actor); Sara Gilbert (actress); Heather Graham (actress); Ann Jillian (actress); Greg Louganis (swimmer); Ernst Lubitsch (director); Victor Mature (actor); Katherine Ross (actress); Tom Selleck (actor); Oprah Winfrey (TV host)

January 30

♒ Aquarius, 3

With their commanding personalities and strong sense of purpose, those born on this date are natural leaders. Nothing seems impossible to you; the greater the challenge, the more likely it is to catch your interest. You're an objective thinker with an inventive mind and unique ideas that are far ahead of their time. Your keen intellect and shrewd insight into the characters of others make you a good judge of people and situations. However, your forte is communication, and you take great pride in your ability to charm, persuade, or bamboozle others into seeing things from your point of view.

Those born on January 30 are self-assured, success-oriented individuals with big ideas. Yet they are also eccentric, freedom loving, and rebellious. This unusual blend of traits gives you an elusive quality that can be difficult to define or pin down. Nevertheless, you shine in public roles, and when called upon to act, you do so decisively and with conviction. Concerned about your image and the impression you're making, you may actively seek the approval of others. But in the end, you do what you think is right and let the chips fall where they may.

In personal relationships, you are sociable, witty, fun loving, and loyal. You enjoy the company of clever, creative people who stimulate you intellectually. Intimate unions can be somewhat more difficult because of your fear of commitment and your intense devotion to your work.

On This Day:

In ancient Rome, the planting festival known as Feriae Sementiva was celebrated annually on this date. Special sacrifices were made to Ceres, fertility goddess of the harvest and the Earth, and Tellus Mater, mother goddess of the Earth, as well as to other lesser-known gods and goddesses associated with planting and agriculture.

★★
★ **Born Today:** Richard Brautigan (writer); Dick Cheney (U.S. vice president); Gene Hackman (actor); Dick Martin (TV comedian); Franklin Delano Roosevelt (U.S. president); Boris Spassky (chess champion); Curtis Strange (golfer); Louis Rukeyser (financial analyst); Barbara Tuchman (historian/writer); James Watt (engineer/inventor)

January 31

♒ Aquarius, 4

The bright, logical-minded individuals born on this date are frequently jolted out of their linear mode of thinking by sudden flashes of inspiration. These instantaneous bolts of psychic awareness awaken your imagination and help you resolve problems you've been wrestling with for a long time. Although your Aquarian nature is basically unconventional and open to all sorts of possibilities, the sensible vibration of the root number four may make it difficult for you to accept psychic impressions as valid information. Nevertheless, when you go with your hunches, you have the wherewithal to combine your intellectual and creative ideas with bursts of intuition and to materialize your avant-garde ideas in the real world.

You're a true humanitarian, someone who cares about the world's troubles and wants to help fix them. Your solutions tend to rely on practical considerations rather than pie-in-the-sky idealism. You have exceptional organizational and managerial skills and a better head for business than most water bearers do. Your strength of purpose keeps you going long after others have run out of steam.

Mentally you are alert and quick-witted, but emotionally you're a rather cool customer who finds it difficult to share deeper feelings. Despite your air of detachment, you're more in need of affection and companionship than you admit. When you're willing to let down your guard, you make a wonderfully loyal, reliable friend or lover.

On This Day:

In China, people celebrate a festival in honor of Kwan Yin. In the Hawaiian Islands, celebrants hold a joyous flower-filled festival for an ancient goddess associated with the narcissus flower. This day is also sacred to the Norns' Urd, Verdandi, and Skuld, who sit under the Yggdrasil tree by the Well of Urd and determine the fate of men and gods.

★★★
★ **Born Today:** Phil Collins (rock star); Minnie Driver (actress); Phillip Glass (composer); Zane Grey (writer); Norman Mailer (writer); John O'Hara (writer); Anna Pavlova (dancer); Nolan Ryan (baseball player); Jackie Robinson (baseball player); Franz Schubert (composer); Justin Timberlake (rock star); Jersey Joe Walcott (boxer)

February Birthdays

February 1

♒ Aquarius, 1

Water bearers born on this day are forthright nonconformists who speak their minds boldly and convincingly. Motivated by this unique mentality and progressive agenda, you state your beliefs unequivocally and without subtlety or subterfuge whenever you're fired up by a cause. Although you sometimes appear to be totally wrapped up in your own ideas, your enthusiastic, pioneering spirit fuels your humanitarian ideals and projects them outward to the world at large.

Intuitive, innovative, and forward looking, you have a knack for zeroing in on possibilities that others miss. Your talent for analyzing situations and sizing up people gives you a decided advantage in your dealings with others. However, you're essentially self-directed, dislike supervision, and generally do your best work on your own. Since you're not much of team player, some view you as distant or arrogant. You don't mean to offend anyone; it's just that you hate hypocrisy and refuse to suffer fools gladly. If the price of honesty and candor is someone else's approval, you're quite willing to pay it.

Despite your self-sufficiency, you're more passionate than most Aquarians. Relationships matter to you, but you don't trade your freedom lightly. In an intimate union, you want friendship and companionship as much as love. In a long-term relationship, you need a partner who won't try to tell you what you can and can't do.

On This Day:

Imbolic, one of the four great fire festivals or Sabbats of the year, is the "feast of waxing light." It is sacred to Brigid, the Celtic goddess of fire and water. In ancient Greece, the three-day Lesser Eleusinian Mysteries began on this day each year in honor of the mother goddess Demeter (Ceres) and her daughter Persephone (Kore).

Born Today: Fritjof Capra (physicist); Herve Filion (harness racing driver); John Ford (director); Clark Gable (actor); Victor Herbert (composer); Langston Hughes (poet); Rick James (singer); Garrett Morris (comedian); S. J. Pearlman (playwright); Jessica Savitch (TV journalist); Emilio Segre (nuclear physicist); Stephanie (princess of Monaco)

February 2

♒ Aquarius, 2

The humanistic individuals born on this day are amiable and more interested in pleasing others than are many of their Sun sign counterparts. The vibration of the number two adds a personal note to the universality of the compassionate Aquarian nature. Consequently, you're always willing to consider the other person's point of view, and you are less stubborn than most Aquarians. You sometimes have trouble saying no, and you can run yourself ragged doing things for people. You're also more emotional than many water bearers and are able to feel things with your mind as well as your heart.

Despite your cooperative nature and diplomatic approach, you're very much the independent Aquarian. You are imaginative and have inspired ideas, an expansive viewpoint, and a great deal of curiosity about the latest technical developments. A highly developed aesthetic sensibility enhances your appreciation of beauty, art, and music. Science and art have a way of blending together in your psyche to produce ingenious innovations. Discordant conditions and a lack of harmony disturb you, and your talents and temperament generally favor success in creative endeavors.

In relationships, you're extremely idealistic. A sucker for glamour and romance, you want someone who will be all things to you. You're capable of real devotion as long as the object of your affection doesn't disappoint you. However, if the union turns sour, you may look elsewhere.

On This Day:

Candlemas, a European celebration of the purification of the Virgin, was called Wives Feast Day in old northern England. The weather on this day is said to mark the progress of winter. In a similar vein, Groundhog Day in the United States is a festival linked to predicting the length of winter based on whether the groundhog sees his shadow on this day.

Born Today: Garth Brooks (singer); Christie Brinkley (supermodel); Havelock Ellis (psychologist); Farrah Fawcett (actress); Stan Getz (jazz musician); Gale Gordon (actor); Jascha Heifetz (violinist); James Joyce (writer); Graham Nash (rock star); Ayn Rand (writer); Elaine Stritch (actress); Shakira (singer); Tom Smothers (comedian)

February 3
♒ Aquarius, 3

ot much gets past the mentally alert February 3rd individual. Ideas are your forte, and you're interested in everything and everyone. You possess an open, friendly nature with tremendous personal magnetism. You learn quickly and have excellent communication skills with flashes of inspiration that allow you to express yourself with fluency and ease. You're particularly adept at coming up with new ideas and then selling them to others. Considerably more flexible and versatile than most Aquarians, you are always on the lookout for exciting new experiences. Your enthusiasm, compassion, and interest in the common good benefit everyone around you, and you set a great example for those with a less positive view of life.

With your refined, intellectual nature, you have a tendency to live more in the mind than in the senses. You literally radiate forward-looking Aquarian individuality. You enjoy people, love to talk, and have a natural understanding of what makes others tick. Yet, while you may be a master at probing everyone else's psyche, you rarely give out intimate details of your own life.

Your charm and charisma attract admirers like flies to honey. Relationships are important to you, but you like your own space and can feel uncomfortable if someone tries to get too close. Although you have a great desire for love, you have an even greater need for freedom and independence.

On This Day:

Saint Blaise's Day (Blaze Day) commemorates a bishop of Sabaste in Armenia who, on his way to execution, miraculously cured a boy who had a fishbone lodged in his throat. An annual ceremony, the Blessing of the Throats, is held to honor Saint Blaise and to invoke his power to ward off throat ailments brought on by the winter's cold.

Born Today: Joey Bishop (comedian); Blythe Danner (actress); Morgan Fairchild (actress); Horace Greeley (journalist); Bob Griese (football player); Emile Griffith (boxer); Felix Mendelssohn (composer); James Michener (writer); Norman Rockwell (artist); Gertrude Stein (writer/critic); Fran Tarkenton (football player)

February 4

♒ Aquarius, 4

The seemingly quirky, slightly eccentric individuals born on this day are actually some of the hardest working people around. This means that although you have an adventurous spirit, you're more purposeful and conventional than the average water bearer. You have tremendous self-discipline and little use for things or activities you consider frivolous or impractical. There is nothing of the typically Aquarian absent-minded professor in your makeup; you have an excellent memory and exceptional powers of concentration.

Basically self-motivated, you have a strong sense of what you want to accomplish and your own ideas about the way things should be done. Humanitarian idealism and the desire to build something lasting fuel your desire to help the world. Innovative ideas and the ability to back them up with practical implementation are your strengths. However, your sense of responsibility and a belief in doing the right thing can cause you to over-extend yourself. You're usually so busy doing your duty that you tend to forget to take time out to relax and enjoy yourself.

You're not strictly a workaholic, but when you get caught up in a project or idea, you tend to forget about everything else. Love is truly important to you, but you are easily disappointed if the person you care about fails to live up to your high standards.

On This Day:

In Japan, the demons of winter are exorcised on this date with a festival called Setsu-bun. In London prior to World War I, a fair was held to honor King Frost Day. People would gather at the Thames River to petition the King of Frost to bring on spring. Along the Welsh border, some still celebrate this day by gathering snowdrops.

Born Today: David Brenner (comedian); Linda Cohen (guitarist); Alice Cooper (rock star); Betty Friedan (feminist activist); Fernand Leger (artist); Charles Lindbergh (aviator); Ida Lupino (actress/director); Rosa Parks (civil rights activist); Isabel Peron (president of Argentina); Dan Quayle (U.S. vice president); Lawrence Taylor (football player)

February 5

♒ Aquarius, 5

The individual whose birthday falls on this day is a quick-witted, fast-talking, one-of-a-kind original thinker with an extremely low threshold for boredom and dull routine. You are inherently curious about everything. People intrigue you, and science and technology fascinate you. However, it's the gathering and communicating of information that is your real passion. You collect facts the way some people collect stamps or coins. After pondering what you've learned, you mentally reprocess and reorganize it and then pass it along to others.

A highly effective multi-tasker, you're capable of juggling several different activities with amazing ease. Despite your reserves of energy, the urge to keep constantly busy and mentally occupied puts a lot of stress on your nervous system. To avoid burnout, you need to learn how to relax and recharge your batteries. You are considerably more in tune with mental applications than emotional ones, and you feel more comfortable expounding ideas than dealing with feelings. Physical agility is associated with this day, and many well-known professional athletes were born on February 5.

In social situations, your charming manner makes people want to get to know you better. As a mate or lover, you are loving and generous, but also independent and anxious about maintaining your personal space. You need a partner who provides you with intellectual companionship and shares your various interests.

On This Day:

This day is for telling fortunes and practicing divination. It is sacred to Fortuna, the Roman goddess of fate, luck, and fertility. Fortuna was patroness of the bathhouses and of married women. Shown with a wheel, sphere, ship's rudder, or cornucopia, she was known to the Greeks as Tyche and to the Anglo-Saxons as Wyrd.

Born Today: Hank Aaron (baseball player); John Guare (playwright); Barbara Hershey (actress); Sir Alan L. Hodgkin (physiologist); Robert Hofstadter (atomic scientist); William Jovanovich (publisher); Janet Leigh (actress); Charlotte Rampling (actress); Arthur Ochs Sulzburger (newspaper publisher); Roger Staubach (football player)

February 6

♒ Aquarius, 6

he potentially legendary individuals born on this day have an elusive, paradoxical quality that's difficult to pinpoint or define. On the one hand, you're among the most relationship conscious and congenial of all Aquarian Sun natives. On the other, you're a nonconformist who chafes at restrictions and consistently marches to the beat of a different drummer. Your foresight and innovative vision are specifically geared towards interaction, and you have tremendous insight into other people and their motivations.

You are fun loving and possess so much natural charm that even your rivals and detractors are forced to acknowledge your likeability. The unique blend of the water bearer's strong sense of personal integrity with the diplomatic vibration of the number six allows you function as a mediator between disparate factions. Moreover, you are more open to ideas you don't agree with than many of your Sun sign counterparts. With your magnetic personality and upbeat amiability, you're a joy to be around. However, it's your positive attitude and willingness to embrace all of humanity that makes it possible for you to use your prodigious talents for the benefit of all.

In personal relationships you are loyal and loving. Partnership is important to you, and you have a romantic streak that makes it possible for you to enjoy courting and being courted. In a committed union, you go out of your way to accommodate your significant other, and you expect similar consideration in return.

On This Day:

In Greece on this day, a festival was held in honor of the love goddess Aphrodite. Throughout northern Japan, a centuries-old winter snow festival takes place around this time of the month every year. The ancient, beneficial spirits that bring life-sustaining water are honored at special shrines erected in huts that resemble igloos.

Born Today: Tom Brokaw (TV journalist/anchor); Aaron Burr (U.S. vice president); Fabian (singer); Mary Leakey (archaeologist); Bob Marley (singer/songwriter); Christopher Marlowe (playwright/poet); Ronald Reagan (U.S. president/actor); George Herman "Babe" Ruth (baseball player); Rip Torn (actor); Francois Truffaut (director)

February 7

♒ Aquarius, 7

The water bearer born on this day projects an alluring magnetism that is hard to resist and impossible to define. Your complex, contradictory personality tends to mystify most people, yet they find themselves drawn to you as if by magic. Although outwardly gregarious and genuinely helpful, you possess a contemplative inner core that demands periods of privacy and solitude. You are an innovative, independent thinker with an otherworldly demeanor and a strikingly original way of looking at things. When your Aquarian intellect merges with the number seven's intuition and imagination, you're capable of visualizing possibilities that others don't even dream about.

Your gentle heart and sensitive, impressionable nature make you a crusader for social causes. Because you identify with people and their problems, you long to help them improve their lives. Your scholarly command of language and talent for communicating your unique insights help you convince others to join you in your humanitarian concerns. Although your solutions to the world's troubles are a rather oddball mixture of logical, scientific ideas and metaphysical principles, they can be surprisingly effective.

In close relationships, you waver between romantic idealism and rational Aquarian detachment. You make a wonderfully loyal friend, but in an intimate union you feel exposed and vulnerable. You want to be involved, yet you're deathly afraid of losing your independence.

On This Day:

A yearly fertility festival known as Li Ch'un, meaning "to welcome back the spring," is still celebrated on this day in China. Bamboo and paper effigies of water buffalo are carried through the streets to the local temple. Once there, the effigies are set on fire so that the prayers of the people may be carried up to heaven on the smoke.

Born Today: Alfred Adler (psychiatrist); Eddie Bracken (actor); Buster Crabbe (actor); King Curtis (jazz musician/bandleader); Charles Dickens (writer); Ashton Kutcher (actor); Sinclair Lewis (writer); Chris Rock (comedian); James Spader (actor); Gay Talese (writer); An Wang (computer entrepreneur); Laura Ingalls Wilder (writer)

February 8

♒ Aquarius, 8

The February 8th individual is a resourceful, hardworking visionary with the requisite enterprise and stamina to succeed in virtually any venture. No matter what path you follow in life, you always seem to know what to do to obtain the best possible results. Your sense of timing is impeccable. In financial matters, instinct tells you when to invest and when to opt out. Despite your rugged Aquarian independence, your ambitions are more universal than personal. You're concerned with society and its woes, and you feel duty bound to create or construct something beneficial to all humanity.

You are more driven and goal oriented than other Aquarians, and your inner strength is awesome. The more tasks and obligations piled on you, the better you function. In business, you always have a plan for dealing with thorny problems and solving them quickly and efficiently. You keep your finger on the public pulse, and you usually know what consumers want before they do.

You are responsible, loyal, and devoted to family and close friends. Nevertheless, you don't go in for wild displays of emotion; losing control is not your style. You're so wrapped up in your own thoughts and plans that you find it difficult to give your all to your mate or partner. Even in intimate relationships, you maintain a certain emotional detachment.

On This Day:

In Japan, the goddess Wakahiru, who oversees weaving, is honored on this day. Broken needles are brought to Buddhist temples along with a variety of sewing objects for the Mass for the Broken Needles. In China, the Star Festival takes place on or around this date. Lanterns are lit to honor the 108 stars that influence the fate of humans.

Born Today: Evangeline Adams (astrologer); Martin Buber (philosopher); James Dean (actor); Robert Klein (comedian); Ted Koppel (TV news analyst/host); Jack Lemmon (actor); Mary I (queen of England); Audrey Meadows (actress); Nick Nolte (actor); Lana Turner (actress); Jules Verne (writer); John Williams (composer/conductor)

February 9

♒ Aquarius, 9

Your birth date signifies a person who is a unique combination of childlike innocence and great wisdom. Although you have to deal with many problems in your own life, you willingly rally to the cause of other people's struggles. You don't merely espouse your spiritual beliefs—you live them. You're compassionate and not overly practical; at times you can be so generous to others as to endanger your own security. Moreover, you could care less. Aquarian stubbornness is marked in February 9th individuals. Once you decide to do something, no power on Earth or in the heavens can change your mind.

You are self-directed and march to a beat that only you can hear. Your innovative ideas often border on genius. You have a reputation for eccentricity that comes as much from other people's misinterpretation of your paradigm-busting brilliance as from your own desire to shock. You have no patience with those who are so focused on the past that they refuse to accept change. You won't hesitate to shake people up if you think it will help get your message across.

Naturally friendly and sociable, you attract all types of acquaintances. You're inherently more romantic and sentimental than many of your Sun sign counterparts. You flourish in the tranquility of a harmonious home and can be rather protective of your loved ones and your private moments with them.

On This Day:

The feast day of Apollo, deity of the Sun, celebrates the increasing light after the darkness of winter. In northern Norway, the annual Narvik Sun Pageant honoring the ancient pagan goddess who rules over the Sun begins at sunrise. The ancient celebration continues throughout the day until the shadows of evening begin darkening the sky.

Born Today: Brendan Behan (writer); Ronald Colman (actor); Mia Farrow (actress); Kathryn Grayson (singer/actress); William Henry Harrison (U.S. president); Carole King (singer/songwriter); Amy Lowell (poet); Joe Pesci (actor); Dean Rusk (U.S. secretary of state); Bill Veeck (baseball owner/manager); Alice Walker (writer)

February 10

♒ Aquarius, 1

T he individual whose birthday falls on February 10 is a dynamic bundle of high energy. Plugged in and ready to go, you zip through your day, and anyone who gets in the way risks being run over. You don't mean to be insensitive; it's just that you are single-minded in your pursuit of any goal or ideal that fires your imagination. The erratic mental processes of Aquarius combined with the number one give you a mind that bounces from idea to idea and thought to thought without following any system of logical progression. This nonlinear method of thinking often produces innovative, inventive ideas that are years ahead of their time.

Nothing is hidden in your personality—what people see is what they get. Words like *secret* and *clandestine* simply have no place in your vocabulary. Although you may not see yourself as a classic do-gooder, you're a freedom-loving idealist and a fervent crusader for the rights of others. You are inherently loyal and naïvely trusting unless given a good reason to be otherwise. You rarely hold a grudge, but once someone betrays your trust, you're quite capable of cutting that person out of your life forever.

You are more ardent and romantic than the typical Aquarian, and close relationships are extremely important to you. Despite your freewheeling nature, you're deeply concerned about the welfare of your loved ones.

On This Day:

The Afro-Brazilian festival of Yemaja, whose name means "fish mother," honors the Nigerian goddess of flowing water. On this day in Brazil, the celebrations begin at daybreak with ocean-bound processions of singers and dancers. In Africa, the start of the fishing season is celebrated on this day each year by the Kebbawa tribe of Nigeria.

Born Today: Stella Adler (acting teacher); Bertold Brecht (playwright); Lon Chaney, Jr. (actor); Laura Dern (actress); Jimmy Durante (comedian); Roberta Flack (singer); Alan Hale, Sr. (actor); Charles Lamb (writer/critic); Greg Norman (golfer); Boris Pasternak (poet/writer); Leontyne Price (opera singer); Mark Spitz (swimmer); Robert Wagner (actor)

February 11

♒ Aquarius, 2

The essential makeup of those born on this day is a fascinating combination of strength and ambition on the one hand and gentleness and imagination on the other. Your magnetic intensity and commanding personality rarely fail to attract attention and admiration. You understand and appreciate the powerful forces that drive you, even if others don't. While your avant-garde and occasionally outlandish ideas may startle some in the mainstream, they can also bring you fame and fortune. Although you're a lot more interested in prestige than money, success has a way of attracting both.

You're highly competitive in a very un-Aquarian manner. Your single-mindedness and desire to make it to the top of your profession help you overcome disappointments and setbacks. Your forte lies in your ability to balance the different areas of your life without losing your focus or emotional center. You are socially aware, sincerely interested in others, and fair and equitable with everyone you meet. Wherever you go, people respond to your friendly, gracious, colorful ways.

You enjoy the good things in life and want to share them with those you love. You also tend to be more romantic and partnership oriented than other water bearers. You have many friends and acquaintances, and you treat them all with the same open-hearted warmth and affection that other Aquarians reserve for their nearest and dearest.

On This Day:

Each year, many pilgrims converge on the shrine of Our Lady of Lourdes in France to commemorate the apparition of the Virgin Mary, who appeared to Bernadette Soubrious on February 11, 1858. A spring in the village is believed to possess curative powers, and some people bathe in the water in the hope that it will heal their illness and disabilities.

Born Today: Jennifer Aniston (actress); Brandy (singer); Sheryl Crow (singer); Thomas Alva Edison (inventor); Tina Louise (actress); Joseph Mankiewicz (director); Sergio Mendes (bandleader); Manuel Noriega (Panamanian dictator); Mary Quant (fashion designer); Burt Reynolds (actor); Sidney Sheldon (writer); Kim Stanley (actress)

February 12

≋ Aquarius, 3

ater bearers born on this day are outgoing, friendly, and brimming with personal magnetism. Aquarian eccentricities are tempered in you by an easy charm and good social skills. In fact, you project so much positive energy and enthusiasm that it almost seems unfair. The warmth of your likeable personality and the appeal of your wonderful, offbeat sense of humor make you very popular. One way or another, you manage to achieve a balance between the independent side of your nature and your desire to be supportive of others.

Leadership abilities are strongly marked in those born on February 12. With this birthday, you possess both a quick wit and a fine objective mind that allow you to accurately assess situations and people. Flashes of inspiration help you zero in on established ideas, take them apart, and then put them together again in entirely new ways. Inherently understanding and sensitive, you are more tactful and cooperative than most other members of your Sun sign. Moreover, you're capable of motivating and inspiring others, and many born on this day find their niche in government service or politics.

You're more of a "people person" than the typical Aquarian. A personal relationship is very important to you, but you want more from a partner than just love and affection. You need someone whose company is as stimulating on a mental level as it is on an emotional one.

On This Day:

This is a holy day sacred to Diana, the Roman Moon goddess, patroness of the hunt and guardian of the forest near Aricia, where her sacred grove stood. Diana is also known as the Lady of the Beasts, and she watches over pregnant animals and their babies. As light returns to the Earth, Diana's powers of protection are invoked for all her creatures.

Born Today: Omar Bradley (U.S. Army general); Dom DiMaggio (baseball player); Charles Darwin (naturalist/evolutionist); Charles Dumas (high jumper); Joe Garagiola (baseball player); Lorne Green (actor); Abraham Lincoln (U.S. president); Christina Ricci (actress); Bill Russell (basketball player); Franco Zeffirelli (director)

February 13

♒ Aquarius, 4

Water bearers born on this date are among the genuine go-getters of the universe. You know what you want to accomplish and refuse to be diverted from your goals by extraneous factors. You're self-motivated and not easily swayed by what others think of your efforts. You know that you have the requisite enterprise and stability to succeed in virtually any venture. A natural workhorse, you're prepared to do whatever it takes—come in early, stay late, work on weekends—to achieve your goals.

In you, the visionary ideals and innovative ideas typically associated with Aquarius are energized by the number thirteen's ambitious nature. You think things through and carefully prepare a course of action before implementing your plans. Like an architect or builder, you know that you must install a good foundation for everything to function correctly. You may be anxious on the inside, but you project a calm exterior, and your shrewd assessments of people and situations inspire confidence. You're proud of your accomplishments and expect recognition in return for all your hard work. If it's not forthcoming, you feel slighted. However, you would rather suffer in silence than admit to hurt feelings.

Your tendency is to work too much and play too little. But when you do take a break, you tend to party heartily. You're someone who enjoys the single lifestyle, yet once you settle on the right person, you make a loyal and devoted partner.

On This Day:

Old Leap Year's Day was observed on this date. In ancient Rome, the eight-day festival of Parentalia began with the senior Vestal Virgin performing rites in honor of the dead. Ancestral tombs were visited with offerings honoring the spirits of the departed, especially parents. During the entire Parentalia period, all the temples were closed and marriages forbidden.

Born Today: Patti Berg (golfer); Stockard Channing (actress); Konstantin Costa-Gavras (director); Tennessee Ernie Ford (singer/actor); Peter Gabriel (rock star); Kim Novak (actress); Oliver Reed (actor); George Segal (actor); William Shockley (physicist); Georges Simenon (writer); Grant Wood (artist); Chuck Yeager (astronaut)

February 14

♒ Aquarius, 5

he quick-witted, silver-tongued February 14th person possesses an analytical intellect with a propensity for tackling extremely complex problems. Lies, even little white ones, and hypocritical pronouncements are abhorrent to your nature. You are inspired to spread the truth abroad, and you feel an obligation to share your beliefs and opinions with the world. Your forte is your capacity for entertaining people and making them laugh. At times you may shock those around you with your devastatingly clever quips and insightful comments, but you rarely fail to make them think.

Those born on this day are apt to go their own way without a giving much thought to possible consequences. It's no wonder that for you, your ideas are your ideas, and you'll stand up for them no matter what others may think. A loyal champion of the underdog, you'll fight the good fight even if your cause seems hopeless. Words are your medium, and your manner of employing them can seem bold and reckless to more timid souls. Although you are extremely generous and compassionate, the emotional detachment of an Aquarius makes your humanitarianism appear more universal than personal.

Individuals born on Saint Valentine's Day are loyal and loving, but not especially romantic. Sincere friendship and companionship rate a lot higher in your estimation than syrupy, sentimental pronouncements. You need a partner who either shares your intellectual interests and crusading ideals or grants you the freedom to pursue them without interference.

On This Day:

This day is the Feast of Saint Valentine, patron saint of lovers. According to legend, a bishop named Valentine conducted weddings for Roman soldiers against an order of Claudius II, who had forbidden them to marry. After being condemned to death, Valentine cured the judge's daughter of blindness and then sent her a letter signed "your Valentine."

Born Today: Mel Allen (sportscaster); Jack Benny (comedian); Carl Bernstein (journalist); Drew Bledsoe (football player); Hugh Downs (TV host); Florence Henderson (actress); Gregory Hines (dancer); James Hoffa (union leader); Johnny Longden (jockey); Vic Morrow (actor); Alan Parker (director); Meg Tilly (actress)

February 15

Ingenuity and enthusiasm are key traits of the person whose birthday falls on this day. You're an innovative thinker with a quick mind and original ideas that are frequently miles ahead of the rest of the crowd. Moreover, as a charismatic communicator, you have a talent for winning other people over to your point of view. Challenges and setbacks don't faze you, because you learn so fast that overcoming difficulties has become your specialty. Despite your inevitable disappointment when plans go awry, you always manage to hang on to your optimistic, positive outlook.

You function best in the company of those who understand and appreciate your broad vision. Consequently, you are attracted by large-scale enterprises and bold ideas. You understand what's required to turn your visions into realities. Some of your dreams may seem "far out" to more conservative types, but you have the wherewithal to back them up with practical plans. You're the original Good Samaritan who refuses to give up on anyone. You have willingly helped many a grateful friend or associate avert disaster.

Your basic nature is warmer and more affectionate than many of your Sun sign counterparts. You're popular and outgoing and have many friends and acquaintances. Home and family mean a great deal to you. Your loved ones provide a quiet haven and anchor of security in your freewheeling, go-go lifestyle.

On This Day:

In ancient Rome, the Lupercalia (Feast of the Wolf) was celebrated in the cave on Palantine Hill where Romulus and Remus were suckled by their wolf foster-mother. The rustic festival marked the beginning of spring with ritual purification and fertility magic. In the Odinist calendar, this day is sacred to the Norse hero Sigfrid.

Born Today: Susan B. Anthony (social activist); John Barrymore (actor); Chris Farley (comedian); Galileo Galilei (astronomer); Harvey Korman (actor); Melissa Manchester (singer); Cyrus McCormick (inventor/manufacturer); Cesar Romero (actor); Jane Seymour (actress); Sir Ernest Shackleton (explorer); Charles Tiffany (jeweler)

THE 366 BIRTHDAYS OF THE YEAR   113

February 16

♒ Aquarius, 7

The February 16th individual is a paradox wrapped in an enigma. At first glance, you come off as a courageous, high-spirited extrovert. However, a second look may reveal the truth seeker within who is fascinated by all things mysterious and mystical. Despite your outgoing exuberance, you're inclined to take the task at hand a lot more seriously than people think. Physically you are fast on your feet, and mentally you're even quicker on the uptake. You are not afraid of responsibility or changes in direction. When opportunity comes knocking, you tend to respond with interest and enthusiasm.

You have a gift for sizing up situations quickly and efficiently. A mixture of wisdom and imagination provides the insight; then your intuition works with your analytical mind to tie everything together. Artistic talent is quite common among those born on this day, and you may be skilled in handicrafts, writing, music, or dance. Whatever you do, you need to make a difference. If the work you're involved isn't meaningful, you won't find it fulfilling. You're quite capable of leaving a job rather abruptly and going off in search of something better.

You may find an intimate relationship difficult to sustain. You breathe the rarefied air of a visionary and can feel misunderstood. You need a partner who understands your moodiness and occasional desire for solitude.

On This Day:

In ancient Tibet, people performed a rite called the Devil's Dance on or near this date when, as part of the New Year Festival, a sorcerer exorcised the demons and evil influences of the prior year. The Celebration of Victoria (Nike) took place in Rome on this day until the year 394 C.E., when Theodosius I destroyed the sacred altar of the goddess.

Born Today: Patty Andrews (singer); Max Baer (boxer); Edgar Bergen (ventriloquist); Sonny Bono (singer/politician); LeVar Burton (actor); Robert Flaherty (documentary filmmaker); Ice-T (rap star); George Kennan (diplomat/political scientist); C. W. Leadbeater (occultist); John McEnroe (tennis player); John Schlesinger (director)

February 17

~~~ Aquarius, 8

Water bearers born on this day are charismatic, ambitious, smart, and successful. Your birthday means you're a leader with executive skills and a very strong presence. You continually push the envelope, and you're constantly challenging yourself to bigger and better accomplishments. Like others born on February 18, you are hard working, persistent, and adept at overcoming obstacles. Your essential nature is obstinate and rebellious, and once you set your mind to a goal, virtually nothing can stop you from achieving it.

You enjoy both physical and mental competition, and your responses on all levels are quick as lightning. While you may act the part of the innovative, eccentric Aquarian where your own affairs are concerned, you're less likely to take risks in ventures involving others. Your concern for your group or team can cause you to stick to the tried and true until you're absolutely convinced that a proposed change is in everyone's best interest. When you get both sides of your paradoxical nature working together, you're capable of inspiring people with your inherent wisdom and farseeing, humanitarian principles and ideals.

In relationships, you're sociable and enjoy the company of interesting people from diverse backgrounds. You are attracted to strong-minded, talented individuals with something worthwhile to contribute to a conversation. You may hesitate, however, before getting involved in a permanent union. When you do make a commitment, you can be quite demanding, yet also loyal and loving.

On This Day:

The Roman Festival of Fornacalia was celebrated in February to honor Fornax, the oven goddess. In early Rome, each area had its own day for performing the Fornacalia. As the city grew, some did not know when to perform the sacrifice, so they held the ritual on the day of the Quirinalia, which was later called "The Feast of Fools."

Born Today: Marian Anderson (opera singer); Red Barber (sportscaster); Alan Bates (actor); Jim Brown (football player); Paris Hilton (socialite); Hal Holbrook (actor); Michael Jordan (basketball player); Arthur Kennedy (actor); Huey Newton (political activist); Lou Diamond Phillips (actor); Chaim Potok (writer); Rene Russo (actress)

February 18

♒ Aquarius, 9

The highly individualistic person whose birthday falls on this day can't help standing out in a crowd. That's because your rather unusual lifestyle stems from an oddball mixture of contradictory ideas. With interests that run in every direction, any attempt to pigeonhole you becomes an exercise in futility. More than anything, you're a reformer, albeit an unlikely one. Your world view is a conglomeration of humanitarian ideals, scientific principles, and metaphysical beliefs. Inherently charitable and capable of tremendous sacrifices for the general good, you do everything in your power to promote a cause once you're convinced of its value.

You are sociable, helpful, sympathetic, and determined to make a difference in the world. When you reach out to people, they respond enthusiastically. You instinctively know what needs to be done, and your talent for persuasive speech helps you convince others to join your work. Although you want to be of service to the world, you're quite capable of serving your own interests as well. While personal success may not be the number one item on your agenda, your efforts on your own behalf are usually well rewarded. In fact, many of those born on February 18 are stars in their own right, with brilliant careers in politics, entertainment, or business.

With other people, you're more accessible emotionally than most other Aquarians. Caring, compassionate, and romantic, you pour your heart and soul into an intimate union. However, you are so idealistic that you're easily disappointed if the relationship fails to live up to your expectations.

On This Day:

This day was sacred to Tacita, the silent Roman goddess who binds hostile speech. In Persia, the annual pagan festival of women known as Spenta Armaiti took place on this date to celebrate the goddess within all women. The temple priestesses performed fertility rites in honor of Spandaramet, goddess of the Earth and the dead.

Born Today: Matt Dillon (actor); Dr. Dre (rap star); Milos Forman (director); John Hughes (director); George Kennedy (actor); Toni Morrison (writer); Yoko Ono (conceptual artist); Molly Ringwald (actress); Andres Segovia (guitarist); Cybill Shepherd (actress); Louis Comfort Tiffany (stained glass artist/silversmith); John Travolta (actor)

February 19

♓ Pisces, 1

Those born on the Pisces/Aquarius cusp, a combination that blends the cool rationality of the water bearer with the intuition of the emotional fish, are among the genuine visionaries of the zodiac. The vibration of the number one adds the dynamic energy of the aggressive doer to your gentle Piscean nature. As a result, you often feel conflicted or pulled in several directions at once. Sometimes you just want to kick back and watch the world go by. However, when your rich imagination is fired by a dream, your strong sense of purpose surprises everyone.

People are drawn to your magnetic personality and bubbly enthusiasm. Many famous people in fields related to the arts and entertainment were born on this day. Although you enjoy the spotlight, too much scrutiny and attention makes you uncomfortable. Your charitable instincts and sympathetic understanding of people's problems incline you toward the helping professions. You have what it takes to accomplish whatever you set your mind to, and your innovative ideas and exceptional powers of persuasion inspire others to try to make a difference in the world as well.

In a one-to-one relationship, you're passionate and sympathetic to your partner's desires. You enjoy being pampered, and you're willing to indulge your lover's desires in return. As a true romantic, you're easily swept off your feet. However, if reality fails to live up to your idealistic notions of love, you are easily disappointed.

On This Day:

The birth of the Roman goddess Minerva (Pallas Athena), who was perceived alternately as a goddess of war and of peace, was believed to have taken place on this date. Minerva, the tutelary goddess of Rome, is also associated with wisdom, arts and crafts, and needlework. This day is also sacred to the Mesopotamian creator and birth goddess Nammu, who was the mother of mortal life.

Born Today: Eddie Arcaro (jockey); Nicholas Copernicus (astronomer); Jeff Daniels (actor); John Frankenheimer (director); Stan Kenton (jazz composer/bandleader); Lee Marvin (actor); Carson McCullers (writer); Merle Oberon (actress); Smokey Robinson (singer/songwriter); Brad Steiger (psychic researcher/writer); Amy Tan (writer)

February 20

♓ Pisces, 2

People born on this day are romantic idealists with a genuine love of beauty, art, and music. The sign of the fish indicates you're a warm, social being with a compassionate personality and a friendly, easygoing manner. As a diplomat and team player, you are naturally polite and receptive to the needs of others. You identify with those in distress and even feel their pain, and to relieve their suffering, you're usually willing to do whatever you can to help them solve their problems. At times you're so eager to be of assistance that you may not even notice when someone is trying to take advantage of your good nature.

Your mysterious, chameleon-like personality fascinates and often confounds people. You have tremendous insight into what motivates others, yet they can't figure you out. You possess an otherworldly quality that can make you seem softer than you actually are. Your forte is your ability to compromise and bring opposing forces together. Courteous, tactful, and sociable, you project a sense of balance and harmony that permeates all of your interactions. Your real aim is to help create a world where everyone is treated equally, with respect and dignity.

You are sentimental, idealistic, and romantic, with some rather unrealistic ideas about relationships. You abhor confrontations and may try to keep the peace by clinging to a bad situation. Instead of dealing with disappointment, you prefer to put on a pair of rose-colored glasses and tell yourself everything's okay, even when it isn't.

On This Day:

This is the Roman Catholic feast day of the Blessed Jacinta and Francisco Marto, children who, along with their cousin Lucia dos Santos, received apparitions of the Virgin Mary at Cova da Iria near Fatima, Portugal. Both Jacinta and Francisco died of influenza at an early age. Lucia, a Carmelite nun, was still living when Jacinta and Francisco were beatified in the year 2000.

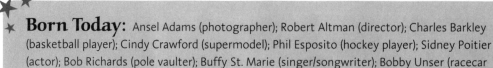

Born Today: Ansel Adams (photographer); Robert Altman (director); Charles Barkley (basketball player); Cindy Crawford (supermodel); Phil Esposito (hockey player); Sidney Poitier (actor); Bob Richards (pole vaulter); Buffy St. Marie (singer/songwriter); Bobby Unser (racecar driver); Gloria Vanderbilt (fashion designer); Nancy Wilson (singer)

February 21

♓ Pisces, 3

The individual whose birthday falls on this day is imaginative, creative, dramatic, and romantic. Charming and resourceful, with a wonderful sense of humor and a chameleon-like adaptability, you fit in everywhere and get along with everyone. You project a dreamy aura that makes you appear one step removed from the real world. Some may see this as an indication that you're a pushover for an adroit sales pitch or heart-wrenching sob story. Nothing could be further from the truth. Despite your compassionate, easygoing nature, you are capable of talking circles around most people, and you rarely agree to do anything you don't want to do.

People born under the sign of Pisces and the number three are self-expressive, enthusiastic, optimistic, and sociable. As one of society's charmers, you probably have many friends and admirers. You possess the logical mind of a scientist with an artistic temperament. Mentally, you are quick-witted and clever. Emotionally, you're impressionable, idealistic, and compassionate. Despite your light-hearted manner, there is nothing superficial about your desire to succeed; you are naturally ambitious and hard working. Multi-talented and extremely versatile, you may have trouble choosing from among several different career options.

You project a magical allure that draws romance into your life. It's a lucky thing too, because you consider love vital to personal happiness. You crave moonlight, poetry, and romance. Before you commit to an intimate union, you need to know you're truly cared about and appreciated.

On This Day:

Feralia, the ancient Roman All Soul's Day, was held annually at the close of Parentalia. Family members came together at the tombs to honor their departed ancestors and the Lares (ancestral guardian spirits) with prayers. On this day, offerings of food were left for the spirits of the dead, who were believed to be abroad in the world.

Born Today: W. H. Auden (poet); Erma Bombeck (writer/humor columnist); Charlotte Church (singer); Tyne Daly (actress); Hubert de Givency (fashion designer); Kelsey Grammer (actor); Rue McClanahan (actress); Anais Nin (writer); Sam Peckinpah (director); Alan Rickman (actor); Ann Sheridan (actress); Nina Simone (jazz singer)

February 22

♓ Pisces, 4

Being born on February 22 gives you a charismatic personality and a compassionate understanding of those around you. You empathize with others, yet a cautious pragmatism lurks beneath your kindhearted Piscean personality. You can be rather secretive, and you rarely talk about your plans until you've set them into motion. A unique combination of intuition and psychic receptivity helps you understand the deeper meaning of things. You have a gift for tuning into wavelengths that aren't available through ordinary channels; it sometimes seems as if you pull information out of the air.

Your unusual blend of creativity and will power make you a good bet for a career in the arts or the media. Your personal agenda revolves around a desire to make your mark in the world. With your many talents, prophetic vision, and strength of purpose, you have the requisite skills to succeed in virtually any occupation. You would do especially well in politics because of your universal appeal. As the consummate humanitarian, you're willing to sacrifice your own interests for the good of society.

In love, you're idealistic and romantic, but also responsible and devoted. You crave affection and may not be truly happy without it. You are generous with your loved ones, but your feelings are easily hurt if you sense that your help is not appreciated.

On This Day:

The festival of the goddess Concordia was an annual Roman celebration of favor and goodwill that followed Feralia. It was a cheerful time, coming after the Parentalia's eight days of somber activities. Families and friends gathered to renew ties and settle disputes. At the end of the festival meal, offerings were made to the gods of the household.

Born Today: Sparky Anderson (baseball manager); Drew Barrymore (actress); Luis Bunuel (director); Frederic Chopin (composer/pianist); Julius Erving (basketball player); Charles O. Finley (baseball manager); Edward "Ted" Kennedy (U.S. senator); John Mills (actor); Jeri Ryan (actress); George Washington (U.S. president); Robert Young (actor)

February 23

♓ Pisces, 5

Those born on this day are an intriguing blend of the intuitive, emotional fish and the rational communicator associated with the number twenty-three. As such, you're fascinated with the occult and metaphysics, yet a lot of common sense is mixed in with your interest in the mysterious and unusual. You are fluent in language, enjoy making conversation, and have a great deal to say. Moreover, you're also a good listener. You may have literary and dramatic ability and possibly a talent in art, music, and dance as well. If you're not a writer, artist, or entertainer yourself, you're probably an avid patron of the arts.

You possess the genuine compassion and caring nature of a true humanitarian. Your sensitivity to others gives you a psychic-like insight into their hearts and minds. Your quick wit and fine intellect attract friends and associates with a broad range of cultural interests. Ambitious and versatile, with a mercurial temperament, you're a natural networker who mixes well with people from all walks of life. Your leadership capabilities and knack for mixing business with pleasure make you a powerful force in the professional world. However, you have a restless nature that can't abide being chained to a desk or tied to a routine job.

In a loving relationship you are generous and passionate. You enjoy the intimacy of a committed partnership. However, you need a partner who shares some of your many interests and can be a friend as well as a lover.

On This Day:

The Teminalia was an annual ritual held in the temple of Jupiter on Capitoline Hill in Rome to honor Terminus, the god of boundary stones. Throughout the country-side, all boundary stones and markers of converging fields were draped with flower garlands, and a sacrifice of blood, wine, and honeycombs was offered to the god.

Born Today: William Edward Burghardt DuBois (founder of the NAACP); Victor Fleming (director); Peter Fonda (actor); George Frederic Handel (composer); Elston Howard (baseball player); Akira Kurosawa (director); Patricia Richardson (actress); Meyer Amschel Rothschild (banker); John Sandford (writer); Julie Walters (actress)

February 24

♓ Pisces, 6

Pisceans born on this day are partnership oriented, sympathetic, and sincerely willing to help out. These qualities give you a nurturing, sympathetic manner that invariably draws people close to you. You accomplish your purposes through charm and diplomacy instead of by making demands. You can be rather elusive and mysterious, and your chameleon-like personality fascinates some and confuses others. Consequently, you usually understand other people a lot better than they understand you.

You absorb emotional vibrations like a sponge. At times you have great difficulty distinguishing between what you are feeling and what you're picking up from those around you. If you find it difficult to remain centered in the midst of a group, you should withdraw to a quiet place where you can calm your swirling feelings and emotions. You always strive for peace and harmony, and you are at your best when things run smoothly and without discord. With your kind heart and creative bent, you're particularly well suited to work in the helping professions or the arts.

You are something of a whimsical free spirit. Nevertheless, your home and family are truly important to you. Sentimental, idealistic, and romantic, you have some pretty unrealistic ideas about love relationships. However, instead of dealing directly with your disappointments, you tend to gloss over the negatives and hope for the best.

On This Day:

In India, Shiva, the multifaceted Hindu Moon god of the mountains, is honored on or around this date every year by a day of fasting. After the ritual fasting, worshipers gather at Shiva's temples and shrines to celebrate his celestial dance of creation. This rite is followed by an oil-lamp vigil known as Shivaratri (Shiva's Night).

Born Today: Edward James Almos (actor); Barry Bostwick (actor); Kristin Davis (actress); Jimmy Ellis (boxer); James Farantino (actor); Steven Jobs (computer executive/co-founder of Apple Computer); Michel LeGrand (composer); Eddie Murray (baseball player); Alain Prost (racecar driver); Lance Reventlow (sports car designer); Billy Zane (actor)

February 25

♓ Pisces, 7

February 25th people are truth-seeking detectives in search of the grail that contains life's secrets. Your mind is your greatest resource, and in many ways you are wise beyond your years. You have a vivid imagination with a strong attraction to all things mysterious, unknown, or unknowable. Your psychic-like intuition gives you tremendous insight into people and their situations. Yet you have a rather secretive nature yourself, much given to solitude and private contemplation.

Those born on this day are natural salespersons and can be witty, charming conversationalists when they feel like it. Whether you choose to channel your talents into the arts, business, or the helping professions, you have a knack for transforming your dreams into profitable realities. Because the combination of the Sun in Pisces and the root number seven is extremely spiritual in nature, you may be traditionally religious or involved in an alternative movement outside the mainstream. Many whose birthdays occur on this date are successful writers, actors, artists, or musicians. Others find that their true calling lies in helping others through teaching, social work, politics, or the ministry.

You're a true romantic, and love could play a major role in your life. However, you need to find a partner who understands your moodiness and is tuned in to your wavelength. Otherwise, you may realize that you are happier on your own.

On This Day:

Ta Anith Esther is an annual Israeli festival held on or near this date to commemorate Queen Esther's strength when she pleaded with King Ahasuerus to save her people, who were being held captive in Persia. It is a quiet time of prayer and reflection that celebrates the feminine nature of the qualities of compassion and mercy.

Born Today: Sean Astin (actor); Meher Baba (mystic); Anthony Burgess (writer); Enrico Caruso (opera singer); Tom Courtenay (actor); Adele Davis (nutritionist); John Foster Dulles (U.S. secretary of state); Carl Eller (football player); George Harrison (rock star); Sally Jessy Raphael (talk show host); Pierre Auguste Renoir (artist)

February 26

♓ Pisces, 8

Pisces natives whose birthdays fall on this date are sensitive, compassionate workaholics who want to make a difference in the community. You may be as dreamy and imaginative as other fish, but the number twenty-six's vibration prompts you to channel your artistic talents into undertakings that are practical as well as creative. Your forte lies in your ability to carefully prepare a foundation and fine-tune your plans before you convey them to others. A caring, idealistic humanitarian, you get along with all kinds of people, and you usually know what the public wants. Your unique combination of intuition, creativity, and will power make you a good bet for success in almost any career.

Those born on February 26 are among the most industrious, efficient, and disciplined members of the Pisces group. Although you're better at dealing with reality than some fish, you may become resentful when practical considerations rain on your illusions. Repeated disappointments can sap your vitality and make you pessimistic about the future. Your saving grace is a surprising sense of humor that helps get you through challenges and setbacks.

In an intimate relationship, you crave affection and understanding. You are romantic, devoted, generous, and protective with your loved ones, but your own feelings are easily hurt if your kind gestures are not appreciated or reciprocated.

On This Day:

In many parts of the Christian world, a joyous pre-Lenten celebration called Carnival takes place on or around this date each year. It was observed during the Middle Ages as Shrove-Tide, a festival of expelling winter by burning or drowning its effigy. In some places, the Carnival celebration is known as Mardi Gras or Fat Tuesday.

Born Today: Michael Bolton (singer); Madeline Carroll (actress); Buffalo Bill Cody (U.S. Army scout/showman); Johnny Cash (singer); Fats Domino (singer); Jackie Gleason (comedian/actor); Victor Hugo (writer); Betty Hutton (actress); Margaret Leighton (actress); Tony Randall (actor); Levi Strauss (businessman/inventor of denim pants)

February 27

♓ Pisces, 9

Those born on this day are the artists, innovators, and crusaders of society. Sensitive and empathetic, you're able to tune in to people and their problems the way others tune in to a TV channel or radio station. A veritable psychic sponge, you absorb the moods and emotions of those around you. You need to separate from the world periodically or risk getting stuck in other people's difficulties. However, your concern for others won't let you to stay disconnected for very long.

Your active imagination and prophetic insight give you the ability to see deep into the core of things. Consequently, you're often aware of portents and omens that others don't even notice. With your flashes of insight and belief in your own hunches, you can achieve almost anything you set your mind to. Because you're attracted to the fantasy worlds of entertainment and the arts, acting is a natural medium for you, as are writing, music, dance, art and design, photography, and filmmaking. Some February 27th individuals find their niche as spiritual leaders, fund-raisers, teachers, therapists, nurses, or doctors.

You give of yourself completely in a love relationship; you are prepared to sacrifice your own needs and desires in favor of those of your partner. In return, your tender, romantic nature requires lots of affection, encouragement, and emotional support.

On This Day:

Equirria was an ancient Roman festival of horseracing held in honor of the god Mars. It was a celebration established by Romulus and took place annually around this date in the Campus Martius on Caelian Hill. Mars was originally a god of agriculture, but later identification with the Greek Ares turned him into a god of war.

Born Today: Marion Anderson (opera singer); Hugo Black (Supreme Court justice); Lawrence Durrell (writer); Mary Frann (actress); Howard Hesseman (actor); Ralph Nader (consumer advocate); David Sarnoff (TV executive); Arthur Schlesinger (historian); John Steinbeck (writer); Henry Wadsworth Longfellow (poet); Elizabeth Taylor (actress)

February 28

♓ Pisces, 1

Among Pisces natives, those born on February 28 stand out as dynamic leaders. Your dreamy, Neptune-ruled nature notwithstanding, you're the one to call on in a crisis. When a problem arises, your gut response is to confront it head on. You proceed full steam ahead to straighten things out; then you direct them to a successful conclusion. Your ability to tune in to your surroundings provides you with a sense of what people are thinking and feeling. Your knack for discerning patterns, tastes, and trends tells you what the public wants and needs.

Those born on this day have a caring, compassionate nature and an idealistic view of the world. As a result, you don't always deal well with rock-bound reality, especially when it intrudes on your dreams and illusions. Although you're less forceful than other people, your unique combination of intuition and ambition helps you hold your own in the competitive milieu of business or the arts. Sometimes you may feel caught between your artistic Piscean temperament and the energy and drive of the root number one. When you send out mixed signals, you confuse even those who think they know you well.

Your many activities and independent spirit can get in the way of close relationships. In an intimate union, you're caring and romantic, but you feel emotionally vulnerable. Nevertheless, you need love in your life. Without it, you feel only half alive.

On This Day:

In ancient times, a Chaldean Sabbat known as Sabbatu was celebrated each year at this time. On this day in 1836, the *Kalevala*, a Finnish poetic folk tale of 22,000 verses, first appeared in print. Prior to that date it was memorized and passed down by bards. Finns mark Kalevala Day by reading the poem and then partaking of a great feast.

Born Today: Mario Andretti (racecar driver); Charles Durning (actor); Frank Gehry (architect); Gilbert Gottfried (comedian); Ben Hecht (journalist/playwright); Gavin MacLeod (actor); Vincent Minnelli (director); Zero Mostel (actor); Bernadette Peters (actress); Linus Pauling (chemist); Tommy Tune (dancer/choreographer)

February 29

♓ Pisces, 2

The special individuals born on Leap Year's Day are likeable, charming, and diplomatic. Your magnetic personality attracts many friends and acquaintances. With your fine social skills and equitable manner, you get along with all types of people. You have an ethereal quality that makes you appear less resilient than you actually are. As a result, your personal agenda is often misinterpreted. Although some may consider you an inconsequential social butterfly, you're actually surprisingly ambitious. And you're not afraid to use your subtle powers of persuasion to get people to see things your way.

Your mysterious, otherworldly air captivates and confuses people. You have a great deal of insight into what motivates them, yet they can't quite figure you out. You are sympathetic and sensitive to people's difficulties and sincere in your desire to help. As you listen to their problems, instinct tells you what they need to do to achieve the best possible results. With your refined and artistic temperament, you may find your best avenues of expression in the arts or the helping professions. However, you are extremely sensitive. If your efforts do not elicit the response you expect, you have a tendency to become discouraged.

In an intimate relationship, you make a loyal, loving, giving partner. You're inherently romantic and idealistic, and you need a mate who is equally caring and affectionate in return.

On This Day:

Leap Year's Day, February 29, occurs only once every four years. Its addition was designed to rectify the discrepancy between the calendar year of 365 days and the solar year of approximately 365 and one-fourth days. Traditionally on this day, a lady was free to propose marriage to a man; if he refused, he was honor bound to give her a gift.

Born Today: Jimmy Dorsey (bandleader); Anne Lee (founder of the Shakers); James Mitchell (actor); Michelle Morgan (actress); Henri "Pocket Rocket" Richard (hockey player); Gioacchino Rossini (opera composer); Antonio Sabato, Jr. (actor); George Seferis (poet); Dinah Shore (singer/actress/TV talk show host); William Wellman (director)

March Birthdays

March 1

♓ Pisces, 1

Those who are born on this day under the sign of the fish are some of the more artistic and creative members of their Sun sign. Since, with this birth date, you're also among the most ambitious and hard working, anyone foolish enough to write you off as passive dreamer soon discovers his or her mistake. Inspired by your personal muse and driven by the energy of the number one's vibration, you have more confidence in your own ability than other Pisces natives. Challenge intrigues you, and you're never afraid to risk failure. When your imagination is fired up by an exciting new idea, your tendency is to plunge right in. Your prophetic vision often goes way beyond mere intuition, and you know instinctively what to do and when to do it.

Inherently idealistic and sympathetic to the feelings of others, you're a true humanitarian. You care about people and their problems, and you are often the first to respond when help is needed. Your compassionate nature and magnetic personality attract many friends and acquaintances. With your abundance of creative talent and charm and your enterprising spirit, you're a natural for success in career areas connected to the arts and entertainment, politics, business, or the helping professions.

In intimate relationships you are the consummate romantic. You're passionate, loving, and responsive to your partner's desires. However, you are so idealistic that your heart may be broken and your illusions destroyed if things don't turn out the way you had hoped.

On This Day:

The Kalends, or first day, of March was the beginning of the year in ancient Rome and was marked by the Vestal Virgins' rekindling of the sacred fire in the Temple of Vesta and by the Festival of Matronalia, sacred to the goddess Juno. Prayers were offered to Juno Lucina for prosperity in marriage, and wives received gifts from their husbands.

Born Today: Harry Belafonte (actor); Sandro Botticelli (artist); Robert Conrad (actor); Roger Daltry (rock star); Ralph Ellison (writer); Hans Hoffman (artist); Ron Howard (director/actor); Alberta Hunter (jazz singer); Oskar Kokoschka (artist); Robert Lowell (artist); Glenn Miller (bandleader); David Niven (actor); Alan Thicke (actor)

March 2

♓ Pisces, 2

The individual whose birthday falls on March 2 is warm and sociable, with a compassionate heart and a friendly, easygoing manner. Temperamentally, you're a romantic idealist with a genuine love of beauty, art, and music. Solitude holds no particular appeal for you, and you actively seek the partnership and cooperation of other people. Invariably tactful and polite, you empathize with others and are extremely receptive to their needs. People in trouble turn to you for help and support because they know that you understand their problems and difficulties.

Despite your amiability, you are nobody's fool. Your psychic-like intuition quickly zeros on any attempt to take advantage of your agreeable nature. Then you let the other person know, in no uncertain terms, that you know the score and refuse to be imposed on. In career matters, you are ambitious and determined to succeed. Your ideas are forward looking and progressive, and your effervescent personality and willingness to work hard help you bring them to fruition. Your essential nature is refined and creative, and your best means of expression will likely be found in the arts.

In an intimate relationship, you're romantic and sentimental, with very idealistic ideas about love. You dislike confrontation, and you'll bend over backwards to keep the peace. In a worst-case scenario, you might decide to leave rather than fight.

On This Day:

This day is sacred to Ceadda, a Celtic deity of holy wells and healing springs, and is symbolized by the Crann Bethadh, the tree of life. On this date in some parts of Europe, women celebrate Mother March, the mother goddess who presides over the third month of the year, by holding a festive parade to honor all women who have created life.

Born Today: Desi Arnez (bandleader/actor/producer); Karen Carpenter (singer); Theodore Seuss Geisel, "Dr. Seuss" (writer/artist); Jennifer Jones (actress); Jon Bon Jovi (rock star); Laraine Newman (comedian); Lou Reed (singer); Martin Ritt (director); Max Lincoln Schuster (publisher/editor); Kurt Weill (composer); Tom Wolfe (writer)

March 3

♓ Pisces, 3

People whose birthdays fall on this day are good-natured and sociable and have a terrific sense of humor. The twinkle in your eyes and your silver-tongued rhetoric may give some the idea that you're too superficial to be taken seriously. However, those who think that way are in for a big surprise. Beneath the showmanship of your hail-fellow-well-met personality, there's a force to be reckoned with. Not only are you a good deal more serious than you appear, but you're clever and ambitious, with a fine intellect and considerable talent along artistic and scientific lines.

Pisceans with the number three are full of plans and schemes. You're adept at juggling your schedule to cram in as much activity as possible. Still, there aren't enough hours in the day for you to do all the things you'd like to do or see everyone you want to see. You're easily distracted and prone to go off on tangents. However, once you get going, you accomplish prodigious amounts of work in relatively short periods of time. Your mind is quick and sharp, and you come up with innovative, inventive ideas that others never even dream about.

In love, you're playful and affectionate. You desperately need the grounding provided by a stable partnership, but you enjoy your freedom too, and you're fearful of too much commitment.

On This Day:

This is the day of Aegir, a Teutonic sea god and controller of the sea's tides and weather. His wife Ran likes to sink ships and then care for the sailors she's drowned. The third day of the third month is also sacred to all Triple Goddesses and all deities of the Moon because the Moon shows itself in three aspects: waxing, full, and waning.

Born Today: Gilbert Adrian (movie fashion designer); Milton Avery (artist); Alexander Graham Bell (inventor); Jessica Biel (actress); James Doohan (actor); Jean Harlow (actress); Jackie Joyner-Kersee (heptathlete/long jumper); George Pullman (industrialist/inventor); Ronald Searle (illustrator); Hershel Walker (football player)

March 4

♓ Pisces, 4

The March 4th person is an odd dichotomy of dreamy idealism and sensible realism. On the one hand, you're creative and intuitive and, on the other, logical and scientific minded. Inherently hard working and dedicated, you have been blessed with a fine intellect and a vivid imagination. As a practical visionary, you long to build something of lasting value. When you can get the two sides of your nature to work together, you're able to translate your innovative plans and ideas into concrete realities.

Practicality, attention to detail, and insight into the public's wants and needs make you a sure bet for success in business or the arts. Although you want stability and security for yourself, your high aims and objectives extend to everyone. Empathetic and sensitive to people's feelings, you care a great deal about the welfare of the less fortunate. You are charitable and self-sacrificing, and your sense of duty and responsibility prompts you to help in any way you can. You're very receptive to the vibrations around you, but you're so prone to fluctuating emotions and worry that you may get stuck in a negative mindset that's accompanied by mild bouts of depression.

Your hidden uncertainty often surfaces in intimate relationships. You are devoted, generous, and protective of your loved ones. You need a partner who provides love and respect in return.

On This Day:

This is the feast of the Welsh mother goddess Rhiannon (great queen), who was known as Rigantona in Ireland and was identified with the horse goddess Epona. In ancient Greece, this day was the beginning of Anthesteria, a three-day ritual to honor the Keres (souls of the dead) and the goddess Hecate, who controls the underworld's dark forces.

Born Today: Chastity Bono (gay pride activist); Jim Clark (racecar driver); George Gamow (physicist); John Garfield (actor); Charles Goren (bridge expert/columnist); Patricia Heaton (actress); Kay Lenz (actress); Miriam Makeba (singer); Paula Prentiss (actress); Knute Rockne (football coach); Antonio Vivaldi (composer)

March 5

♓ Pisces, 5

The versatile individual born on this day is an intriguing combination of intellect and emotion. Your attention is quickly caught, yet just as easily diverted. You require constant mental stimulation, and your restless curiosity sends you off on one tangent after another. A freewheeling adventurer, you refuse to be boxed in by monotonous routine. You're drawn to the strange and unusual. Nothing appeals to you more than traveling and exploring exotic new places. Still, there's plenty of common sense mixed in with your vivid imagination and your fascination with everything weird, mystical, and mysterious.

Those born on March 5 are idealistic dreamers with the courage to stand up and fight for their convictions, so it's fortunate that communication is your forte. You are naturally talkative and friendly, with a wonderful sense of humor. You make your case with so much grace and charm that even your detractors find your arguments difficult to resist. It's important for you to be able to share your ideas and feelings, but whether other people agree with you or not, their opinions rarely influence your actions.

In a love relationship, you're caring and considerate, but considerably more independent than many of your Sun sign counterparts. Your ideal partner is someone who understands your need for freedom and for time on your own to pursue your many interests.

On This Day:

On this day in ancient Rome, people celebrated Navigum Isis (Blessing of the Ship of Isis) in honor of the Egyptian goddess's invention of the sail. Isis Elupoia (Isis of Good Sailing) protects boats and shipping and is also a guide on the final voyage of life. During the festival, flowers were floated down a river, and boats were blessed with incense.

Born Today: Samantha Eggar (actress); Eugene Fodor (violinist); Andy Gibb (singer); Rex Harrison (actor); Henry II (king of England); Randy Matson (shot-putter); James Noble (actor); Frank Norris (writer); Dean Stockwell (actor); Niki Taylor (supermodel); Heitor Villa-Lobos (composer); Michael Warren (actor); Frank Williamson (actor)

March 6
♓ Pisces, 6

The basic temperament of most fish born on this day is refined, artistic, and poetic. Attracted to elegance and beauty, you appreciate everything that is pleasant and harmonious. Easygoing by nature, you function best when life's running smoothly, with a minimum of stress and discord. Essentially an idealist, you dream of a peaceful world where all people are treated with respect and dignity. Since you have such high expectations, you can become disheartened if things don't turn out the way you would like.

Pisces natives linked with the number six love their homes and enjoy entertaining. You are quite willing to spend lavishly for parties and other social affairs, and personal magnetism and a warm friendly attitude are the hallmarks of your personality. A genuine "people person," you like being surrounded by family and friends. Diplomacy and cooperation come naturally to you. You're sympathetic and sensitive, and you possess an intuitive understanding of what makes others tick. Consequently, you're usually the one who is called upon to mediate when there is a difference of opinion.

Warm-hearted and sentimental, you place a high priority on the importance of love in your life. If you are without an intimate relationship, you feel lonely and incomplete. If your relationship turns sour, it can be difficult for you to accept that it's over. Instead, you may try to retreat into the rich fantasy world of your imagination where romance reigns.

On This Day:

This day is sacred to Eriu, the Irish goddess of the De Danaan, from whose name Eire (Ireland) comes. On this date in Rome, people celebrated the festival of Mars, god of agriculture and war and father of the Roman people. During the Whale Festival in northern California, people visit the shore hoping to glimpse the annual whale migration.

Born Today: Elizabeth Barrett Browning (poet); Michelangelo Buonarroti (artist); David Gilmour (rock star); Alan Greenspan (economist/Federal Reserve Board chairman); Ring Lardner (writer); Gabriel Garcia Marquez (writer); Ed McMahon (TV host); Shaquille O'Neal (basketball player); Valentina Tereshkova (cosmonaut); Mary Wilson (singer)

March 7
♓ Pisces, 7

Pisces natives whose birthdays fall on this date are a curious combination of creative imagination and rational thought. Your psychic-like intuition is complimented by the practicality and efficiency of your fine intellect. You receive a psychic impression or a "feeling" about something, and then you think it through to a logical conclusion. Conversely, you gather all the facts and data you can on a subject, process the results, and then convey what you've learned to others via words and images.

The versatile, multi-talented March 7th individual is an inveterate seeker of knowledge and wisdom. As an idealist and perfectionist, you prefer to study all sides of an issue before coming to a decision. Although you put on a confident front, you're prone to worry and frustration. In business, you know what people want and can discern patterns and predict trends. However, with your unique combination of a sharp mind and artistic talent, you may fare better in a career in education, scientific research, the media, or the arts. Whatever you chose to do in life, you should surround yourself with people and things that induce harmony and beauty.

In a loving relationship, you are caring, sensitive, tenderhearted, and romantic. You have lots of affection to give to the right person, but you need a great deal of encouragement, pampering, and emotional support in return.

On This Day:

The day of Junonalia honored the Roman goddess Juno with a procession of twenty-seven girls dressed in long flowing robes and accompanied by an image of the goddess carved from the wood of a cypress tree. In Thailand, the Phara Buddha Bat Fair is held in honor of the Buddha's footprint. Local shrines receive offerings of flowers, food, thread, and yarn.

Born Today: Tammy Faye Bakker (TV evangelist); Luther Burbank (horticulturist); Janet Guthrie (racecar driver); Franco Harris (football player); Anna Magnani (actress); Piet Mondrian (artist); Maurice Ravel (composer); Roger Revelle (oceanographer); Anthony Armstrong Jones, Lord Snowdon (photographer); Lynn Swann (football player)

March 8

♓ Pisces, 8

People born on this day are hard working and ambitious, as well as insightful and highly imaginative. In fact, you are considerably less dreamy and otherworldly than many who share your Sun sign. You enjoy nice things and comfortable surroundings and can feel insecure without a strong financial base. A compelling blend of sensitive artist and stoic worker, you prefer to channel your creative ideas into practical undertakings. Commitment and responsibility don't frighten you. Your dedication to the job at hand becomes even more evident when your imagination is fueled by a challenging new project.

Those born on March 8 are naturally secretive and tend to play their cards close to the chest. Consequently, you don't usually talk about your plans until you're ready to set them into motion. Your ambition is rooted in the desire to make your mark in the world, thereby gaining the recognition and remuneration you believe you deserve. A sensible idealist, you are genuinely sympathetic to those who need help. You're generous and charitable, but you don't let people impose on your good nature. You refuse to give free handouts to the undeserving, and you know instinctively when someone is trying to pull a fast one.

Although you can be somewhat serious in company, you're actually a secret romantic. In an intimate union with the right person, you make an ardent, caring, and devoted lover.

On This Day:

Welsh Witches' Day is celebrated on this date. Throughout China, Mother Earth Day is celebrated to honor the Earth as mother goddess. The festival consists of street parades, firecrackers, and feasting. Coins, flowers, incense, paper dolls, and other things are placed in the ground, blessed, and then covered with soil and left as birthday presents for the goddess.

Born Today: Cyd Charisse (actress/dancer); Otto Hahn (chemist/physicist); Oliver Wendell Holmes, Jr. (Supreme Court justice); Kathy Ireland (supermodel); Anselm Kiefer (artist); Freddie Prinze, Jr. (actor); Aidan Quinn (actor); Lynn Redgrave (actress); Jim Rice (baseball player); Claire Trevor (actress); James Van Der Beek (actor)

March 9

♓ Pisces, 9

The sensitive, intuitive individuals born on this day are inherently caring and courageous. Both a humanist and idealist, you're prepared to stand up for the underdog and fight for those causes you believe in. You are naturally supportive of people who are in need, yet a part of you remains detached and emotionally uninvolved in their problems. You're far more concerned with examining and exploring the space around you. Your journeys of discovery may be physical, mental, emotional, or spiritual in nature. Whatever form your travels take, you're not inclined to give up on them until you've uncovered some of the secrets of the universe.

Extremely curious, with a penetrating intellect and vivid imagination, you're fascinated by the strange, mysterious, and unknown. Challenges rarely faze you, because you view them as precursors to change and transformation. Many individuals born on this day are prophetic visionaries interested in initiating new ventures. Some are particularly interested in philosophy and metaphysics. Others strive to find their personal answers in science, art, or religion. No matter what path you follow, the knowledge you gain from your studies and experiences helps you grow in wisdom and understanding.

In love, you are tenderhearted and romantic. Nevertheless, you're afraid of your own vulnerability and want a partner you're sure can be trusted. You're probably best suited to a union with someone who shares your high ideals and aspirations.

On This Day:

In Tibet, the Butter Lamp Festival takes place annually on this date. Monks parade through the streets carrying yak-butter sculptures of Buddhist heroes, hoping to secure the favor of the gods and render the demons powerless. After the procession is over, the sculptures are taken down to the river and cast into the water.

Born Today: Samuel Barber (composer); Juliette Binoche (actress); Andres Courreges (fashion designer); Bobby Fischer (chess champion); Yuri Gagarin (cosmonaut); Raul Julia (actor); Floyd B. McKissick (civil rights leader); Irene Papas (actress); Keely Smith (singer/actress); Micky Spillane (writer); Trish Van Devere (actress)

March 10

arch 10th births are Pisceans with attitude, adept at drawing the spotlight and keeping it focused on them. Inherently ambitious, enthusiastic, and super-idealistic, you make a dramatic and courageous leader. A battler with an authoritative manner and a strong sense of purpose, you inspire others to follow in your wake when your imagination is fired by a cause. You're motivated by an insistent inner voice that continues to nag at you until you do something about your ideals. You like to know that you're not alone in your pursuit of your dreams, and you actively seek out the company of like-minded people.

Caught somewhere between the gentle fish's willingness to extend a helping hand and the "me first" philosophy of the number one's vibration, you may feel conflicted and at odds with yourself. Nevertheless, your drive for personal accomplishment colors much of what you do in life. Still, when your poetic side surfaces, you reveal a deep-seated love of beauty and an exceptional taste and/or talent in the fine arts. You're no pussycat, yet you're a perceptive, sympathetic, caring person with a pragmatic approach to problem solving.

You have a charming social manner that attracts many friends and admirers. You enjoy surrounding yourself with intelligent people who can introduce you to new ideas. In an intimate relationship, you're ardent and romantic, but so idealistic that you may wind up disillusioned or disappointed.

On This Day:

On this day in ancient Greece, themes of love, romance, and forgiveness prevailed in honor of the numerous reconciliations of Hera and Zeus. The celebration was held next to an old oak tree. Small pieces of fallen wood were collected to symbolize the reunion of the divinities, and then they were burned in a ritual fire to keep love warm.

Born Today: Bix Beiderbecke (jazz musician/composer); Gerard Croist (psychic); Barry Fitzgerald (actor); Tamara Karsavina (dancer); Pamela Mason (actress); Shannon Miller (gymnast); Chuck Norris (actor/martial arts champion); David Rabe (playwright); Sharon Stone (actress); Fou T'song (pianist); Harriet Tubman (abolitionist)

March 11

♓ Pisces, 2

Many of the gentle yet determined individuals with birthdays on March 11 sense that they have a purpose that is higher than mere existence. You too may feel that the universe has something special in store for you. If you do, it's up to you to figure out what it is. Your individual path may lead to a spiritual journey of self-discovery or a lifetime of service to society, but no matter which end of the political spectrum you're on, your beliefs may frequently be out of step with the mainstream. You're drawn to extremes and have some specific—and occasionally unrealistic—ideas about how the world can be improved.

Being born on this day makes you sensitive, versatile, and receptive to situations going on around you. Yours is a sociable, courteous nature that brings balance and harmony to all your interactions. People with problems trust you because they realize you understand their difficulties and empathize with their pain. Your knowledge of the public's wants and needs allows you to influence people's choices. Although you have an artistic temperament, you like things to be useful as well as beautiful.

In intimate relationships you're sensual and affectionate. A true romantic, you enjoy courting and being courted. During your youth, you may have a tendency to fall in and out of love quite often. However, when you find your special someone, you make a loyal and devoted partner.

On This Day:

This day is sacred to Hara Ke, African goddess of sweet water and gentle spring rains, who lives under the river Niger. At the beginning of the sowing season, people in Nyambinyambi, West Africa, take out all their garden tools and seeds and bless them. This ensures plentiful rains (the water of Hara Ke's spirit) and a good harvest.

Born Today: Ralph Abernathy (civil rights leader/NAACP head); Douglas Adams (writer); Dorothy Gish (actress); Bobby McFerrin (jazz singer); Rupert Murdoch (media mogul); Marius Petipa (choreographer); Antonin Scalia (Supreme Court justice); Dorothy Schiff (publisher); Raoul Walsh (director); Lawrence Welk (bandleader/TV host)

March 12

♓ Pisces, 3

The engaging March 12th individual breezes through life radiating charm and personality. The youthful vitality and enthusiasm you emit has little to do with your chronological age. Courage and determination help you overcome obstacles and deal with disappointments. Although you've had your share of hard knocks, your scars don't show on the outside. With your easygoing nature and whimsical sense of humor, people welcome you wherever you go. Fluency of self-expression is the hallmark of your existence. Versatile, artistic, and articulate, you have a particular strength that lies in your ability to communicate your thoughts and ideas visually as well as verbally.

You're a born entertainer, with a cheerful manner and a gift of gab that endears you to people. Your erratic nature, however, makes you somewhat unpredictable and difficult to pin down. You are multi-talented and interested in so many things that some may consider you superficial. The truth is, you can't stand being boxed in by a monotonous job or dull company. Your restless nature requires variety and change, and your attention is quickly sidetracked by anything new or interesting that comes along.

You are extremely sociable and friendly, and your flirty ways can earn you a reputation for being fickle. Although you tend to shy away from romantic commitment, you are devoted to friends and family. With the right partner, you can forge a relationship that will last a lifetime.

On This Day:

The feast of Marduk, in honor of the creator god of Babylonia and the patron of the city of Babylon, takes place on this day. Marduk was venerated in Mesopotamia from as early as the Third Dynasty of Ur. Marduk's consort was the goddess Zarpanitu, his symbol was an agricultural tool, and his sanctuary in Babylon was the Esagila and the E-temen-anki-ziggurat.

Born Today: Edward Albee (playwright); Barbara Feldon (actress); Paul Kantner (rock star); Jack Kerouac (beat poet); Liza Minnelli (singer/actress); Gordon MacRae (singer); Vaslav Nijinsky (dancer); Wally Schirra (astronaut); Darryl Strawberry (baseball player); James Taylor (singer); Andrew Young (civil rights leader/statesman)

March 13

♓ Pisces, 4

Pisceans born on this day are more pragmatic and down to earth than most of their dreamy Sun sign counterparts. This quality is strengthened by your infinite capacity for hard work and your refusal to let anything derail your carefully formulated plans. Yet, despite your ingrained sense of responsibility, you are a Pisces after all. You keep the more serious aspects of your character hidden behind a sunny smile and a warm, amiable disposition. Your magnetic personality and the subtle aura of mystery you project make you a sought-after friend and companion.

Your greatest potential for achievement lies in your ability to combine the sensitivity and perception of the Neptune-ruled with the persistence of the number thirteen. Many with birthdays on this date are artistically inclined and enjoy successful careers in the worlds of entertainment or the arts. Others find their niche in business, where they use their unique blend of intuition and common sense to make money by giving customers what they want. In the helping professions, you're able to employ your humanitarian ideals without losing site of practical considerations.

In an intimate relationship, you're very idealistic. You tend to imagine that this other person in your life actually is whatever you wish he or she could be. You may become disillusioned if your significant other lets you down or fails to live up to your high expectations.

On This Day:

In Luxembourg, a pagan fire festival, Burgsonndeg, is celebrated on this day with the lighting of great bonfires to welcome spring and the rebirth of the Sun. Also on this day, the Balinese Festival of Purification takes place, when the lord of the underworld cleans out his lair. With demons roaming free, people must purify the island and their own homes.

Born Today: Walter H. Annenberg (publisher); Eugene A. Cernan (astronaut); Dana Delany (actress); Roy Haynes (jazz drummer); L. Ron Hubbard (writer/founder of the Church of Scientology); Sammy Kaye (bandleader); Percival Lowell (astronomer); William H. Macy (actor); Neil Sedaka (singer/songwriter); Alexi von Jawlensky (artist)

March 14
♓ Pisces, 5

People born on this day are creative visionaries and are frequently out of step with the status quo. A dreamer and paradigm buster, you're a font of innovative ideas and imaginative plans for the future. Your particular brand of intuitive logic stems from the combination of your scientific mentality and artistic temperament. Although your mind is open to all possibilities, you never make assumptions without verification. Before you arrive at a judgment, you question everything. Then you carefully scrutinize your own conclusions.

Those with March 14th birthdays have an otherworldly quality that makes them appear removed from the people around them. With your quirky sense of humor and somewhat skewed image of the world, you accept the odd, bizarre, and outrageous as normal. At heart you're a humanitarian and deeply concerned about society and its problems. You have a knack for getting along with all types of people and quickly make friends out of strangers. You believe in truth and beauty, and your ingrained idealism and sincerity are obvious to everyone your meet. Despite your tolerance for dissenting ideas, you come across as rather preachy when expressing your personal views.

In a close relationship, you're devoted and understanding. It's easy for you to tune in to your mate to find out what he or she is thinking and feeling. However, when you're seized by the creative impulse, you can just as easily tune your partner out.

On This Day:

This day is sacred to Ua-Zit, the Lady of the Night, a serpent goddess of the ancient Egyptian religion. Also, the annual thirteen-day Ghanian New Year celebration begins on this date. Traditionally, a series of special ritual dances are performed during the first eleven days to dispel evil spirits and to honor the souls of the departed.

Born Today: Frank Borman (astronaut); Les Brown (bandleader); Michael Caine (actor); Billy Crystal (comedian/actor/director); Paul Ehrlich (immunologist); Albert Einstein (physicist); Quincy Jones (arranger/composer/producer); Hank Ketcham (cartoonist); Robert Rimmer (writer); Johann Strauss, Sr. (composer/conductor)

March 15

♓ Pisces, 6

The March 15th individual is sensitive and perceptive, with delicate sensibilities. Because of this, you thrive in harmonious surroundings and steer clear of things you consider crude or vulgar. Your social skills and amiable personality attract a large circle of friends and acquaintances. A natural diplomat with a fair and equitable nature, you're often called upon to mediate differences. You have a talent for bringing out the best in people by helping them recognize their own potential.

Creative artists of all kinds are born on this date. The combination of the Pisces Sun and the number fifteen bestows an eye for line, form, color, and texture. You may also be drawn to the fantasy world of entertainment. Acting is a natural medium for you, as are writing, music, dance, art and design, architecture, and filmmaking. Yours is a curious, inquiring mind with a vivid imagination. You're fascinated by anything that is the least bit strange or mysterious. Your prophetic vision goes far beyond mere intuition, and your innate understanding of patterns and cycles lets you detect upcoming trends and changes in taste and fashion.

Being both partnership and family oriented, you don't like living or working alone. Your super-romantic, idealistic view of the world keeps you focused on love and relationships, sometimes to the exclusion of everything else. Without someone to share your life, you may feel only half alive.

On This Day:

This day is the Ides of March, the festival of the river nymphs, and the holy day of Rhea, Greek goddess of the Earth. On this date in ancient Rome, people celebrated the annual festival of the great mother goddess Cybele and her consort Attis, which began with a procession of reed bearers to commemorate the discovery of the infant god Attis among the reeds.

Born Today: Alan Bean (astronaut); Macdonald Cary (actor); Terrence Trent D'Arby (singer); Fabio (supermodel); Ruth Bader Ginsberg (Supreme Court justice); Judd Hirsch (actor); Andrew Jackson (U.S. president); Harry James (bandleader/trumpet player); Phil Lesh (rock star); Mike Love (rock star); Sly Stone (singer)

March 16

♓ Pisces, 7

Pisceans born on this day are a complex blend of artistic, mystical, and material impulses. In addition, you possess a type of intellectual curiosity that is sometimes found among individuals of genius mentality. On the one hand, you have the requisite ability to successfully compete in the commercial world. On the other, you feel compelled to remain true to your personal vision no matter what the cost. You are keenly perceptive, with acute powers of observation that allow you to see through anyone's façade. Yet, personally, you are rather secretive and prefer keeping the details of your private life to yourself.

Thoughtful, philosophical, and wise, you probably have clairvoyant or psychic abilities. Your creative imagination seeks expression in writing, music, or art. Although some people write you off as an impractical dreamer, your qualifications for worldly success are grossly underestimated. Your groundbreaking innovations are generally light years ahead of what others are doing. Your alien ideas may be regarded with skepticism at first, but sooner or later people begin to recognize their value.

Idealistic and romantic, you willingly make sacrifices for your loved ones. You yearn for an intimate union but have an independent streak that can make close relationships difficult. You need to find a partner who understands your need for occasional periods of solitude.

On This Day:

This is the start of the two-day festival of the Greek wine god Dionysus (Bacchus). Traditionally on this day, prisoners are set free, and the possessions of debtors may not be seized. In India, the Hindu festival of Holi welcomes spring. A fire is lit and dedicated to the god Krishna. Then ashes from the fire are rubbed on people's foreheads for luck.

Born Today: Rosa Bonheur (artist); Bernardo Bertolucci (director); Erik Estrada (actor); Isabelle Huppert (actress); Jerry Lewis (comedian/director/producer); James Madison (U.S. president); Leo McKern (actor); Daniel Patrick Moynihan (U.S. senator); Pat Nixon (U.S. first lady); Simon Ohm (physicist); Henny Youngman (comedian)

March 17

♓ Pisces, 8

The dreamy gaze of the person whose birthday falls on this date veils an eminently practical inner nature. Ambitious and hard working, you'll do whatever it takes (as long as it's honorable) to achieve your goals. You're efficient and disciplined, and you resent it when you see other people slacking off on the job. You're not a perfectionist per se, but your high ideals and even higher aspirations make you a stickler for quality. However, the materialism of the root number four is tempered by the compassion of your Pisces Sun. You are sympathetic to the plight of the less fortunate, and you readily volunteer your services whenever help is needed.

Many fish born on this day are psychic receptors and subject to powerful premonitions. Your ability to pick up vibrations provides insight into impending events. In business, your intuition regarding the public taste keeps you one step ahead of the competition. Creative imagination is another of your strong suits, and you may find professional fulfillment in a field related to the arts or entertainment. No matter what you choose to do in your life, the chances are you will do it successfully.

In an intimate relationship you are sensitive and loving. Although you enjoy your solitude, you flourish in a caring, committed union with a partner who understands your serious side and respects your work ethic.

On This Day:

Saint Patrick's Day marks the celebration of the patron saint of Ireland, who is most famous for driving all the snakes from the country, even though scientists claim that at the time Ireland had no snakes. This holiday has roots in Trefuilnid Treochair, the national day of Ireland, and the feast for "the triple bearer of the triple key," the trident-bearing Celtic deity that was later assimilated into Saint Patrick.

Born Today: Sammy Baugh (football player); Nat King Cole (singer/jazz pianist); Patrick Duffy (actor); Eileen Garrett (psychic); Paul Horn (jazz musician); Mia Hamm (soccer player); Bobby Jones (golfer); Rob Lowe (actor); Thomas Mattingly (astronaut); Rudolf Nureyev (dancer); Kurt Russell (actor); John Sebastian (singer/songwriter)

March 18

♓ Pisces, 9

T he mystical beings celebrating birthdays on this date are blessed with the uncanny ability to see right to the core of things. Sometimes your psychic insight is so strong it seems as if you have access to divinely inspired information. At other times your tendency to see omens and meanings where others see only ordinary objects makes you appear to be losing your grip on reality. You're a dreamer, a visionary, an artist, and a poet. Moreover, you're not afraid to embrace your unusual talents or confront whatever challenges life throws at you. You march to your own tune and don't worry about what others think of you.

The highly imaginative, multi-talented, artistic March 18th individual needs an outlet for creative self-expression. Sensitive and deeply emotional, you're more likely to be motivated by feelings and instinct than thoughts and ideas. You project a kind of magical allure that draws people to you. Your tender heart and understanding nature make you a willing recipient of everyone's confidences. People trust you because they can see that you really care about them and their problems. Besides, you're not a gossip and won't betray anyone's secrets.

Your super-romantic nature and fanciful view of the world mean that a loving relationship is everything to you. Warm and caring, you're willing to make any sacrifice for your partner. You want to know that you are cherished and appreciated in return.

On This Day:

This is the Day of Saint Edward the Martyr, an Anglo-Saxon monarch who was assassinated on the orders of his step-mother in the year 979 C.E. In ancient times, Sheelah-Na-Gig, the Irish goddess of fertility, was honored on this day. In Ireland, Sheela's Day is celebrated by the downing of a shamrock in a glass of whisky to bring luck.

Born Today: Bonnie Blair (skater); Edgar Cayce (clairvoyant/healer); Robert Donat (actor); Grover Cleveland (U.S. president); Peter Graves (actor); Edgar Everett Horton (actor); Queen Latifah (rap star/actress); Wilson Pickett (singer); Charlie Pride (singer); Nicolai Rimsky-Korsakov (composer); John Updike (writer)

March 19

♓ Pisces, 1

People with birthdays on this day are a strange mix of dreamer and doer. A dynamic, powerful, persuasive crusader on the one hand, you're a gentle, dreamy poet on the other. When your aggressive, pioneering spirit takes charge, you feel as if nothing can stop you from reaching your worldly goals. But when the gentle, dreamy side of your nature surfaces, your creativity and artistic talent point your attention in another direction entirely. No matter which mode you're in, when your imagination is fueled by an exciting project, your determination can surprise everyone.

March 19th births lead to idealistic reformers inclined to dramatize their own lives. Typically, you rush to the aid of those who need help and then see yourself as some kind of mythological hero. You are exceptionally kindhearted and generous to a fault. However, you tend to be more outspoken and aggressive than other Pisces natives. Although your help is appreciated, your habit of telling people what to do is not. Some with birthdays on this day are explorers destined to break new ground in the physical world. Others prefer staying home and exploring the inner worlds of the psyche.

Because you are impetuous, you are likely to rush into a love relationship without prior thought. As a lover, you are caring and considerate as long as the union lives up to your expectations. But if you become disillusioned, you'll make a beeline for the exit.

On This Day:

This is a day of observance for Nametona, the Roman/Celtic goddess of the sacred grove. In ancient Greece, a festival called the Lesser Panathenaea was celebrated on this date in honor of the goddess Athena. In classical Rome, the Quinquatrus, one of three annual festivals for the birth of the goddess Minerva, took place annually on this day.

Born Today: Ursula Andress (actress); Sir Richard Burton (adventurer); William Jennings Bryan (U.S. congressman/statesman); Serge Diaghilev (ballet producer/founder of the Ballet Russe); Wyatt Earp (U.S. marshal); Glenn Close (actress); David Livingstone (explorer); Moms Mabley (comedian/singer); Irving Wallace (writer); Bruce Willis (actor)

March 20

♓ Pisces, 2

The paradoxical individuals born at the end of the astrological year, a period of intense creativity, often possess unique talents and abilities. Because your birthday falls on the Pisces/Aries cusp, you're the recipient of a combination that brings together the universality of the fish with the individuality of the ram. At times you feel that you're being pulled back and forth between the cooperative instincts of Pisces and the independent nature of Aries. However, your Pisces side usually wins out, because the root number two's vibration makes you more of a team player than a loner.

Imaginative, idealistic, and purposeful, you know how to put your plans and ideas to practical use. You are intuitive, compassionate, and sensitive to the problems of others. When you sense that someone is in trouble, you jump right in and offer your help. You're able to reach out with more skill and understanding than most people, and your counsel is received in the same spirit in which it's given. Many born on this day forge successful careers in the arts or entertainment; others may find fulfillment in counseling, education, or professional sports.

In a love relationship, you're fun loving, charming, and spontaneous. However, your emotional nature is complex, and you go through periods of restlessness. You long for the stability of a committed union, but you also crave change and excitement.

On This Day:

The annual observance for the Norse goddess Iduna, bearer of the magic apples of life that keep the gods young, falls on this day. Iduna appears on this date as a sparrow bringing joy to humans. Elsewhere around the world, this day is sacred to the goddess Fortuna, the Morrigan, the Norns, the Three Fates, and the Three Mothers (Lakshmi, Parvati, and Sarasvati).

Born Today: Holly Hunter (actress); William Hurt (actor); Spike Lee (director); Hal Linden (actor); Erwin Meher (physiologist); Bobby Orr (hockey player); Michael Redgrave (actor); Carl Reiner (comedian/actor/director); Pat Riley (basketball coach); Fred Rogers, Mr. Rogers (children's TV host); B. F. Skinner (behaviorist/psychologist)

March 21

♈ Aries, 3

The vivacious rams celebrating birthdays on this first day of the astrological year are easily recognized by their "can-do" attitude. As one of them, you have great faith in yourself and an intense desire to always be number one. You tend to move around a great deal because you like being where the action is. At times you set such a fast pace that others find themselves struggling just to keep up. You are an up-front, outgoing free spirit, with nothing hidden behind your open, friendly manner. What people see is what they get.

Ariens born March 21 are inherently enthusiastic and brimming with youthful vitality, no matter what their chronological age. You view life as an ongoing adventure, and you're continually on the lookout for exciting new ways to implement your many plans and ideas. Your impulsive temperament, courage, and pioneering spirit fuel your willingness to gamble and take risks. Independent in thought and action, you are much better at giving orders than taking them. Endowed with the gift of gab, you're one of the world's great persuaders. In fact, creative self-expression and the ability to mix words with action are your specialties.

You are ardent and romantic, but you fall in and out of love quite easily. In a committed relationship, you'll stay the course unless things get really dull and boring. If you should become truly disenchanted, your inclination is to leave and never look back.

On This Day:

Spring commences with the Vernal Equinox when the Sun enters Aries. Celebrations for the birth of spring include lighting bonfires at sunrise and decorating eggs like the goddess Ostera (Eostre), who protects small children. On this date in ancient Irish tradition, two Milesian princesses, Tea and Tephi, founded the city of Tara.

Born Today: Johann Sebastian Bach (composer); Matthew Broderick (actor); Peter Brook (director); Timothy Dalton (actor); J. B. J. Fourier (mathematician); Rosie O'Donnell (comedian/actress/TV host); Gary Oldman (actor); Walter Gilbert (molecular biologist); Aryton Senna da Silva (racecar driver); Florenz Ziegfeld (producer)

March 22

♈ Aries, 4

Determination is the touchstone of those born on this date. Aries' habit of throwing caution to the winds is greatly moderated by the root number four's fondness for meticulous planning. As a result, you're considerably more controlled than other rams. You possess a strong inner drive toward success that is unequaled among your Sun sign counterparts. Adventurous, independent, and virtually fearless, you view life as a series of challenges to be overcome. Motivated by a combination of idealism and practicality, you know exactly what you want to accomplish. Moreover, you believe that you're up to the task.

People with birthdays on March 22 are born pioneers. This quality make you partial to innovative projects that venture into previously unexplored territory. Although your leadership abilities are marked, excessive enthusiasm can make you seem dictatorial. Since you refuse to mince words, some people may find your honest, outspoken manner hard to take. Basically sensible and opportunistic, you dislike squandering time and energy on unproductive enterprises. Your restless nature continually urges you forward, and lack of activity usually makes you feel frustrated.

In an intimate relationship, you're ardent and romantic, yet quite capable of directing and managing your passion. With the right person, you can be truly loyal and devoted. However, you're something of a workaholic, and even true love may be forced to take a backseat to your personal ambitions and career plans.

On This Day:

On this day in ancient Rome, members of the cult of Attis conducted the Procession of the Tree Bearers. As part of an annual ritual to mourn the god's demise, they carried uprooted pine trees through the streets to the sacred temple of Attis. In Hopi tradition, the Butterfly Maiden, a kachina who rules spring and fertility, flutters to life on this day.

Born Today: Bob Costas (TV and radio sportscaster); Keira Knightley (actress); Matthew Modine (actor); Robert Andrew Millikan (physicist); Pat Robertson (preacher/politician); Steven Sondheim (composer/lyricist); William Shatner (actor); Elvis Stojko (skater); Andrew Lloyd Webber (composer/impresario); Reese Witherspoon (actress)

March 23
♈ Aries, 5

The freedom-loving Aries native whose birthday falls on this day is a perpetual motion machine. Driven by mercurial spurts of nervous energy, you seek constant change and mental stimulation. A rugged individualist, you maintain your independence by following your own course. Moreover, you're a thinker as well as a doer. First you study a situation, and then you act on what you've learned. As an idea person, you are particularly adept at networking and communicating. As a person of action, you view life as an ongoing quest for adventure and excitement.

Although those born on March 23 are not usually considered dreamers, they are decidedly optimistic. Once you make up your mind to do something, you convince yourself it's doable, no matter what the risks or obstacles. You are so lucky, however, that even your failures have a way of paying off in the end. Sociable and outgoing, you're a born storyteller with a gift for demonstrating and illustrating your plans. You enjoy initiating new projects, but you're a better starter than finisher. With everything up and running, you may get bored and suddenly decide to leave.

A delightful, fun-loving companion, you just can't help attracting friends and admirers. In love, you're ardent and generous, yet fearful of too much intimacy. You value freedom more than security and, above all, treasure the companionship of shared interests.

On This Day:

The Norse festival of the ascendancy of the light of spring over the darkness of winter takes place this day. In ancient Rome on this date, priests performed the Dance of Salii. Brandishing spears and shields, they invoked the gods Mars and Saturn. The observance drove the spirits of the winter from the city and encouraged the growth of spring crops.

Born Today: Dr. Roger Bannister (mile runner/neurologist); Joan Crawford (actress); Erich Fromm (psychologist); Juan Gris (artist); Chaka Khan (singer/songwriter); Akira Kurosawa (director); Moses Malone (basketball player); Amanda Plummer (actress); Dane Rudhyar (astrologer); Werner von Braun (rocket scientist)

March 24

♈ Aries, 6

People born on this day are bombarded by contradictory impulses. Aggressive, independent Aries is a born instigator who cannot abide inactivity. As soon as life quiets down, the ram's inclination is to stir things up and get them moving again. However, the root number six represents peace and harmony. Those subject to its vibration are happiest when everything runs smoothly, with a minimum of stress and discord. With your head telling you one thing and your heart another, your actions can conflict with your deepest needs and feelings.

Those with birthdays on March 24 have magnetic personalities and tons of charm and sex appeal. You're considerably more sensitive and tactful than the typical Aries native. You love your home and derive great joy from hosting social affairs for your many friends and associates. You have a vivid imagination and a deep appreciation for art, beauty, and culture. Many with birthdays on this date possess an abundance of creative talent and enjoy successful careers in the world of entertainment and the arts.

You are a dichotomy of independence versus dependence. However, relationships are what matter to you, and you rarely lack for romance in your life. You don't like going it alone, and without a loving relationship, you tend to feel incomplete. In an intimate union with Mr. or Ms. Right, you make a loyal, affectionate mate or partner.

On This Day:

Today is sacred to Britain's guardian goddess Albion (also known as Prytania or Britannia), whose image appears on British coins. This is the Day of Heimdall, the Norse horn-sounding god of light and guardian of the Bifrost Bridge that links heaven and earth. A god of orderliness, Heimdall is often equated with the archangel Gabriel.

Born Today: Louie Anderson (comedian); Roscoe "Fatty" Arbuckle (actor); Clyde Barrow (bank robber); Harry Houdini (magician/escape artist); Peyton Manning (football player); Steve McQueen (actor); William Morris (poet/artist); Bill Porter (hurdler); John Wesley Powell (geologist); Joseph Priestley (chemist); Annabella Sciorra (actress)

March 25

♈ Aries, 7

Rams born on this day are wise, street-smart warriors who thrive in difficult or challenging environments. At the same time, you project an aura of mystery that people find intriguing and possess a magnetic quality that draws them to you. Dynamic and extremely competent, you believe in yourself and your capacity for success. A natural risk taker, you're not afraid to tackle something you know very little about. Your ability to compartmentalize tasks and shift focus on demand helps you absorb new information and learn as you go along. Once you've decided on a goal, virtually nothing can stop you from reaching it.

The typical March 25th person is an individualist with a crusading nature and eloquent powers of persuasion. Although your demeanor gives the impression of great forcefulness, your basic temperament is that of a poet or mystic. Your vivid imagination and creative talent bode well for a professional career in areas related to music, drama, dance, writing, painting, sculpting, or broadcasting. The spiritual side of your nature helps you appreciate higher values and intangible beauty. Some people with birthdays on this date are drawn to traditional religions, while others prefer alternative movements.

Home and family hold great appeal, yet a close relationship may be difficult for you to sustain. You function best when you are the authority in your own realm. When your partner tries to tell you what to do, your restlessness kicks in and you begin to think about leaving.

On This Day:

The Hilaria (Festival of Joy) was celebrated annually on this date in ancient Rome. A joyous event, Hilaria commemorated the triumph of day over night after the equinox, as well as the ascendancy of the goddess Cybele over death. The festivities were brought to a close with a ceremony of washing that was believed to promote fertility.

Born Today: Bela Bartok (composer); Howard Cosell (sportscaster); Aretha Franklin (singer); Paul Michael Glazer (actor); Elton John (singer/songwriter); David Lean (director); Sarah Jessica Parker (actress/producer); Simone Signoret (actress); Gloria Steinem (feminist activist/writer); Arturo Toscanini (conductor)

March 26

♈ Aries, 8

People who celebrate their birthdays on this day are inclined to stop and think before they act. By steering clear of hasty decision making, you manage to avoid many of the blunders committed by your more impulsive Sun sign counterparts. You are a natural leader, and your enthusiasm and idealism are harmoniously counterbalanced by practicality and common sense. You have the requisite energy, enterprise, and ambition to succeed in virtually any undertaking. Moreover, you are not afraid of hard work, and you're willing to sacrifice a great deal for success.

Inspiration is everything to those born March 26. Without it, you feel restless and frustrated. When you find a worthy objective that fires your imagination, you stick with it until you reach your goal. You are an innovative, independent thinker with big ideas. You can be very persuasive and usually have little difficulty convincing others to follow your lead. You have an intuitive grasp of situations, a driving determination to get things done, and a compelling desire to get them done properly. Although you expect the best from those you work with, you wouldn't dream of asking anyone to do anything you're not prepared to do yourself.

You are helpful and caring, with a genuine interest in the problems of others. In personal relationships, however, you sometimes feel torn between the inclinations of your independent nature and a sense of obligation to those closest to you.

On This Day:

Today is the observance for the Celtic god of youth, liberation, harmony, unity, and music, Mabon ap Modron. According to Welsh tradition, Mabon was held captive after being stolen from his mother when he was three days old. His prison was at Caer Loyw (Gloucester), a far-away location that is meant to symbolize the Otherworld.

Born Today: Marcus Allen (football player); Alan Arkin (actor); James Caan (actor); Joseph Campbell (mythologist); Robert Frost (poet); Erica Jong (writer); Leonard Nimoy (actor); Sandra Day O'Connor (Supreme Court justice); Diana Ross (singer); Martin Short (comedian); Tennessee Williams (playwright); Bob Woodward (journalist)

March 27

♈ Aries, 9

The versatile individuals with birthdays on this day have eclectic tastes and universal interests. As an idealist and humanitarian, you refuse to tolerate injustices. You're not afraid of anything or anyone, yet you're a warrior with the soul of a poet. When you allow your heart to overrule your head even in the face of common sense, you tend to get carried away by impractical ideas. If this happens, your potential for doing good may become lost in aimless dreaming.

Your March 27th birth gives you a curious mix of sensitivity and bravado. You may be likened to a prickly pear that has a tough and thorny outer skin but is surprisingly soft and sweet on the inside. Despite the your gutsy outer demeanor, inwardly you may be shaking in your boots. But your desire to win helps you overcome any uncertainty you're feeling. You're an inventive originator of ideas, with an intuitive understanding of social trends. You know what the public wants, and your innovative mentality helps you give it to them.

A born romantic, you enjoy being courted and pampered by your significant other. In return, you're sympathetic to his or her needs and willing to satisfy them. Your idealism can cause you to place your beloved on a pedestal. If your partner fails to live up to your ideal, you may end up heartbroken and disillusioned.

On This Day:

The Liberalia, an ancient Roman festival that annually honored the wine god Liber Pater, was celebrated on this date. It was believed that the young men who participated in this coming of age festival would be gifted with strong sons and bountiful crops. In Egypt, Smell the Breeze Day honored the great creator and sky goddess Nut.

Born Today: Mariah Carey (singer); Randall Cunningham (football player); Miller Huggins (baseball manager); David Janssen (actor); Harold Nicholas (dancer); Henry Royce (co-founder of Rolls-Royce Motors); Gloria Swanson (actress); Quentin Tarantino (director); Sarah Vaughan (singer); Michael York (actor); Xuxa (singer/dancer/model)

March 28

♈ Aries, 1

Like the Knight of Wands in the tarot deck, the energetic, self-motivated March 28th individual has a temperament that can only be described as "fire of fire." Those born on this date are outgoing leaders with sunny personalities and tons of initiative. A true individualist, you have faith in yourself and in your own way of doing things. With a mind that's as active as your body, you're easily bored by repetition and dull routine. You thrive on the challenges involved in initiating and carrying out new projects.

Although extremely friendly and sociable, your March 28th birthday means you're not really a team player (except when in charge of the team). Essentially a strategist and idea person, you possess a creativity, resourcefulness, and enthusiasm that make you an excellent manager and planner. In addition to your pioneering spirit, sharp mentality, and forward-looking idealism, you are something of the visionary. A courageous champion of the underdog, you boldly rush to the aid of those who cannot defend themselves.

In personal relationships, you're ardent, loving, and loyal. Family and home are important to you, but you also value your freedom and independence. In romantic situations, you sometimes enjoy the pursuit even more than the consummation. You like change and excitement. If a relationship goes too smoothly, you may get antsy. When this happens, your tendency is to stir things up in order to get the sparks flying again by deliberately (if unconsciously) creating conflict.

On This Day:

The birth of Artemis, Greek goddess of the Moon, is celebrated on this day, as are the ancient Roman sacrifice at the Tombs of the Ancestors and the birthday of the goddess Kwan Yin, which is celebrated in Taiwan. According to the treatise *De Pascha Comutus* (243 C.E.), the Sun and the Moon were created on March 28. Before 336 C.E., this day was associated with the nativity of Jesus.

Born Today: Dirk Bogarde (actor); Auguste Anheuser Busch, Jr. (brewer); Maxim Gorky (writer); Ken Howard (actor); Reba McEntire (singer); Edmund Muskie (U.S. senator); Raphael (artist); Rudolf Serkin (pianist); Julia Stiles (actress); Saint Theresa of Avila (mystic); Paul Whiteman (orchestra conductor); Dianne Wiest (actress)

March 29

♈ Aries, 2

People with birthdays on March 29 are constantly being bombarded by contradictory impulses. Your head tells you one thing, your heart another. You are naturally ambitious, determined, and geared toward accomplishment, but your energy comes in spurts, causing you to alternate between periods of intense activity and all-out laziness. Yet, despite your penchant for stopping along the way to smell the flowers, you have what it takes to reach your goals and make your dreams come true.

You are affectionate, outgoing, and sociable. Although you possess all the courage and initiative of the Mars-ruled individual, you don't feel a compelling need to take charge. Teamwork and partnership suit you just fine, and you generally prefer sharing power and responsibility. You seek acceptance and approval, and your desire for peace and cooperation makes you a lot more sensitive and tactful than other Aries natives. The inherent aggression and independent nature of your Sun sign is greatly mitigated by your deep-seated concern for the feelings of others.

Sometimes you appear to be a dichotomy of independence versus dependence. Relationships are truly important to you, yet you prefer being on your own to being involved in an unhappy union. In love and romance, you are passionate and caring, but you look carefully before leaping into an intimate relationship. You need to be with someone you can trust, a partner who inspires and brings out the best in you.

On This Day:

On this day, the ritual reenactment of the "fixing of the destinies," a rite of holy marriage between the Sumerian god Dumuzi and the goddess Inanna, took place. The current king represented the god, and a temple priestess represented Inanna of Uruk. This is also the date of the annual masquerade ritual of the Bobo people of Africa that's believed to help restore the balance of nature and ward off evil spirits.

Born Today: Pearl Bailey (singer); Jennifer Capriati (tennis player); Bud Cort (actor); Walt Frazier (basketball player); Eric Idle (actor/writer); Lucy Lawless (actress), Elle MacPherson (supermodel); John Major (U.K. prime minister); Eugene McCarthy (senator/presidential candidate); John Tyler (U.S. president); Sam Walton (founder of Wal-Mart)

March 30

♈ Aries, 3

The dynamic Aries native born on this day has a talent for mixing social amiability with commercial savvy. There are two distinct sides to your character. One is a happy-go-lucky, social butterfly; the other is ambitious and motivated toward success. With your silver-tongued charm, you could lure the birds from their nests and then talk them into going back. Intuition tells you what people want and what you need to do to give it to them. Brimming with energy and enthusiasm, you let nothing stop you once you set your mind to something.

The person born on March 30 has a sunny nature and a wonderful sense of humor. You love mixing and mingling in a social setting, where people are drawn to you as if by a magnet. Although you get along with almost anyone, you gravitate toward those who share your fondness for gracious living. You have a vivid imagination and either possess artistic talent of your own or have a fine appreciation for art and beauty. You're popular, adaptable, and well suited to public life, especially in politics or the arts. A willing worker, you also have what it takes to be successful in a business milieu.

You have a tendency to fall in love with love, and you can't endure boredom. In a close relationship, you stick around as long as your partner is able to hold your interest. If the excitement goes, you may go too.

On This Day:

The Roman festival of Janus and Concordia honors the patron god and goddess of beginnings and doorways and of peace and harmony, respectively. In Norse tradition, this day begins the runic half-month of Ehwaz, the horse. It's a time of partnership between humans and nature, as represented by the relationship between rider and horse.

Born Today: John Astin (actor); Warren Beatty (actor/director); Eric Clapton (rock star); Celine Dion (singer); Francisco de Goya (artist); Frankie Lane (singer); Jerry Lucas (basketball player); Peter Marshall (TV game show host); Sean O'Casey (playwright); Paul Reiser (comedian/actor); Anna Sewell (writer); Vincent van Gogh (artist)

March 31

♈ Aries, 4

March 31st people are groundbreaking visionaries who are much too realistic to chase after unattainable dreams. Your artistic talent and temperament provide you with a deep appreciation for intangible beauty, yet you rarely let the creative impulse stand in the way of practical considerations. A born executive, you're particularly good at motivating people and managing money. Despite your sound business sense, you're not afraid to take risks. Your adventurous Aries nature goads you into taking chances, especially when you believe the odds are in your favor.

This birthday blends the battering power of the ram with the root number four's self-discipline and efficiency. You possess great powers of concentration and a mentality that is logical, scientific, and technical. You don't like wasting time and energy on nonproductive enterprises. Your need for stability prompts you to build strong, lasting structures and institutions. You tend to take life more seriously than others of your Sun sign. You are usually willing to sacrifice some of your independence in return for material success. On an emotional level, however, you are a crusading idealist. When you adopt a cause, you pursue it with passion.

Prone to falling in love with love, you prefer being half of a couple to living on your own. However, in an intimate relationship, you often feel torn between your freewheeling nature and your sense of obligation to your partner.

On This Day:

On this day, the old Roman festival of Luna celebrated the goddess of the full Moon, whose temple on Aventine Hill was the focus of her worship. As the Full Moon goddess, Luna represents growing awareness, the fulfillment of love, and the mystery of enchantment. She surrounds March's exit with her soft, shimmering light.

★★
★ Born Today: Liz Claiborne (fashion designer); Rene Descartes (philosopher); Albert Gore, Jr. (U.S. vice president/senator); Franz Joseph Haydn (composer); Gordie Howe (hockey player); Shirley Jones (singer/actress); Moses-ben-Miamon, "Maimonides" (philosopher/physician); Volker Schlondorff (director); Christopher Walken (actor)

April Birthdays

April 1
♈ Aries, 1

The audacious individuals who celebrate birthdays on April Fool's Day really are the fools who "rush in where angels fear to tread." However, there is nothing foolish about your reasons for venturing into the unknown. You are action personified, a crusading champion of the underdog who fights for those who are unable to wage their own battles. Driven by a volatile combination of courage, impatience, and the need to always be *first*, you will let no power on Earth stop you once you've made up your mind to do something.

Ariens born on April 1 can't abide inactivity. When nothing is happening, their inclination is to stir the pot in order to get things moving again. No matter what the project, you just want to get on with it. With your pioneering spirit and "go-go" nature, it's very difficult for you to follow established guidelines. Besides, you have some very strong opinions and a warrior-like confidence in your own ideas and abilities. People cannot fail to be impressed by your aura of invincibility, and inevitably some of them will start depending on you to lead the way. That is okay with you, so long as they don't start making too many suggestions about how things should be done.

In an intimate relationship, you're ardent and romantic. However, you thrive on challenge and change, and if the union becomes dull or routine, you may lose interest.

On This Day:

April Fool's Day (All Fools' Day) is the date of the Festival of Fools, the classic day of tricks and practical jokes ruled over by the Norse trickster god Loki. In Rome, this day was the women's festival of Fortuna Virilis, for women who were seeking good relations with men. In Egypt, this was the Day of Hathor, mother of the gods and holder of the eye of Ra.

Born Today: Wallace Beery (actor); Lon Chaney, Sr. (actor); Sir William Harvey (physician/discoverer of blood circulation); Jan Kadar (director); Abraham Maslow (psychiatrist); Ali MacGraw (actress); Jane Powell (actress); Sergei Rachmaninoff (composer); Debbie Reynolds (dancer/actress); Edmond Rostand (writer)

April 2
♈ Aries, 2

In people born on this day, the bold individualism of Aries is complimented and harmoniously counter-balanced by the cooperation and diplomacy of the root number two. You have all of the typical ram's directness, yet you're more willing to listen to the other person's side of the story before making decisions. Consequently, you function better in a partnership situation than most other members of your Sun sign. Nevertheless, you sometimes you feel as if you are being bombarded by contradictory impulses. At those times, your actions may conflict with your deepest needs and feelings.

You're an ambitious, determined go-getter, yet your energy tends to come in spurts. Physically, you alternate between industrious periods of intense activity and times of pure relaxation and social interaction. Your mental processes also follow a rather erratic pattern in which your mind bounces from idea to idea without following any system of logical progression. You have an artistic temperament and possess either creative talents of your own or a fine appreciation for beauty and culture. You enjoy the good things in life and relish the company of amiable, interesting people.

Affectionate, outgoing, and sociable, you probably don't lack for romantic partners. But you may feel torn between your desire for independence and the need for a close relationship. However, without an intimate relationship, you feel incomplete, so partnership usually wins out in the end.

On This Day:

In some regions of Germany, the old pagan custom of Rejoicing Day, a celebration of the return to warm weather, takes place on this date. Straw effigies representing winter are carried through the streets and then placed atop a central bonfire. The belief is that when the flames consume the last effigy, winter succumbs to spring.

Born Today: Hans Christian Andersen (writer/playwright); Sir Jack Brabham (racecar driver); Dana Carvey (comedian/actor); W. P. Chrysler (car manufacturer); Buddy Ebsen (actor/dancer); Max Ernst (artist); Marvin Gaye (singer); Sir Alec Guinness (actor); Emmylou Harris (singer); Jack Webb (actor); Emile Zola (writer)

April 3

The exuberant, charismatic rams born on this day have the sort of universal appeal that makes them welcome wherever they go. Your eternally youthful outlook and bubbling personality exude sparks of life. You're such a delightful companion that you just can't help attracting friends and admirers. You love people and truly enjoy the interaction of lively social gatherings, yet you value your freedom and independence above all else. A consummate bundle of energy, you always seem to be on your way to or from someplace new and exciting. You're not afraid to take risks, because you believe that things will work out your way—and they usually do.

Aries, when combined with the number three, produce multi-talented, hard working, and ambitious individuals. This makes you a natural leader with a genuine distaste for occupying subordinate positions. Charm, intelligence, foresight, and versatility make it easy for you to climb the ladder of success. You're best known for your strong powers of persuasion and your ability to communicate your ideas to others. You like to talk and exchange information and will rarely pass up a chance to join a spirited debate or discussion.

In intimate relationships, you're ardent, straightforward, and sincere, but you fall in and out of love rather easily. Since you prefer variety and excitement to safety and security, fidelity is probably not your strongest suit.

On This Day:

Persephone's return from the underworld, signifying the beginning of spring, was celebrated on this date in ancient Rome. In Iran, on the thirteenth day of the New Year, special bowls containing sprouted seeds are traditionally cast into the rivers as offerings in the belief that they will carry away bad luck left over from the previous year.

Born Today: Alec Baldwin (actor); Marlon Brando (actor); Doris Day (actress/singer); Jane Goodall (anthropologist/conservationist); Gus Grissom (astronaut); Leslie Howard (actor); Washington Irving (writer); George Jessel (comedian); Henry Luce (publisher); Marsha Mason (actress); Eddie Murphy (comedian/actor); Richard II (king of England)

April 4

♈ Aries, 4

The people born on this day are among the most grounded of all the rams. Hard working, pragmatic, ambitious, and focused, you have little trouble directing your prodigious energy into concrete achievements. Your practicality and the ability to transform big ideas into workable realities often come as a surprise to those who think they know what to expect from an Aries. The inner tensions you often feel come from the discordant nature of the conflicting signals you receive from your freewheeling Sun sign and the cautious vibration of the number four. Sometimes you rush ahead to meet a challenge head on, but on other occasions you organize and plan before attacking.

The creative, capable April 4th individual can make his or her mark in virtually any professional field. However, you may find that you're most comfortable pursuing a career in business or the arts. You have a vivid imagination and a knack for mixing your artistic talent with commercial know-how. You're a builder who thoroughly enjoys working on things that are as practical and useful as they are innovative and unusual. Instinct tells you what the public wants and what you need to do to provide it.

Your close relationships also tend to be full of contradictions. On the one hand, you desire freedom and independence, yet on the other, you want the security of a solid, long-term union.

On This Day:

This is the first day of the weeklong celebration of Magalesia Mater in honor of Cybele, or Magna Mater, the great mother goddess. Her cult originated in Phyrgia. It was brought to Rome during the war with Carthage, following a prophecy in the Sibylline Books that stated the invaders would be driven back once Magna Mater was in Rome.

Born Today: Maya Angelou (writer/poet); Robert Downey, Jr. (actor); Marguerite Duras (writer/screenwriter); Edward Hicks (artist); Gil Hodges (baseball player/manager); Kitty Kelley (writer); Chloris Leachman (actress); Arthur Murray (dance instructor); Anthony Perkins (actor); Muddy Waters (singer/guitarist); Emmett Williams (poet)

April 5

♈ Aries, 5

The most obvious thing about those whose birthdays fall on April 5 is their star quality. Typically, you can talk circles around most people, and your forte is the ability to mix persuasive words with bold actions. You view life as a performance with you in the leading role. Because you equate admiration with love, you constantly worry about the impression you're making on other people. Unlike other Aries natives, you're very concerned with your public image—so much so that you may have difficulty separating your true self from the dramatic persona you've created.

The free-spirited rams born on this day are drawn to innovative ventures and progressive enterprises. Those around you are attracted by your genial personality and open-minded acceptance of all types of people. It's no surprise that you're popular and make friends easily. Your restless nature needs a creative outlet, but thanks to your abundant energy and sharp intellect, there is constant feedback between your ideas and your actions. You usually know exactly what you want to do, and you're not afraid to plunge right in and do it.

Although you can be as fiery and ardent as any ram, you prize your freedom and independence too much to get overly intimate or clingy. In a long-term relationship, sharing interests and companionship are as important to you as passion and romance.

On This Day:

On this day in China and Japan, people celebrate the festival of Kwan Yin, goddess of compassion, healing, mercy, and forgiveness. Offerings of incense and violet-colored candles are placed on Kwan Yin's altar, along with rolled-up petitions for healing and protection that have been written by her supplicants on pieces of rice paper.

Born Today: Bette Davis (actress); Roger Corman (director); Melvin Douglas (actor); Joseph Lister (physician); Michael Moriarty (actor); Gregory Peck (actor); Colin Powell (U.S. Army general/secretary of state); Judith Resnick (astronaut); Spencer Tracy (actor); Booker T. Washington (educator/founder of the Tuskegee Institute)

April 6
♈ Aries, 6

Rams born on this day are charming and diplomatic, but they're also bold, determined go-getters. Your happiness may depend on your ability to maintain some kind of balance between your driving need to "make it" in the material world and your inner desire for peace and harmony. No matter what you do in life, you want to come out on top. Yet you'll go out of your way to avoid stepping over people on your climb up the ladder of success. Your instincts as an idealist and Good Samaritan can even cause you to suppress your own powerful ambition in the interest of fairness and justice.

You are one Aries who is generally content working with partners. Although you may realize your greatest potential in tandem with others, what you really want is to be first among equals. You can be a team player when the occasion demands, but you still prefer being at the head of the team. You're extremely sociable and able to get along with almost anyone you meet. However, you tend to gravitate toward those who share your cultural interests and love of art and beauty.

In intimate relationships, you're affectionate and warm-hearted. More sentimental than the typical forthright Aries, you enjoy the stylized rituals of courtly romance almost as much as the earthy passion of physical lovemaking.

On This Day:

In France, the Boat Festival commemorates the return of spring. Children celebrate this day by making a wish and then launching a miniature boat into the estuaries of the Mozelle River. Each boat holds a burning candle and symbolizes sailing on the "sea of life." Anyone finding a boat may also make a wish while bringing it to the shore.

Born Today: D. W. Douglas (airplane manufacturer); Harold Edgerton (physicist); Anthony Fokker (airplane manufacturer); Merle Haggard (singer); Barry Levinson (director); Gustave Moreau (artist); Gerry Mulligan (jazz musician); Andre Previn (conductor); Peter Tosh (reggae star); James Watson (biologist); Billy Dee Williams (actor)

April 7

♈ Aries, 7

Like the Tarot's Page of Swords or the members of the monastic military order of the Knights Templar, the April 7th person is a fascinating bundle of contradictions. Are you a warrior or a mystic, an aggressive fighter for what you believe or a spiritual hermit in search of solitude? Linked to the Greek Athena, a warrior goddess and a goddess of wisdom, those born on this date are an uneasy combination of the outspoken crusader and contemplative scholar. Nevertheless, your capacity for blending your pioneering spirit, creative imagination, and inventive, logical thinking is truly impressive.

Thanks to your Aries Sun, you come off as self-motivated and extremely confident, yet you're considerably more open minded and receptive to outside influences than most other rams. Part doer and part idealistic dreamer, you truly believe in your own ability to overcome any adversity and win out in the end. Although personal success is important to you, you also enjoy using your talents and abilities to improve conditions for everyone. As a leader or manager, you inspire the entire team with your novel ideas and fresh approach to problem solving.

Your loving, passionate nature yearns for a long-term relationship with a home and a family, but you may be too preoccupied with your own interests and career commitments to settle down in one place and actually stay put.

On This Day:

On this day, the feast of Coventina honors the Celtic goddess of sacred water sources. In Romania, children throw red Easter eggshells into streams as gifts for water spirits known as the Blajini. This is also the feast day of sixth century Saint Finnian, founding abbot and patron of a monastery in Kinitty, Ireland.

Born Today: Jackie Chan (actor/martial arts expert); Francis Ford Coppola (director); Russell Crowe (actor); Tony Dorsett (football player); David Frost (TV host); James Garner (actor); Billie Holiday (jazz singer); Wayne Rogers (actor/businessman); Ravi Shankar (musician); Walter Winchell (gossip columnist); William Wordsworth (poet)

April 8

♈ Aries, 8

People born on this day are the ultimate go-getters. You view life as a series of challenges, and you're determined to overcome them all. Whether as a creative entrepreneur or the executive of an established corporation, you have a knack for gaining the respect and cooperation of others. A dynamic mix of realism and idealism has you upholding tradition one moment and flying in the face of it the next. Some of your innovative ideas may seem a bit far-fetched, yet they succeed because they're built on a firm foundation of common sense and business acumen.

Those who celebrate birthdays on this date are rather less colorful than others of their Sun sign. The ram's inclination to race full speed ahead is tempered by the number eight's more cautious approach. Innately practical and opportunistic, you keep your eye on the prize and waste little time or energy on nonproductive enterprises. You automatically assume that you're right until proven wrong, so when you make a request, you usually refuse to take no for an answer.

Your emotional nature is more controlled than that of the typical ram, and you may have difficulty sharing your deepest feelings with your significant other. Where love is concerned, you're not into playing games. You are loyal and dependable; when you make a commitment, you stick by it.

On This Day:

On this day in ancient Greece, people honored the Moon goddess Artemis with the Feast of the Moon Cakes. The Buddha's birthday is celebrated this day in temples in Japan and America. An altar is draped in flowers, and a figure of the infant Buddha is set in a tub. Temple members then pour licorice tea over the baby's image to signify bathing.

Born Today: Jacques Brel (singer/songwriter); Ilka Chase (actress/writer); Franco Corelli (opera singer); Betty Ford (U.S. first lady/founder of the Betty Ford Center); Sonja Heine (skater); Jim "Catfish" Hunter (baseball player); Julian Lennon (singer/songwriter); Carmen McRae (jazz singer); Donald Whitehead (journalist)

April 9

♈ Aries, 9

People with birthdays on April 9 are a fascinating blend of charisma, artistry, and spirituality. Despite your assertive personality, inside you're more of a poet than a warrior. Your compassionate, kind nature can make you an easy mark for a good sob story. As a gallant crusader for truth and justice, you're not afraid to fight for the things you believe in. However, you much prefer the peaceful path of compromise and mutual agreement. Moreover, you're more receptive to outside influences than the average ram and less likely to make mistakes based on rash decisions.

Rams born on this day are fond of animals and humans. If you come upon a stray of any species, your impulse is to take it in and care for it. You're capable of motivating and inspiring those around you because you understand their problems. Forward looking and intuitive, you zero in on possibilities others usually miss. With your enterprising spirit, eloquent powers of persuasion, and insight into society's needs, you can be a dynamic force for change in the world. No matter what you do in life, your talent for correctly sizing up situations gives you a decided edge over the competition.

You're so romantic and idealistic that you let your heart rule your head. Although you are perfectly willing to make sacrifices for a loved one, you expect similar treatment in return. If it is not forthcoming, you may be severely disillusioned.

On This Day:

In England, the Hocktide Festival takes place on this date to celebrate the triumph of the Saxon female warriors who battled the Danish invaders in 1002 C.E. In Macao, the birthday of the ancient goddess A-Ma, patroness of fisherman and sailors, is celebrated on this day every year with a religious festival known as the Feast of A-Ma.

Born Today: Severiano Ballesteros (golfer); Jean-Paul Belmondo (actor); Justine Hill (anthropologist/archaeologist/magazine editor); Mary Pickford (actress); Dennis Quaid (actor); Charles Steinmetz (electrical engineer/inventor); Efrem Zimbalist, Sr. (violinist)

April 10
♈ Aries, 1

Rams born on this day are the pioneers and trailblazers who always seem to be one step ahead of their companions. Energetic, adventurous, and courageous, you're a dynamic force for progress and change. Your sunny disposition and generous nature attract people and guarantee you a warm welcome wherever you go. Inherently sociable, you enjoy time spent with friends and acquaintances. However, it's difficult for you to slow down, even with your closest associates. Restless and impatient, you have a tendency to race through life as if you're afraid of missing out on something important.

The April 10th individual is an extremely self-confident nonconformist with razor-sharp perceptions. When called upon to make a snap decision, you go with your intuition, and your choice is usually the right one. Once you decide to do something, you don't seek anyone's approval but your own. Since you find it easier to compete than cooperate, the only team you care to play on is one you lead. With your abundant, fiery energy, you are action personified. You cannot abide inactivity. If life gets too quiet, you stir things up just to get them moving again.

You are passionate and romantic. Although you like being half of a couple, responsibility and fidelity are not your strongest points. When the thrill begins to fade, you may decide to leave or look elsewhere for excitement.

On This Day:

In ancient Celtic tradition, the Sun dances each year on this day. Even today, in many parts of Ireland, people arise at first light in order to view the Sun's dance reflected in a shimmering bowl of water. In ancient Babylonia, the great goddess Bau, mother of Ea, was honored in a sacred religious festival known as the Day of Bau.

Born Today: William Booth (founder of the Salvation Army); Chuck Connors (actor); John Madden (football coach/sports commentator); Haley Joel Osment (actor); Commodore Matthew Perry (U.S. Navy admiral/opened Japan to the West); Frances Perkins (U.S. secretary of labor); Omar Sharif (actor/champion bridge player)

April 11

♈ Aries, 2

The enigmatic individuals who celebrate birthdays on April 11 are a curious mix of bravado and sensitivity. Although outwardly adventurous and brimming with enthusiasm, inwardly you're more of a dreamer than a doer. However, you're extremely idealistic and can usually be found in the forefront of any crusade for social justice. You have a good heart, and you empathize with the problems of others. With your originality, unconventional ideas, and incomparable imagination, you come off as part artist and part prophet. The unique combination of Aries' daring with the powerful vibration of the root number two's make it possible for you to do a lot of good in the world.

Rams born on this day are psychic and responsive to everything and everyone around them. Despite your air of aggressive determination, you feel things very deeply. When life refuses to conform to your ideal of how things should be, you take your disillusionment to heart. Still, you know that you are capable of reaching your goals. More than anything, it is your belief in yourself and in your own abilities that virtually guarantees your success.

You are open minded, with eclectic views regarding companionship. Although you're a romantic with poetic sensibilities, the thin line between love and friendship tends to blur when you're with someone you care about.

On This Day:

In Greece on this day, children wore branches of evergreen, myrtle, or bay as protection against the evil eye. Anahita, a Persian love goddess, was honored on this date. A deity of lunar power, she dwells inside the silvery light of the Moon. Today is also the festival of the Anglo-Saxon spring goddess Ostara, who hides eggs for children to find.

Born Today: Oleg Cassini (fashion designer); Clive Exton (playwright/screenwriter); Alonzo Jake Gaither (football coach); Joel Grey (actor); Charles Evan Hughes (Supreme Court justice); Masaru Ibuka (Japanese industrialist); Louise Lasser (actress); Manuel Neri (sculptor); Elmer Ochs (U.S. Army general); Meshach Taylor (actor)

April 12

♈ Aries, 3

If there is such a thing as an Aries who is relatively cool and collected, you're it. You are philosophical, curious, and a keen observer of the human condition. Your sunny nature and upbeat, fun-loving personality attract many friends and admirers. Communication is your forte. You prize knowledge and enjoy sharing what you've learned with others. You have tremendous insight into what makes people tick and can usually spot a phony a mile away. An idea person, you're continually on the lookout for exciting new ways to implement your plans. A born entertainer, you possess a finely honed sense of humor and a gift for gab that endears you to those around you.

You're ambitious and adventurous and love traveling to exotic foreign places. Because you dislike occupying subordinate positions, your preference for taking charge fuels your climb to the top. You are multi-talented and an inveterate networker. Luck and good fortune seem to follow you around—so much so that it's as if you're under the protection of a guardian angel. Whatever the reason, even your disappointments and setbacks often turn out for the best.

In love, you can be fiery and ardent one moment and cool and detached the next. You appear to be a dichotomy of independence versus dependence, yet relationships are important to you. With a like-minded person, you can forge a bond that lasts a lifetime.

On This Day:

This is the first day of the Cerealia, honoring Ceres, goddess of grain. The ancient Romans celebrated the annual eight-day festival to insure the fertility of their crops. In Taiwan, Chu-Si-Nu, the goddess who presides over childbirth, is honored on this day. Pregnant women go to the temples to ask for blessings for their unborn children.

Born Today: David Cassidy (singer); Tom Clancy (writer); Claire Danes (actress); Shannen Doherty (actress); Andy Garcia (actor); Vince Gill (singer); Tama Janowitz (writer); David Letterman (TV host); Ann Miller (dancer/actress); Ed O'Neill (actor); Scott Turow (writer); Jane Withers (comedienne/actress)

April 13

♈ Aries, 4

Rams born on this day are ambitious, efficient, and disciplined. You possess exceptional organizational skills, and you're not afraid of hard work. A natural leader, you like being the one in charge calling the shots. As a manager, you set high standards for yourself and everyone else. You really resent it if you see others slacking off on the job. You want to be involved in long-lasting accomplishments that you consider worthwhile. When you decide to undertake a project, you stick with it until you reach your goal.

Aries born on April 13 view life as a series of challenges. Even so, you relate to the world realistically, and there is nothing frivolous or superficial about you. You have an inner drive to succeed that is rarely equaled. You know what you want, and you firmly believe that you can get it. You're also prepared to sacrifice a great deal for security and success. Although status and material wealth are important to you, fame and recognition are your top priorities. You have an innate wisdom and a practical understanding of the world, qualities that people respect.

In your approach to romantic relationships, you're considerably more cautious than most of your Sun sign counterparts. Intimacy may be important to you, but then so is your career. Consequently, love may be forced to take a backseat to your lofty ambitions.

On This Day:

The festival of Libertas, the Roman goddess of liberty, was celebrated on this day. In Thailand, the Buddhists hold their annual Water Festival. Temples are cleaned and purified with incense, and the statues of the Buddha are ritually bathed. Then the water is thrown on the attendees to wash away the evil spirits of the previous year.

Born Today: Samuel Beckett (writer/playwright); Stanley Donen (producer/director); James Ensor (artist); Al Green (singer); Thomas Jefferson (U.S. president); Gary Kasparov (chess player); Howard Keel (singer); Ron Pearlman (actor); Lyle Waggoner (actor/announcer); Eudora Welty (writer/critic); Langford Wilson (playwright)

April 14
♈ Aries, 5

The April 14th individual is even more of a rebel and nonconformist than the average Aries native. You sustain your individuality by following your own course in life. Although you fervently resist any attempts to boss you around, you're not particularly interested in telling anyone else what to do either. You're a genuine maverick, and the herd mentality so prevalent in society just doesn't sit well with you. You regard social justice as a vitally important concept. You want the freedom to be yourself, and you are prepared to extend that freedom to everyone on Earth.

Those born on this day are drawn to innovative ventures and progressive enterprises. A crusader by nature, you're quick to commit to an idea or cause you believe in. No matter what the job or project, you're wholehearted about getting it done. Thanks to your abundant energy and sharp intellect, there is constant feedback between your thoughts and actions. Because you are a natural salesperson, you're especially good at promoting yourself, your products, and your services.

In personal relationships, you're loving, generous, and warm-hearted. Since you're drawn to the new and unusual, it may be difficult for you to commit to a long-term union. However, if you find the right person, you make a surprisingly devoted, loyal partner.

On This Day:

In India, this day is the beginning of the sacred festival honoring Maryamma (or Mariamme), the Hindu goddess of the sea. On this date, the Norse festival of Sommarsblot is celebrated to welcome the arrival of summer. Also, the runic half-month of Man is a time to meditate on the archetypal reality of the human condition.

Born Today: Julie Christie (actress); Bradford Dillman (actor); Brad Garrett (actor); Sir John Gielgud (actor); Sarah Michelle Gellar (actress); Loretta Lynn (singer); Pete Rose (baseball player); Rod Steiger (actor); Annie Sullivan (social worker/teacher); Arnold Toynbee (historian/writer); Erich von Daniken (writer)

April 15

℣ Aries, 6

The aim of the person whose birthday falls on this day is to strike a balance between the urge toward aggressive action and an inner desire for peace and harmony. In you, the independent Aries nature conflicts with the partnership orientation of the root number six, resulting in a mass of contradictions. You are inherently ambitious and adventurous, yet you hate turmoil and strife. Your greatest assets are your superb people skills. You are not the type of ram who rushes out to meet every challenge head on. Instead of running roughshod over the competition, you win them over with charm and diplomacy.

Because of your April 15th birthday, you have a magnetic personality that draws people into your orbit. You love your home and find great joy in being surrounded by family and friends. You particularly enjoy entertaining and playing host at parties or other social affairs. You have good luck in material matters and a tendency to attract money and property. You also possess a fine appreciation for art, beauty, and culture, and you like owning beautiful things. However, people mean more to you than material possessions.

Despite an ongoing struggle between independence on the one hand and dependence on the other, your relationships are truly important to you. Partnership invariably wins out over the long term because your need for love and affection is stronger than your desire for freedom.

On This Day:

In ancient Egypt, this day was the festival of the beloved cat-headed goddess Bast, who embodied the creative force of the Sun and was partial to black cats. The Roman festival of Tellus Mater, great mother goddess of the Earth, took place on this date. It was devoted to prayers for the environment and the continued health of the Earth.

Born Today: Jeffrey Archer (writer); Claudia Cardinale (actress); Hans Conried (actor); Leonardo da Vinci (artist/scientist/inventor); David Gilhooly (sculptor/ceramic artist); Henry James (writer/playwright/critic); Elizabeth Montgomery (actress); Bessie Smith (blues singer); Emma Thompson (actress); Emma Watson (actress)

April 16
♈ Aries, 7

Rams born on this day have two distinct sides to their personalities. On the outside, you are bold and confident, but the inner you harbors numerous doubts and insecurities. Sometimes you come off as a truth-seeking intellectual with a deep reservoir of wisdom. At other times, your dreamy, faraway look and vivid imagination reveal a more spiritual side to your nature. Your instinct and intuition work in tandem with your analytical mind to tie it all together. This unusual blend of scientific mentality and poetic temperament is the source of your ongoing fascination with life's deeper mysteries.

Musical, artistic, and dramatic talent, as well as athletic ability, are common among those born on April 16. Independent in mind and spirit, you are more of an individualist than a team player. In fact, some may regard you as a genuine paradox. You're basically outgoing and friendly, yet you require periods of solitude for private contemplation. You combine your enterprising spirit with a sympathetic understanding of what other people need. When there is a cause to fight for, you suit up for battle and readily answer the call.

There is a changeable aspect to your nature that makes you moody and apprehensive in a romantic relationship. However, when you relax enough to let yourself get close to the other person, you make a romantic and steadfast partner.

On This Day:

In Greece, the festival of Hiketeria was celebrated on this date to honor the god Apollo. The Celtic observance of Saint Padarn's Day was the customary time for weeding the crops. In old Rome, offerings of first fruits were made to Pomona, goddess of orchids and gardens, and her consort Vertumnus, who also presided over the gardens.

Born Today: Kareem Abdul-Jabbar (basketball player); Edie Adams (actress); Evelyn Ashford (sprinter); Ellen Barkin (actress); Charlie Chaplin (actor/director); Merce Cunningham (choreographer); Martin Lawrence (actor); Herbie Mann (jazz musician); Barry Nelson (actor); Bobby Vinton (singer); Sir Robert Wilson (astrophysicist)

April 17

♈ Aries, 8

Nothing stops the dynamic individuals who celebrate birthdays on this day. Your essential nature is confident, ambitious, and opportunistic. You simply refuse to quit; when you are knocked down, you bounce right back up again. You know your own mind and have a clear idea of where you are going and how you'll get there. Poised for success yourself, you also possess a talent for recognizing suitable opportunities for other people.

Aries' inherent restlessness and impatience are tempered considerably by the patience and self-discipline of the vibration of the number seventeen. Consequently, you are much better at waiting for what you want than most other members of your Sun sign. Although it may seem as if you were born successful, you actually have to work hard to get to the top. Hard work isn't a problem, though, because you're willing to do whatever it takes to make it in the world. Your executive skills are well developed, and your perceptions razor sharp. Inventive and farseeing, you have the ability to come up with fresh ideas and creative innovations.

You may not be as outwardly romantic as other rams, but underneath your rather restrained exterior, you are deeply passionate, extremely sensitive, and very much in need of love and friendship. When you are willing to take time away from work to settle down, you make an ardent, caring partner.

On This Day:

In the Himalayan kingdom of Nepal, the Chariot Festival of the rain god begins on this day. Lasting for eight consecutive days, the festival is dedicated to Machendrana, the ancient and powerful Indian god of rain. Prayers and offerings are made in homes and temples to secure the god's continued protection for the region.

Born Today: Victoria "Posh Spice" Adams (singer); Jennifer Garner (actress); William Holden (actor); Olivia Hussey (actress); Nikita Khrushchev (Soviet premier); Don Kirshner (rock concert promoter); J. P. Morgan (financier); Harry Reasoner (TV journalist); Thornton Wilder (playwright); Buster Williams (jazz musician)

April 18
♈ Aries, 9

Those born on April 18 are compassionate and sensitive, with a tremendous capacity for understanding human frailties. A champion of causes and ideals, you are not afraid to step up and fight for what you believe. A dedicated protector of your own interests, you're even more interested in defending the less fortunate who cannot protect themselves. You refuse to recognize limitations or acknowledge the boundaries that keep people from fulfilling their destinies. In your nature, the artistic, spiritual, and material combine in such a way that you may be thought of as a person "for all seasons."

The merger of the root number nine's sympathy and intuition with the pioneering enthusiasm of your Aries Sun confers an uncanny ability to succeed. You have an extremely fertile imagination and a gift for combining creativity with commercial savvy. You know what people are looking for and zero in on shifting trends and patterns in the public's taste. Creative, capable, and hard working, you could probably make your mark in any field. However, you may find your career niche in business, the arts, or the helping professions.

There is a sentimental side to your nature that makes it possible for you to have total faith in your romantic dreams. In love, you're so idealistic and devoted that you may be tempted to sacrifice everything for your beloved.

On This Day:

The festival of Rama-Navami is celebrated on this date at shrines in India. Rama is the seventh incarnation of Vishnu, the Vedic Sun god who sustains the order of the cosmos and is reborn each morning. In Burma, all the sacred statues are cleansed and polished during the New Year's Festival of Water, which takes place on or around this date.

Born Today: Clarence Darrow (lawyer); Joseph Goldstein (molecular geneticist); Melissa Joan Hart (actress); George Hitchings (biochemist); Robert Hooks (actor); Hayley Mills (actress); Conan O'Brien (TV talk show host); Eric Roberts (actor); Leopold Stokowski (conductor); Max Weber (artist); James Woods (actor)

April 19

♈ Aries, 1

Power is the name of the game for persons born on the Aries/Taurus cusp, and these people play the game very well. Decidedly ambitious, you have a dominant personality and the ability to do pretty much as you please and get away with it. Even those who refuse to be intimidated by the aggressive aspects of your character still fall under the spell of your charm and personal magnetism. You instinctively take charge and provide vision and direction in cooperative ventures. Your confidence and poise under fire inspire trust, making your advice and leadership difficult to resist or ignore.

The biggest challenge for those born on April 19 is to find a way to combine Aries' sense of adventure with bullish practicality. In addition, your underlying need for security is often at odds with the persistent desire for change and excitement. You are an innovator and idea person, and you've been endowed with a pioneering spirit and superior executive skills. Your forte is the ability to combine creativity with common sense and a head for commercial ventures, traits that can lead to success in business, politics, or the arts.

In love, you're a genuine romantic. Caring, ardent, and sensuous, you can be truly loyal and devoted to the right partner. However, you thrive on challenge and change and may lose interest if the union becomes dull or routine.

On This Day:

This is the feast day of Roman Catholic Saint Appollonius the Apologist, a martyr whose defense of the faith (Apologia) is considered to be one of the most valuable documents of the early church. A Roman senator, Appollonius was denounced by his own slave and martyred by the Roman authorities when he refused to renounce his Christian beliefs.

Born Today: Ken Carpenter (discus thrower); Tim Curry (actor); Kate Hudson (actress); Richard Hughes (writer); Ashley Judd (actress); Andrea Mead Lawrence (skier); Jayne Mansfield (actress); Dudley Moore (comedian/actor); Hugh O'Brien (actor); Paloma Picasso (jewelry designer); Constance Talmadge (actress); Al Unser, Jr. (racecar driver)

April 20
♉ Taurus, 2

Bulls born on this day are the practical and talented artists, artisans, musicians, and performers of the zodiac. Your approach to creativity is simple: Does it work, and is it both functional and beautiful? Although you may acquire a reputation for conventionality, there is a decidedly mystical side to your nature that is intuitive and innovative. Your vivid imagination and inquisitive mind fuel your desire to explore the unexplained mysteries of life. However, you staunchly refuse to accept the existence of ghosts or fairies, unless you see them yourself. You believe in results—not abstract theory.

Those with April 20th birthdays are not lazy, but they refuse to waste energy. Your personal credo might be, "Don't do anything today that can be put off until tomorrow." You think and plan, and you have great difficulty taking the first step. However, once a project is underway, you will stick with it until the end. When you're allowed to set your own timetable, you usually do a great job. You make a superior manager because you have infinite patience, good business sense, and the ability to remain calm when others become stressed and frazzled.

In a relationship, you're rather possessive, but your devotion is solid and guaranteed to withstand the test of time. Once you make up your mind about someone, your rarely change it, and you do what you can to keep your partner happy and interested.

On This Day:

In Japan, the Furukawa Matsuri takes place each year on April 19 and 20. On April 20, elegant ritual ceremonies are held. The festival procession is escorted by the performance of the lion dance, the music of the cockfight, and court music. Nine festival floats are displayed on the streets, adding a gorgeous atmosphere to the holiday.

Born Today: Carmen Electra (actress); Nina Foch (actress); Lionel Hampton (jazz musician/bandleader/composer); Adolf Hitler (German Nazi dictator); Jessica Lange (actress); Harold Lloyd (actor/director); Don Mattingly (baseball player); Joan Miro (artist); Ryan O'Neill (actor); Tito Puente (musician/bandleader/composer)

April 21
♉ Taurus, 3

The enigmatic individuals who celebrate birthdays on April 21 are as much a puzzle to themselves as they are to everyone else. Nevertheless, your sharp mind and friendly nature make you an outstanding communicator. Your forte is your talent for distilling the highlights of a plan or idea and then conveying them to others. Your natural eloquence is enhanced by the ability to paint vivid word pictures that make it possible for you to share your personal experiences. However, if you allow yourself to be seduced by rumor and gossip, your facile tongue can convert your strength into a weakness.

Those born on this day are home loving and security minded. However, you are also possessed of an exuberant, adventurous spirit that makes you eager to be off somewhere exploring new ground. Artistic and creative on the one hand, yet serious and responsible on the other, your good business sense helps you turn dreams into practical realities. An intriguing mix of patience and restlessness, you have a way of flipping back and forth between serenity and nervous anxiety. At times you seem very flexible, yet, when emotion takes over, you can become remarkably stubborn and determined.

As a romantic partner, you are sensual and exciting. Although you desire the affection and safety that family life offers, you would also like to the freedom to pursue your own plans and interests.

On This Day:

The Roman festival of Pales was held annually on this date. Connected to the birth of Rome, this festival involved the purification of the sheep, whose pens were cleaned and decorated with greenery. Large bonfires were built, and sheep and shepherds were ritually cleansed in the smoke. Sweet offerings were then left for the pastoral gods.

Born Today: Charlotte Bronte (writer); Catherine the Great (empress of Russia); Charles Grodin (actor); Tony Danza (actor); Elizabeth II (queen of England); Silvana Mangano (actress); Rollo May (psychotherapist/writer); Iggy Popp (singer/songwriter/musician); Anthony Quinn (actor); Max Weber (sociologist/philosopher)

April 22

♉ Taurus, 4

The April 22nd person is industrious, ambitious, and extremely well grounded. Consequently, you're totally clear about what you want out of life, and you have the determination to make it happen. You love the beauty of nature, art, and music, yet your stable, sensible attitude keeps you concentrated on the practical necessities of life. Despite an artistic temperament, you're a lot more interested in preservation than innovation. As resistant to change as the Rock of Gibraltar, whatever you agree to today, you deliver tomorrow.

Because of your ability to stay calm no matter what's happening around you, you may come across as cool or calculating. Actually, nothing could be further from the truth. You're as emotional as other bulls, but you're just not as comfortable letting your deepest feelings show. Your head may be filled with dreams, but you keep your feet planted firmly on the ground. Your unswerving devotion to physical reality and the security of the tangible world causes you to resist the attraction of nebulous ideas. If you can't see it, feel it, hear it, smell it, or taste it, you refuse to acknowledge that it exists.

You're a secret romantic, but you're rather hesitant when it comes to your love life. Your passionate, sensual nature requires the type of emotional reassurance that can only come from a caring, faithful, and devoted mate. Within the safety of a loving union, you are the staunchest and most loving of partners.

On This Day:

The festival of Ishtar, goddess of love, sexuality, and fertility, took place in ancient Babylonia on this day. Offerings were made to the goddess to promote health and fruitfulness. Since 1970, Earth Day has been celebrated on this date. Dedicated to Gaia, the Earth mother, it marks a time to remember everyone's responsibility to the environment.

Born Today: Eddie Albert (actor); Paul Chambers (jazz musician); Peter Frampton (singer/songwriter); Alexander Kerensky (Bolshevik revolutionary/communist ideologist); Vladimir Lenin (Russian revolutionary leader); Jack Nicholson (actor); Robert Oppenheimer (nuclear physicist); Aaron Spelling (producer)

April 23
♉ Taurus, 5

There is an elusive quality to people born on this date that is difficult to pinpoint and even harder to define. Although you're a nonconformist with beliefs that often run counter to conventional wisdom, your affable surface personality can mask your determination to do what you think is right—regardless of other people's opinions. As an innovator and visionary, you can sense future trends, and by staying in touch with practical reality, you're able to put your cutting-edge ideas to use in enterprises that are productive and profitable.

Although you may act as a guide for others, you'd rather do your own thing than follow in someone else's footsteps. When dealing with facts and figures, your clear-headed, forthright manner of presentation helps you make a convincing case for your ideas. Your progressive outlook allows you to see future possibilities that the less imaginative can't even conceive. Intellectually, you are usually light years ahead of your peers. Emotionally, however, you can be set in your ways. You normally don't welcome change in your personal life, especially not abrupt changes to your habitual way of doing things.

You attract many casual friends and acquaintances, yet you're quite particular when it comes to close relationships. There is a possessive streak to your nature that belies your own desire for freedom and independence. Ultimately, your deep-seated need for the stability and consistency of a loving, intimate union helps you overcome your inner reservations.

On This Day:

England's patron, Saint George the dragon slayer, is commemorated with parades and other festivities on this day. Today is also a time for remembrance of the northern European hero Sigurd, another famous dragon slayer. In ancient Rome, the Vinalia, a wine festival in celebration of Jupiter and Venus, was held annually on this date.

Born Today: Scott Bairstow (actor); Valerie Bertinelli (actress); Shirley Temple Black (actress/U.S. ambassador); Sandra Dee (actress); Michael Moore (documentary filmmaker); Vladimir Nabokov (writer); Sergei Prokofiev (composer/pianist); William Shakespeare (playwright/poet); Warren Spahn (baseball player)

April 24

♉ Taurus, 6

The seemingly easygoing individuals born on April 24 like the good life and enjoy sharing its pleasures with others. Your desire for beauty and luxury impels you to seek out the very best. You're continually looking for ways to improve your surroundings by making them more attractive and harmonious. Despite your low threshold for discord, you refuse to let people take advantage of your good nature. Underneath the glamour and charm, you're considerably more resolute and practical than you seem. Moreover, you rarely agree to do anything that you don't want to do.

Creativity is your strong point, and your artistry manifests in all your activities. At times your keen instincts in monetary matters make you look like a financial genius. Savvy about investments, you know what is hot and getting hotter. You have big dreams and the talent to match. Although you can have difficulty making up your mind, once you decide what you want, you know exactly what to do to get it.

More than anything, you crave love. You may find that you're not truly happy without a partner. In intimate relationships you're ardent and romantic, but you can also be rather possessive and demanding. You view romance as an ongoing ritual, and when you're in love, you are lavish in expressing your feelings for your significant other. And you expect no less in return.

On This Day:

Traditionally, Saint Mark's Eve is a time for divining the future. According to the folklore of the English countryside, any young woman wishing to see her future lover should fast from sunset. She should then prepare a cake containing salt, wheat meal, and barley meal. Her true love will come to the house during the night and turn the cake.

Born Today: Chipper Jones (baseball player); Johnny Griffin (jazz musician); Joe Henderson (jazz musician); William de Kooning (artist); Jill Ireland (actress); Shirley MacLaine (actress/dancer/writer); Bridget Riley (artist); Barbra Streisand (singer/actress/songwriter); Anthony Trollope (writer); Robert Penn Warren (writer)

April 25
♉ Taurus, 7

Those with birthdays this day are generally quicker on the uptake and more adventurous than other bulls. Mentally and physically, you're open to virtually any challenge. Ever the optimist, you are not afraid to take chances, especially when the rewards outweigh the risks. You are a practical idealist and very receptive to people's needs, yet you project an aura of mystery that may have them wondering who you really are. Your friendly, outgoing personality occasionally gives way to moodiness and the need for solitude. Nevertheless, you like people and they like you. In social situations, your charm, wit, and intelligence attract many admirers.

People born on April 25 are truth seekers with a deep reservoir of wisdom and a vivid imagination. Because you see life as a learning experience, you are more interested in the journey than the destination. With your creativity and love of knowledge, you can succeed in any number of educational or artistic pursuits. Music figures prominently in the lives of some born on this date. However, you express yourself in so many different ways that virtually any career is a viable possibility.

In an intimate relationship, you want the emotional security sought by all bulls. But you also need freedom and independence. You become bored and restless if you stick close to home for too long. Consequently, your ideal mate is someone who shares your love of travel and adventure.

On This Day:

The Roman festival of Robigalia took place on this date. It focused on the deity Robigus, who was associated with the god Mars and able to prevent and destroy the dreaded rust or red mildew that sometimes attacked the corn that was the city's principle food crop.

Born Today: Hank Azaria (actor); Ella Fitzgerald (jazz singer); Meadowlark Lemon (basketball player); Guglielmo Marconi (physicist/radio and telegraph inventor); Paul Mazursky (director); Edward R. Murrow (radio and TV journalist); Al Pacino (actor); Talia Shire (actress); Cy Twombly (artist); Renee Zellweger (actress)

April 26
♉ Taurus, 8

The person born on this day is artistic and creative, with a first-rate head for business and finance. Serious about your long-term goals, you have the requisite persistence and determination to turn your visionary ideas into practical realities. Outwardly gracious and charming, inside you are extremely shrewd and sensible. A flair for management and problem solving furthers your prospects for success. Whether you're promoting your own talents or someone else's, you are mainly concerned with results, not abstract theories. While material rewards may appear to be your main concern, what you really want is recognition, prestige, and authority.

Individuals with birthdays on April 26 are builders who work slowly and steadily to make their dreams come true. Mentally inquisitive, you enjoy exploring new territory and have a knack for translating your innovative ideas into forms that can be communicated to others. You're fascinated by the unexplained mysteries of life, yet you generally prefer keeping your controversial beliefs and opinions hidden. However, there may be times when you feel compelled to share your experience of the mystical and unusual with the world at large.

You have a deep-seated need to be loved and understood, but you must be able to trust the other person before you can commit to an intimate relationship. You want the affection and emotional reassurance of a devoted mate, but you'd rather be alone than with the wrong partner.

On This Day:

On New Year's Day in the African republic of Sierra Leone, the people perform an ancient seed-sowing ceremony in honor of their powerful fertility goddess, Mawu. Filled with spring's creative energy, she watches over their crops. To the Africans, this goddess is the lunar-aligned deity and mother figure who created people from clay.

Born Today: John James Audubon (ornithologist/artist); Carol Burnett (comedienne); Eugene Delacroix (artist); Donna De Varona (swimmer); Michel Fokine (choreographer); Alfred Krupp (industrialist); Anita Loos (scriptwriter); Bernard Malamud (writer); Charles Richter (seismologist); Jess Stern (writer); A. E. Van Vogt (writer)

April 27

♉ Taurus, 9

The April 27th individual is a compassionate humanitarian who is very receptive to the needs of others. People trust you and look to you for assistance because they believe that you empathize with their pain and can help them solve their problems. The passionate dedication that drives your crusading nature impels you toward action, rather than the procrastination so common among other members of your Sun sign. You aim to make a difference in the world. However, if your efforts are not appreciated, you may become temporarily despondent.

Although making money is not a prime concern of those born on this day, their excellent business instincts help them rake in the big bucks. There is actually very little that you can't do when motivated by an intriguing challenge. Your considerable charm and personal magnetism make an unforgettable impression on those you meet. You are sensitive and imaginative, with a genuine love of art and beauty. Although your temperament is that of an artist and a dreamer, your Taurian stability and practicality help you deal with your creativity in a down-to-earth, rational manner.

In personal relationships, you're the consummate idealist. You need to be especially wary of placing your beloved on a pedestal, because you're sure to be severely disillusioned if he or she is unable to live up to your high expectations.

On This Day:

Tyi Wara, a mythical half-man, half-animal, is honored every year on this date by members of the Bambara tribe of the African Republic of Mali. They believe that Tyi Wara was sent down to Earth by the gods of nature in order to teach human beings the necessary skills of farming. The farmers celebrate this sacred day with songs and dances.

Born Today: Sandy Dennis (actress); Sheena Easton (singer); Edward Gibbon (historian); Ulysses S. Grant (U.S. president/Union Army general); Rogers Hornsby (baseball player); Jack Klugman (actor); Walter Lanz (cartoonist); Samuel Morse (electric telegraph and Morse Code inventor); Herbert Spencer (philosopher)

April 28
♉ Taurus, 1

The seemingly placid outer nature of those who celebrate their birthdays on this day hides the extremely ambitious go-getter within. Like most bulls, you need roots and a sense of security. Yet your restless, pioneering spirit craves change and excitement. You long to try new things and explore virgin territory. Your life's challenge is to find a way to combine the adventurous spirit of the number one's vibration with the inherent practicality of your Taurus Sun sign.

As a natural leader, you provide vision and direction in cooperative ventures. You expect a lot from others, but you're prepared to do as much or more yourself. When you really want something, you go after it and stick with it to completion. Your single-minded pursuit of your goals may earn you a reputation as a ruthless competitor, especially in business. You are generally open minded and tolerant of other people's ideas, yet you can be surprisingly dogmatic if your own beliefs are called into account. However, your inherent enthusiasm, coupled with your plausible reasoning, usually helps you win people over to your point of view.

In a love relationship, you're sensuous and fun loving, with a lively zest for life. You can be difficult and demanding, but you're also very loyal and caring. Your own need for freedom and independence makes you less clingy than most other bulls.

On This Day:

In ancient Rome, the beginning of the growing season was marked each year with a three-day festival known as the Floralia, dedicated to Flora, goddess of flowers, sexuality, youth, and springtime. Flora was honored with offerings of flowering plants in the hope that she would use her powers to ward off the possibility of famine.

Born Today: Jessica Alba (actress); Lionel Barrymore (actor); Penelope Cruz (actress); Nancy Lee Grahn (actress); Saddam Hussein (Iraqi dictator); Harper Lee (writer); Jay Leno (comedian/TV talk show host); Ann-Margret (actress/singer/dancer); James Monroe (U.S. president); Kaneto Shindo (director); Charles Sturt (explorer)

April 29

♉ Taurus, 2

People born on this day are steadfast in their devotion to the safety and security of the material world. Level headed and concerned with the practical necessities of life, you like to be prepared for any eventuality. Accumulating money, property, and possessions is your way of protecting yourself from life's uncertainties. Your persistence in pursuit of your objectives is legendary. Nevertheless, you rarely make the first move. You prefer waiting until opportunity comes knocking, and with fortunate Venus as your planetary ruler, it usually does.

The artistic bent of those born April 29 arises from a deep aesthetic appreciation for beautiful things. You may also possess considerable talent as a musician, dancer, painter, writer, or actor. Very much the craftsperson, you're probably skilled in cooking and gardening too. Closely allied to your refined taste is a love of pleasure. Comfort, luxury, and good food and drink are high on your list of important things. You're a great host who loves entertaining family and friends. Nothing makes you happier than a home filled with the sounds of music, laughter, and scintillating conversation.

In love, you're romantic, ardent, and sensuous. It may take you awhile to come to a firm decision, but once you've made up your mind about someone, you rarely change it. When you agree to stick around "for better or for worse," you keep your promise.

On This Day:

This is the beginning of the runic half-month of Lagu, representing the flowing, mutable forces of water and symbolizing life, growth, and the waxing power of spring. On this day each year, in the ancient city of Teotihuacan, Mexico, the setting Sun aligns to the entrance of a ritual cave and to the setting point of the Pleiades star cluster overhead.

Born Today: Andre Agassi (tennis player); Daniel Day-Lewis (actor); Dale Earnhardt, Sr. (racecar driver); Duke Ellington (jazz composer/pianist/bandleader); Zubin Mehta (conductor); William Randolph Hearst (publisher); Kate Mulgrew (actress); Michele Pfeiffer (actress); Jerry Seinfeld (comedian); Uma Thurman (actress)

April 30

♉ Taurus, 3

Those born on this day are open hearted, warm, and friendly. You enjoy lively conversations and have a decided knack for conveying thoughts and ideas. In social situations, your intelligence, charm, and wit tend to attract many admirers. You possess a fine sense of humor and can be hysterically funny as long as the joke is not on you. Despite your good nature, you can't stand looking silly or foolish. Like most bulls, you carefully guard your dignity and image of respectability. Although you are not a snob, there is a touch of pomposity in your character that may give people that impression.

Mentally, you're sharp and versatile, with a large variety of diverse interests. On an emotional level, you flip back and forth between the placid bull's need for peace and serenity and the sociable root number three's desire for change and excitement. The lighthearted social butterfly inside you usually wins the day, and your overall response to new people is considerably freer than that of other Taurians. Although you can succeed in virtually any career field, you're most likely to be attracted to one that calls upon your talent as a communicator.

As a romantic partner, you are sensual and exciting. However, too much togetherness can make you uncomfortable. You want the love and security of a committed union, but you also want the freedom to pursue your personal ambitions.

On This Day:

Walpurgis Night derives from an ancient Teutonic holiday when the arrival of spring was celebrated with nocturnal bonfires. In Germany, birch boughs are placed on doors to protect homes from sorcery. Fires and torches of rosemary and juniper are lit, and according to legend, witches may be seen riding broomsticks across the sky.

Born Today: Eve Arden (actress); Corinne Calvert (actress); Jill Clayburgh (actress); Kirsten Dunst (actress); Herbert Ferber (artist); Cloris Leachman (actress); Willie Nelson (singer/songwriter); John Crowe Ransom (poet/critic); Don Schollander (swimmer); Isaiah Thomas (basketball player); Jeff Timmons (singer); Burt Young (actor)

May Birthdays

May 1
♉ Taurus, 1

Bulls celebrating their birthdays on this day are a complex blend of persistence and patience on the one hand and restless impatience on the other. The energy and enthusiasm of the number one engenders immediate action. Unlike many natives of your Sun sign, you're a doer rather than a procrastinator. Self-motivated and more assertive than other Taurians, you rarely worry about what others think of you or your activities. When a good opportunity presents itself, you seize it by the horns. Once committed to a project, you'll stick with it to completion.

A born executive, it is natural for you to assume a leading role in all your endeavors. Your energy level is exceptionally high, but you need to take time out to recharge your batteries from time to time. There is a genuine division between your intellect and your emotions. You can be calm and rational one moment, yet upset and temperamental the next. It's not unusual for you to hold rigidly to a belief about how things should be done and then, unexpectedly, switch sides and take the opposite position.

In relationships, you crave security and can be difficult if your stability is threatened. Yet you are a true romantic and likely to be swept off your feet by love. If you meet the right person, you won't shy away from a long-term commitment.

On This Day:

The ancient Celtic fire festival of Beltane is celebrated on this date. It honors the rebirth of the Sun, the death of winter, and the union of the goddess and the horned god. In ancient Rome, the deity worshipped on this day was Maia, namesake of the month of May, who uses her divine powers to encourage the growth of crops.

Born Today: Chuck Bednarik (football player); Steve Cauthen (jockey); Rita Coolidge (singer); Judy Collins (singer); Glen Ford (actor); Joseph Heller (writer); Ollie Matson (football player); Tim McGraw (singer); Kate Smith (singer); Terry Southern (screenwriter); Valentina (fashion designer); Theo van Gogh (art dealer)

May 2
♉ Taurus, 2

The individual born on May 2 has an earthy, here-and-now world view that accounts for his or her no-nonsense approach to dealing with problems. As a materialist, you believe in results, not theories. Nevertheless, you refuse to let your rock-hard realism interfere with the abiding charm of your amiable personality. Inclined toward collaboration and teamwork, you will go out of your way to avoid conflict and controversy. However, a bullish Taurian temperament lurks just beneath the surface of your placid exterior; with sufficient provocation, you'll fly into a terrible rage.

People with birthdays on this date often exhibit exceptional artistic or musical talent. Your creativity tends to be of the practical variety. When coupled with intuition, it provides you with keen insight and a deep understanding of the public's needs and desires. Strong-willed, dependable, and resolute, you have a powerful memory and tons of common sense. Although many career fields are open to someone of your capabilities, you could have a particular interest in the performing arts, teaching, counseling, architecture, designing, cooking, or catering.

You are deeply caring and passionate, yet you can be rather shy about love. You fear rejection and may take a passive approach, preferring to attract romantic partners instead of pursuing them. Once you make up your mind about someone, you rarely change it. However, if you should change your mind, the relationship is as good as over.

On This Day:

In India, Ysahodhara, consort of the Buddha, is honored in a festival that takes place annually on this date. This day is also sacred to Elena, or Helen, goddess of the holy road or four royal roads of Britain. In Wales, her causeways and roads are known as Sarn Helen. Elena is also Elaine, mother of Sir Galahad of the Authurian romances.

Born Today: David Beckham (soccer player); Theodore Bikel (singer/actor); Leslie Gore (singer); Engelbert Humperdinck (singer); Dwayne "The Rock" Johnson (wrestler/actor); Baron Manfred "The Red Baron" von Richthofen (WWI fighter pilot)

May 3
♉ Taurus, 3

Those born on this day are personable, articulate, determined, and tenacious. You have a wide range of interests and a mentality that is well equipped with intelligence, foresight, and intuition. The unusual mixture of a breezy personality associated with the number three's vibration and the practical intellect of the Sun in Taurus makes you a master communicator. You're a charming, witty conversationalist, but your propensity for saying whatever you're thinking can sometimes get you into trouble.

Taurians with birthdays on May 3 enjoy gardening and cooking and have a gift for nurturing plants, animals, and people. Even when you're stuck inside a city of concrete, you take advantage of every opportunity to get close to nature. Like most bulls, you are creative, have excellent taste, and feel a deep appreciation of all things beautiful and artistic. With your extraordinary common sense and facility for handling money, you're well suited to a career in the world of business and finance. Those born on this day often go on to become successful artists, actors, singers, musicians, songwriters, poets, novelists, architects, interior designers, chefs, restaurateurs, florists, or fashion designers.

As a romantic partner, you are affectionate, sensual, and exciting. You take your commitments seriously, and devotion and loyalty tend to be key elements in your relationships. Although you want the love and security of family life, you also enjoy the freedom to pursue your many interests.

On This Day:

In ancient Rome, the festival of the Bona Dea was held annually on this date. A goddess of the Earth, the Bona Dea was the deity of women's mysteries. Men were never admitted to her secret ceremonies. The rites, which took place in the house of the praetor of the city, were usually presided over by his wife and the Vestal Virgins.

Born Today: Mary Astor (actress); James Brown (singer); Bing Crosby (singer); Christopher Cross (singer); Doug Henning (magician/escape artist); William Inge (playwright); Golda Meier (Israeli prime minister); Sugar Ray Robinson (boxer); Pete Seeger (folksinger/environmental activist); Frankie Valli (singer)

May 4

♉ Taurus, 4

People who celebrate birthdays on this date are ambitious, hard working, and practical. You're pretty clear about what you want from life, and you have the confidence and determination to get it. You are a builder, someone who works slowly and steadily toward an accomplishment. You pursue your plans and dreams with resolve and dogged determination. Once you decide what you're going to do, you refuse to let anything or anyone deter you from your goal. In addition, you have a good head for business and finance, and you're a shrewd judge of people and their needs.

Although safety and security may seem to be your main concerns, you are actually very sensitive and imaginative, with a genuine love of beauty, art, and nature. Moreover, you're extremely sociable, warm, and gracious— so much so, in fact, that some may regard you as an easy mark for a sob story. However receptive you may be to the needs of others, you're not prone to letting them take advantage of your good nature. Your sympathy is of the practical variety, and you're much more likely to hand out sensible advice than money.

In love, you may come off as rather cool and collected. You are as emotional as any other bull, however, just not as comfortable letting your true feelings show. At heart you're a secret romantic, but when discouraged by insecurity, you repress your emotions.

On This Day:

The hawthorn tree is honored on this day at the festival of the Veneration of the Thorn. Hawthorns marking sacred places and holy wells are acknowledged by tying scraps of new cloth to their branches. According to Irish folklore, this date marks Fairy Day, when mischievous fairies emerge from their hiding places to cause confusion.

Born Today: Manuel Benites, "El Cordobes" (bullfighter); Frederick Church (painter); Howard Da Silva (actor); Maynard Ferguson (jazz musician/bandleader); Audrey Hepburn (actress); John Hanning (explorer); Keith Haring (artist); Horace Mann (educator); Roberta Peters (opera singer); Randy Travis (singer)

May 5
♉ Taurus, 5

People born on May 5 are genuine originals. With your independent spirit and far-reaching mentality, you're not shy about sharing your discoveries or articulating your innovative ideas and opinions. You are all about intellectual pursuits and idealistic causes. Your forward-looking, progressive outlook allows you to see future possibilities that the less innovative can't even imagine. Your fierce independence is reinforced by Taurus's dogged determination. You feel perfectly capable of telling others how to improve their lives, yet you stubbornly resist any attempt to get you to change your own.

Affable, open, and friendly, with a gregarious personality and a gracious manner, you obviously care a great deal about people. However, there is a detached, impersonal side to your nature that makes you seem cool and serene under even extreme emotional pressure. You're a good listener as well as a persuasive talker, and you're something of an expert in human relationships. You like getting inside people's heads and figuring out what makes them tick. Whether in business, the arts, or the professions, you long to use your talents and abilities to help make the world a better place for everyone.

Although one part of you is afraid of intimacy and togetherness, the other part craves a relationship that offers stability and consistency. When you do decide to commit to a partner, you do it wholeheartedly, and you make a loyal and devoted mate.

On This Day:

Cinco de Mayo commemorates the victory of the Mexicans over the French troops at the Battle of Puebla in 1862, which eventually led to the expulsion of Napoleon III's army from Mexico. In some parts of Mexico and Central America, the shamanic priests and priestesses perform ancient rain ceremonies each year on this date.

Born Today: James Beard (chef/food writer); Pat Carroll (actress); Ann B. Davis (actress); Alice Faye (actress); Soren Kierkegaard (philosopher); Karl Marx (political theorist); George Muche (artist); Michael Palin (comedian/actor); Robert Prescott (Flying Tiger Airlines founder); Tyrone Power (actor); Tammy Wynette (singer)

May 6

♉ Taurus, 6

Bulls who celebrate birthdays on this date are warm, sociable, charming "people who need people." Your diplomatic manner draws others into your orbit, and cooperative ventures and shared activities are all-important to you. You don't favor spending time alone, and thanks to your outgoing, friendly personality, you rarely have to. Despite your ability to get along with virtually anyone, you tend to gravitate toward those with similar tastes and interests. If cooperation is one of your strengths, persuasion is another. You have a knack for talking your way into or out of almost any situation.

Those with May 6th birthdays are seeking balance and harmony. Your special gift is to bring people and things together and help synthesize the various parts into a comprehensive whole. You particularly enjoy entertaining family, friends, and associates, and you never stint on the cost of a dinner party or other social affair. You're sure to be successful at any undertaking that allows you to combine your impeccable taste and love of beauty with your desire to please others.

Relationships are the glue that holds your life together. More than anything, you enjoy the companionship of a loving partner. Sensual and idealistic, you're capable of loving passionately and with total commitment. In return, you fully expect your significant other to respond with affection, poetry, and romance.

On This Day:

This day is sacred to Eyvind Kelve, a Norwegian pagan martyr who was killed on the orders of King Olaf Trygvason for refusing to renounce his pagan beliefs. In many Buddhist traditions, the holiday Vesak is celebrated on or around this date. It honors Buddha's birthday, his enlightenment, and his death in one all-encompassing festival.

Born Today: Tom Bergeron (TV host); Tony Blair (British prime minister); George Clooney (actor); Sigmund Freud (founder of psychoanalysis); Willie Mays (baseball player); Robert E. Peary (explorer/first person to reach the North Pole); Rudolph Valentino (actor); Orson Welles (actor/screenwriter/director/producer)

May 7
♉ Taurus, 7

Those born on this day are an unusual blend of the conventional practicality of solar Taurus and the adventurous spirit of the number seven. On the one hand, you're a truth-seeking intellectual with a deep reservoir of wisdom, and on the other, you're something of a mystic or occultist. Creative imagination is your forte, and you possess all the sensitivity of a true artist. You have tremendous empathy for other people and considerable talent as a psychic, which allows you to "tune in" to what people are feeling.

When your own deepest emotions come into play, logic and reason tend to fall by the wayside, and you think with your heart instead of your mind. There is a solitary side of your nature that requires frequent "down time" for private contemplation. As a result, even people close to you may regard you as rather mysterious. You can be torn and uncertain about what you want to do in life. However, when you find an idea or project that truly excites you, your enthusiasm won't quit until the goal is achieved.

In an intimate union, you make a sentimental, tender, caring lover. However, at times you can be depressed or moody, especially if you feel that your efforts are not appreciated. If a close relationship turns sour, the inevitable breakup can leave you feeling heartbroken and betrayed.

On This Day:

On or around this date each year, the ancient Greeks and Ionians celebrated the festival known as the Thargelia. The festival was held in honor of Apollo, god of the Sun, prophecy, music, medicine, and poetry. It took place on the sacred island of Delos, the traditional birthplace of Apollo and his twin sister, the Moon goddess Artemis.

Born Today: Ann Baxter (actress); Johannes Brahms (composer); Teresa Brewer (singer); Robert Browning (poet); Gary Cooper (actor); Gabby Hayes (actor); Edward Land (Polaroid Land Camera inventor); Darren McGavin (actor); Tim Russert (TV journalist); Peter Ilyitch Tchaikovsky (composer); Johnny Unitas (football player)

May 8
♉ Taurus, 8

The amiable, good-natured facade of individuals who celebrate birthdays on this day masks an extremely practical inner nature. With your executive abilities and excellent judgment in evaluating people and situations, you're well suited to positions of authority. You have a realistic approach to life that is quite helpful in various career fields, from business to politics. Your organizational skills and capacity for zeroing in on the causes of a problem are the heart of your business acumen.

People born on May 8 have a knack for recognizing the funny side of any situation and are renowned for their sense of humor. You're very outspoken and rarely afraid to say what you're thinking. Despite your own self-sufficiency, you speak up for the rights of others when you deem it necessary. Your ability to get your message across can make you quite influential with regard to raising people's consciousness. Since you gravitate toward the higher echelons of business, the arts, government, or academia, you may find yourself in a position to implement progressive improvements in the system.

You tend to be shyer and less sure of yourself in personal matters than you are professionally. You want love and romance in your life, but you're hesitant about making the first move. However, once involved in loving union, you are the staunchest and most reliable of partners.

On This Day:

In Cornwall, England, the annual Furry Dance is performed in the streets of Helston. One of the oldest surviving springtime festivals in the world, the Furry honors the Celtic horned god in the guise of Robin Hood. Also known as Flora Day, it coincides with the feast of the Apparition of Saint Michael the Archangel, Helston's patron saint.

Born Today: Peter Benchley (writer); Melissa Gilbert (actress); Gabby Hayes (actor); Enrique Iglesias (singer); Ricky Nelson (singer); Don Rickles (comedian); Jane Roberts (writer/channeled the Seth material); Fulton J. Sheen (Roman Catholic bishop); Gary Snyder (poet); Toni Tennille (singer); Harry S. Truman (U.S. president); Sloan Wilson (writer)

May 9

♉ Taurus, 9

The person whose birthday falls on this day has the temperament of an artistic dreamer and the practicality and determination of the Taurian bull. You are sensitive and imaginative, with a genuine love of art and beauty. Yet you possess the wherewithal to employ your artistry in a very down-to-earth manner. You derive great satisfaction from using your talents to create things that are useful as well as beautiful. Many born on this date become the artists, writers, musicians, actors, filmmakers, architects, and inventors who turn their visionary ideas into commercial success stories.

Being born on March 9 makes you very receptive to the needs of others. People naturally trust and depend on you. You have a deep spirituality that makes you selfless and courageous. Others realize that you understand their pain and are willing to go the extra mile to help them solve their problems. Mixed in with your empathy, compassion, and material assistance, there is likely to be some very sound, sensible advice. Sometimes, however, problems may arise with those you are trying to help, particularly if they equate your advice and assistance with possessiveness.

You want a stable, tranquil home life, and you enjoy the closeness of an intimate union. However, you have a definite tendency toward moodiness and over-sensitivity. Living with you can become a complex roller-coaster ride of frequent ups and downs.

On This Day:

In ancient Rome, the first day of the three-day festival of the Lemuria took place on this date. Its purpose was to appease the spirits of the dead (lemurs), who haunted homes where they had once lived. The master of the house went through the rooms tossing black beans (symbolizing the underworld) as offerings to the ghosts.

Born Today: Ralph Boston (long jumper); James L. Brooks (producer/director); John Brown (militant abolitionist); Howard Carter (archaeologist); Albert Finney (actor); Pancho Gonzales (tennis player); Glenda Jackson (actress); Henry Kaiser (industrialist); Billy Joel (singer/pianist/songwriter); Mike Wallace (TV journalist)

May 10

♉ Taurus, 1

Bulls who celebrate birthdays on this day are the ambitious, independent go-getters of their Sun sign. You possess an innovative, pioneering spirit that prompts you to strike out in new and previously unexplored directions. Once you make up your mind to do something, you succeed because your energy and determination are backed by your powerful will. Whenever life gets too quiet for your taste, you make things happen by throwing yourself into exciting new enterprises. You're a self-starter and don't relish waiting around for anyone's permission or approval before beginning a new adventure.

Despite your love of action and fresh experience, you desperately need roots and a sense of security. Since your intellect and emotions don't always function on the same wavelength, you may not even be aware of your own inconsistencies. Consequently, you often feel as if you're being pulled in several different directions. You may be tranquil one moment, upset and temperamental the next. It's not unusual for you to hold rigidly to an idea or belief and then suddenly switch sides and express an opinion that is exactly the opposite.

In relationships you are caring, generous, fun loving, and exciting. However, you crave security, and you can be quite difficult when your stability is threatened. Yours is an extremely impulsive nature, and you're easily swept off your feet by love and romance.

On This Day:

In Madurai, India, the faithful celebrate the sacred marriage of the god Shiva to the goddess Meenakshi. Hymns are sung and offerings made of incense and white flower petals at all the temples dedicated to Shiva. On this day each year in Hong Kong, Tin Hau, the Chinese goddess of the North Star, is honored with a festival.

Born Today: Fred Astaire (dancer/actor); Amanda Borden (gymnast); Donovan (singer/songwriter); Phil Mahre (skier); Steve Mahre (skier); David O. Selznick (producer); Max Steiner (composer); Sid Vicious (rock star); Nancy Walker (actress)

May 11
♉ Taurus, 2

Individuals who celebrate birthdays on this day are possibly the only Taurians with a facility for handling two tasks at once or balancing two careers simultaneously. As a practical idealist, you face the zodiacal task of finding a way to integrate your spirituality with the bull's earthy materialism. On one level you are pragmatic, ambitious, and determined to "make it" in the material world. However, on a deeper level you need to know that your personal achievements contribute something to your community's development. You feel most rewarded when your humanitarian efforts help people to help themselves.

Your abundant charm and personal magnetism draws friends and admirers. You possess tremendous creative potential that may be used in the arts, business, or the helping professions. Although some born on this day choose to become ministers, teachers, nurses, or missionaries, others who are more artistically inclined prefer vocations associated with the fine arts. In business, you employ sound financial practices while making sure that customers get what they pay for. Whatever you decide to do in life, you have a gift for turning the ordinary in to something very special.

In relationships, you like being surrounded by clever, interesting people. In love, you are affectionate, romantic, and genuinely devoted to your partner. You're capable of great sacrifice, but at times you may need to guard against jealousy and possessiveness.

On This Day:

In German and Swiss folklore, this date marked the first of three feast days of Eisheilige (Ice Saint Days), honoring the saints Mamertius, Pancratius, and Servais. These three were known as the Three Chilly Saints because their feast days were most likely to bring a late frost. Traditionally, it was not safe to plant until the icemen were gone.

Born Today: Irving Berlin (composer); Eric Burdon (singer/songwriter); Salvador Dali (artist); Charlie Gehringer (baseball player); Martha Graham (dancer/choreographer); Andre Gregory (director/actor/writer); Natasha Richardson (actress); Margaret Rutherford (actress); Mort Sahl (comedian); Phil Silvers (comedian/actor)

May 12
♉ Taurus, 3

Bulls who celebrate birthdays on this date are an intriguing mix of dogged endurance and restless impatience. Although you are security minded and home loving, your adventurous spirit thrives on travel and exploration. You're more articulate than the typical Taurus native, and your wonderfully witty sense of humor enlivens all your comments and conversations. More than anything, you're a philosopher with a deep understanding of nature and the world around you. Your forte is the ability to translate your intuitive ideas into words and communicate them to others.

May 12th Taurians are artistic and self-expressive, but they're rather inclined to take their creative talents for granted. Nevertheless, you have what it takes to turn your dreams into reality by forging a successful career in music, art, dance, or sports. Individuals born on this day do their homework. With your practical intelligence, excellent memory, and skills as a researcher, you would make an outstanding writer, educator, actor, lawyer, politician, or preacher. Your natural eloquence is enhanced by your ability to paint vivid word pictures that allow you to share your personal experiences with others.

Emotionally, you blow hot and cold. Your basic makeup is a mixture of the number twelve's freewheeling independence and the rock-solid dependability of Taurus. You want the comfort of a secure relationship, but you also crave the freedom to pursue your dreams.

On This Day:

In Belgium, people dress up as cats for the annual cat parade that features the Egyptian cat-headed goddess, Bast, as Queen of the Cats. In India on this date, people hold the annual festival in honor of Anranya Sashti. A god of the woodlands, Anranya Sashti is usually identified with the pagan horned deities Pan and Cernunnos.

★★
★ **Born Today:** Burt Bacharach (songwriter); Yogi Berra (baseball player/manager); George Carlin (comedian); Emilio Estevez (actor); Tony Hawk (skateboarder); Katharine Hepburn (actress); Jiddu Krishnamurti (philosopher/teacher); Florence Nightingale (nurse/founder of modern nursing as a profession); Tom Snyder (TV host)

May 13
♉ Taurus, 4

The charismatic individuals born on this day are discriminating, practical, and pragmatic. Your sweet-natured, gracious exterior hides an iron will and a deep inner sense of your own worth. You are very clear about what you want out of life, and you possess the self-confidence and determination to make it happen. Because you appear more easygoing than you actually are, few people realize that what you crave most are authority, prestige, and recognition.

The creative individuals with birthdays on May 13 generally love art and music and often have considerable artistic talent of their own. Many people born on this date become successful singers, musicians, songwriters, actors, writers, architects, or designers. Like them, you're hard working and ambitious and have a facility for handling money and finances that could prove extremely useful in a career in business. Your desire for security and stability motivates you to build strong structures, both literally and figuratively. You like seeing the tangible results and practical applications of your efforts.

With your close associates, friends, and family, you're generous, loyal, dependable, and totally trustworthy. In an intimate union, you are passionate and loving, but you can also be quite possessive and demanding. You willingly give your all to those you love, but you want and need the same kind of love and devotion in return.

On This Day:

On May 13, 1917, three children, Lucia, Francisco, and Jacinta, were tending sheep in the Cova da Iria, outside Fatima, Portugal. They saw a bright flash, and in the center of the light a lady appeared who was "brighter than the Sun." She told the children that she had come "from heaven" and would appear before them six more times.

Born Today: Bea Arthur (actress); Georges Braque (artist); Bruce Chatwin (writer); Daphne du Maurier (writer); Jane Alison Glover (conductor); Harvey Keitel (actor); Joe Louis (boxer); Sir Arthur Sullivan (composer); Ritchie Valens (singer/songwriter); Stevie Wonder (singer/songwriter); Roger Zelazny (writer)

May 14

♉ Taurus, 5

People with this birthday are practical visionaries whose view of the future is based on a sound understanding of the past and present. You're not afraid to go against the tide of tradition, because you believe in yourself and your farseeing, innovative ideas. Intellectually, you're light years ahead of other members of your generation. Your forward-looking, progressive outlook allows you to see future opportunities that your more conservative peers can't even imagine. Consequently, you may be the one to come up with groundbreaking ideas capable of changing the world.

Those born on May 14 are generally more restless and likely to be propelled by nervous energy than most of their Sun sign counterparts. Despite an inner streak of stubbornness, you are affable, sociable, and well liked by your friends and associates. A proud and independent self-starter, you rarely seek help from others. Nevertheless, there are usually influential people standing by who are prepared to offer you assistance if you ask. Despite your professional image as a poster child for progress, in your personal life you're rather set in your ways. You neither welcome nor adapt readily to abrupt changes to your habitual way of doing things.

In a love relationship, you want stability and consistency, but your independent spirit makes you somewhat fearful of intimacy and togetherness. However, once you decide to make the commitment to a long-term union, you do it wholeheartedly.

On This Day:

In northern Scandinavia, the Festival of the Midnight Sun begins a ten-week-long celebration of daylight that pays homage to Dag, the ancient Norse goddess of the Sun. This day is also sacred to Ing, male consort of the Earth-mother goddess Nerthus. His rune, the symbol of light, expresses the energy potential of the abundance of summer.

Born Today: Cate Blanchett (actress); Kurt Browning (skater); David Byrne (singer/song-writer); Bobby Darrin (singer/actor); Gabriel Daniel Fahrenheit (physicist); Joseph Fruton (biochemist); Thomas Gainsborough (artist); George Lucas (producer/director); Patrice Munsel (opera singer); Robert Zemeckis (director)

May 15
♉ Taurus, 6

Those born on May 15 are among the more civilized, cooperative, and peaceable members of the zodiacal community. Your personal charm, compassionate attitude, and easygoing nature have a way of drawing people into your orbit. Although you get along with almost anyone, you tend to gravitate toward individuals who share your cultured tastes and interests. You're devoted to the good life and enjoy sharing its pleasures with others. You appreciate having a nice home where you can entertain your family and friends. A gracious host or hostess, you have a special knack for bringing people together.

People with birthdays on this day are self-expressive and imaginative. You are likely to be happiest in a profession that makes use of your creative talents. Since you're personable and make an excellent first impression, you should do particularly well in the performing arts, the diplomatic service, politics, fashion and interior design, catering, or the production and sale of luxury items. Cooperation and teamwork are your strengths, and you'll certainly succeed in any career that allows you to combine your love of beauty with your sense of fair play and your desire to please.

You are extraordinarily romantic, and you may not feel complete without a partner. Because of your inclination to think in pairs, when you are involved in an intimate relationship, you pepper your conversation with words like *we, us,* and *our.*

On This Day:

On this day in ancient Rome, the Vestal Virgins performed an annual purification rite to ensure the water supply for the coming year. It consisted of the "sacrifice" of twenty-seven straw puppets to the river god of the Tiber. This day was also sacred to Maia, goddess of springtime and fertility and wife of the blacksmith god, Vulcan.

Born Today: Anna Maria Alberghetti (singer); Madeleine Albright (U.S. secretary of state); Richard Avedon (photographer); L. Frank Baum (writer); George Brett (baseball player); David Charvet (actor); Joseph Cotton (actor); Jasper Johns (artist); James Mason (actor); Jamie-Lynn Sigler (actress); Emmitt Smith (football player)

May 16
♉ Taurus, 7

Bulls who celebrate their birthdays on this date are intelligent and honorable. You have a very generous disposition, and you don't limit your kindness to material things. Always gracious with your time and attention, you're a teacher who inspires by example. You have an inquiring mind that is open to any type of mental challenge. Your congenial, breezy outer personality hides the more serious side of your nature, the part of you that is interested in philosophical subjects and the whys and wherefores of existence.

May 16th individuals are enthusiastic and optimistic and are not afraid to take chances when the rewards seem worth the risks. Those born on this day are often deeply spiritual or religious, albeit in a most unorthodox fashion. You may also possess psychic powers or be interested in various aspects of mysticism or the occult. You are hard working and discerning, but also extremely creative, imaginative, and intuitive. You may be gifted with the kind of musical, artistic, dramatic, or literary talent that can lead to a successful professional career.

In love relationships, you're the consummate romantic. Caring, sensual, and affectionate, you're both giving and responsive as a mate or partner. You tend to fall in love rather easily, and virtually any sign of passion brings out the lover in you. You're loyal and devoted, but you can be rather possessive as well.

On This Day:

The voyages of Saint Brendon the Navigator are remembered on this date. An Irish Celtic priest, he is believed to have been the first European to find North America. It was during the sixth century C.E. that he set sail in search of the Garden of Eden. His voyage lasted seven years and forty days and produced an adventurous itinerary.

Born Today: Pierce Brosnan (actor); Henry Fonda (actor); Tracey Gold (actress); Janet Jackson (singer); Olga Korbut (gymnast); Liberace (pianist); Billy Martin (baseball player/manager); Kenji Mizoguchi (director); William Seward (U.S. secretary of state who purchased Alaska); Tori Spelling (actress); Debra Winger (actress)

May 17
♉ Taurus, 8

The most obvious trait of those whose birthdays fall on May 17 is their determination. A self-starter with a plan, you've probably known from an early age what you want to accomplish and how to go about it. Unlike some members of your Sun sign, you're not particularly concerned with other people's opinions of your actions. You run right up and grab the bull by the horns without waiting for permission or approval from anyone. Honesty is your touchstone. Despite your charming manner and winning personality, you're not known for tact. You prefer saying exactly what you're thinking and letting the chips fall where they will.

People celebrating their birthdays on this date have an eye for quality and a sensible approach to finances that insures material security. Business is your forte, and you know how to commercialize your talents and use them to the best advantage. You are a born executive with a gift for organization and a firm, take-charge manner. As a shrewd judge of character, you know which of your associates can be trusted and depended on to get the job done.

In an intimate union, you make a loving, reliable, and discerning partner. You're naturally bull-headed, however, and at times you can be quite demanding. You know exactly what you want in a mate or lover, and you're not willing to settle for less.

On This Day:

The Green Corn Dance of the Florida Seminoles takes place annually on this date. A very old harvest ceremony, it is also celebrated by the Cherokee, Natchez, and Creeks. In addition to the sacred dances, there are ball games, council meetings, a feast of barbecued beef, and a purifying black beverage made from a creek holly shrub.

Born Today: Alfonso XIII (king of Spain); Enya (singer); Gaylord Hauser (nutritionist); Dennis Hopper (actor); Edward Jenner (physician/discovered the smallpox vaccine); Sugar Ray Leonard (boxer); Zinka Milanov (opera singer); Brigit Nilsson (opera singer); Maureen O'Sullivan (actress); Bill Paxton (actor); Dewey Redman (jazz musician)

May 18

♉ Taurus, 9

People born on this day are an interesting blend of creativity, spirituality, and idealism. Physically and mentally alert, you have quick reflexes and heightened intellectual perceptions. A compassionate humanitarian, you possess great empathy for the human condition and an intuitive understanding of other people's experiences. Your ultimate aim is to help improve the world. You are able to accomplish this in a direct way by speaking out against injustices politically, in the media, in the classroom, or from the pulpit; or you may prefer to communicate your ideas in an indirect manner through your work as an artist, musician, writer, or athlete.

May 18th individuals are highly creative and imaginative, but they're also eminently practical and able to get things done with a minimum of fuss. A born fighter, you're not afraid of anything or anyone. You absolutely refuse to tolerate prejudice, discrimination, or inequity. Impatient, impulsive, and extremely outspoken, you can hurt your own cause if you forget to stop and think before you speak. When you are disappointed by the insensitivity of some people or the world in general, you may become temporarily despondent or withdrawn.

You need a stable personal life to offset the turbulence of your passionate crusading. A true romantic, you are a sentimental, tender, caring partner who revels in the closeness of a committed relationship. In love and friendship, you're loyal, dependable, and very responsive to the other person's needs.

On This Day:

Apollon Day is sacred to Apollo, the Greco-Roman god of sunlight, medicine, music, poetry, and divination. Annually on this day in Greece, seventeen-year-old males were initiated and welcomed into adult society. In the Republic of Nigeria, the Yoruba people celebrate the Feast of Twins in honor of all the twins in the community.

Born Today: Pierre Balmain (designer); Frank Capra (director); Perry Como (singer); Margo Fonteyn (dancer); Dwayne Hickman (actor); Reggie Jackson (baseball player); Jacob Javits (U.S. senator); John Paul II (Roman Catholic Pope); Robert Morse (actor); Pernell Roberts (actor); Brooks Robinson (baseball player); Bertrand Russell (philosopher)

May 19
♉ Taurus, 1

Bulls born on this date are the future-oriented pioneers and leaders of our society. Sometimes it seems as if you came into this world just to try to change it. You have extraordinary instincts when it comes to managing and controlling situations. But your achievement quotient is more highly developed than your understanding of human nature. You tend to run roughshod over people in your attempts to help them. Something of a benevolent dictator, you expect cooperation from others, yet rarely give it in return.

Those with a May 19th birthday are independent and extremely self-confident. Full of initiative, you are driven by your humanitarian ideals and convictions. Your modus operandi is to act first and ask questions later. You love travel, change, and excitement, but you also require roots and a feeling of security. When you feel that you're being pulled in two opposite directions at the same time, you become impatient and irritable. It's not unusual for you to spend years holding on to a belief or idea and then suddenly switch sides and take the opposite position.

In a personal relationship, you are warm and passionate. Inherently romantic and sentimental, you're easily swept off your feet by love. Despite your inclination to do everything your own way, your need for intimacy and close connections usually overcomes your desire for freedom and independence.

On This Day:

This is the feast day of Roman Catholic Saint Theophilus of Corte. Born in Corsica of noble parents, Theophilus entered the Franciscan order at a young age. His love of solitude, prayer, and the austere life of the Franciscans inspired him to start retreat houses in Corsica and Tuscany. Saint Theophilus was famous for his preaching as well as his missionary efforts.

Born Today: Andre the Giant (wrestler/actor); Nora Ephron (director/writer); Kevin Garnett (basketball player); Lorraine Hansberry (playwright); Grace Jones (model/singer/actress); Jim Lehrer (TV journalist); Malcolm X (political activist/writer); Nellie Melba (opera singer); Joey Ramone (singer); Pete Townshend (rock star)

May 20

♉ Taurus, 2

The individual born on the Taurus/Gemini cusp is charming and friendly, with the easy manner of someone who has been blessed with a winning personality. You are versatile, original, communicative, and imaginative. A creative thinker with an artistic temperament, your hands and brain seem to work together in perfect harmony. You possess all of the bull's artistry coupled with the twin's mental and physical dexterity. Sociable and lighthearted, you generally respond to people and situations more quickly and openly than do other bulls.

Placid, stable Taurus exerts a calming effect on Gemini's nervous, restless nature. Even so, you tend to flip back and forth between one mood and another. You like things safe and serene, yet crave change and diversity. With your Gemini side in control, you're logical and coolly detached, but you become remarkably emotional and stubborn when Taurus takes over. A good listener and a persuasive talker, you're also astute at working behind the scenes. When you're thwarted or blocked in your efforts, you mix a bit of cunning with your charm to help turn things around.

As a romantic partner, you are affectionate, sensual, and exciting. Although physical closeness poses little difficulty, emotionally you may be totally unavailable. You want the love and security of family life, but you also want the freedom and independence to pursue your own dreams.

On This Day:

The Norse festival of Mjollnir celebrates Thor's hammer. In medieval times, this day was viewed as a good time to hold ritual trials by combat, for which the will of the gods would decide the winner. On this date in ancient Greece, the goddess Athena, patroness of war and wisdom, was honored with the festivals of Kallyntaria and Plynteria.

Born Today: Honore de Balzac (writer); Cher (singer/actress); Joe Cocker (singer); George Gobel (comedian); Leroy Kelly (football player); Stan Mikita (hockey player); Bronson Pinchot (actor); Busta Rhymes (singer); Socrates (philosopher); Owen G. Smith (pole vaulter); Jimmy Stewart (actor); Constance Towers (actress)

May 21
♊ Gemini, 3

Twins with birthdays on this day are the whirling dervishes of the zodiac. You rush around from place to place, meeting people and gleaning bits of news and information as you go. A consummate communicator, you can barely wait to share what you've learned with others. Although you skim the surface of most subjects, you have a knack for zeroing in on essentials and important elements. As a result, you often have a better understanding of people and situations than those who pride themselves on probing deeply for the facts.

People born on May 21 are optimistic, versatile, and independent. You believe in yourself and in your ability to overcome difficulties. Surprisingly lucky, you are not afraid to act on your hunches. You're always on the lookout for new challenges and adventures because you are convinced that variety is the spice of life. Your restless temperament abhors a vacuum, and your chameleon-like adaptability allows you fit in anywhere. You fervently resist attempts to box you in, and dull situations or boring company won't hold you for long.

In love and romance it takes both intellectual and physical stimulation to keep you interested. Effusive emotion and unremitting intimacy can scare you off. When the closeness becomes cloying, you're inclined to take off in search of greener, less restrictive pastures.

On This Day:

In ancient Rome, Agnoalia was held annually on this date to honor the god Vediovis (or Vedius), who was Jupiter's counterpart in the underworld. Vediovis was also a deity of swamps and volcanic activity. At the Festival of Vediovis, a she-goat was sacrificed in an attempt to placate the eruptive forces of nature and the underworld.

Born Today: Raymond Burr (actor); Peggy Cass (actress); Dennis Day (singer); Albrecht Durer (artist); Stephen Girard (financier); Armand Hammer (businessman); Philip II (king of Spain); Robert Montgomery (actor); Harold Robbins (writer); Henri Rousseau (artist); Mr. T. (actor); Andre Sakharov (physicist); Fats Waller (jazz musician)

May 22
♊ Gemini, 4

The geniality, sociability, and quick wit of those born on this day mask a steely inner core of ambition. A born leader, you know how to use your persuasive charm to encourage others to live up to their highest capabilities. Since you communicate well and understand people's motivations, you're able to steer them in the right direction. The single-mindedness of the root number four's vibration conflicts sharply with the carefree versatility of your Gemini Sun. You may develop a reputation as a workaholic because, once you get caught up in a project, you develop so much enthusiasm that you lose track of time.

Although May 22nd people are decidedly materialistic, some have very marked interests in mysticism and the occult. No door is closed to you; whatever you wish to accomplish materially or spiritually is possible. Creativity and intelligence are your best assets. You're skilled at organizing and communicating information and can prosper in any career related to teaching, broadcasting, writing, acting, sales, public relations, advertising, or promotion.

Because you operate on a mental level, you refuse to let your feelings get in the way of your good judgment. Actually, your inclination is to distance yourself from your emotions as much as possible. At times, you're not quite sure what you are feeling. In a close personal relationship, mental harmony and shared interests are as important to you as love and romance.

On This Day:

Viking leader Ragnar Lodbrok is remembered on this day. He was captured by the Northumbrians and killed by being thrown into a pit of poisonous snakes. His death song, which reflects his faith in the afterlife, has been passed down from generation to generation to provide hope and reassurance about what lies beyond.

Born Today: Richard Benjamin (actor); Naomi Campbell (supermodel); Mary Cassatt (artist); Sir Arthur Conan Doyle (writer); Judith Crist (film critic); Sir Laurence Oliver (actor/director); Alexander Pope (poet); Michael Sarazin (actor); Susan Strasberg (actress); Richard Wagner (composer); Paul Winfield (actor)

May 23

♊ Gemini, 5

ndividuals whose birthdays fall on this date are quick-witted, independent, original thinkers. With your uncanny foresight, you're able to anticipate and plan for future developments. Your unique, innovative ideas are often one step ahead of those of your contemporaries. Naturally curious about everything and everyone, you're a great talker and theorizer. You have a special gift for understanding the importance of small details, without losing sight of big picture.

Those born on May 23 are genuine paradoxes. Open-minded, unconventional, and unpredictable one moment, you can become quite stubborn and intractable the next. Your universe is composed of thoughts and words, and you gather information from as many sources as possible. After pondering and processing the true meaning of what you've discovered, you reorganize it to suit your own beliefs and ideas. A born teacher, writer, and speaker, your clarity of mind, feel for language, and fluency of expression help you share your knowledge with others.

Everyone wants to be your friend or associate because you have an instinctive understanding of how to get along with people. However, you're extremely wary of putting yourself in a position of emotional vulnerability. You enjoy the closeness and passionate intensity of an intimate relationship, yet what you want most are mutual understanding and companionship. You're loyal to those you love, but you won't tolerate too many restrictions on your freedom.

On This Day:

In ancient Rome, the Rosalia, a sacred rose festival, was celebrated each year on this date. The festival was dedicated to springtime and to the flower goddess Flora and the love goddess Venus. Since flowers, especially roses, were plentiful at that time of the year, they were used in many different kinds of perfumes, cosmetics, and teas.

Born Today: Drew Carey (comedian); Rosemary Clooney (singer); Joan Collins (actress); Scatman Crothers (actor); Douglas Fairbanks, Sr. (actor); Marvin Hagler (boxer); Jewel (singer/songwriter); Anatoli Karpov (chess player); Franz Kline (artist); Franz Anton Mesmer (hypnotist/physician); Helen O'Connell (singer); Artie Shaw (bandleader)

May 24
♊ Gemini, 6

Twins whose birthdays fall on this day are extremely sociable. Intelligent, clever, and persuasive, you're able to get around anyone and get away with almost anything. You know exactly what to say to convince people to do your bidding, and you're not above using your silver-tongued charm for your own benefit. In your sweet-natured, diplomatic way, you're usually able to win others over to your way of thinking. Nevertheless, you're flexible enough to be able to adjust yourself to people and events if the occasion demands it.

Individuals born on May 24 enjoy entertaining and will spend lavishly for parties and other social affairs. You love your home and derive great joy from congenial surroundings. More than anything, you like being in a place filled with music, laughter, and the scintillating conversation of interesting, intelligent people. You have a knack for mixing work with pleasure, and you make the most of every possible opportunity. Your quick thinking, creativity, and ability to see possibilities that others may miss can take you far in business or the arts.

Although you tend to live on a mental plane rather than and emotional one, you're still an incurable romantic. It's so easy for you to fall in love with the idea of love that you often ignore the reality of it. Part of you wants to settle down with one perfect person for a lifetime, but another part rates freedom and independence above love and affection.

On This Day:

In Celtic countries, this day was sacred to the Mothers, three goddesses who were worshiped as bringers of prosperity and a good harvest. In France, these beings were known as the Three Marys of Provence. In Cambodia, the harvest ritual was called Sacred Furrow Day. Members of the royal family plowed the land to appease the gods.

Born Today: Gary Burghoff (actor); George Washington Carver (botanist/chemist); Rosanne Cash (singer); Tommy Chong (actor); Bob Dylan (singer/songwriter); Patti LaBelle (singer); Elsa Maxwell (columnist/press agent); Samuel I. Newhouse (publisher); Priscilla Presley (actress/businesswoman); Victoria (queen of England)

May 25
♊ Gemini, 7

Intelligence, imagination, and psychic ability are associated with this birth date. You're a study in paradox and sometimes as much a puzzle to yourself as to those who think they know you best. Cerebral and rational solar Gemini dwells mainly in a mental atmosphere of words and ideas. However, the vibration of the number twenty-five connects you to the mysteries of the subconscious. As a result, you're as likely to be interested in mysticism and the occult as you are in science and technology. You're considerably more emotional than other twins, yet your basic mistrust of emotion can cause you to suppress your feelings or rationalize them away.

People born on May 25 are many-faceted, creative communicators. No matter what the message, you have a knack for getting it across fluently and convincingly. You gather information through study, research, and an intuitive understanding of the facts. Your insight works in tandem with your analytical mind to blend bits of information together into a comprehensive whole. Musical, poetic, and artistic ability are quite common among those born on this day, and you could be skilled in handicrafts, writing, dancing, or painting.

In a love relationship, you're romantic, affectionate, and thoughtful. You care deeply, but you are emotionally vulnerable and easily hurt if love turns sour. You want the grounding that partnership offers, but you fear commitment and the loss of your freedom.

On This Day:

In France, the Fete of May takes place in the town of Saintes-Marie-de-la-Mer. The grand celebration honors the two Marys, Saint Mary Jacobé and Saint Mary Salomé, as well as Saint Sarah-la-Kali, patron of the Gypsies. Gypsies from all over the world gather in the seaside community to honor Saint Sarah with colorful traditions that are uniquely their own.

★★★
★ **Born Today:** Miles Davis (jazz musician/bandleader/composer); Ralph Waldo Emerson (poet/essayist/philosopher); Anne Heche (actress); Robert Ludlum (writer); Sir Ian McKellan (actor); Mike Meyers (comedian/actor); Frank Oz (puppeteer/director); Bill "Bojangles" Robinson (dancer/actor); Beverly Sills (opera singer)

May 26

♊ Gemini, 8

The dynamic individuals celebrating birthdays on this day are hard-working realists. Unlike other Gemini natives, you're not concerned with accumulating knowledge for its own sake. Unless what you're learning has practical applications, you may quickly lose interest. Your genial sociability and quick wit mask a strong, determined inner core. However, the ambitious nature of the root number eight conflicts with the twins' carefree, easygoing manner. On the surface you appear to be taking everything in stride, but deep down you may dream of kicking over the traces and breaking away.

A talented executive, you have a fervent need to run the show. Your work must allow room for movement, because you can't stand being chained to a desk all day. Communication is your forte, and your computer, telephone, and fax machine are rarely out of reach. Your inherent shrewdness and presence of mind make you a great problem solver, especially in a crisis. With your creativity, versatility, and physical dexterity, there is little you can't accomplish. Many career fields are open to you. If business is not to your liking, you could find success in the media, the arts, politics, or sports.

Emotionally you want commitment, but mentally you require variety and challenge. Your ideal romantic partner is intelligent and has a great sense of humor. To keep you interested, he or she should be open to debating and sharing thoughts and ideas.

On This Day:

In many villages in Ireland, England, and Western Europe, Sacred Well Day, or Well-Dressing Day, is celebrated on this date with beautiful wreaths and flower offerings to honor the deities and spirits of the wells. The custom dates back to the Fortinalia, an ancient Roman well festival that took place each year on this day.

Born Today: James Arness (actor); Peter Cushing (actor); Al Jolson (singer); Lenny Kravitz (singer); Peggy Lee (singer); Robert Morley (actor); Brent Musburger (sportscaster); Stevie Nicks (rock star); Sally Ride (astronaut); Jay Silverheels (actor); John Wayne (actor); Hank Williams, Jr. (singer/songwriter)

May 27
♊ Gemini, 9

Gemini natives whose birthdays fall on this date have a dreamy, illusive quality that makes them appear one step removed from the real world. A true humanitarian, you refuse to tolerate injustices of any kind. Never one to look before you leap, you rush headlong to the defense of all those who can't defend themselves. Sometimes, however, you get so carried away by impractical plans and ideas that your potential for helping gets lost in the shuffle. Nevertheless, you are innately compassionate and empathetic. You understand the human condition, and you're courageous and selfless in your work with others.

With your May 27th birthday, you are a natural communicator and witty speaker with few equals in argument and debate. In addition to first-rate verbal skills, you have a mind that is crammed with interesting information and innovative ideas. You have a penchant for the spotlight that gets you noticed, even in a crowd. If you allow your heart to rule you head, you may become so sympathetic to the plight of the less fortunate that you give away everything you own.

In romantic relationships, your paradoxical nature can puzzle even those closest to you. You are sincerely devoted to your loved ones and prepared to sacrifice everything for them. However, when the reality doesn't live up to your expectations, you react with deep disappointment and a desire to move on to another "ideal" partner.

On This Day:

On this day each year in ancient Rome, a festival was held honoring Diana of the Wild Wood. The evening celebrations were dedicated to the goddesses Diana and Prosperina and to the Three Fates, who were honored with night-time healing ceremonies. A festival at Bath honors the Celtic goddess Sulis, who oversees the sacred hot spring.

Born Today: John Barth (writer); Isadora Duncan (dancer); Joseph Fiennes (actor); Lou Gossett, Jr. (actor); Jay Gould (financier); Dashiell Hammett (writer); Hubert Humphrey (U.S. vice president); Henry Kissinger (U.S. secretary of state); Christopher Lee (actor); Vincent Price (actor); Georges Rouault (artist); Sam Sneed (golfer)

May 28

♊ Gemini, 1

People born on this day are active, versatile, restless, and impatient. Intellectually curious, mentally sharp, and physically agile, you think and act with lightening speed. You enjoy participating in activities that are exciting, unusual, or dangerous. More than anything, you adore traveling, visiting exotic places, meeting new people, and trying new things. Sameness and dull routine bore you. Friends and acquaintances seek you out because you're fun to be with. In fact, there is never a dull moment when you're around.

You're more passionate and emotional that the average Gemini. People usually find your dynamic energy and silver-tongued charm hard to resist. Temperamentally, you're an individualist, and you will fervently resist attempts to pigeonhole or typecast you. You're a doer as well as a thinker and talker. You can master any subject or skill that is exciting enough to hold your interest and attention. Driven by a competitive nature, youthful exuberance, and assertiveness, you're well positioned for success.

Yours is a loving, romantic nature, and an intimate relationship means a great deal to you. You need to be able to admire your partner and respect his or her intelligence, and you expect your significant other's unconditional love and admiration in return. Your perfect match is friendly, sociable, and hospitable and shares your many interests.

On This Day:

Every four years on this date in ancient Greece, the Pythian Games were held at Delphi. A sacred rite was enacted honoring the great serpent goddess Python. According to some legends, Python was the child of the Earth goddess Gaia and the mud left after the great deluge. The god Apollo killed her when he took over the sacred Delphi shrine.

Born Today: Jesse Bradford (actor); Carroll Baker (actress); Ian Fleming (writer); John Fogerty (rock star); Kirk Gibson (football player); Rudy Giuliani (New York City mayor); Gladys Knight (singer); Kylie Minogue (singer); Glen Rice (basketball player); Jim Thorpe (pentathlon and decathlon Olympic athlete); Jerry West (basketball player)

May 29
♊ Gemini, 2

The finest asset of the enchanting May 29th individual is the magnetic charm that attracts many friends and admirers. You are affable, easygoing, and popular, with a lively intellect and a wonderful, wry sense of humor. The flexibility of your nature allows you to adjust yourself to people and events. In your sweet, diplomatic way, you are usually able to win others over to your way of thinking. Your powerful mentality and fluency with language help make you an outstanding communicator. You have a knack for understanding complex information and translating it into forms that can be easily understood by the world.

Those born on this day are more tranquil than most other members of their Sun sign. Highly civilized and refined, you dislike disharmony or discordant conditions. Your creativity, foresight, and ability to see possibilities that most people miss can take you far in politics, business, or the arts. A genius at mixing work with pleasure, you make the most of every possible opportunity. Your many influential friends and acquaintances are prepared to help you advance socially and professionally.

Although you yearn for a permanent life partner, your spontaneous, freedom-loving Gemini Sun tends to prefer flirting to commitment. It's not unlikely that you will go through a string of romances before settling down with your special someone.

On This Day:

In England, the popular festival of Oak Apple Day is held annually on this date. It commemorates the return of King Charles II from exile and his success in escaping from Cromwell's army by hiding in an oak tree. The Roman Ambarvalia festival was celebrated on this day in honor of Ceres, and farmers honored the god Mars with feasts and prayers.

Born Today: Annette Bening (actress); Charles II (king of England); Paul R. Ehrlich (ecologist); Melissa Etheridge (singer); Anthony Geary (actor); Patrick Henry (U.S. patriot); Bob Hope (comedian); John F. Kennedy (U.S. president); Bea Lillie (comedienne); Al Unser, Sr. (racecar driver); T. H. White (writer); Tony Zale (boxer)

May 30
♊ Gemini, 3

Twins born on this date are intelligent, versatile, and witty. A bundle of nervous energy, you move from place to place with the speed of a whirlwind. You're particularly adept at juggling various tasks and keeping several balls in the air at the same time. Your forte is your amazing ability to switch back and forth among them with ease. Your many-faceted, lively, creative mentality is a continuous source of innovative plans and ideas. A born entertainer, you endear yourself to all types of people with your cheerful, easygoing manner and gift for gab. You like people and they like you, and therefore you're never at a loss for friends and companions.

Your sparkling personality is open and easygoing. People have a hard time resisting your dynamic energy and silver-tongued charm. Your facile mind and extraordinary communicative abilities enable you to get your ideas across swiftly and convincingly. Words are your medium, and you can usually talk anyone into or out of anything. At times you may come off as bit shallow or something of a social butterfly. However, your tendency to move from experience to experience and person to person is part and parcel of your restless search for knowledge and understanding.

In relationships, as in everything else, you dislike being boxed into a monotonous routine. You need a partner who respects your need for time and space to pursue your many personal interests.

On This Day:

This day is sacred to the Norse goddess Frigg, queen of heaven and consort of Odin. In the United States, Memorial Day, or Decoration Day as it was once known, is observed on this date. The earlier custom of cleaning cemeteries and decorating graves as a way of paying homage to the dead has largely been replaced with picnics and reunions.

Born Today: Keir Dullea (actor); Peter Carl Faberge (goldsmith/jeweler); Benny Goodman (clarinetist/bandleader); Howard Hawks (director); Wynonna Judd (singer); Meredith MacRae (actress); Lydell Mitchell (football player); Michael J. Pollard (actor); Gale Sayers (football player); Cornelia Otis Skinner (writer)

May 31
♊ Gemini, 4

The charming and genial exterior personality of the intensely ambitious individuals born on this day covers a world of determination. You operate mainly from a mental plane and refuse to let feelings get in the way of good judgment. You distance yourself from your emotions as much as possible—so much so, in fact, that much of the time you're not aware of what you are really feeling. Creativity and intelligence are the great strengths that help you cope with difficult situations. When you encounter a problem, your instinctive reaction is to try to "think" it through to a successful conclusion.

May 31st individuals are versatile, animated, and entertaining, with a sharp wit and a pleasingly wry sense of humor. A wonderful communicator, you invariably have a thought to share or a point of view to express. You're a dramatic speaker with few equals in argument and debate. Moreover, your innate practicality is allied to a deep understanding of and appreciation for art and beauty. Many who celebrate birthdays on this date forge successful careers in areas related to the media, literature, art, entertainment, architecture, politics, or education.

Romantically, you're more passionate, responsible, devoted, and decidedly less flirtatious than many of your Sun sign counterparts. You need a partner who understands your deep-seated desire to "make it" in the world, even if that leaves you with considerably less time for a personal life.

On This Day:

Theravada Buddhists observe the annual Triple Blessing of the God Buddha on this day. Shrines and houses are decorated with flowers and special prayer flags in celebration of the Buddha's birthday, enlightenment, and passage into nirvana. Offerings of flowers, incense, and rice are made during the festival's three days.

Born Today: Fred Allen (comedian); Clint Eastwood (actor/director); Colin Farrell (actor); Rainer Werner Fassbinder (director); Sharon Gless (actress); Ellsworth Kelly (artist); Joe Namath (football player); Norman Vincent Peale (clergyman/writer); Brooke Shields (actress); Lea Thompson (actress); Walt Whitman (poet); Peter Yarrow (singer)

June Birthdays

June 1
♊ Gemini, 1

emini natives born on this day are mentally sharp and physically agile, with few equals in argument and debate. Your interest and attention are easily caught, and you follow your thoughts and ideas wherever they happen to lead you. With your share of Gemini's quick wit and love of mischief, there is rarely a dull moment when you're around. You're restless and impatient; sameness and monotonous routine bore you to tears. When life gets too quiet, your tendency is to stir things up and get them moving again.

The June 1st individual is a naturally curious master of nonlinear thinking. Your zodiacal task is to gather and disseminate information. A dangerous adversary in any battle of words, you respond to verbal challenges with clever, persuasive answers delivered with lightning-like speed. Although specialized, in-depth knowledge is not your thing, you generally manage to acquire a broad spectrum of useful information. Driven by your competitive nature and the winning combination of exuberance, ambition, and assertiveness, you are well positioned for success in any field connected to the media, entertainment, sports, or politics.

Your personality sparkles, and your manner is open and easygoing. Because of your youthful good nature and wonderful sense of humor, you're much sought after as a friend and companion. In a love relationship, you're often mistrustful of your own feelings, and too much intimacy can scare you off.

On This Day:

This day was sacred to Carna, the Roman goddess of doors and locks. Carna was the equivalent of the Norse goddess Syn. This is also the day of Tempestas, the goddess of storms, who tests the doors and locks without mercy. Today's pagan festival of the Oak Nymph honors the hamadryads, the female nature spirits who inhabit oak trees.

Born Today: Rene Aberjonois (actor); Pat Boone (singer); Morgan Freeman (actor); Andy Griffith (actor); John Masefield (poet); Colleen McCullogh (writer); Marilyn Monroe (actress); Alanis Morissette (singer); Molly Picon (actress); Jonathan Price (actor); Nelson Riddle (bandleader); Ron Wood (rock star); Brigham Young (Mormon leader)

June 2

♊ Gemini, 2

The "people who need people" celebrating birthdays on this day are clever, charming, and popular. You are interested in everything and everyone, and very little of what happens escapes your notice. Communication is your strength and your weakness. You generally assume the role of the impartial journalist, passing along whatever you've learned without getting emotionally involved. However, sometimes you get so caught up in the drama of what's going on that you forget to check your facts. When that happens, you're capable of swallowing and repeating all kinds of rumors and exaggerations.

Those born on June 2 are innately intelligent and shrewd, with a marvelous flexibility that helps them adjust to people and events. Yet, in your sweet, diplomatic way, you manage to win most people over to your way of thinking. You possess good organizational skills and a decided knack for mixing business with pleasure. Artistic talent and a love of luxury are typical of those born on this date. Your tendency to "go with the flow" may give the impression that you are rather shallow. However, your inclination to move from one experience to another is actually part of your ongoing search for truth and beauty.

As an incurable romantic, you're prone to falling in love with the idea of love. You want a permanent relationship, but you like to party and flirt. Ultimately, you may go through a string of romances before deciding to settle down.

On This Day:

Saint Elmo's Day honors the Syrian bishop who became the patron of sailors. The electrical charges that flicker around ships during June storms and are known as Saint Elmo's Fire are believed to be a sign of his protection. This day is also sacred to Ursula Sontheil (Mother Shipton), a Yorkshire prophet who is the patron saint of laundresses.

Born Today: Wayne Brady (comedian); Kevin Brownlow (producer/director); Dana Carvey (comedian); Marvin Hamlish (composer); Thomas Hardy (writer); Hedda Hopper (gossip columnist); Stacey Keach (actor); Sally Kellerman (actress); Jerry Mathers (actor); Milo O'Shea (actor); Johnny Weissmuller (swimmer/actor)

June 3

♊ Gemini, 3

The exuberant, fun-loving charmers born on this day project an infectious brand of optimism that is virtually impossible to resist. You have a way of convincing yourself, and others, that no matter what happens, everything will turn out for the best. One reason you have so many friends and acquaintances is that people just love being with you. When fired up by a subject, you talk a blue streak. And what you have to say is much more than simple, aimless chatter. You cut directly to the heart of a matter in a swift, incisive way that involves your listeners and holds their attention.

Those celebrating birthdays on this date are among the busiest bees in the zodiac. Perpetually in a hurry, you always have places to go, things to do, and people to see. Multi-talented, ambitious, and hard working, you know your own worth and have a genuine distaste for occupying subordinate positions. Well rounded and well informed, with a magnetic personality, you're a born entertainer and salesperson with a penchant for the spotlight. Since the number three's vibration stands for self-expression, you should have little trouble forging a successful career in any field that requires confidence and creativity.

In love, your best possible partner is someone who is easygoing, sociable, and hospitable and who doesn't mind sharing you with your many friends and acquaintances.

On This Day:

The festival of Cataclysmos is celebrated on this day on the island of Cyprus. The seaside ritual consists of prayers for the souls of the departed, water games, and a sacred dance. In ancient Rome, this date was set aside to worship the Bellona, the goddess of war and the personification of force, who was the wife/sister of the war god Mars.

Born Today: Josephine Baker (singer/dancer/actress); Tony Curtis (actor); Jefferson Davis (U.S. Confederacy president); Colleen Dewhurst (actress); Raoul Dufy (artist); Maurice Evans (actor); Allen Ginsberg (beat poet); Paulette Goddard (actress); Hale Irwin (golfer); Curtis Mayfield (singer/songwriter); Alain Resnais (director)

June 4
♊ Gemini, 4

The trustworthy, reliable twins born on this day tend to be better organized and more analytical than many of their Sun sign counterparts. Although you are as clever and adaptable as any other Gemini, you're less likely to scatter your energies or waste time on impractical pursuits. When you're fired up by a dream, you refuse to let anything stand in your way. Your forte is your ability to harness your creative artistry through disciplined action. As an idea person and master communicator, you're able to promote your innovative plans in a way that virtually insures their successful implementation.

You are inherently charming, versatile, animated, and entertaining, with a sharp wit and a pleasingly dry sense of humor. Despite your psychic-like intuition, your logical mind has you questioning everything. Although your talents are mainly intellectual, your mental discrimination is closely allied to a deep appreciation of art and beauty. You have a knack for understanding complex information and translating it into forms that can be easily understood by the general public. You could do well in a large variety of career fields, particularly those related to art, architecture, publishing, science, or business.

Close relationships are important to you. Family and friends provide you with a sense of security and fulfillment. Romantically, you are loving, dependable, and considerably less flirtatious than most other twins.

On This Day:

Whitsunday occurs on or near this date each year. The pagan fertility festival of Whitsunday marks the death of the spirit of winter and the birth of the spirit of summer. As an annual Christian festival, Whitsunday celebrates the descent of the Holy Ghost upon the disciples. Its observance takes place on the seventh Sunday after Easter.

Born Today: Gene Barry (actor); Bruce Dern (actor); William A. Eaton (molecular biologist); Sam Harris (singer); Angelina Jolie (actress); Morgana King (jazz singer); Darci Kistler (dancer); Robert Merrill (opera singer); Michelle Phillips (actress); Rosalind Russell (actress); Dennis Weaver (actor); Noah Wyle (actor)

June 5
♊ Gemini, 5

The individual who celebrates his or her birthday on this day is a profound thinker and a great theorizer. A quick-moving, fast-talking bundle of nervous energy, you possess a very low threshold for boredom and dull routine. Innovation and communication are your twin specialties. Naturally curious about everything and everyone, you gather information from as many sources as possible. After pondering what you've learned, you reprocess it and pass it along to others in an updated form. Many-faceted and inventive, you are as adept as any juggler when it comes to keeping several balls in the air at once.

With your humane ideals and genial manner, you tend to get along with everyone and easily make friends out of strangers. As one of life's great observers, you're fascinated by people and interested in knowing what makes them tick. Your witty, breezy outer personality covers a seriously reflective inner nature. At heart you're a philosopher seeking answers to age-old questions about the meaning of life. June 5th individuals possess an uncanny insight and the ability to look ahead and foresee future developments. In some ways you are living ahead of your time, always anticipating changes and improvements.

While you may think that you want romance and passion in a love relationship, what attracts you most are companionship and mutual understanding. Although you're loyal to those you love, you refuse to tolerate any restrictions on your personal freedom.

On This Day:

This day is sacred to the Irish saint Gobnatt, who is a version of Domna, the Irish goddess of sacred stones and cairns. To insure an abundant harvest, an annual Corn Dance is held at this time at San Ildefonso Pueblo in the southwestern United States. Legend also has it that on this date in 8498 B.C.E., the ancient continent of Atlantis sank into the sea.

Born Today: John Couch Adams (astronomer); Margaret Drabble (writer/editor); Ken Follett (writer); Kenny G (jazz musician); Frederico Garcia Lorca (poet/playwright); David Hare (playwright); Bill Moyers (TV journalist/writer); Tony Richardson (director); Richard Scarry (writer/artist); Mark Wahlberg (singer/actor)

June 6
♊ Gemini, 6

An inherent sociability and outgoing manner make those born on June 6 well liked and popular with almost everyone they meet. People are swiftly captivated by your offbeat charm and slightly mischievous sense of humor. You are charismatic, optimistic, and entertaining, with a very strong sense of your own individuality. A born peacemaker, you're fluent in the language of diplomacy and believe in the importance of making a good impression. Your magnetic personality and way with words captivate your audience and rarely fail to win people's attention and cooperation.

Gemini twins born on this day are both intellectual and intuitive, yet they tend to prefer a mental atmosphere to an emotional one. Temperamentally, you are artistic and individualistic and will resist any attempt to pigeonhole or typecast you in any way. However, when the instinctual and rational portions of your character work together, each reinforces the other, and you operate like a well-oiled machine. Ideas are extremely important to you, but people are even more important. Your overriding consideration in every situation is your family and friends, who invariably come first in your mind and heart.

Yours is a loving, partner-oriented, romantic nature, and relationships mean a great deal to you. You need to be able to admire your lover and respect his or her intelligence. You expect your significant other's admiration and fidelity in return.

On This Day:

On this day in the ancient country of Thrace, a festival called the Bendidia was held in honor of the lunar goddess Bendi. Each year on or around this date in Nigeria, the ancestral spirits are honored during a weeklong festival. Offerings of food and gifts are made to Egungun-Oya, mother of the dead and mistress of spiritual destinies.

Born Today: Bjorn Borg (tennis player); Robert Englund (actor); Jimmy Lunceford (bandleader); Thomas Mann (writer); Alexander Pushkin (writer); David R. Scott (astronaut); Robert F. Scott (polar explorer); Dame Ninette de Valois (choreographer); Diego Velazquez (artist); Billie Whitelaw (actress)

June 7
♊ Gemini, 7

The ambitious, success-oriented Gemini twins born on this day have an eye for opportunity that helps them turn their artistic dreams into concrete realities. You're a truth seeker with a mind that functions like a perpetual motion machine. In fact, you sometimes wish you could just turn off your thoughts. However, the constant thinking allows you to swiftly evaluate people and situations and understand what they're really about. Unlike some members of your Sun sign, you rarely skim the surface of things. Instead, you keep on digging and probing until you get to the very root of a problem.

The Gemini natives celebrating birthdays on this date have the open, easygoing manner and sparkling personality that usually attract many friends and acquaintances. People born under the influence of the number seven tend to possess vivid imaginations, psychic abilities, and an interest in various aspects of mysticism and the occult. An inveterate multi-tasker, you possess a secret weapon in your ability to switch back and forth among several different undertakings with amazing agility. It's not unusual for you to watch TV and talk on the phone, while simultaneously jotting down notes for your next major project.

In intimate relationships, you are often mistrustful of your own feelings and may try to rationalize them out of existence. To hold your love, your significant other needs to find ways to engage your mind along with your heart.

On This Day:

The Vestalia, a festival in honor of the hearth goddess Vesta, began on this date in ancient Rome. During the eight-day period, the temple doors were opened to married women. The sacred fire inside the temple was rekindled, and prayers were offered to the goddess. Then the shrine was once again closed to all except the Vestal Virgins.

Born Today: Philippe Entremont (pianist/conductor); Rocky Graziano (boxer); James Ivory (director); Jenny Jones (TV talk show host); Tom Jones (singer); Dean Martin (singer); Thurman Munson (catcher); Liam Neeson (actor); Prince (singer/songwriter); Georges Szell (conductor); Jessica Tandy (actress); Randy Turpin (boxer)

June 8

♊ Gemini, 8

People born on this day are ambitious and hard working. You are well suited to the business world, because you don't let personal feelings cloud your judgment. Although it may take awhile for you to come to a firm decision, once you do, you seldom make a mistake. Success is important to you, and you're not deterred by disappointments or setbacks. When things don't go according to plan, you take time out to rethink your position. Then you pick yourself up, dust yourself off, and start over again.

Socially, June 8th individuals are charming, charismatic, and fun to be around. However, your sharp tongue and incisive wit can get you into big trouble. Your penchant for speaking your mind could be your undoing in professional situations, where saying the wrong thing often costs more than a mere loss of popularity. Nevertheless, your intellect is powerful, and you're an outstanding communicator and careful researcher. You are a natural for any job that requires objectivity, intuition, and innovation. You know what the public wants, and you have the wherewithal to give it to them. Your great strength is your ability to harness your various talents and direct them into productive enterprises.

In intimate relationships, you're loyal, dependable, and caring. Naturally sensual and loving, you want and need a stable relationship in your life. Without the right partner, you could turn into a bit of a workaholic.

On This Day:

In China during the celebration of the Grain in Ear Festival, the grain gods are honored with old rituals to ensure a harvest of plenty. Also around this time of year when the daylight and nighttime hours grow close to equal, the Chinese hold a dragon boat festival to honor the dragon-bodied creator goddess Nugua, who represents balance.

⭐**Born Today:** C. C. Beck (cartoonist); Willie Davenport (hurdler); Grant Lewi (astrologer); LeRoy Neiman (artist); Sarah Peretsky (writer); Joan Rivers (comedienne); Robert Schumann (composer/music critic); Nancy Sinatra (singer); Alexis Smith (actress); Keenen Ivory Wayans (comedian); Frank Lloyd Wright (architect)

June 9

♊ Gemini, 9

Gemini twins born on this day are compassionate humanitarians who refuse to put up with intolerance and injustice. An intelligent listener and articulate communicator, you're never afraid to speak out in defense of your own rights or those of others. However, you're impatient and impulsive and don't always think things through before speaking. When your heart rules your head, you may become so overly sympathetic that logic and good sense fly right out the window. If you allow yourself to get carried away by impractical plans, your potential for getting things done can get lost in the shuffle.

People born on June 9 are intuitive and mentally receptive. When a subject truly interests you, you absorb knowledge like a sponge. However, you're impressionable and easily distracted, and you have a dreamy, illusive quality that keeps you somewhat remote from the real world. Restlessness can lead to dissatisfaction and a tendency to scatter your energy in too many directions. Temperamentally, you're probably better suited to a creative career than to the structured world of business. Your zodiacal challenge lies in learning to develop concentration and continuity of purpose.

In relationships, you are a romantic, thoughtful lover. You care deeply, but your emotional vulnerability means that you can be easily hurt if love turns sour. If things get really bad, you may be tempted to seek escape by overindulging in sweets or alcohol.

On This Day:

In many Japanese villages, an ancient rice festival is held annually on this date. Women wearing traditional kimonos recite prayers and light rice-straw fires to bless the crops and honor Wakasaname No Kami, or Young Rice-Planting Maiden, who is the goddess of rice and oversees the rice transplanting that takes place at this time of year.

Born Today: Robert Cummings (actor); E. M. Delafield (writer/women's rights activist); Johnny Depp (actor); Michael J. Fox (actor); Marvin Kalb (TV journalist); Jackie Mason (comedian); Carl Nielsen (composer); Les Paul (musician); Cole Porter (composer); Natalie Portman (actress); Fred Waring (orchestra leader)

June 10
♊ Gemini, 1

The versatile individuals celebrating birthdays on this date have an abundance of talent and ideas and the necessary energy to put them to good use. The only problem you're likely to encounter is deciding what you want to accomplish first. Intellectually curious, mentally sharp, and physically agile, you think and act with lightning speed. Nimble fingered and fast on your feet, you're constantly in motion and always on the lookout for something new and exciting to do or learn. Sameness and dull routine bore you to tears. You adore traveling, visiting exotic places, and meeting different people.

Those born on this day are chatty, witty, dramatic speakers with few equals when it comes to communicating thoughts and plans. Driven by your competitive nature and the winning combination of youthful exuberance and assertiveness, you're well positioned for success in a large variety of vocations. Your innovative ideas, athletic prowess, mechanical ability, and ease of self-expression provide you with many career choices, including broadcasting, writing, acting, teaching, sales, advertising, sports, law, politics, engineering, and the military.

In romantic relationships, you are generous and eager for love and affection. However, you need a certain amount of freedom to pursue your numerous interests. Although your partner may tire of your repeated comings or goings, he or she will never be bored when you're at home.

On This Day:

In Celtic tradition, this day is the beginning of Duir, the month of the oak tree. Oak is the tree most often associated with the Druids, who revered it as the "king of the trees." This is a time of total empowerment. Duir means "door," and it signifies the door of the year that stands as an opening to the greater wisdom of life at its very peak.

Born Today: F. Lee Bailey (attorney); Judy Garland (actress/singer); Nat Hentoff (journalist); Elizabeth Hurley (supermodel/actress); Tara Lipinski (skater); Robert Maxwell (publisher); Hattie McDaniel (actress); Grace Mirabella (editor/publisher); Maurice Sendak (writer); Howlin' Wolf (blues singer/songwriter)

June 11

♊ Gemini, 2

Gemini natives born on this day are very often atypical of their Sun sign. You're more likely to be guided by your feelings and emotions than by intellect or logic. An inspired thinker, you possess the ability to communicate ideas nonverbally as well as through the written and spoken word. Naturally psychic and highly intuitive, you're capable of bypassing the usual Gemini thought processes and relying on your hunches instead. As an inventor and pioneer, you have the wherewithal to discover new truths that go well beyond the accepted realities of the time and place in which you live.

Those with June 11th birthdays are basically tranquil and dislike disharmony or discordant conditions. Offended by crudeness and vulgarity, you function best when surrounded by beautiful things in a harmonious environment. Your quick mind, innate creativity, foresight, and ability to see the possibilities that others miss can take you far in business or the arts. You have a knack for making the most of every opportunity. Your many influential friends and acquaintances appreciate your elegance and diplomacy and are usually willing to help you advance socially and professionally.

A large circle of friends and acquaintances gives you a sense of security and fulfillment. Romantically, you're considerably less flirtatious than many of your Gemini counterparts. However, you need a partner who stimulates you mentally as well as physically, or you may lose interest and start looking elsewhere.

On This Day:

In ancient Rome, the Matralia was held on this day in honor of the fertility and nature goddess Matuta. The festival was presided over entirely by free women, the only ones allowed to participate in its rituals. Matuta's temple was in the Forum Boarium, alongside the temple for the beloved goddess Fortuna, who was also worshiped on this date.

Born Today: John Constable (artist); Jacques Cousteau (oceanographer/writer/producer); Chad Everett (actor); Vince Lombardi (football coach); Joe Montana (football player); Hazel Scott (jazz singer); Rise Stevens (opera singer); Jackie Stewart (racecar driver); Richard Strauss (composer); William Styron (writer); Gene Wilder (actor/director)

June 12
♊ Gemini, 3

The individual whose birthday falls on this date is physically and mentally alert and constantly on the move. Like your planetary ruler Mercury, the messenger god, you're extremely clever, quick-witted, and fast on uptake. Some may consider you a rather smooth operator because of your ability to talk your way out of sticky situations. You are sociable and genuinely popular with everyone you meet. You love people, make new friends easily, and tend to keep the old ones for many years.

Although interested in virtually everything, people born on June 12 are not inclined to dig very deeply into any single subject. Resourceful and flexible, you have a gift for rolling with the punches that often gets you through tough situations that would overwhelm more rigid personalities. You thrive on diversity and change, and with your quick mind and multi-tasking abilities, you're quite capable of keeping several different balls in the air at once. Since it is so easy for you to switch back and forth among different undertakings, there is a danger of spreading yourself too thin or having difficulty deciding on a specific career path.

Young at heart and a natural entertainer, you want a fun-loving mate or partner who shares your many interests. You're particularly attracted to bright, lively individuals with whom you can have intelligent, spirited discussions.

On This Day:

In ancient Greece, people honored the god Zeus on this day by wearing oak leaves in their hair. In Korea, rice farmers wash their hair in a stream on this date as part of an annual ritual to dispel bad luck, ward off evil, and ensure an abundant crop. The traditional meal for this festival consists of fresh fish, steamed rice, and greens.

Born Today: Marv Albert (sportscaster); Irwin Allen (producer); Brigid Brophy (writer); George Herbert Walker Bush (U.S. president); John Charles Clifford (choreographer); Chick Corea (jazz musician); Anthony Eden (British prime minister); Rona Jaffe (writer); Jim Nabors (actor/singer); David Rockefeller (banker)

June 13

♊ Gemini, 4

The friendly, self-expressive personalities of twins born on this day serve as protective covering for the practicality, ambition, and hard work typically associated with the root number four. Restless, energetic, and enthusiastic, you routinely tackle difficult tasks and solve thorny problems that other people would rather not deal with. You're artistic and creative, with a gift for synthesizing and communicating your knowledge and ideas. Yours is an active, logical mentality. In business situations, your cleverness and versatility make it easy for you to out think and out maneuver the competition.

Your realistic view of the world grounds you and heightens your sense of purpose and desire for material success. Like other members of your Gemini Sun sign, you sometimes have difficulty reaching concrete decisions. Nevertheless, in an emergency you can be counted on to respond with swift, appropriate action. Your shrewdness and quick physical responses help you cope with circumstances that you hadn't anticipated. Since you function best on a intellectual plane, you rarely let feelings and emotions get in the way of your good judgment.

In a love relationship, you may be torn between your need for freedom and the desire for a serious commitment. Mental harmony is probably as important to you as romance. Your ideal partner is smart, with a great sense of humor and a penchant for exploring thoughts and ideas.

On This Day:

The feast of the Celtic goddess Epona was celebrated on this day. The popular horse goddess was sacred to the soldiers of the Roman garrisons in occupied territories, who looked to her to protect their horses. Epona is the only Celtic goddess to have been honored in Rome, where she was known as Epona Augusta or Epona Regina.

Born Today: Tim Allen (comedian/actor); Christo (artist); Ralph Edwards (TV game show host); Paul Lynde (comedian); Malcolm McDowell (actor); Ashley Olsen (actress); Mary-Kate Olsen (actress); Basil Rathbone (actor); Dorothy L. Sayers (writer); Ali Sheedy (actress); Richard Thomas (actor), William Butler Yeats (poet/mystic)

June 14

♊ Gemini, 5

The straightforward individual celebrating a birthday on this date has no stomach for hypocrisy or pretense. You're in a class by yourself when it comes to understanding and communicating your personal ideas and beliefs. You're not someone who's easily fooled by smooth talk, yet you have relatively little trouble getting around the defenses of others and persuading them of the merits of your ideals and causes. Your winning personality and penetrating intelligence enhance your leadership potential. Consequently, after listening to what you have to say, people are usually willing to go along with your innovative policies and plans for the future.

Twins born on this day are always on the lookout for fresh challenges and adventures. Your restless temperament abhors a vacuum, and your chameleon-like adaptability allows you fit in almost anywhere. Your need to continually learn and grow may be satisfied through actual physical travel or by mentally exploring the world around you through study. Basically a free spirit, you'll fervently resist any attempt to cramp your style. A boring job or dull company will not hold you for long.

You are sociable and gregarious, with an instinct for getting along with virtually anyone. Your breezy personality and witty sense of humor attract loads of friends and acquaintances. In romantic relationships you often feel emotionally vulnerable, making you somewhat wary of too much intimacy.

On This Day:

In modern Asatru, this day is sacred to Vidar, son of Odin, who survived the destruction of Ragnarok. Patron of leatherworkers, Vidar placed a stout leather boot in the mouth of the demonic Fenris wolf in order to kill it. Nordic leatherworkers would save their scraps and bury them in a pit for Vidar as a means of warding off bad luck.

Born Today: Yasmine Bleeth (actress); Margaret Bourke-White (photographer/first female war correspondent); Marla Gibbs (actress); Steffi Graf (tennis player); Eric Heiden (skater); Jerzy Kosinski (writer); "Boy George" O'Dowd (rock star); Harriet Beecher Stowe (writer); Donald Trump (real estate developer); Sam Wanamaker (actor)

June 15

♊ Gemini, 6

Gemini twins born on this day are the epitome of the proverbial "iron fist in the velvet glove." Rarely augmentative or abrasive, you get your way though charisma and charm. Even when you decide to play hardball, others may not realize that they've been in a fight. You're extremely shrewd, yet flexible enough to adjust yourself to people and events. In your search for harmony and perfection, you consider all sides of an issue. At times, you have great difficulty coming to a concrete conclusion. The paralyzing effects of indecision can cause you to miss out on some of life's best opportunities.

The June 15th individual knows a little about a lot of things, yet gives the impression of being deeply knowledgeable. A quick study, you absorb the pertinent points of new subjects with surprising ease. Your agile mentality makes it possible for you to field most questions with witty, off-the-cuff remarks. Your extraordinary ability for communication allows you to get your ideas across swiftly and convincingly. You're a natural for any career related to advertising, sales, athletics, education, writing, speaking, or acting.

Although you yearn for a permanent life partner, your freedom-loving Gemini Sun tends to prefer flirting to commitment. You may go through a fairly long string of romances before eventually finding and settling down with your one true soul mate.

On This Day:

Saint Vitus' Day honors the patron saint of Bohemia who was said to have been boiled in oil, thrown to the lions, and stretched on a rack, only to emerge unscathed and die peacefully at home. As patron of dancers, Vitus is credited with having cured the Tanzwut, or dancing mania, that led to mass hysteria and fainting among girls and women.

Born Today: Jim Belushi (actor); Wade Boggs (baseball player); Courteney Cox (actress); Erik Erikson (psychologist); Erroll Garner (jazz musician/composer); Edvard Grieg (composer); Malvina Hoffman (sculptor); Helen Hunt (actress); Waylon Jennings (singer/songwriter); Harry Langdon (actor); Dina Meyer (actress)

June 16
♊ Gemini, 7

The caring, empathetic people born on this date project a dreamy, ethereal quality that makes them appear somewhat removed from reality. Despite a temperament that is receptive and intuitive, you also possess all the attributes of the sharp-witted, logical mentality typically associated with Gemini natives. As a wonderful communicator, you invariably have a thought to share or a point of view to express. Your rational, scientific side causes you to question everything and then analyze the answers you receive. Your mystical, spiritual side accounts for your deep appreciation of music, art, and the beauties of the natural world.

June 16th Gemini natives are extremely curious and willing to experiment outside the norms of the mainstream when it suits their purposes. Well hidden beneath your sociable, friendly personality, there is a rather solitary inner nature that is much given to meditation and private contemplation. Driven by tension and nervous energy, you feel compelled to try to exert mental control over your deepest emotions. Since you believe in the old saw about the grass being greener in other people's yards, you may experience feelings of dissatisfaction with your own efforts and achievements.

Your innate mistrust of emotion can make close relationships seem problematic. You want and need the space and freedom to pursue your many personal interests, but you also long for the love and security of a long-term, committed union.

On This Day:

The Incan Festival of the Sun, originally an elaborate Peruvian celebration of the power and beauty of the all-seeing deity, still takes place on this date in some of Mexico's more remote areas. This Mexican version of the festival usually includes a family picnic and the ancient custom of burning one's old clothing to banish bad luck.

Born Today: Alice Bailey (theosophist/social worker); Roberto Duran (boxer); Nelson Doubleday (publisher); Katherine Graham (newspaper publisher); Stan Laurel (comedian); Barbara McClintock (geneticist); Joyce Carol Oates (writer); Erich Segal (writer); Adam Smith (economist); Lucky Thompson (jazz musician)

June 17

♊ Gemini, 8

Gemini natives born on this day are seriously concerned with making a success of their lives and careers. Although you have a vision of what you want, you're not always sure how to achieve it. Fueled by ambition, you are so intent on reaching your goals that you may not be aware of the spirit of rebellion lurking beneath your seemingly conservative façade. Although you give the impression of having it all figured out, the carefree twins' love of excitement and change can exert itself at any time, prompting you to try to kick over the traces and break away.

Your sociability and warm, outgoing manner make you well liked and popular with just about everyone. Although you enjoy a scintillating conversation as much as any of your Gemini Sun counterparts, you're less inclined to pass along rumors, gossip, or other information obtained from questionable sources. You are imaginative and artistic, and your innate common sense gives you the ability to turn your creative ideas into solid realities. You could be successful in various fields of endeavor, including those related to art, music, the media, architecture, publishing, and athletics.

In love and romance, you are ardent, affectionate, trustworthy, and dependable. Gemini's roving eye is greatly mitigated by the number seventeen's desire for companionship and for the lasting rewards of a serious, long-term commitment.

On This Day:

In Japan on this date, the ancient Shinto purification rite of the Cleansing Lily takes place. Lily stalks are gathered and blessed as an offering to entreat the deity to prevent flooding by bringing an end to the rainy season. In ancient Greece, Eurydice, the nymph who was later transformed into an underworld goddess, was honored on this day.

Born Today: Art Bell (radio talk show host); Ralph Bellamy (actor); James Brown (singer/songwriter); Andre Derain (artist); John Hersey (writer); Dan Jansen (speed skater); Alfred Knopf, Jr. (publisher); Barry Manilow (singer/songwriter); Joe Piscopo (comedian); Igor Stravinsky (composer); Venus Williams (tennis player)

June 18

♊ Gemini, 9

The paradoxical personality of the person born on this day runs the gamut from the profoundly serious to the ridiculously light-hearted. Nevertheless, your unique mixture of insight and humor attracts friends and helps you get along with all kinds of people. You possess an extremely perceptive mentality with intuitive capabilities bordering on the psychic. At times you seem intriguingly mysterious and chameleon-like, yet on other occasions you appear to be totally open and relaxed. You are selfless and courageous, with a tremendous capacity for tolerance and spiritual achievement.

Active, impatient, and restless, individuals with birthdays on June 18 are indefatigable fighters for the rights of others. A clever, witty, and dramatic speaker, you have few equals in argument and debate and absolutely refuse to tolerate injustice and intolerance. Despite your sincerity, intelligence, and charisma, however, your incisive wit and sharp tongue can get you into big trouble. Nevertheless, when you see things that you believe to be wrong, you're not afraid to stand up and be counted among the opposition. You're willing to sacrifice everything you have in defense of those who cannot defend themselves, no matter how unpopular the cause.

You are very devoted to those you love. However, you are so idealistic that if your significant other does not live up to your expectations, you may drop him or her like a hot potato and start looking around for someone who fits your image of the ideal partner.

On This Day:

This date marks the feast day of Roman Catholic Saint Elizabeth of Schonau, a Benedictine abbess and gifted mystic. She had her first vision in 1152 and was best known for ecstasies, prophecies, and diabolical visitations. In old Rome, this day was sacred to the ancient Etruscan goddess of the fruitful Earth, Anna Perenna, who ruled human reproduction.

Born Today: Richard Boone (actor); Sammy Cahn (songwriter); Roger Ebert (film critic); Carol Kane (actress); Keye Luke (actor); Jeanette MacDonald (singer); Paul McCartney (rock star); E. G. Marshall (actor); George Mikan (basketball player); Sylvia Porter (newspaper columnist/financial expert); Isabella Rossellini (actress)

June 19

♊ Gemini, 1

The fast-talking, dynamic individual whose birthday falls on this date can always come up with a plausible reason for each impulsive act or utterance. However, the truth is that you tend to speak or act without thinking. Although sometimes your impulses get you into big trouble, more often than not it turns out that you've said exactly the right thing or taken the most appropriate action. Your spontaneity and youthful exuberance serve as proof of your sincerity. Even when others happen to disagree with things you've said or done, they appreciate your conviction and realize that you mean well.

You love to talk and will rarely pass up a chance to join in a lively discussion or debate. Your thirst for knowledge and information is virtually unquenchable. You are fun loving and sociable, with a personality that sparkles and attracts many friends and acquaintances. You lead an action-packed life that causes you to skim the surface of many different things. You adore traveling, visiting exotic places, and meeting new people. You particularly enjoy living on the edge and participating in dicey activities that prove to be exciting, unusual, or dangerous.

You're in love with the romantic ideal of the perfect romance, but when push comes to shove, you prefer being free and unfettered to being locked a dull relationship.

On This Day:

In ancient Greece, the Day of All Heras was celebrated each year on this date. The festival honored Hera, Queen of Heaven and wife and sister to the god Zeus, as well as all wise women and the goddess within each woman. In Brazil, the Feast of the Holy Ghost, a weeklong religious festival that is celebrated annually, begins on this day.

Born Today: Paula Abdul (singer); Lou Gehrig (baseball player); Moe Howard (actor); Louis Jordan (actor/singer); Pauline Kael (film critic); Guy Lombardo (bandleader); Phylicia Rashad (actress); Gena Rowlands (actress); Salman Rushdie (writer); Wallace Simpson (Duchess of Windsor); Kathleen Turner (actress)

June 20

♊ Gemini, 2

emini natives born on this day are dramatic, charismatic, outgoing charmers who love to talk and adore being in the spotlight. First-rate verbal skills and an innovative mind crammed with interesting information make you a vibrant, witty conversationalist. With your warm sociability, you are popular and well liked by just about everyone you meet. You know how to enjoy yourself and keep others entertained at the same time. Because you care about people's opinions and the impression you're making, you go out of your way to establish and maintain harmonious relationships in every area of your life.

For those celebrating birthdays on this date, artistic talent often goes hand in hand with literary fluency. Many go on to become successful artists, writers, actors, or musicians. Your June 20th birthday also makes you particularly skilled at mixing business with pleasure. Your easygoing manner and organizational abilities virtually guarantee success in commercial ventures. You are highly intuitive and quite capable of assessing the public mood. You generally know exactly what the people want and need, and thanks to your foresight and innovative ideas, you're usually able to give it to them.

In an intimate union, you are tender and considerate. Partnership and sharing are the very touchstones of your essential nature. Less independent and more cooperative than others of your Sun sign, you're willing to sacrifice some of your freedom in return for the security of a loving union.

On This Day:

Cerridwen, the ancient Welsh lunar goddess and keeper of the Otherworld's Sacred Cauldron of Wisdom, where inspiration and divine knowledge are brewed, is honored on this day. Her sacred herb, Vervain, is burned in small cauldron-like pots, green ribbons are tied to trees, and green candles are lit on altars dedicated to her.

Born Today: Danny Aiello (actor); Chet Atkins (jazz musician); Olympia Dukakis (actress); Errol Flynn (actor); John Goodman (actor); Lillian Hellman (playwright); Nichole Kidman (actress); Martin Landau (actor); Audie Murphy (WWII hero/actor); Anne Murray (singer); Lionel Richie (singer/songwriter); Brian Wilson (rock star)

June 21

The individual born on the Gemini/Cancer cusp is chatty, quick-witted, self-expressive, imaginative, and approachable. This combination typically produces people who are inspired to use their energies and talents in the service of a higher purpose, such as political or social causes, philosophy, education, the arts, family, or religion. While you are sensitive to everything going on around you, your rationality keeps you from over-dramatizing situations. You may be ambitious for material success, but you are also extremely idealistic and determined to accomplish things that will make a difference in the lives of others.

Since you have the easygoing twins' facility with words, you're not as vulnerable to emotional overload as most other crabs. You're willing to discuss your own feelings and ideas, and you encourage other people to share their thoughts and emotions with you. As a result, you are able to respond to their problems with insightful feedback and helpful solutions. The Cancer/Gemini mix of curiosity and prodigious memory make you a natural student and a wonderful teacher. This combination of intellect, imagination, and creativity produces many successful writers, artists, musicians, educators, and politicians.

In a love union, you're romantic without being sentimental. Although you make a caring, affectionate partner, you're unwilling to forgo friendship and companionship in favor of moonlight and roses. Without mental affinity and common interests, you may become bored and lose interest in the relationship.

On This Day:

Summer Solstice, Midsummer's Day, the Druidic festival of Alban Helfin, the Anglo-Saxon festival of Litha, and the longest day of the year all fall on this day. At Stonehenge, the heel stone marks the summer sunrise as seen from the center of the stone circle. In ancient Russia, people worshiped the fertility goddess Kupala on Midsummer's Day.

Born Today: Meredith Baxter (actress); Norman Cousins (editor/writer); Al Hirschfeld (artist); Juliette Lewis (actress); Michael Gross (actor); Mariette Hartley (actress); Mary McCarthy (writer); Jane Russell (actress); Francoise Sagan (writer); Jean-Paul Sartre (existentialist/philosopher); Maureen Stapleton (actress)

June 22

♋ Cancer, 4

Those born on this day are warm and friendly, with a wonderful, somewhat loony sense of humor. Outwardly you come off as chattier and less moody than most Cancer natives. However, on the inside you're as practical and determined to succeed as any other crab. Material security is one of your main concerns. Because of your complete devotion to family and friends, you worry as much about their security as your own. You're careful with money and possessions, but it's not that you're ungenerous. You just detest waste. You have an eye for quality and only buy things you know will last.

The root number four represents the builder. It evokes the power to build structures for the betterment of humankind. As a leader, you thrive on responsibility. You have a tough, but fair, management style and organizational ability that make you top executive material. You're predisposed to go a little further and work a little harder than the next person. In negotiations, you are hardheaded and focused on the bottom line. However, you're so nice about it, the other person doesn't realize that he or she has been out maneuvered until after the deal is signed.

Trust doesn't come easily to you. Whenever you feel insecure in love and romance, you retreat into your protective shell. Yet, once your confidence has been won, you'll remain loyal and loving forever.

On This Day:

This is the feast day of Roman Catholic Saint Thomas More, patron of lawyers. Thomas More was the Lord Chancellor under King Henry VIII, but when he refused to accept the king's claim to the position of head of the Church of England, he was convicted of treason. From the scaffold he told the crowd that he was going to his death as "the King's good servant—but God's first."

Born Today: Ed Bradley (TV investigative journalist); H. Rider Haggard (writer); Carl Hubbell (baseball player); Kris Kristofferson (singer/songwriter); Joseph Papp (producer); Freddie Prinze, Sr. (comedian); Meryl Streep (actress); Lindsay Wagner (actress); Kurt Warner (football player); Billy Wilder (director/screenwriter)

June 23

♋ Cancer, 5

The individual celebrating his or her birthday on this date is a study in contrasts, poised between the emotional sensitivity of solar Cancer and the cerebral mentality of the root number five. Bright, understanding, and sympathetic, you have a great deal to contribute to society. You're something of a visionary with intuitive capabilities that allow you to foresee and anticipate future possibilities. Your innovative ideas may seem rather far out to some people, but your magnetic personality helps you get through to them and bring them around to your way of thinking.

Your free-spirited urge for independence and adventure is often at odds with your home-loving inner crab's need for emotional and material security. Your head may want safety, but your heart longs for freedom and excitement. You have a wide-ranging mentality that relates well to philosophical ideas. Something of an idealist and a crusader, you feel strongly about social problems and community issues. You're particularly well suited to a career in any field connected to the literary or performing arts, education, medicine, law, scientific research, government, or politics.

You probably have a wide range of interesting associates, but few truly close friends. In a love union, you are passionate and romantic. While you may long for roots, commitment, and permanence, your less emotional, more intellectual side thrives on mental companionship and a more independent or unconventional lifestyle.

On This Day:

Until recently, Saint John's Eve, or Bonfire Night, was celebrated throughout Ireland. The ancient fire festival began with the lighting of the bonfires exactly at sunset on June 23. The fires were then watched and tended until long after midnight. Prayers were offered to obtain God's blessing for the crops, which were at the peak of summer bloom.

Born Today: Ray Davies (singer/songwriter); Edward VIII (king of England/Duke of Windsor); Bob Fosse (dancer/choreographer/director); Alfred Kinsey (psychologist); Ted Lapidus (designer); Frances McDormand (actress); Wilma Rudolph (sprinter); Clarence Thomas (Supreme Court justice); Alan Turing (mathematician)

June 24

♋ Cancer, 6

Crabs born on this day are ambitious and hard working, yet they rarely let the pursuit of worldly success take precedence over their relationships. Although family and friends come first with you, you have the capacity to make everyone feel comfortable. You are nurturing and hospitable, and your consideration for others immediately puts them at ease. You refuse to run roughshod over people's feelings just to get what you want. You're a tactful, equitable mediator who prefers diplomacy to confrontation.

Those born on June 24 are cultured individuals with refined sensibilities. You revel in the comfort of a harmonious environment. Your innate creativity and appreciation for everything beautiful may lead to a career in art, interior design, fashion design, or architecture. With your inherent intelligence and artistic talent, you could garner success in any field associated with teaching, acting, writing, painting, sculpting, or music. In business, your keen understanding of human nature makes you a good manager of people. You are quick to figure out what the public wants and even quicker to understand what has to be done to give it to them.

In love, you're a romantic idealist. You'll hold off making a commitment until you are reasonably sure that your feelings are reciprocated. However, once the commitment is made, you expect the union to last forever.

On This Day:

The old Egyptian festival of the Burning of the Lamps is celebrated on this date in the city of Sais on the Nile delta. In ancient Rome, the Fors Fortuna was held annually on this day to honor Fortuna, the goddess of good luck, and to gain her blessings. In Peru, the Inti Raymi, the Sun-god festival, takes place each year on this date.

Born Today: Jeff Beck (rock star); Ambrose Bierce (writer); George Sanford Brown (actor); Billy Casper (golfer); Claude Chabrol (director); Jack Dempsey (boxer); E. I. DuPont (industrialist); Mick Fleetwood (rock star); Michele Lee (actress); William George Penney (astrophysicist); Joe Penny (actor); David Rose (orchestra leader)

June 25

Like the Greek philosopher Diogenes, the individual whose birthday falls on this date is a truth seeker who spends a lifetime in search of honesty and sincerity. The crusader in your makeup causes you to feel strongly about social problems and community issues. Your nurturing, compassionate nature makes you something of a "fixer" of people and their problems. You are extremely sensitive to what others need, and you enjoy doing things for them.

Most of your actions are closely allied to your feelings and emotions. However, your insight and intuition tend to work hand in hand with your analytical mind. As a result, you always seem to know when it's really okay to be emotional and when it's better to be completely practical. You prefer playing your cards close to your chest as a means of avoiding confrontation. Your real opinion of things often remains hidden or disguised. A natural detective, you love suspense and mystery. Musical, poetic, and artistic abilities are common among those with this vibration, and you may be quite skilled in handicrafts, writing, dancing, or painting.

In an intimate relationship, you're cautious and vulnerable, but also very affectionate and caring. Naturally nurturing and giving, you're capable of touching the other person's soul. When you're feeling insecure, you become jealous and over-protective. You need a partner who makes you feel cherished and appreciated.

On This Day:

On this day in the Blekinge province of Sweden, a Midsummer Bride or May Queen is chosen from among the young women. She then selects a Bridegroom. Money is collected from the onlookers for the "happy couple." At the end of the daylong festivities, the collected money is distributed among the local charities and churches.

Born Today: Antonio Gaudi (architect); Phyllis George (sportscaster); June Lockhart (actress); Sidney Lumet (director); George Michael (singer); Nancy Mikuriya (psychic medium); George Orwell (writer); Robert C. Venturi (architect); Willis Reed (basketball player); Carly Simon (singer); Scott Terra (actor)

June 26

♋ Cancer, 8

The dynamic individuals born on this day possess enormous drive and persistence. The determination associated with the root number eight is fairly well camouflaged by the congenial charm and sociability of your Cancer Sun sign. Although sensible, practical, and ambitious, you're also self-expressive, imaginative, and artistic. Financially, you're shrewd, intuitive, and able to establish and maintain a healthy bank balance. With all these talents added to your reliability and willingness to work hard, you can make your mark in virtually any field in the arts, sports, business, or the professions.

Those with June 26th birthdays are outwardly strong and powerful, yet thin-skinned and emotionally fragile within. You function best when you are able to maintain a balance between your inner and outer natures. While you're empathetic and understanding with regard to other people's problems, secrecy and mistrust prompt you to keep your own difficulties to yourself. You have an inner defense system that springs into action when you are feeling insecure. If things don't go the way you've planned, you conceal your disappointment in order to keep up appearances.

You are sensitive, but also self-reliant. When hurt, your instinct is to retreat into Cancer's protective shell and stay there until you've worked things out to your own satisfaction. In your personal relationships, you don't like to appear vulnerable. However, once your love and confidence have been won, you will remain loyal forever.

On This Day:

According to Icelandic legend, every year at noon on this date, the tip of the shadow of Mount Scartaris points to the secret entrance of "Centre Earth," in which giant humanlike creatures and prehistoric monsters dwell. Annually on this day, Salavi, the Spruce Tree Rain God, is honored in Native American corn-ripening ceremonies.

Born Today: Claudio Abbado (conductor); Pearl S. Buck (writer); Abner Doubleday (U.S. Army officer/inventor of baseball); Derek Jeter (baseball player); Greg Le Mond (cyclist); Peter Lorre (actor); Chris O'Donnell (actor); Eleanor Parker (actress); Colin Wilson (writer); Babe Didrickson Zaharias (Olympic athlete/golfer)

June 27

♋ Cancer, 9

rabs born on this day possess a heightened spiritual awareness that helps them empathize with the pain and problems of others. This sympathetic, compassionate nature makes you extremely protective of those who can't protect themselves. As a born fighter and champion of the underdog, you refuse to put up with intolerance and inequity. When trouble surfaces, you're the first one to don battle armor and join the fray. Your volatile temperament often prompts you to act on impulse, without rational consideration. When this happens, you may get so carried away by your crusading ideals that your potential for doing good gets lost in a flurry of aimless activity.

Individuals born on June 27 have perceptive mentalities with intuitive powers bordering on the psychic. Nevertheless, when you speak or act without thinking, you can do or say things you later regret. Your basic nature is charitable, caring, creative, musical, and poetic, and you love suspense and mystery. Your professional possibilities run the gamut from entertainment to counseling, detecting, healing, writing, filmmaking, teaching, social work, and preaching.

In intimate relationships, you are cautious and vulnerable. Yet you're so completely devoted to those you love that you're prepared to sacrifice everything for them. As romantic as you are compassionate, you're more likely to fall passionately in love with an ideal than with a real person. When reality doesn't live up to your expectations, you're deeply disappointed.

On This Day:

The Roman festival of Aestatis, goddess of summertime, is a celebration of the beginning of summer and was held annually on this date. On this day in 363 C.E., the Roman emperor Julian died from a battle wound. Known to Christians as "The Apostate" and to pagans as "The Blessed," Julian reinstated the pagan cults in Christianized Rome.

Born Today: Isabel Adjani (actress); Julia Duffy (actress); Emma Goldman (socialist/activist); William Thomas Grant (merchant); Philip Guston (artist); Bob Keeshan (actor/Captain Kangaroo); Helen Keller (educator/writer); Tobey Maguire (actor); Willie Mosconi (pocket billiards champion); H. Ross Perot (businessman)

June 28
♋ Cancer, 1

Those with birthdays on this day are considerably more aggressive than most other Cancer Sun natives. Even so, a wonderful sense of fun permeates every area of your life. Moreover, you're able to laugh at yourself if the joke happens to be on you, a trait that is extremely unusual among proud, sensitive crabs. Motivated and enterprising, you eagerly latch onto every opportunity to further your plans and ambitions. Security may be important to you, but you're adventurous enough to take a calculated risk.

Creative, capable, intuitive, insightful, and hard working, the typical individual born on this day can make his or her mark in virtually any field. However, many born under this combination find their career niche in business or the arts. Not surprisingly, you have an extremely fertile imagination and a gift for mixing your artistic talent with commercial savvy. Your public persona is confident, genial, and outgoing, but behind the scenes you tend to be rather moody and insecure. Although you try to hide your true feelings behind a mask of indifference, you are determined to "make it" in the world.

Your emotional life resembles a roller coaster. In intimate relationships, you're likely to be quiet and understanding one minute and passionately explosive and demanding the next. Yet you're protective of your loved ones and quick to leap to their defense if anyone else should make the mistake of calling them to task.

On This Day:

The celebration of the birth of Hemera, the ancient Greek goddess of day, occurs on this date. Festivals in her honor begin at sunrise and last until sunset. Today is also the runic New Year's Eve, which is ruled by Dag and marks the final day of the runic year. It signifies completion.

Born Today: Kathy Bates (actress); Mel Brooks (writer/director); Steve Burton (actor); John Cusack (actor); John Elway (football player); Henry VIII (king of England); Pat Morita (actor); Charles Stewart Parnell (Irish independence leader); Gilda Radner (comedienne); Richard Rogers (composer); Jean Jacques Rousseau (philosopher)

June 29

The intuitive individuals celebrating birthdays on this date have a knack for anticipating other people's actions and reactions. While you are ambitious and determined, with a strong sense of purpose and a need to be successful, you are also quite amiable and extremely sensitive to the prevailing mood. In business, you're quick to figure out what the public wants and able to understand what must be done in order to give it to them. Since you go out of your way to avoid arguments and unpleasantness, you usually know the right thing to do or say to get others to go along with your plans and ideas.

Those born on June 29 are typically compassionate, home loving, and gracious. Although you usually put your family and friends first, you know how to make everyone feel welcome. You are helpful and accommodating, but you cannot be pushed too far. When you're upset, you turn sullen and moody. Shrewd in business and finance, your practical side keeps you focused on your material goals. However, the artistic side of your nature yearns for the tranquility of beautiful things and harmonious surroundings.

Because you think in pairs, you're much happier sharing your life with a partner than going it alone. You are innately warm-hearted, affectionate, and responsive. You're also rather sentimental, and romance and courtship are particularly important to you.

On This Day:

In East Anglia, today is the optimum time for gathering herbs. On this date in Appleton, England, the boughs of a very old hawthorn tree are decorated with flowers, flags, wreaths, and ribbons in a ceremony known as Bamming the Thorn. In Voodoo belief, this day is sacred to the Sun deity Papa Legba, a spirit-master of the pathways and crossroads.

Born Today: Gary Busey (actor); Stokely Carmichael (political activist); Nelson Eddy (singer/actor); Robert Evans (producer/actor); Oriana Fallaci (journalist); Fred Grandy (actor); Harmon Killebrew (baseball player); Richard Lewis (comedian); Claude Montana (designer); Slim Pickens (actor); Luisa Tetrazzini (opera singer)

June 30

♋ Cancer, 3

The quick-witted, intuitive crab born on this day is emotionally approachable and generally responds to problems with helpful solutions. Your psychic-like intuition helps you anticipate negative eventualities and prevent them from happening. Although sensitive to most things going on around you, your rationality keeps you from over-dramatizing situations. You enjoy talking about your feelings and ideas, and you encourage others to share theirs with you. You possess a mentality that combines curiosity with a prodigious memory, making you an excellent student and teacher.

More than anything else, those with birthdays on June 30 want to find satisfying ways to fulfill their creative potential. Typically, this combination of intellect and imagination produces individuals with writing ability and artistic talent. The media and the performing arts are your most obvious career choices. When business problems arise, you have an instinctive understanding of what needs to be done and what is the best way to go about doing it. You're likely to find success in areas relating to the dissemination of ideas, such as the media, advertising, publishing, and travel. In financial matters, you like taking risks, and Cancer's shrewdness with money usually protects you from foolhardy mistakes.

In your personal relationships, you're more relaxed than most crabs. Socially, you are outgoing, charming, and personable. However, you are also subject to Cancer's mood swings. When real life doesn't live up to your romantic view of how things ought to be, you can become despondent or depressed.

On This Day:

This day is sacred to Earth goddesses of the Americas like Chicomecoatl, maize goddess of the Aztecs; Changing Woman, the Earth goddess of the Apache; Spider Woman of the Zuni, Hopi, and other Native American tribes of the southwestern desert; and Tonantzin, the Aztec mother goddess associated with Mexico's Virgin of Guadalupe.

Born Today: Florence Ballard (singer); Harry Blackstone, Jr. (magician/illusionist); Winston Graham (writer); Susan Hayward (actress); Lena Horne (singer/actress); Billy Mills (Olympic runner); Tony Musante (actor); Vincent D'Onofrio (actor); Linda J. Roberts (nutritionist)

July Birthdays

July 1

♋ Cancer, 1

C rabs born on this day are inherently more aggressive than other Cancer Sun natives. Enterprising and determined to get ahead in life, you eagerly latch onto projects and challenges that further your personal plans and ambitions. You possess an adventurous spirit, a shrewd mind, and a remarkable memory. You tend to think faster on your feet and reach important decisions more quickly than most of your Sun sign counterparts. Creative, intuitive, insightful, and imaginative, you have the originality and innovative ideas you need to serve as a stimulus for your creativity and self-expression.

Many of the extraordinary individuals born on this day are great humanitarians. Helping people is important to you, and you are capable of making enormous sacrifices for those close to you and for society as a whole. Your public persona is genial and outgoing, but in private life you are often moody and changeable. You have a volatile, artistic temperament that can cause you to act on impulse, without rational consideration. When you speak or act without thinking, you may do or say things that you later regret.

In your love relationships, you can be nurturing and understanding one moment and explosively demanding the next. The pattern of your inner life is one of repeated ups and downs, because you're continually being pulled between the number one's need for freedom and independence and solar Cancer's desire for continuity and security.

On This Day:

In Napal on this date, people celebrate the festival of Naga Pachami, which is devoted to the snake gods called Nagas. Sacred snake images are adorned with flower garlands and displayed on religious altars, and offerings are made at snake holes. People line the streets for elaborate parades featuring beautifully costumed participants and live serpents.

Born Today: Dan Aykroyd (actor); Leslie Caron (actress/dancer); Diana (Princess of Wales); Olivia De Haviland (actress); Deborah Harry (rock star); Charles Laughton (actor); Carl Lewis (track and field athlete); Sydney Pollack (producer/director); Twyla Tharp (dancer/choreographer); Liv Tyler (actress); William Wyler (director)

July 2
♋ Cancer, 2

Cancer natives celebrating birthdays on this day are warm, gracious, and compassionate. You have a knack for reaching out to other people and making them feel like family. Although you enjoy being helpful and accommodating, you cannot be pushed too far. Your public face is one of compassion for everyone. However, your hidden side can be rather less sympathetic, especially when your own life isn't working out as planned. You feel extremely vulnerable if things aren't going your way, and you'll protect yourself by retreating into your shell or building a wall around your emotions.

There is a decidedly practical, material side to the character of those born July 2. Something of a genius with money, you have what it takes to attract and accumulate wealth. You're sensitive, creative, and artistic, yet you have a very good head for business. Your persistence and tenacity of purpose keep you on course. Your intuitive understanding of what makes people tick allows you to tune in to their wants and needs.

You are sensual, warm, affectionate, responsive, and devoted. Relationships are central to your life, and you value your loved ones above all else. Romance and courtship are particularly important to you, and you know exactly what you want from an intimate union. You need to be with someone you regard as a soul mate, and you're not likely to settle for less.

On This Day:

On this day in ancient Rome, female citizens celebrated the Feast of Expectant Mothers. Pregnant women gathered at various temples throughout the city to receive blessings for themselves and their babies. They honored the goddesses of fertility, including the Bona Dea, known as the good goddess, and Juno, Lucina, Diana, and Carmenta.

Born Today: Michelle Branch (singer); Jose Conseco (baseball player); Vincente Fox (president of Mexico); Jerry Hall (supermodel); Hermann Hesse (writer); Lindsay Lohan (actress); Thurgood Marshall (Supreme Court justice); Carlos Menem (president of Argentina); Richard Petty (racecar driver); Dan Rowan (comedian); Ron Silver (actor)

July 3

♋ Cancer, 3

The cheerful, easygoing manner of people born on this day effectively conceals their strong determination to succeed. Unlike most other crabs, you enjoy being the center of attention, and much of what you do reflects your flair for the dramatic. Self-expression is your forte. You have a strong creative streak that, while not limited to the language arts, often manifests in the way you communicate your feelings and ideas. A forward-looking curiosity permeates everything you do. A perennial student, you rarely pass up the opportunity to test the usefulness of any intriguing new method or idea.

The typical July 3rd individual is both mentally intuitive and analytical. You're an excellent spokesperson for your own ideals and beliefs and those of other people as well. You won't compromise on issues you consider important, yet you're adaptable enough to get along with most people and fit in just about anywhere. Whereas many who celebrate birthdays on this day choose careers that allow them to tap into their natural abilities as writers and speakers, others find their best means of expression in art, music, dance, sports, business, politics, or science.

You are extremely sociable and mildly flirtatious, but you're also completely sincere in your affections. When you make a promise or commitment, you keep it, and you fully expect others to do the same.

On This Day:

In rural villages of Wales, the festival of the Celtic mother goddess Cerridwen celebrates the fertility of the land and the labors of summer. Cerridwen is also a goddess of the grain and the embodiment of lunar attributes. In Italy, this day was sacred to the witch of Gaeta. In Greece, the goddess Athena was honored on this date.

Born Today: Tom Cruise (actor); Franz Kafka (writer); Dorothy Kilgallen (newspaper columnist/radio and TV personality); Stavros Niarchos (shipping magnate); Ken Russell (director); George Sanders (actor); Tom Stoppard (playwright); Montel Williams (TV talk show host)

July 4

♋ Cancer, 4

ancer natives born on this day are among the most successful people on the planet. Tradition and practicality go hand in hand with your ambition and willingness to work twice as hard anyone else. You know exactly what you want and usually have a carefully laid out strategy for obtaining it. Moreover, you're not likely to be satisfied with purely personal gains. You want to be involved in a larger effort where you know that you're contributing something important to your group, community, or society as a whole.

The tendency of many celebrating birthdays on this day is to push so hard on the job that they short circuit other important areas of life. Consequently, it's really important for you to learn to lighten up and slow down from time to time. Although a little fun now and again won't add anything to your bank account or make you famous, it can help you live longer and make your life worth living. You can succeed at virtually anything you set your mind to, but you may feel most comfortable in a field related to business, science, education, politics, the media, or the arts.

You need love in your life, and your domestic side craves a home and a family. In an intimate relationship, you're a caring, responsive lover and a dependable, if somewhat demanding, partner. However, the intensity of your desire to create a safe and secure haven can make your loved ones feel somewhat claustrophobic.

On This Day:

U.S. Independence Day, the official birthday of the United States, celebrates the anniversary of the adoption of the Declaration of Independence in 1776. In ancient times on this date, Pax, the Roman goddess of peace and harmony, who was also identified with the Greek goddess Concordia, was honored with a considerable amount of feasting and revelry.

Born Today: Calvin Coolidge (U.S. president); Rube Goldberg (cartoonist); Ann Landers (advice columnist); Gina Lollobrigida (actress); Geraldo Rivera (TV talk show host); Eva Marie Saint (actress); Neil Simon (playwright); George M. Steinbrenner (principal owner, New York Yankees baseball team); Abigail Van Buren (advice columnist)

July 5
♋ Cancer, 5

The basic character of people celebrating birthdays on this day is one of sharp contrast between the emotionally sensitive nature of solar Cancer and the cerebral mentality associated with the number five's vibration. You can be rational and objective one moment and moody and unpredictable the next. A need for personal freedom is the hallmark of your existence; but you don't like being embroiled in disagreements, so you keep future plans to yourself until you're ready to implement them. By then, if someone objects to your actions, its usually too late for them to do anything about it.

Those with July 5th birthdays are intelligent, understanding, and sympathetic. You possess an inquiring mind with a deep-seated need to know why things are the way they are. There is a visionary aspect to your intuition that allows you to foresee and anticipate future possibilities. Whether in business or the professions, your forte is working with people. You are well suited to fields of endeavor connected to medicine, education, psychology, and the social services. Your magnetic personality has a way of getting through to an audience and can lead you to a successful career as an entertainer, lecturer, or politician.

In a love union, you're passionate and romantic. You long for roots, commitment, and permanence, but your intellectual side needs mental companionship and could be drawn to a more unconventional lifestyle.

On This Day:

In ancient Egypt, this day was sacred to the goddess Maat, who presides over truth and wisdom. On Tynwald Hill on the Isle of Man, the people gather to celebrate a Norse assembly established more than 1,000 years ago. It's believed that the hill is atop an old burial mound that made it a place of pagan gatherings in Celtic times.

Born Today: P. T. Barnum (showman); Jean Cocteau (writer/director/critic); Dwight Davis (tennis player/Davis Cup founder); Katherine Helmond (actress); Shirley Knight (actress); Huey Lewis (singer); Del Miller (harness race driver/trainer); Warren Oates (actor); Georges Pompidou (president of France); Milburn Stone (actor)

July 6

♋ Cancer, 6

The July 6th individual is people oriented and doesn't like being alone. Your main focus is on family, either your own or the larger family of man. You thrive on the affection and attention of those around you. No matter how busy you happen to be, you will always take time to help a friend or associate. Since intuition allows you to anticipate people's reactions, you usually know the right thing to do or say to calm a seemingly volatile situation.

People born on this date are a curious mixture of dependence and independence that some may view as confusing and contradictory. Generally well liked and sociable, you have an easygoing charm that appeals to people and puts them at ease. Yet beneath your amiable façade, you're brimming with drive, ambition, and a strong desire for recognition and success. Despite your sweet, gentle nature, you like having your own way. If things don't go as you planned, you react in a passive-aggressive manner. You are also imaginative and artistic. With your charm, creativity, and talent, you can do well in any occupation related to the media, the arts, entertainment, politics, or religion.

In a love union, you're a romantic idealist looking for a fairytale romance. When you think you've found it, you'll bend over backwards to make the relationship fit your dream of perfect love.

On This Day:

This date marks the celebration of the birth of the ancient Babylonian creator goddess Tiamat, the mother of the Babylonian gods. This day is sacred to various goddesses of the ancient world's pagan religions, including the Deer Mothers, Europa, Hathor, Hera, Io, Ishtar, Isis, Luna, Selene, Naphthys, and Pasiphae.

Born Today: Ned Beatty (actor); George W. Bush (U.S. president); Dalai Lama XIV (Tibetan Buddhist spiritual leader); Merv Griffin (singer/TV host/producer); Frieda Kahlo (artist); Janet Leigh (actress); Nancy Davis Reagan (actress/U.S. first lady); Della Reese (singer/actress); Jennifer Saunders (actress); Sylvester Stallone (actor)

July 7

♋ Cancer, 7

Crabs born on this day are truth seekers who seem to learn more through their instincts and emotions than from actual study. Like a psychic sponge, you absorb vibrations from your surroundings. In fact, you sometimes have great difficulty distinguishing between what you're feeling and what you are picking up from other people. This innate ability to shrewdly assess what people are thinking can be a wonderful career asset, helping you gain success by acting on your hunches.

People who celebrate birthdays on July 7 are fascinated with the unknown and unknowable and intrigued by the mysterious secrets of religion, spirituality, mysticism, and the occult. Some people, however, regard *you* as the mystery because of your rather solitary nature and the time you spend in private contemplation. The type of imagination and creativity you possess tends to produce individuals of exceptional talent in the artistic fields. Many born on this date make their mark as artists, musicians, or dancers. Others choose to earn their living as mystery writers, social workers, athletes, or preachers.

Family and friends are important to you. In an intimate union, you're sensual, affectionate, responsive, caring, and extremely generous. You will do just about anything for those you love. However, if you are hurt or disappointed, your nurturing attitude can morph into jealousy and possessiveness.

On This Day:

In China, the Chih Nu, the Feast of the Milky Way, takes place each year on this date. It commemorates the romantic encounter between Vega, the weaver maid, and Aquila, the herd boy. In Japan, this is the day of the Tanobata, the Star Festival, which celebrates the reunion of two celestial lovers who bridged a raging river with their bodies.

Born Today: Pierre Cardin (designer); Marc Chagall (artist); Ezzard Charles (boxer); George Cukor (producer); Vittorio de Sica (actor); Shelley Duvall (actress); Robert A. Heinlein (writer); Michelle Kwan (skater); Gustav Mahler (composer); Satchel Paige (baseball player); Doc Severinson (bandleader); Ringo Starr (rock star)

July 8
♋ Cancer, 8

People celebrating birthdays on this day are an intriguing blend of toughness and tenderness. Outwardly you are charming and friendly, but your amiability should not be mistaken for weakness. Your ability to focus on your goals is one of your strongest assets. You take things slowly, one step at a time, and you seldom change either your mind or your agenda. Once you've set your course, you refuse to give up, even if you encounter formidable obstacles. This birth date bodes extremely well for worldly success, and many noteworthy people were born on July 8.

You are ambitious, responsible, and authoritative, but you're also sensitive and intuitive. Whatever you lack in flexibility, you make up for with hard work and persistence. New ideas come easily to you, and you have a knack for formulating them into practical, workable plans. Your skills at organizing and planning a strategy are your great strength. But it's your shrewd handling of people and your ability to communicate approval or disapproval without words that make you a respected leader.

Although you come across as strong and powerful, you're rather thin-skinned and emotionally fragile within. Moreover, there is an intensely private side to your nature that makes it difficult for you to share your deepest feelings. However, once you decide to commit to another person, you make a loyal, generous, devoted companion.

On This Day:

Today is the feast of Saint Sunniva, the Christianized version of the ancient festival of the Norse goddess Sunna, the solar maiden. In Rome on this date, a nature celebration known as the Nonae Caprotinae, or Festival of the Wild Figs, was held in honor of the goddess Juno. It's believed to be one of the oldest of the women's festivals.

Born Today: Kevin Bacon (actor); Billy Eckstein (singer/songwriter); Marty Feldman (comedian); Anjelica Huston (actress); Elizabeth Kubler-Ross (psychologist); Jack Lambert (football player); Steve Lawrence (singer); John D. Rockefeller (founder of Standard Oil); Nelson Rockefeller (U.S. vice president/governor of New York State)

July 9

♋ Cancer, 9

The receptive, intuitive crab born today combines a fertile imagination with the foresight to act on his or her hunches and impressions. First, you conjure up a workable idea, and then you search for a way to turn your dream into a reality. You are sociable and charismatic, with a flair for people that allows you to make friends easily. You have strong convictions and speak your mind without hesitation. Your idealistic nature and sense of justice make you a tenacious fighter for the rights of others. Inherently daring and fearless, you're not easily discouraged or distracted from the pursuit of your goals. You aim high, and you generally get whatever you go after.

Your popularity and ability to shrewdly assess what others are thinking are your strengths. People seek you out because they enjoy your affability and charming sense of humor. Deeply sensitive and emotional, you're as likely to be motivated by feelings and intuition as by thoughts and ideas. Since you identify so closely with the pain and problems of others, your instincts tell you when and where help is needed.

In matters of the heart, you're a total romantic. You are either in love, looking for love, or involved in a rich fantasy life where love rules. You thrive when all goes well in a relationship, but if your partner doesn't live up to your expectations, you feel devastated.

On This Day:

In ancient Greece, this day was sacred to Dionysus, the god of wine and fertility, and to Rhea, the mother of the Olympian gods. In honor of Athens' patron goddess Athena, the Greeks celebrated the Panathenaea on this date every forth year. It was a six-day festival of sacrifices, citizens' processions, and sports competitions.

Born Today: Barbara Cartland (writer); Brian Dennehy (actor); Tom Hanks (actor); Elias Howe (inventor of the sewing machine); David Hockney (artist); Richard Roundtree (actor); Oliver Sacks (neurologist); Fred Savage (actor); Jimmy Smits (actor); Dorothy Thompson (columnist); Nikola Tesla (physicist/electrical engineer/inventor)

July 10
♋ Cancer, 1

Those celebrating birthdays on this day are more courageous, impulsive, and impatient than most of their Sun sign counterparts. Your pioneering spirit and openness to change make you more willing to break with tradition than other Cancer natives. However, you're not in favor of change for its own sake. An inner need to be cautious about the important things tells you how far you can go without stepping over the line. Intensely dedicated to achieving your personal goals, you often feel torn between your devotion to family responsibilities on the one hand and your keen sense of your own worth and your need to make a mark in the world on the other.

July 10th individuals are extremely creative and imaginative. Yours is a quick mind and a remarkable memory, coupled with a moody, artistic, and somewhat volatile temperament. The originality of your innovative ideas stimulates your deep-seated need for creative self-expression. You are sensitive to everything going on around you, and you respond to problems with emotional insight and helpful solutions. In business and the professions, your psychic-like intuition helps you anticipate negative eventualities and prevent them from happening.

Socially, you're outgoing, charming, and personable. In love and romance you are sensuous, passionate, and generous, and you rarely lack for companionship. Despite a strong independent streak, you're very devoted to friends and family and prefer the safety and security of a settled home life.

On This Day:

Today is the Day of Holda, Hela, and Skadi. It honors the goddesses of Niflheim, the Norse underworld. Holda is the Snow Queen. Hela is the goddess of disease. Skadi is the destroyer goddess. They hold power over death and the shadows. This day is also sacred to Knut, the Death Reaper, who swings the hay-cutting scythe.

Born Today: Arthur Ashe (tennis player); Saul Bellow (writer); David Brinkley (TV journalist/news anchor); John Calvin (Protestant reformer); Arlo Guthrie (folksinger/songwriter); Fred Gwynne (actor); Jake La Motta (boxer); Camille Pissaro (artist); Marcel Proust (writer); Jessica Simpson (singer)

July 11
♋ Cancer, 2

People born on this day are personally ambitious, yet amiable and sensitive to the moods of others. Basically peaceable and tactful, you go out of your way to avoid arguments and unpleasant situations. As a clever diplomat, you're particularly good at working around problems and sidestepping confrontations. Afraid of hurt feelings and rejection, you have a tendency to withdraw into your crab shell at the first sign of serious discord.

The chameleon-like quality of those born on July 11 allows them to blend in no matter where they happen to find themselves. You're generally well liked and have an easygoing charm that appeals to people and puts them at ease. Your basic nature is an interesting blend of creativity that may include artistic and musical talent and a shrewd head for business and finance. In business and the professions, your tact and your understanding of human nature make you a good manager. Moreover, you are inherently nurturing and enjoy helping people. In short, you have what it takes to succeed in virtually any career field that appeals to you.

A romantic idealist, you have a tendency to think in terms of "we" and "us." You value your family and friends above all else. In an intimate union, your desire for a fairytale romance may cause you to go to great lengths to make the relationship conform to your sentimental dream of love.

On This Day:

On this date in ancient times in the city of Athens, the Greek deities Kronos, known as Father Time, and Rhea, known as Mother Earth, were honored in an annual religious festival called the Kronia. It also commemorated Theano, wife of the Greek philosopher Pythagoras, a philosopher in her own right and patron of vegetarians.

Born Today: John Quincy Adams (U.S. president); Georgio Armani (designer); Yul Brynner (actor); Tab Hunter (actor); Bonnie Pointer (singer); Lisa Rinna (actress/TV talk show host); Robert the Bruce (king of Scotland); Marie Serneholt (singer); Leon Spinks (boxer); Suzanne Vega (singer); E. B. White (writer)

July 12

♋ Cancer, 3

Self-expression is a major concern of the typical individual celebrating a birthday today. You're very ambitious, yet reluctant to admit how much you crave success. Your cheerful, easygoing personality effectively conceals a strong inner determination. You possess a pronounced creative/dramatic/artistic streak, and you enjoy being the center of everyone's attention. Mentally, you're quick-witted and blessed with the gift of gab. As a perennial student with a curious, innovative mind, you're usually among the first to test the usefulness of any intriguing new method, product, or idea.

Although your talents are not limited to the language arts, your creative genius tends to manifest in the way you communicate your thoughts and feelings. Your charisma and self-confidence are so strong that you rarely have difficulty convincing others to help you turn your grandiose dreams into practical realities. While many July 12th people are drawn to careers that allow them to tap into their natural abilities as writers and speakers, others find their best means of expression in painting, design, music, dance, sports, business, or politics.

On a personal level, you are devoted to your friends and family. Generous, warm, and loving, you like interacting with people at social gatherings and in intimate one-on-one situations. In a close relationship, you're loving and romantic, but not starry-eyed. Without the mental affinity and common interests of true companionship, you eventually become bored and lose interest.

On This Day:

According to an age-old superstition, today is "the luckiest day of the year." It is believed that a child with the foresight to be born on this date is destined for a life of great wealth and success. On this day in Tibet, Yama, the Buddhist/Hindu god of death and the underworld, is honored with an ancient festival known as the Old Dances.

Born Today: Milton Berle (comedian); Julius Caesar (dictator of Rome); Bill Cosby (comedian/actor/producer); R. Buckminster Fuller (engineer/inventor); Oscar Hammerstein II (lyricist); Henry David Thoreau (writer/philosopher/naturalist); Richard Simmons (TV fitness instructor); Andrew Wyeth (artist); Kristy Yamaguchi (skater)

July 13

♋ Cancer, 4

The serious, determined crab born on this day thrives on duty and responsibility. Material security is one of your main concerns, and your determination to succeed is obvious to all who know you. You are intensely devoted to your loved ones, your work, and your community. A true believer in the work ethic, you're fully prepared to try a little harder than the next person to achieve your goals. You're extremely careful with money and possessions. It's not that you are ungenerous, but you detest waste. With your excellent eye for quality, you generally manage to get full value for your dollar.

Professionally, you're tough but fair. Your management style, business efficiency, and organizational skills make you top executive material. In negotiations you are hardheaded, pragmatic, and focused on the bottom line. However, you're so nice about it that the other person often fails to realize that he or she has been out maneuvered until after the deal is closed. Loyal, nurturing, and sensitive to what people are feeling, you're a pillar of strength to family and friends who turn to you in time of trouble.

In intimate relationships, you're very loving and caring. However, if you are hurt or disappointed by your significant other, your protective attitude swiftly morphs into possessiveness, and you attempt to control your mate or partner.

On This Day:

This day marks the birth of Osiris, Egyptian god of vegetation, law, and the underworld. In Japan, the annual Obon, or Bon Festival of the Dead, is celebrated in honor of ancestral spirits. It's believed that the spirits of the dead return during Obon, and families make special preparations to receive and honor them with the Feast of Fortune.

Born Today: Albert Ayler (jazz musician); Bob Crane (actor); John Dee (astrologer); Father Flanagan (Roman Catholic priest/Boy's Town founder); Harrison Ford (actor); Cheech Marin (comedian/actor); Erno Rubik (inventor of Rubik's cube); Charles Scribner III (publisher); Patrick Stewart (actor); David Thompson (basketball player)

July 14

♋ Cancer, 5

The unique individuality of people born on this day gives them an elusive quality that can be difficult to pigeonhole or define. Not only are you extremely sociable, with a genial personality that allows you to make friends easily, but you are also considerably more independent and impersonally detached than the typical Cancer native. Moreover, there are sharp contrasts between the sensitivity of your emotional nature and your cerebral mentality. As a result, you can be rational and objective one moment and quite dreamy and unpredictable the next.

Your strength lies in your ability to merge your personal feelings with your well-developed social conscience. When you get all sides of your humanistic approach working together, you can achieve wonderful things in the helping professions as a teacher, counselor, healer, social worker, or preacher. In business, you're shrewd, yet popular and well liked by clients and associates. Your magnetic personality has a way of getting through to an audience and, combined with your artistic temperament, can lead to a successful career as an entertainer, writer, painter, musician, lecturer, or politician.

In intimate relationships, you often feel conflicted because of your desire for personal freedom and your longing for stability and security. However, you need roots and commitment more than independence. Eventually, your nurturing, romantic side will overcome any reluctance you may have about entering into a long-term union.

On This Day:

The falcon-headed Egyptian god Horus is honored on this day by lighting royal blue altar candles and burning frankincense and myrrh. The runic half-month of Ur commences on this date. Ur represents primal strength and collective action, and the month of Ur is the time when society's powers are best applied to projects that serve the common good.

Born Today: Polly Bergen (actress); Ingmar Bergman (director); John Chancellor (TV journalist/anchor); John Singleton Copley (artist); Gerald R. Ford (U.S. president); Roosevelt "Rosy" Grier (football player/minister); Woody Guthrie (singer/songwriter); Gustav Klimt (artist); Dale Robertson (actor); Isaac Bashevis Singer (writer)

July 15
♋ Cancer, 6

The family-oriented, hard-working July 15th person is the nurturing worker bee of society. Whether at home or on the job, you're an enthusiastic, responsible member of your community. You're drawn to everything that is peaceful and beautiful, including the beauties of the natural world. Moreover, you are appreciative of, and possibly gifted in, the musical, dramatic, and literary arts. Although you are ambitious and determined to "make it" professionally, people mean more to you than material things. Charming and generally easy to get along with, you know how to make others feel comfortable and welcome in any setting or situation.

Those born on this date are very much a part of the world, despite being deathly afraid of hurt and rejection. You love having people around you, even though your sensitivity to their vibrations makes you feel extraordinarily vulnerable. An observer of the human condition, you delight in watching other people's reactions and studying their moods and temperaments. Your powers of observation and analysis make you especially well suited to an artistic, literary, or scientific career.

Relationships are all-important to you, but they don't always turn out as you hope they will. An idyllic vision of love has you imagining a life of endless harmony. At the first sign of serious trouble, you may withdraw to the solitude of your crab shell.

On This Day:

This day is sacred to Rowana, or Rauni, the goddess of the rowan tree. Rowana is patroness of the secret knowledge of the runes. The rowan is a tree of protection, and its wood, used in making defensive amulets, is especially effective if cut on this day. The celebration of the birth of Set, or Seth, the Egyptian god of darkness and magical arts, also takes place on this day.

Born Today: Brian Austin Green (actor); Philly Joe Jones (jazz musician); Alex Karras (football player); Iris Murdoch (writer); Brigitte Nielson (actress); Linda Ronstadt (singer); Rembrandt van Rijn (artist); Jesse Ventura (wrestler/Minnesota governor); Jan Michael Vincent (actor); Forest Whitaker (actor)

July 16

♋ Cancer, 7

ancer natives born on this day are a curious mix of shyness and sociability. A seemingly complaisant façade covers your strength of purpose and innate sense of destiny. As a genuine visionary with a deep reservoir of wisdom and a vivid imagination, you have big dreams and the wherewithal to see them through to completion. You generally function best when left to your own devices. You require extended periods of solitude to formulate your plans and recharge your batteries. Consequently, your true potential for bringing your ideas to a successful conclusion is sometimes overlooked by your friends and associates.

Those with July 16th birthdays are an unusual blend of innocence and sophistication. You project an other-worldly quality that confuses people and can cause them to misread your intentions. The romantic, spiritual, idealistic side to your nature sets you apart from other people. You need to believe in everything you do, and your work may become more of a crusade than a job. In fact, when you get caught up in your passionate ideals, you may not be able to resist proselytizing to others in an attempt to convert them to your way of thinking.

In love, you are protective and self-sacrificing. Your nature is romantic and caring, but also emotionally erratic. You're easily hurt by indifference or rejection. Your ideal partner is someone who accepts your moodiness and your occasional need for seclusion.

On This Day:

On this day in Haiti, pilgrims begin an annual pilgrimage to the Saut d' Eau Waterfall, sacred to Erzulie Freda, the voodoo loa of love and beauty. They bathe in the blessed waters near Ville Bonheur, tie pink ribbons to the trees closest to the falls, and leave offerings of food for Erzulie Freda in the hope that she will grant them good luck.

Born Today: Roald Amundsen (polar explorer); Mary Baker Eddy (Christian Science founder); Ruben Blades (singer/actor); Corey Feldman (actor); Michael Flatley (dancer/choreographer); Bess Meyerson (Miss America/actress); Ginger Rogers (dancer/actress); Barbara Stanwyck (actress); Pinchas Zuckerman (violinist/conductor)

July 17
♋ Cancer, 8

July 17th individuals are outwardly strong and powerful, but also rather fragile and thin-skinned on the inside. Deep down you are serious, practical, and determined to succeed. You possess a defense system that springs into action whenever you're feeling nervous or insecure. You need to feel liked and respected, and you worry about the impression you make on others. When you're not on the defensive, you are warm-hearted and friendly, with a charming manner and a wickedly entertaining sense of humor. You are at your very best when you're able to maintain a balance between your reserved public persona and the sensitivity, compassion, and consideration of your inner nature.

The typical individual born on this day is shrewd, ambitious, and totally committed to excellence in achievement. A tenacious determination to gain worldly recognition keeps you focused on your long-term goal of success. Professionally, you thrive on responsibility. A good executive, you drive a hard bargain, yet usually manage to get people to do your bidding without hurting anyone's feelings. Whatever you decide to do in life, you do with total dedication.

In relationships, you hold off making a commitment until you are reasonably sure that your feelings are reciprocated. However, once the commitment is made, you expect the union to last a lifetime. When you're feeling unsure of your loved ones, you tend to become possessive and overly protective.

On This Day:

The Japanese Sun goddess Amaterasu-Omikami is honored annually on this date with a Shinto procession. This day is sacred to the Egyptian mother goddess Isis, sister/wife to Osiris and mother of Horus. In Romania, Amari De's folk festival is held on this day. It was originally a marriage fair where young people came looking for partners.

Born Today: John Jacob Astor (financier); Diahann Carroll (singer/actress); James Cagney (actor); Phyllis Diller (comedienne); Earle Stanley Gardner (writer); David Hasselhoff (actor); John Paul Jones (U.S. naval commander); Nicolette Larson (singer); Donald Sutherland (actor); Brian Trottier (hockey player)

July 18
♋ Cancer, 9

Crabs born on this day are deeply emotional and more likely to be motivated by feelings than ideas. Even so, your practical and intuitive senses are so keen that you usually find yourself out in front of the crowd at the end of the day. You are so tactful, agreeable, and affable that it's difficult to know where you really stand on any issue. The truth is that you often don't know yourself. You're just so impressionable and open to suggestion that you seem to change with the wind. However, your flexibility often proves to be your best asset. While others remain wedded to outmoded dreams, you move on to new and better things.

The July 18th person is a champion of the underdog. You possess a naturally sympathetic and compassionate nature. Kindhearted and diplomatic, you go out of your way not to offend people. You are imaginative and artistic, and more than anything else you need to develop an outlet for your creativity. Your sunny, outgoing temperament and magnetic personality gets people's attention and draws them into your orbit. Still, when life doesn't go your way, you can be as crabby as any other Cancer native.

In matters of the heart, you are an idealistic dreamer, and romance is rarely very far from your thoughts. Without a partner to share your life, you may retreat into your rich fantasy world where love always rules.

On This Day:

According to Lothian legend, Princess Thenew of Taneu was the daughter of a sixth century king, Leudonus of Scotland. When she became pregnant without the benefit of marriage, her family threw her from the summit of Traprain Law. She survived the fall and gave birth to a son, Kentigern. Thenew is the patron saint of unwed mothers.

Born Today: Tenley Albright (skater); Richard Branson (businessman/adventurer/founder of Virgin Records); Dick Button (skater/TV commentator); Hume Cronyn (actor); Vin Diesel (actor); Nick Faldo (golfer); John Glenn (astronaut/U.S. senator); Nelson Mandela (South African president); Red Skelton (comedian); Hunter Thompson (writer)

July 19

he complex individual whose birthday falls on this date is bright, independent, and self-protective. Adventurous and courageous on the one hand, you're guarded and cautious on the other. Your paradoxical nature is subject to a variety of moods that can change from joy to dejection in the blink of an eye. When the pioneering spirit takes hold, your tendency is to rush headlong into new ventures. There may be times when you regret your impulsive actions, but on most occasions everything works out even better than you expected.

In business and at home, July 19th individuals are good at motivating people and managing money. You are proud, sensitive, and capable, and you're determined to live up to the best that is in you. Despite your innate shrewdness, you're something of a risk taker. Financial security is important to you, yet you're brave enough to follow your hunches. You size up most situations intuitively, and you have a knack for saying and doing the right thing at the right time. Moreover, you're able to influence other people by appealing to both their heads and their hearts. Actually, there is very little that you can't accomplish, once you set your mind to it.

At once independent and dependent, your emotional life is rather like a roller coaster. You're pulled between your need for freedom and independence and a desire for continuity that only the love and support of a long-term union can provide.

On This Day:

In ancient Greece, people celebrated the Adonia on this date, the midpoint of Adonis' traditional six months' presence on Earth and the anniversary of his wedding to Aphrodite. The ancient Egyptian New Year falls on this day, which is the birthday of the mother goddess Isis and the anniversary of her marriage to Osiris, the god of vegetation.

Born Today: Natalya Bessmertnova (dancer); Vicki Carr (singer); Samuel Colt (firearms inventor/manufacturer); A. J. Cronin (writer); Edgar Degas (artist); Anthony Edwards (actor); Pat Hingle (actor); Charles Mayo (surgeon, co-founder of the Mayo Clinic); George S. McGovern (U.S. senator); Ilie Nastase (tennis player)

THE 366 BIRTHDAYS OF THE YEAR   285

July 20

♋ Cancer, 2

The tactful, adaptable individuals born on this day will do everything possible to avoid arguments and disagreements. With your charming, chameleon-like quality, you are able to blend into the environment whenever it suits your purpose. Your intellectual and emotional sensitivity to the needs of others helps you feel your way along when you're dealing with volatile situations. Naturally compassionate and gracious, you have a decided knack for reaching out to people and making them feel like family.

Despite being more cooperative than competitive, you are ambitious for social and professional success. You aim to make your mark in the world, and given your tenacious determination, there is little doubt that you will succeed. In addition to intuition and imagination, you've been blessed with a unique style and a flair for the dramatic. At once creative and practical, and with the likelihood of having artistic and/or musical talent, you may discover your niche in one of the entertainment or art-related fields. No matter which career path you choose, your psychic-like intuition helps you anticipate and avoid many of the pitfalls.

You care about the impression you make on others, because you want to feel that you are liked and respected. In love and romance, you're nurturing, passionate, and generous. Essentially, you're a family person who longs for the safety and security of a committed partnership and a settled home life.

On This Day:

In Lithuania, the ancient goddesses of love are invoked during an annual lovers' festival called the Binding of the Wreaths. At sunset, all the participants go into the forest and gather summer flowers. The flowers are then made into wreaths, crown circlets, and streamers to be exchanged between the lovers on the days that follow.

Born Today: Theda Bara (actress); Gerd Binnig (physicist); Kim Carnes (singer); Chuck Daly (basketball coach); Sir Edmund Hillary (adventurer/mountain climber); Giorgio Morandi (artist); Tony Oliva (baseball player); Diana Rigg (actress); Carlos Santana (guitarist/songwriter); Natalie Wood (actress); Cesare Zavattini (screenwriter)

July 21

♋ Cancer, 3

People born on this day have a way with words that makes them fine writers, debaters, politicians, and salespersons. Although you're an innovative thinker, you often feel caught between the innate originality of the root number three's vibration and the conventionality of your Cancer Sun sign. You can cloak your insecurities in bravado, but they'll continue to thrive just beneath the surface of your consciousness. Half the time, you're the sensitive, imaginative, intuitive person who understands the world through feelings and emotions. During the other half, you are a cerebral, rational being living in a mental atmosphere of words and ideas. When one side or the other gains the upper hand, you can experience feelings of distraction, anxiety, or uncertainty.

Your strengths lie in creative self-expression and ease of communication. You enjoy talking about your ideas and your feelings, and you encourage others to share theirs. You possess excellent money-making capabilities and know the worth of most goods and services. Whether in business, the professions, or the arts, you know what people will buy and how much they are willing to pay.

In an intimate relationship, you make a loving partner. Perceptive and caring, you want the very best for your loved one. Nevertheless, you are unwilling to forgo companionship in favor of romance. Without a meeting of minds, you may get bored and lose interest.

On This Day:

The Mayan New Year is still celebrated annually on this date in parts of Mexico and Central America, where indigenous people welcome the sacred day with special feasts and prayers in honor of the old gods. Today honors the Greek seer Damo, daughter of the sage and philosopher Pythagoras, who entrusted all of his secrets to her.

Born Today: Hart Crane (writer); Josh Hartnett (actor); Ernest Hemingway (writer); Norman Jewison (producer/director); Hatty Jones (actress); Marshall McLuhan (professor of media culture/writer); Don Knotts (comedian/actor); Jon Lovitz (comedian); Isaac Stern (violinist); Cat Stevens (singer/songwriter); Robin Williams (comedian/actor)

July 22

♋ Cancer, 4

Those born on the Cancer/Leo cusp are creative individuals with artistic temperaments and a flair for the dramatic. Ambitious for worldly success, you are self-assured enough to continue believing in yourself in the face of obstacles and setbacks. You prefer a position of leadership, yet you work exceedingly well within a team environment. You need to be in the thick of things rather than sitting on the sidelines. You always seem to know the best way to promote yourself and your ideas, and you have a gift for inspiring others to do the same.

The charming, sunny personality of the July 22nd individual covers a proud inner nature with a concentrated drive to win. You project the illusion of tractability, but you generally manage to get your own way in the end. An incorrigible optimist, you enjoy the material trappings of the good life. When you want something, you buy it, even if you can't afford it. You figure that by the time the bills arrive, the money will miraculously be there to pay them, and often that proves to be the case.

You believe that love makes the world go 'round, and in an intimate relationship, you're romantic and affectionate. You may flirt a good deal, but you do it more for the attention than anything else. Once committed to another person, you're a loyal and devoted partner.

On This Day:

On this date in 1930, the first sighting of the famous Loch Ness monster was officially recorded in Scotland. Old Nessie, as the monster was affectionately nicknamed, has since been sighted by thousands of people and continues to attract countless numbers of tourists armed with cameras to the vicinity of the loch every year.

Born Today: Alexander the Great (conqueror of much of the known world); Albert Brooks (actor/writer/director); Alexander Calder (sculptor); Louise Fletcher (actress); Danny Glover (actor); Don Henley (singer/songwriter); Alan Menken (composer); Bobby Sherman (singer); Alex Trebek (hockey player/TV game show host)

July 23
♌ Leo, 5

Lions born on this day are creative, imaginative individualists who are bent on doing things their own way. You are naturally outgoing and friendly, with an upbeat, sunny disposition. However, it's your fiery zest for life that draws the interest and admiration of those around you. Idealistic and high-minded, you envision yourself as a noble hero whose destiny it is to blaze a path for others to follow. On one level, you are a socially conscious humanitarian concerned about people and their problems. But on another level, you're a lot more interested in making your own way in the world.

Blessed with intuition, originality, and a flair for the dramatic, July 23rd individuals are natural born performers. Your inherent interest in progress and new ways of doing things can help you create career opportunities for yourself and others. You could be successful in just about any job or occupation as long as you love what you are doing. Those areas most likely to attract your interest include the media, the arts, entertainment, the sciences, education, politics, and professional sports.

With your independent spirit, you can't be truly happy in a romantic relationship that is emotionally or mentally confining. Once you've found your soul mate, you make a loyal, loving partner, as long as you're given a little freedom and some breathing room.

On This Day:

The ancient Roman festival of the Neptunalia celebrates the divinity of the sea god Neptune and his wife Salacia, goddess of the wide-open salty sea and the inland springs of highly mineralized waters. It is believed that the goddess Sulis, who is still worshiped at the sacred hot springs in Bath, England, is an aspect of the goddess Salacia.

Born Today: Coral Browne (actress); Bert Convy (actor/TV game show host); Gloria De Haven (actress); Don Drysdale (baseball player); Don Imus (radio talk show host); Nomar Garciaparra (baseball player); Woody Harrelson (actor); Max Heindel (theosophist/Rosicrucian leader); Harold "Pee Wee" Reese (baseball player)

July 24
♌ Leo, 6

The friendly disposition and warm, sympathetic nature of lions celebrating birthdays on this day gain them respect and popularity wherever they go. The natural aggressiveness of fiery Leo is greatly diminished by the charming diplomacy associated with the root number six. You still want to be the boss, but you're also willing to be part of the team. When you take charge, you generally manage it do it without offending anyone. Although you meet most challenges with enthusiasm, you rarely jump into new situations without careful consideration.

Those born on July 24 project a type of confidence and personal magnetism that people tend to notice. It's not surprising that you surround yourself with drama and excitement, and your flamboyant personality can make you seem larger than life. Your magnanimous charm, managerial and organizational skills, creative talents, and physical vitality make you a good bet for success in just about any career that catches your fancy. You enjoy art and music and may have artistic and creative talents of your own. Your love for the spotlight can lead to a career in acting, music, dance, writing, or politics.

As a super-romantic, you expect a lot from a love union. You are warm-hearted and passionate, and you thrive on intimacy and the feeling of being part of a couple or family. You want to be with someone who can share all aspects of your life, but your need for constant appreciation, love, and attention can be hard on your partner.

On This Day:

Today is the birthday/anniversary of Simon Bolivar, who was born in Caracas, Venezuela on July 24, 1783. His victories over the Spaniards won independence for Bolivia, Panama, Colombia, Ecuador, Peru, and Venezuela. In these Latin countries, Bolivar is referred to as The Liberator and the George Washington of South America.

Born Today: Ruth Buzzi (comedienne); Lynda Carter (actress); Julie Crone (jockey); Alexandre Dumas, Sr. (writer); Zelda Fitzgerald (writer/painter/dancer); Robert Graves (writer/critic/mythologist); Jennifer Lopez (actress/singer/model); Anna Paquin (actress); Amelia Earhart Putnam (pilot); Michael Richards (actor)

July 25
♌ Leo, 7

The individual whose birthday falls on this date is a complex mixture of extroversion and introversion. Ever the outgoing, gregarious lion, you actively pursue attention and companionship even though your more contemplative inner nature yearns for privacy and quiet. You are imaginative and intuitive, with humanitarian instincts and an artistic temperament. Naturally empathetic and compassionate, you're easily moved by the problems and difficulties people face. Your generosity makes you a soft touch, and you should be careful lest others take advantage of your good nature.

The July 25th person is more reflective and internally focused than the typical Leo Sun native. You are a truth-seeking intellectual with a gift for sizing up people and situations quickly and correctly. You have a deep reservoir of wisdom and an extremely creative imagination with possible psychic abilities. You project an air of mystery that fascinates people and draws them into your sphere of influence. Idealistic and high-minded, you see yourself as a noble hero whose destiny it is to blaze a path for others to follow. Your many innovative ideas provide the fuel for translating your plans and dreams into action.

In love and romance, you're passionate, loyal, and sincere, but you're also determined to have things your own way. Although you treasure your own independence, you may have some difficulty granting the same freedom to your mate or partner.

On This Day:

In Osaka Japan on this day, people celebrate the thousand-year-old Tenjin festival of paper dolls. The handmade dolls are rubbed on the bodies of the faithful in order to absorb sickness, negativity, and evil spirits. Then the dolls are taken to the Dojima River and dropped in. It is believed that ill health is discarded with the dolls.

Born Today: David Belasco (actor/producer); Walter Brennen (actor); Stanley Dancer (harness racing driver); Thomas Eakins (naturalist/artist); Estelle Getty (actress); Barbara Harris (actress); Johnny Hodges (jazz musician); Omar Khayyam (poet); Matt LeBlanc (actor); Maxfield Parrish (artist); Walter Payton (football player)

July 26
♌ Leo, 8

T he confident, dynamic people born on this day command respect and thrive on prestige and responsibility. You have a decided flair for the dramatic that draws you toward the center of the stage, where you bask in the admiration and applause of your audience. Your jovial nature and sunny façade mask a proud, ambitious nature bent on achievement. You want to be in the forefront of all your activities, and you'll work as hard as you need to in order to get there. Your tremendous self-confidence, unswerving faith in your own destiny, and ability to stay focused on your goals virtually guarantees your success in any field of endeavor.

Lions born on July 26th possess a wonderfully dry wit, and they enjoy a good joke as much as anyone, as long as the joke's not on them. Your magnetic charm catches people's attention, and your creative talents and sense of humor hold their interest and keep them entertained. Leo's pride makes worldly recognition and material achievement very important in your scheme of things. Your excellent organizing skills and knack for solving problems in times of crisis make you an ideal leader and valued executive.

In a love relationship, you are romantic, loyal, and devoted. You may be somewhat touchy and demanding, but when you're in a secure, lasting union, you make a generous, caring, dependable partner.

On This Day:

Today is the festival of Sleipnir, Odin's eight-legged horse that can take the rider between the three worlds: Asgard (heaven), Midgard (Earth), and Utgard (the underworld). As the Norse sky god, god of war, and god of the dead, Odin had the ability to transcend the planes of consciousness, which allowed him to oversee the fate of human beings.

Born Today: Sandra Bullock (actress); Blake Edwards (director); Dorothy Hamill (skater); Aldous Huxley (writer); Mick Jagger (rock star); Carl Jung (psychologist); Stanley Kubrick (director); Helen Mirren (actress); Jason Robards, Jr. (actor); George Bernard Shaw (writer); Kevin Spacey (actor); Vivian Vance (actress).

July 27
♌ Leo, 9

The regal lions born on this day are self-assured, enterprising, and ambitious. You are outgoing and magnanimous, with a generous nature and a genuine understanding of people and their problems. Your sociability and compassion make you extremely popular with friends and associates. Their acceptance, recognition, and praise mean the world to you. However, your frank, outspoken manner and the inclination to say whatever you're thinking may not go over so well. You are intuitive to the point of being a visionary, and your psychic-like perception allows you to tune in to prevailing conditions. As a result, you pick up on things that others tend to miss.

Despite the sensitivity of lions born on this day, no one would ever accuse them of being shy or retiring. Ambitious and determined to get ahead in the world, you have an abiding faith in your own abilities and a tendency to see yourself as the star of the show. High-minded and idealistic, you believe that you have something important to contribute to the world. You are inherently courageous and aggressive, and you think and act quickly and decisively when carrying out your ideas and ideals.

In intimate relationships, you are fiercely loyal, passionate, and generous, but you're equally jealous and demanding. Your ego requires a lot of stroking, and it can take constant attention and repeated assurances of love and affection from your partner to keep you happy.

On This Day:

On this day, the celebration of the Kachina Dances takes place among the Native American Hopi tribe in Arizona. The Kachinas are the ancient spirits that guide and protect the Hopi people. The religious ceremonies and dances begin at sunrise and end at sunset. Their purpose is to bring the rain that will benefit and heal the community.

Born Today: Christopher Dean (skater); Alexander Dumas, Jr. (writer); Leo Durocher (baseball manager); Peggy Fleming (skater); Bobby Gentry (singer); Norman Lear (TV producer); Maureen McGovern (singer/actress); Sir Joshua Reynolds (artist); Alex "A-Rod" Rodriguez (baseball player); Charles Vidor (director)

July 28

♌ Leo, 1

Those celebrating birthdays today seem to have twice the passion and vitality of most people. A true pioneer and innovator, you're always on the lookout for fresh challenges and adventures. Confident and self-motivated, you tear through life propelled by your fiery energy. You throw yourself into every project with dynamic intensity. You don't shirk responsibility, and you meet your obligations head on. Once you've chosen a course of action, there is not much that anyone can do to stop you.

The other side of your nature is romantic and idealistic, and you tend to dramatize and mythologize every aspect of life. Mediocrity and dull routine are definitely not your style. A natural leader and independent thinker, you resent being told what to do. However, like many lions, you can be rather bossy, and you don't think twice when telling others what to do. It really doesn't matter to you whether you become a champion athlete, a star entertainer, a noted politician, a famous artist or writer, or a business executive as long as you're in a position to stand out from the crowd.

Relationships are the heart and soul of your existence. Your open-hearted personality draws people to you. Your fun-loving, sunny nature makes them want to stay. As a lover, you can be a rather demanding. You expect your significant other to flatter and pamper you. In return, you offer generosity, romance, and passion.

On This Day:

The Irish god Domhnach Chrom Dubh and the John Barleycorn personification of barley are associated with the cutting of the grain, which dies at this time so that people may live. Peruvian Independence Day commemorates the country's separation from Spain on this day in 1821. Spanish rule ended in 1824 with Simon Bolivar's final defeat of the Spanish troops.

Born Today: Vida Blue (baseball player); Bill Bradley (basketball player/U.S. senator); Joe E. Brown (comedian); Jim Davis (cartoonist); Marcel Duchamp (artist); Peter Duchin (pianist); Riccardo Muti (conductor); Jacqueline Kennedy Onassis (U.S. first lady/editor); Beatrix Potter (writer/artist); Sally Struthers (actress)

July 29

♌ Leo, 2

The fiery aggressiveness of the Leo native born on this day is tempered by the courtesy and sociability associated with the root number two. Your aim is to bring balance and harmony to all your undertakings. Although you meet challenges with enthusiasm, you're less apt than some lions to jump into new situations without cautious consideration. You prefer thinking things through very thoroughly and consulting with others before reaching a final decision. Even after you've made up your mind, you're prone to reservations and second thoughts.

Those celebrating birthdays on this date like comfort and luxury. You may be idealistic, but you are also practical and realistic. Materially and emotionally, you're someone who wants to have it all, and you never lose sight of your objectives. Your magnanimous charm, creative talents, and physical vitality make you a good bet for success in almost any career that catches your fancy. Occupational fields with obvious appeal include the arts and entertainment, politics, the diplomatic service, business, law, and professional sports.

In your personal life you are generous and loving. You think in pairs, and people and relationships mean more to you than material things. You want to be with someone who is prepared to share all aspects of your life. However, your romantic idealism and need for constant attention can be rather hard on your partner.

On This Day:

This is the first day of the runic half-month of Thorn. Northern tradition honors the god known to the Anglo-Saxons as Thunor and to the Norse as Thor. In Tarascon, France, the Festival of Tarasque takes place. A dragon float is paraded through the streets to commemorate the ancient victory over a fierce, fire-breathing dragon.

Born Today: Marvin Belli (attorney); Clara Bow (actress); Ken Burns (documentary filmmaker); Don Carter (bowler); Elizabeth Hanford Dole (Red Cross president/U.S. senator); Bill Forsyth (director); Dag Hammarskjold (United Nations secretary general); Peter Jennings (TV news anchor); William Powell (actor); Booth Tarkington (writer)

July 30
♌ Leo, 3

Those celebrating birthdays on this date are witty and fun loving, with an attractive personality that makes them extremely popular. You're a born entertainer who thoroughly enjoys the attention and adulation of the crowd. Naturally self-expressive and silver-tongued, you could probably talk anyone into anything. You're a much sought-after companion who prefers company to solitude. People and the details of their lives fascinate you, but your nose for news sometimes turns into a nose for gossip. Nevertheless, you're no mental lightweight. You have a clear understanding of what's important in life and the ability to communicate that insight to others.

You have lots of innovative ideas and the know-how to translate them into concrete actions. The image you project is magnetic and exciting, and your conversations are never dull or boring. Your dramatic personality and facility with words make writing and acting top career choices. Also high on the list of possible occupations for those born on this day are all aspects of the media, from publishing to TV journalism. While some born on July 30 become successful show business personalities, others may make their mark in advertising, sales, education, or professional sports.

You enjoy flirting, so you're in no hurry to make a firm commitment. You're not an easy person to pin down, let alone catch and hold onto. Yet, once you settle down with your special someone, you make a fiercely loyal, devoted partner.

On This Day:

The weeklong Swan-Upping festival on the River Thames begins on this day. In England, all swans are regarded as the property of the crown, except those that were given by royal grant to two guilds, the Vintners and the Dyers. During the "annual swan voyage," the guilds' cygnets are "upped" from the water and marked by their owners.

Born Today: Paul Anka (singer/songwriter); Peter Bogdanovich (director); Emily Bronte (writer); Bill Cartwright (basketball player); Henry Ford (automotive inventor/founder of Ford Motors); Tom Green (comedian); Lisa Kudrow (actress); Arnold Schwarzenegger (actor/governor of California); Casey Stengel (baseball manager)

July 31
♌ Leo, 4

The fiery, energetic lion whose birthday falls on this day is ambitious, hard working, and tenacious. Your strong sense of purpose provides you with the wherewithal to see your plans through to a fruitful conclusion. You may be an idealist and a dreamer, but your dreams are practical ones. Moreover, you have what it takes to make them come true. Although you are not always as confident as you appear, you're much too proud to admit that you have any doubts or fears regarding the outcome of your efforts.

Worldly recognition and material achievement are all-important in the eyes of people born on July 31. Your urge to shine is matched only by your desire to achieve a position of wealth and status. You aim high, but your inner core of steely determination practically guarantees that you'll reach your goals. Although your leonine enthusiasm is sometimes dampened by an inner desire to maintain emotional control, your public face is relentlessly cheerful and upbeat. You enjoy a good joke as much as anybody, so long as people are laughing with you, not at you.

In a love union, you are romantic, passionate, loyal, and devoted. You have a great deal of respect for the traditional ideas of marriage and family, and you want permanence in an intimate relationship.

On This Day:

The Norse trickster god Loki and his consort Sigyn are honored on this day. Loki is the god of strife, discord, and evil, as well as tricks and practical jokes. On this date, the annual Celtic festival of Oidche Lugnasa was celebrated at the end of the harvest in honor of the solar deity Lugh to ensure the fertility of the corn and grain for the next season.

Born Today: Kenny Burrell (jazz musician); Dean Cain (actor); Geraldine Chaplin (actress); Curt Gowdy (radio and TV sportscaster); Evonne Goolagong (tennis player); Hank Jones (jazz musician); Stanley Jordan (jazz musician); J. K. Rowling (writer); Wesley Snipes (actor); Whitney Young (civil rights leader)

August Birthdays

August 1

♌ Leo, 1

Lions born on this day thrive on recognition and prestige. You throw yourself into things with a dynamic intensity. Although your essential nature is proud, assertive, and demanding, you are also warm-hearted, open handed, and extremely loyal to friends and associates. You are inclined to mythologize your life and live out your own myth, yet the role you assume is a noble one. You are a born leader and a chivalrous crusader for what you believe. Your forte is an uncanny ability to influence others and bring them around to your way of thinking.

You have an upbeat, jovial personality. Your sunny optimism wins people over, and your charisma and keen sense of humor charms and entertains them. A fiery vitality and the ability to focus your energies on your goals guarantees your success in virtually any field of endeavor. Performing is second nature to you, and your flair for the dramatic draws you toward the center of the stage. Lions born on this date often go on to become well-known entertainers, politicians, writers, or professional athletes.

Your tendency to view your love relationships as larger than life can lead to unusually high expectations and ultimate disappointment. You need to find a significant other who is willing to pamper you and stroke your ego. In return, you offer your beloved passion, romance, and undying loyalty.

On This Day:

The festival of Lammas, or Laghnasadh (loaf-mass), is the feast of the first fruits that was held in celebration of the bread loaves baked from the first grain harvested. The loaves were taken to the local church where the priest blessed them. Pagans celebrate Lammas by weaving corn dollies and offering the first loaves to their goddess and god.

Born Today: William Clark (explorer); Claudius I (emperor of Rome); Dom DeLouise (comedian); Jerry Garcia (rock star); Giancarlo Giannini (actor); Geoffrey Holder (dancer); Francis Scott Key (attorney/poet/author of "The Star Spangled Banner"); Yves Saint Laurent (fashion designer); Herman Melville (writer)

August 2

♌ Leo, 2

People celebrating birthdays on this day usually surround themselves with drama and excitement. Like most lions, you are sociable and need love and companionship to be truly happy. Whether you're in the company of just one other person or a large group, you play to your audience and glory in the adulation you receive. Your splashy personality makes you seem larger than life, and your confidence and personal magnetism get people to notice you. With a character that is shaped by lofty ideals, you sincerely believe in everything you say and do.

Materially and emotionally, those born on August 2 want to have it all. Your personal brand of idealism has its practical side. You have a proud, ambitious nature that is bent on achievement, and you thrive on comfort and luxury. In order to turn your dreams into realities, you will sometimes powerhouse your way through obstacles without considering possible consequences. Well spoken and versed in literature, art, and music, you possess creative talents that can lead to a successful career in the arts, entertainment, the media, politics, or professional sports.

As a super-romantic, you expect a lot from an intimate relationship, and real life often fails to live up to your expectations. You want someone with whom you can share all aspects of your life, but your need for appreciation and attention may be rather hard on your partner.

On This Day:

This day is sacred to the ancient Persian goddess Anahita, a deity associated with love and lunar power. Lady Godiva Day is celebrated annually on this date in the village of Coventry, England, with a medieval-style parade. Today is also the anniversary of the death of the second Norman king of England, William Rufus.

Born Today: James Baldwin (writer); Frederic Auguste Bartholdi (monument builder/designer of the Statue of Liberty); Victoria Jackson (actress); Linda Fratianne (skater); Myrna Loy (actress); Gary Merrill (actor); Carroll O'Conner (actor); Louis Pauwels (writer); Peter O'Toole (actor); Jack Warner (founder of Warner Bros.)

August 3

♌ Leo, 3

Those whose birthdays fall on this date are the consummate promoters of their own ideas. Adventurous, multi-talented, creative, and inspired, you possess a bright intellect with flashes of intuition and insight that put you on the cutting edge of innovative thought. Words are your forte, and your gift for dramatic presentation allows you to communicate your vision to others. Although you're often ahead of your time, your persuasive manner helps bring people around to your point of view. As a practical visionary, you know what needs to be done to commercialize your ventures and make them profitable for everyone involved.

August 3rd individuals are big-hearted and generous, and they detest pettiness of any kind. A shrewd judge of character and circumstances, you make quick assessments of people and situations. You are up front about what you happen to be thinking and feeling at any given moment. Your optimism, sociability, and enthusiasm make you extremely popular with people, but at times your outspoken manner can get you into trouble. Nevertheless, your versatility, quick wit, and ability to confront challenges head on make it possible for you to carve out a successful career in virtually any field that interests you.

Your passionate Leo nature yearns for love, affection, and a sense of permanence. However, if a relationship gets too confining, you may get restless and find yourself longing for the excitement of fresh, new experiences.

On This Day:

The Japanese harvest festival of Aomori Nebuta, which takes place annually on this date, is designed to help farmers stay awake long enough to complete their harvesting duties. The celebration and parade of bamboo effigies with grotesquely painted faces and the rituals that follow are used to frighten away the spirits of sleep.

Born Today: Tony Bennett (singer); Tom Brady (football player); Marcel Dionne (hockey player); P. D. James (writer); Anne Klein (fashion designer); John Landis (director); Jay North (actor); Ernie Pyle (WWII newspaper correspondent); Martin Sheen (actor); Martha Stewart (lifestyle guru); Leon Uris (writer)

August 4

♌ Leo, 4

The ambitious, hard-working lion born on this day is determined to achieve something important in life. In fact, you're so totally dedicated to your plans for success that nothing can stop you from gaining your objectives. On the outside you appear so playful and relaxed that few people really understand just how intensely dedicated you are to your dreams for the future. Moreover, you're patient enough to realize that there is no need to rush, because eventually you will reach your goals. Unlike many other lions, you're a consummate planner, and you strategize most of your important moves in advance. Once you decide exactly what it is you need to do, you set about doing it.

You are blessed with tremendous self-confidence and unswerving faith in your own destiny. Even more important than wealth and status is your need to shine and occupy the center of the stage. People who celebrate birthdays on August 4 are born to be stars. You thrive in the limelight and bask in the adulation of the admiring throng. Whether in the arts, sports, business or the professions, you want to see tangible results from your efforts.

In relationships, you are loyal, passionate, and generous, but you're also possessive and demanding. Your ego requires a lot of stroking, and it may take a great deal of attention and repeated assurances of love and affection from your partner to keep you happy.

On This Day:

Each year on this date, it was believed that Scotland's Loch-mo-Naire became charged with miraculous powers to heal all those who drank its waters or bathed in the loch. It was the custom for the people who came to Loch-mo-Naire to toss in a silver coin as an offering to the benevolent, magical spirits that dwelled within the lake.

Born Today: Louis Armstrong (jazz musician/singer); Roger Clemens (baseball player); Herb Ellis (jazz musician); William Hamilton (physicist/mathematician); Maurice Richard (hockey player); Percy Bysshe Shelley (poet); Mary Decker Slaney (runner); Billy Bob Thornton (actor/screenwriter); Raoul Wallenberg (diplomat/negotiator)

August 5
♌ Leo, 5

The individual born on August 5 possesses extraordinary powers of self-expression. With your sharp wit and sublime sense of humor, you're rarely without a clever quip or retort. Your special blend of intellect and creativity supplies you with lots of innovative ideas and the necessary tools to translate them into action. New people and places provide you with welcome stimulation, and your deep-seated need for variety and change impels you to continually seek out new ventures and fresh challenges.

People celebrating birthdays today are open hearted, friendly, and magnanimous, with naturally upbeat, sunny dispositions. On one level you are socially conscious and concerned about the world and its problems. On another, you're a rebel and individualist, determined to do everything your own way. You are intuitive to the point of being a visionary, and your ability to think outside the box gives you tremendous insight into future trends and possibilities. Your predilection for exchanging ideas with as many different people as possible makes you something of a networking genius.

Those born on this day are never dull or boring. Friendship and companionship are so important to you that you may sometimes confuse them with love. In an intimate union, you require a certain amount of breathing room. You make an ardent, exciting, dramatic partner as long as the relationship is not too confining.

On This Day:

This is the first day of the Celtic tree month of Coll, the hazel. Hazel is symbolic of wisdom and Druidry. The annual Native American Crow Fair takes place on the banks of the Little Big Horn River during the first week of August. The fair is a combination of secret rites and public performances designed to unite the tribe and validate its traditions.

Born Today: Conrad Aiken (poet); Loni Anderson (actress); Neil Armstrong (astronaut); Guy De Maupassant (writer); Patrick Ewing (basketball player); Roman Gabriel (football player); John Huston (director/actor); Maureen McCormick (actress); Sydney Omarr (astrologer); John Saxon (actor); Robert Taylor (actor)

August 6
♌ Leo, 6

The fiery nature of the lion born on this day is tempered considerably by the courtesy and diplomacy of the number six's vibration. Your friendly disposition and warm, sympathetic nature garner respect and popularity wherever you go. Although you meet most challenges with typical Leo enthusiasm, you are inherently less aggressive and demanding than many of your Sun sign counterparts. Nevertheless, you know your own worth. You are exceptionally ambitious and determined to live up to your fine potential.

August 6th individuals are generally charming and attractive, with magnetic personalities that draw people to them. With your sunny, outgoing, fun-loving nature, it's not surprising that you like to party and entertain or that you're willing to spend lavishly for social events. Warm and generous by nature, you open your home and your heart to family, friends, associates, and even strangers without hesitation. Everything that is beautiful and harmonious appeals to you. You love art, music, and drama and have creative talents of your own that may lead to a career that puts you in front of an audience.

Lions really don't like being alone, and without a loving, intimate relationship in your life, you may feel incomplete. As a super-romantic, you have very high expectations. You can be severely disappointed if life fails to conform to your idealistic vision of how things ought to be.

On This Day:

The Tan Hill festival commemorates Tienne or Tan, the Celtic deity of holy fire. Related to the festival of Lammas, it takes place two days after the end of the Celtic tree month of Tienne. The Egyptian god Thoth is honored on this date, and this day is also sacred to the Cherokee Earth goddess Elihino and her sister Igaehindvo, the goddess of the Sun.

Born Today: Lucille Ball (comedienne); Charles Crichton (director); Alexander Fleming (bacteriologist/discoverer of penicillin); Charlie Haden (jazz musician); Robert Mitchum (actor); David Robinson (basketball player); M. Night Shyamalan (director/screenwriter); Alfred Lord Tennyson (poet); Andy Warhol (artist)

August 7

♌ Leo, 7

Persons celebrating birthdays today enjoy the limelight as much as other Leos, but they don't like feeling vulnerable or exposed. An exuberant outer personality effectively conceals your rather mysterious and somewhat solitary inner nature. Still, your charisma and personal magnetism fascinate people and draw them into your orbit. Because you breathe the rarefied air of a visionary, you often feel misunderstood and unappreciated. Nevertheless, you are proud and passionately dedicated to your goals. You know what you want to accomplish, and you won't give up until you've achieved your purpose.

Those born on August 7 are imaginative and intuitive, with artistic temperaments. You also are sensitive and more easily distressed and distracted than other lions. Your humanitarian instincts are strong, and you're easily moved by the problems and difficulties that people must face. Although you may think you want a tranquil life, your fiery leonine nature craves excitement and drama. Your unique combination of creativity and idealism incline you toward career fields concerned with entertainment, writing, art and design, social work, politics, religion, and philanthropy.

Despite your need for occasional periods of solitude, love and romance are vital to your happiness. In a love relationship, you're as sensitive to your partner's needs as you are to your own. You pour yourself so totally into an intimate union that your joy quickly turns to despair if it sours.

On This Day:

On this day in ancient Egypt, the beloved cow-headed goddess Hathor, who was worshiped as the mother of the pharaohs, was honored with an annual festival known as the Breaking of the Nile. The festival was also dedicated to all the water and river goddesses. It celebrated the rising of the fertile waters of the mystical River Nile.

Born Today: Ralph Bunch (statesman); Billie Burke (actress); David Duchovny (actor); Stan Freeberg (comedian); Don Larsen (baseball player); Louis Leakey (paleontologist); Alan Leo (astrologer); Alan Page (football player); Nicholas Ray (director); Alberto Salazar (marathon runner); Charlize Theron (actress)

August 8

♌ Leo, 8

The take-charge attitude of the dynamic lions born on this day reveals a strong sense of purpose. Hard working and ambitious, you are determined to get ahead in life. You're a born leader and executive, with unlimited staying power. Once you get started on something, you are virtually unstoppable. Many who celebrate birthdays on this date are graduates of the school of hard knocks. Although you may have to climb a difficult road to success, when you reach the top, you'll have the assurance that comes from making it on your own and the knowledge that no one can take it away from you.

The practicality and common sense of August 8th individuals bodes well for major accomplishment in the world of commerce and finance. Whether in business, the arts, or the professions, you understand what the public wants and have the means to provide it. Your flair for the dramatic means that performing comes easily to you. You gravitate toward the center of the stage and bask in the applause of the audience. You may attain a place of distinction in entertainment, sports, architecture, interior design, or fashion.

Because you have difficulty expressing your true feelings, sometimes you appear cool and distant. However, you are simply self-disciplined and in control of your emotions. Despite a tough outer shell, you often experience deep feelings of loneliness.

On This Day:

On this night in ancient Rome, the people celebrated the Eve of the Festival of Venus with songs, poetry, libations, and passionate love-making. The goddess of love and beauty was invoked and honored with prayers. It was also a time when sorceresses performed love magic and divinations were done for romance and marriage.

Born Today: Rory Calhoun (actor); Keith Carradine (actor/singer/songwriter); Ken Dryden (hockey player); Roger Federer (tennis player); Rudi Gernreich (fashion designer); Dustin Hoffman (actor); Isabelle Allende (writer); Danny Most (actress); Nigel Munsell (racecar driver); Connie Stevens (actress/singer); Esther Williams (swimmer/actress)

August 9
♌ Leo, 9

Those whose birthdays fall on this day are idealistic, impressionable dreamers easily moved by the suffering of others. Your generosity makes you a soft touch, and you should be careful lest people try to take advantage of your good nature. You are moody and sensitive, with paradoxes in your makeup that propel you back and forth between willfulness and self-denial. At times you feel torn between your desire for worldly success, with its accompanying acceptance and approval, and your deep-seated inner need for privacy and tranquility.

The sensitivity and psychic-like receptivity of people born on this day allows them to tune in to prevailing conditions. You rarely miss a major opportunity, because instinct tells you when it's time to move forward and when it is better to hold back. Although you can be aggressive when you think it necessary, you're prudent enough not to push beyond the reasonable limits of good sense. You are athletic, artistic, and compassionate; and your creativity and idealism incline you toward career fields concerned with acting, music, art, social work, sports, and religion.

Sincerely devoted to those you love, you will sacrifice everything for them. However, your tendency is to fall passionately in love with a romantic ideal. If reality fails to live up to your expectations, you may move on to another "ideal" partner.

On This Day:

Witches and Wiccans hold the annual Feast of the Fire Spirits on this date. Also on this day, the Seven Sisters Festival is celebrated in China. According to legend, the stellar goddess Zhinu and her six sisters came to Earth to bathe. A herdsman stole her dress so that she could not return to the heavens and would have to stay on Earth and marry him.

Born Today: Gillian Anderson (actress); Bob Cousy (basketball player); John Dryden (poet); Sam Elliot (actor); Melanie Griffith (actress); Ralph Houk (baseball manager); Brett Hull (hockey player); Whitney Houston (singer); Rod Laver (tennis player); Deion Sanders (football player/baseball player); Robert Shaw (actor)

August 10

♌ Leo, 1

The people born on this day are confident, optimistic, ambitious executive types. Your essential nature blends Leo's personal warmth and magnanimity with the energy and enthusiasm of the root number one. You wield considerable power and influence through the force of your aggressive, dominant personality. A natural leader and independent thinker, you're much better at giving orders than following them. However, you refuse to shirk your responsibilities. You throw yourself into every project with dynamic intensity and a daring pioneer spirit that's fueled by the proud lion's need to win at everything.

Those celebrating birthdays on August 10 tend to be popular and well liked wherever they go. Your charm and charisma draw people to you, and you thrive on their acceptance and approval. Dull routine and mediocrity are definitely not your style. With your flair for the dramatic, you see yourself as larger than life, and you enjoy doing things in a big way. You've been blessed with tremendous creative potential and unswerving faith in your own destiny. No matter what professional path you choose in life—whether business executive, actor, musician, politician, or sports champion—you're practically guaranteed a position of prominence.

You are extremely sociable, and relationships are the heart and soul of your existence. In a love union, you are passionate, warm-hearted, and generous. Although you have a hair-trigger temper, you forgive and forget just as quickly.

On This Day:

A centuries-old festival known as Gharnta Karna Day takes place annually around this date in the ancient kingdom of Napal in the Himalayan Mountains. The festival celebrates the death of Gharnta Karna, a horrible bloodthirsty Hindu demon who haunts the crossroads and is the sworn enemy of the venerated creator god Vishnu.

Born Today: Rosanna Arquette (actress); Patti Austin (singer); Antonio Banderas (actor); Jimmy Dean (singer); Eddie Fisher (singer); Rhonda Fleming (actress); Red Holzman (basketball player/coach); Herbert Hoover (U.S. president); Martha Hyer (actress); Wolfgang Paul (physicist); Norma Shearer (actress); Jane Wyatt (actress)

August 11
♌ Leo, 2

The magnetic, imaginative individual born on this date has lofty aspirations and the wherewithal to put his or her innovative plans into action. Moreover, you tend to inspire a similar idealism in others and can usually get them to follow your lead. You are passionate, strong-willed, tenacious, and determined. Thanks to your amazing staying power, once you get started on something, you're pretty much unstoppable. Inherently romantic and idealistic, you enjoy dramatizing and mythologizing your existence. By surrounding yourself with drama and excitement, you seem larger than life.

You yearn to bring light to the world by leading people towards a better way of life. The powerful combination of solar Leo and the number two vibration adds a touch of humility to your characteristic leonine confidence and pride. Although you want personal success, money, and status, you also want to use your knowledge and skills to help the less fortunate. Intuitive to the point of being psychic, you're an inspired thinker who is able to communicate on all levels. Some with birthdays today become teachers or evangelists, while many of the more artistically inclined find their vocations in the arts.

As a friend or lover, you're generous and loyal. However, you sometimes appear distant and detached from your immediate environment. You may become so involved in your efforts to help the world that you forget about the needs of your own family.

On This Day:

The goddess Oddudua, known as the mother of all the gods, is honored on this day by followers of the Santeria religion in Africa and South America. Today is the first day of the three-day Irish fertility festival known as the Puck Faire. The medieval-style festivity pays homage to the mischievous forest sprite known as Robin Goodfellow.

Born Today: Arlene Dahl (actress); Mike Douglas (singer/TV talk show host); Jerry Falwell (TV evangelist); Alex Haley (writer); Hulk Hogan (wrestler); David Henry Hwang (playwright); Allegra Kent (dancer); Richard Mead (physician); Phil Ochs (folk singer/songwriter); Steve Wozniak (co-founder of Apple Computer)

August 12

♌ Leo, 3

Lions born on this day are witty, versatile, and curious. Communication is your forte, and you put forth your ideas with dramatic intensity. Your interest in everything around you tends to radiate outward and attract people who share your ideals. Your enjoyment of intellectual discourse draws you into spirited discussions where each person is trying to get his or her point across. However, you generally find a way to take over center stage and explain your own views with more drama and clarity than anyone else.

Capable of doing two tasks at once, some August 12th individuals can also handle two careers simultaneously. New people and places provide you with welcome stimulation, and your need for variety and change impels you to continually seek out fresh challenges. An original thinker, you sometimes discover new truths beyond accepted realities, especially when you follow your intuition. With your theatrical personality and facility with words, writing and acting may be your top career choices. Also high on any list of possible occupations is the media, from publishing to TV journalism.

One thing is certain: you are never dull or boring. The image you project is exciting and romantic. You like to flirt and may not be in any hurry to make a firm commitment. You're not an easy person to pin down, let alone catch and hold.

On This Day:

On this day in ancient Egypt, people celebrated the Lychnapsia, or the Festival of the Lights of Isis, which commemorates the search of the goddess Isis for the body of her husband Osiris. On this date in ancient Rome, the festival of Hercules Invictus was celebrated with a sacrifice at the Ara Maxima, or great altar, near the Circus Maximus.

Born Today: Cecil B. DeMille (director); John Derek (actor); Samuel Fuller (director); William Goldman (writer); Edith Hamilton (writer); George Hamilton (actor); Mario "Cantinflas" Moreno (comedian/actor); Mary Roberts Rinehart (writer); Pete Sampras (tennis player); Robert Southey (poet); Jane Wyatt (actress)

August 13

♌ Leo, 4

With Leo's pride joined to the root number four's unyielding sense of responsibility, those celebrating birthdays today are super-competent workaholics. As ambitious as you are enterprising, you're consistently ahead of the pack. You have sound business judgment and a knack for commanding the respect and cooperation of others. Yet, despite your skills as an executive, you have a hard time delegating responsibility. You just can't believe that anyone can do the job as well as you.

People born on this date are high minded and idealistic, with abiding faith in their own capabilities and a tendency to see themselves as the stars of the show. Although you act as if you don't care for anyone's opinion except your own, nothing could be further from the truth. The acceptance, recognition, and praise of others mean the world to you. Inherently industrious and persevering, you don't anticipate having success handed to you on a silver platter. Since most of life's rewards come to you as the result your own accomplishments, you need not feel beholden to anyone.

In matters of the heart, you are warm, passionate, and extremely generous. However, in an intimate union you can be rather demanding and possessive. You require a good deal of emotional pampering, and you're happiest when you get the devotion and attention you crave.

On This Day:

The festival of Hecate, Greek goddess of darkness, is traditionally held at moonrise on this date. This date also marks the first day of the runic half-month of As, the ash tree. The As rune is sacred to the divinities of Asgard and represents stability with the divine force in the world. The world ash, Yaggdrasil, is a symbol of continuity in times of change and chaos.

Born Today: Kathleen Battle (opera singer); Fidel Castro (Cuban dictator); Dan Fogelberg (singer/songwriter); Pat Harrington, Jr. (actor); Sir Alfred Hitchcock (director); Ben Hogan (golfer); Burt Lahr (actor); Annie Oakley (sharpshooter/stage performer); Frederick Sanger (biochemist); George Shearing (jazz musician)

August 14

♌ Leo, 5

Lions celebrating birthdays on this day are open hearted, friendly, and magnanimous, with naturally upbeat, sunny dispositions. Inspired to spread the truth abroad, you possess a sincerity that is the hallmark of your existence. Even little white lies are abhorrent to your honest, up-front nature. However, there is a touch of flamboyance and a definite flair for the dramatic in your brand of honest rebelliousness. You truly want to help people, but you don't mind drawing a little attention to yourself while doing it.

Those born on August 14 can be successful in just about any occupation, as long as they love their work. You possess a zest for life that causes you to totally immerse yourself in everything you do. Your optimism, sociability, and enthusiasm make you popular with your many friends and associates. You are interested in progress and new ways of doing things, and your ability to think ahead of the curve provides you with amazing insight into future trends and possibilities. Your knack for coping with the unexpected gives you the confidence to try things that are unusual and exciting.

You are loving, affectionate, and likely to jump in and out of romantic relationships. Although you rarely admit to being fickle, there is a fear of intimacy in your basic makeup. When you settle down, you're likely to choose someone who shares many of your interests and can be a friend as well as a lover.

On This Day:

Every year on this date in many of the highland towns and fishing villages along the coast of Scotland, a man wearing a costume of thistles and burrs walks through the streets collecting donations from the villagers. Called the Burryman, he's said to represent an ancient fertility god, but the true origins of this tradition remain a mystery.

Born Today: Russell Baker (writer/newspaper columnist); Halle Berry (actress); David Crosby (rock star); Earvin "Magic" Johnson (basketball player); Gary Larson (cartoonist); Steve Martin (comedian/actor); Robyn Smith (jockey); Susan St. James (actress); Danielle Steele (writer); Wim Wenders (director)

August 15

♌ Leo, 6

People born on this day are innately sociable, courteous, and hospitable. A positive turn of mind causes you to seek the best that life has to offer, and you usually find it. You love your home and derive great joy from harmonious surroundings and beautiful things. The welcome mat is always out at your house. You're friendly toward everyone, but family and close friends are particularly important to you. You crave attention and approval, and your upbeat, sunny temperament and sympathetic nature bring you the respect and popularity you desire.

Leo's fiery aggressiveness is tempered in you by the inherent charm and diplomacy of the root number six. You are quietly ambitious and determined to get ahead in life. Although you want to be boss as much as any other lion, you have a knack for taking charge without offending anyone. Whether in the arts, the professions, or business, you understand the public mind and know its wants and needs. You could find a creative outlet for your vivid imagination in art, acting, music, filmmaking, or writing.

Truly romantic and protective, you thrive on intimacy and the feeling of being part of a couple, family, or group. In relationships, you are warm and passionate, but you're also inclined to become overly dependent on your loved ones for emotional fulfillment.

On This Day:

The Assumption of the Virgin Mary is celebrated in Roman Catholic churches on this date. In the Irish church, it's known as the Feast of Mary in the Harvest. Formerly on this day in Rome, women were admitted to the Sistine Chapel between first and second vespers; they were excluded the rest of the year lest they disturb devotions with their chatter.

Born Today: Ben Affleck (actor); Ethel Barrymore (actress); Napoleon Bonaparte (military commander/French emperor); Julia Child (TV chef/food writer); Mike Connors (actor); Linda Ellerbee (TV journalist); Huntz Hall (actor); Rose Marie (actress); Nicholas Roeg (director); Sir Walter Scott (writer); Jimmy Webb (composer)

August 16

The dynamic truth seekers born on this date possess a deep awareness of personal destiny. Even so, others may regard you as a genuine mystery because of the apparent contradictions in your personality. Since you are smarter or better educated than most people, you can be impatient with those who are slower on the uptake. Yet you're a genuine idealist and crusader for causes you believe in. Although you bask in the attention your humanitarian work attracts, the spiritual side of your nature is much given to private contemplation and reflection. You could be deeply religious in the traditional sense or attracted to alternative belief systems such as mysticism and the occult.

August 16th individuals are extremely curious and not afraid to experiment outside mainstream norms when it suits them. Your charming façade masks a proud, ambitious nature bent on achievement. You have the mentality of a visionary with innovative ideas that are often misunderstood by those around you. Consequently, you function best in an individual capacity where you are the authority in your own realm. Even when you are not the boss, you're a good deal more comfortable dispensing advice than taking it.

In a romantic union, you are passionate, but also complex and determined to have your own way. Fervently loyal, you can also be jealous and possessive. Although you treasure your own independence, you have difficulty granting the same freedom to your partner.

On This Day:

Salem Heritage Day in Massachusetts falls on this day. Also, on this date in 1987, the first Harmonic Convergence was observed worldwide by New Age enthusiasts to celebrate the Grand Trine, or alignment of the planets. Today also marks the birthday of the Persian prophet Zoroaster, or Zarathustra, the founder of the first world religion—Zoroastrianism.

Born Today: Angela Bassett (actress); Ann Blyth (actress); James Cameron (director); Vanessa Carlton (singer); Robert Culp (actor); Kathie Lee Gifford (TV talk show host/singer); Eydie Gorme (singer); Timothy Hutton (actor); Madonna (singer/actress); Fess Parker (actor); Lesley Ann Warren (actress)

August 17
♌ Leo, 8

The strong-minded, capable, persistent people celebrating birthdays on this date know exactly what they want and how to get it. It's no wonder that you hold fervent views on many subjects, and you spend a considerable amount of time trying to convince others of the validity of your ideas. You have a talent for excluding extraneous thoughts from your mind and concentrating totally on the task at hand. You systematically organize all your knowledge of the facts in order to avoid unnecessary confusion and uncertainty.

Lions born on August 17 can be successful in almost any career or profession. While you may be less sure of yourself than you appear, you still possess all the aggressiveness and self-confidence you need to get the job done. In business and the arts, your farseeing approach to changing trends helps you decide what is worth keeping from the past and what should be discarded. Your speaking and writing talents, physical vitality, and technical skills combine to give you an edge in occupations concerned with business, entertainment, literature, professional sports, science, and education.

In your personal life, you're generous and loving. In an intimate union, you are both giving and demanding. You expect constancy from your mate, but your need for adoration makes you a bit of a flirt. Nevertheless, in a committed relationship with the right person, you're dependable and exceedingly loyal.

On This Day:

This day marks the first of the nine days that Odin, the chief Aesir sky god, hung from the World Tree (Yggdrasil) in order to discover the meaning of the runes. In ancient Rome, the festival of Diana, beloved goddess of the Moon, chastity, and hunting, was celebrated on this date each year with feasting, mirth, and magic making.

Born Today: Mikhail Botvinnik (chess player); Robin Cousins (skater); Davy Crockett (frontiersman/scout/U.S. congressman); Robert De Niro (actor); Samuel Goldwyn (producer/studio founder); Maureen O'Hara (actress); Sean Penn (actor); Larry Rivers (artist); Donnie Wahlberg (actor); Mae West (actress)

August 18

♌ Leo, 9

The fiery lion celebrating a birthday on this day has a tremendous capacity for spiritual growth and material achievement. A natural leader and independent thinker, you dislike taking orders from others, yet you rarely think twice about telling everyone else what to do. Nevertheless, you understand the human condition, and in your work with people you're a selfless crusader for justice. Moreover, you refuse to tolerate inequity or discrimination of any kind. A born fighter, you're not afraid of anything or anyone. You possess a hair-trigger temper that readily explodes when you encounter oppression or exploitation.

August 18th individuals are a complex mix of confidence and uncertainty, action and inaction. Your leonine nature craves excitement, drama, and the opportunity to shine, while the inner you yearns for the serenity of a tranquil existence. You are imaginative and intuitive, with an artistic temperament that makes you more sensitive and more easily distressed than other members of your Sun sign. The combination of creativity and idealism inclines you toward career fields concerned with acting, music, dance, writing, art and design, politics, social work, and religion.

In love as in life, you are impulsive and likely to forget to think before speaking. When you allow your heart to rule you head, you can get so carried away by romantic ideals that your potential for a happy union becomes lost in maze of aimless dreaming.

On This Day:

On or around this date each year, the Chinese celebrate the Festival of the Hungry Ghosts with offerings for the dead. It is believed that during this time the gates of hell are opened to free the ghosts, who then wander the Earth seeking food. The offerings are made to pay them tribute, appease them, and ward off bad luck from the prior year.

Born Today: Rosalynn Carter (U.S. first lady); Rafer Johnson (Olympic decathlon champion); Meriwether Lewis (explorer); Martin Mull (actor); Roman Polanski (director); Robert Redford (actor/director); Christian Slater (actor); Patrick Swayze (actor); Malcolm-Jamal Warner (actor); Shelley Winters (actress)

August 19

♌ Leo, 1

The dynamic Leo native celebrating a birthday today was born to shine and lives to be noticed. You have a courageous spirit that thrives on drama and excitement and is willing to try anything, at least once. Your inner lion's desire for approval is less compelling than your need to do things your own way. Many of your more outrageous actions are deliberately designed to shock people and shake them out of their complacency. You have a talent for knocking the wind out of the sails of self-righteous hypocrites that would make any Aquarian envious.

Individuals born on August 19 are enthusiastic, optimistic, and industrious. Your personal magnetism, warmth, and vitality tend to attract people and draw them to you. Confident and self-motivated, you like being in charge, and you gravitate toward a central role in most situations. You throw yourself into every project with dynamic intensity and never shirk your responsibilities. You could be a champion athlete, star entertainer, noted politician, top business executive, well-known artist, or best-selling author. Whatever you choose to do, you'll seek a position of prominence where you can stand out from the crowd.

Yours is a glowing presence with a great zest for life and love. In an intimate relationship, you're loyal, passionate, and generous. However, it may require a lot of ego stroking and repeated assurances of love and affection to keep you truly happy.

On This Day:

In ancient Rome, the ripening of the grapes and beginning of the winemaking season was celebrated with an agricultural festival known as the Vinalia Rustica. The first grapes were broken off and offered to Jupiter and Venus. The first wine would then be saved and later opened at the Vinalia Parilia on August 23.

Born Today: Adam Arkin (actor); Bill Clinton (U.S. president); Malcolm Forbes (business analyst/publishing tycoon); Ogden Nash (poet/humorist); Matthew Perry (actor); Gene Roddenberry (writer/creator of *Star Trek*); Willie Shoemaker (jockey); John Stamos (actor); Lee Ann Womack (singer); Orville Wright (aviation pioneer/inventor)

August 20
♌ Leo, 2

The romantic, sentimental lion born on this day is an inveterate "people pleaser" who sees relationships as the primary force in life. More than most of your Leo counterparts, you enjoy joint ventures and cooperative activities, and you tend to think in terms of "we" and "us." Charming, gracious, and magnanimous, you move back and forth between diverse social circles with considerable ease. There are few who can match you in social skills or diplomacy. Still, no matter how much you may want to be a part of the team, pride and ambition fuel your need to be first among equals.

The confidence and personal magnetism of individuals celebrating birthdays today gets people to notice them. Fun loving and fun to be with, you enjoy being the center of everyone's attention. Nevertheless, you're anything but a mental lightweight. You have a clear understanding of what's really important in life, as well as the ability to share your insight with others. You have excellent organizing skills and a knack for taking over in times of crisis and resolving problems and disputes. Your enterprise, creativity, and congeniality virtually guarantee your success in any field of endeavor that interests you.

In a love union, you have a knack for always doing the right thing. A model mate, you don't forget birthdays, anniversaries, or other special dates. You like being petted and admired, and in return you make your lover feel pampered and adored.

On This Day:

This feast day celebrates Roman Catholic Saint Bernard, who was nobly born in Burgundy, France. He revived the near-failing Cistercian order of monks and then went on to found 163 monasteries in different parts of Europe. Bernard wrote the outline for the Rule of the Knights Templar and helped Pope Innocent II triumph over the antipope, Anacletus.

Born Today: Connie Chung (TV journalist/anchor); Benjamin Harrison (Civil War general/U.S. president); Isaac Hayes (singer/songwriter); H. P. Lovecraft (writer); James Marsters (actor); George Mitchell (U.S. senator); Robert Plant (rock star); Al Roker (TV weatherman/amateur chef/food writer); Jacqueline Susann (writer)

August 21
♌ Leo, 3

The enchanting personalities of those born on this day make them popular, sought-after companions. A born multi-tasker, you're considerably more versatile than the average Leo. New people and places provide you with welcome mental stimulation, and your need for variety impels you to continually seek out fresh challenges. Like the Energizer bunny, your drive and vitality keep you going day after day. Your restless mind is always on the lookout for new subjects to study and new questions to ask and answer.

August 21st lions are idealistic and high minded, with a tendency to see themselves as noble heroes whose destiny it is to blaze a path for others to follow. While you have an intuitive grasp of the overall picture in most situations, you often lose interest when faced with the nitty-gritty of routine details. You could probably carve out a successful career in any field you choose. However, with your independent spirit, you might not be happy in a job that is physically or mentally confining. Areas most likely to provide fertile ground for your talents include show business, sports, the media, advertising, education, and sales.

You fall in love quickly, but if the relationship starts to feel confining, you may begin to get antsy. When your desire for permanence conflicts with your need to feel free and unfettered, you will usually choose love over freedom.

On This Day:

The Consualia, a harvest festival held in honor of Consus, the Earth god, took place on this day in ancient Rome. There were sacrifices and offerings of the first fruits, followed by horse racing in the Circus Maximus. The annual festival of Heraclia was also held on this date in honor of the god Heracles and included sacrifices at his shrines.

Born Today: Janet Baker (opera singer); Count Basie (bandleader/composer); Aubrey Beardsley (illustrator); Kim Cattrall (actress); Wilt Chamberlain (basketball player); Arthur Janov (psychologist/developer of Primal Scream therapy); Jim McMahon (football player); Kenny Rogers (singer); Peter Weir (director); Jack Weston (actor)

August 22
♌ Leo, 4

The person born on the Leo/Virgo cusp is an unusual blend of introvert and extrovert. With the intuitive understanding of the fiery lion and the virgin's analytical mentality, you're able to see the big picture and the tiny details of any situation. You may be sensitive and rather shy on the inside, but on the outside you're the star of the show. Leo's artistic temperament, sense of style, and flair for the dramatic, combined with practical Virgo's concern for the welfare of others, provide you with the wherewithal for success in virtually any career field you find appealing.

Those celebrating birthdays on August 22 are typically gregarious, fun-loving, social beings striving to live life to the fullest. Yet you can come off as picky or overly critical to people who are less precise and discriminating than you. Despite your inherent optimism, you're inclined to exaggerate personal problems and setbacks. Because of your tendency to rely as much on feelings as on logic, your heart can tell you one thing and your head another. In the end, however, you usually follow the dictates of your emotions.

In matters of affection, you're warm and caring, but your idealism and desire for perfection can undermine your intimate relationships. You require a considerable amount of pampering and ego boosting, and when you get them, you make a loving, loyal, and extremely devoted partner.

On This Day:

This day is sacred to the Chinese creator goddess Nu Kwa. A primordial deity, she fashioned mankind from lumps of yellow clay. On this date in 1623, the order of the Rosy Cross was established in Paris, France. Since the mysterious Rosicrucian brotherhood was a secret sect associated with alchemy, it was condemned by the church.

Born Today: Tori Amos (singer/songwriter); Ray Bradbury (writer); Denton Cooley (cardiac surgeon); Claude Debussy (composer); Valerie Harper (actress); Bill Parcells (football coach); Dorothy Parker (writer); H. Norman Schwarzkopf (U.S. Army general); Cindy Williams (actress); Carl Yastrzemski (baseball player)

August 23

♍ Virgo, 5

Quick thinking and fast talking, the August 23rd individual is known for physical dexterity and a freewheeling, mercurial temperament. Highly intellectual, rational, and analytical, you are extremely fluent in the spoken and written word. Your emphasis on mind and body can come at the expense of your feelings and emotions. You're not unsympathetic or unfeeling, but intense emotion makes you uncomfortable. Since you give the appearance of being aloof and detached from much of what is going on around you, you may strike others as selfish. You're not selfish per se, but you can be rather self-involved and narrowly focused on your work.

People born on this day are among the most intriguing and enigmatic members of the Virgo group. You're a one-of-a-kind visionary, yet quite capable of materializing your dreams and ideas in the real world. Social concerns loom large in your mind, and with your desire to help people, you'd make an excellent psychologist, teacher, social worker, doctor, nurse, or politician. Well spoken, artistic, creative, and physically adroit, you may discover that your niche is in athletics, the media, or the arts.

In relationships, you're nurturing and caring one moment and nit picking and fault finding the next. You can be loyal and devoted, but you need your space. If your partner tries to cramp your style, you're liable to shut down emotionally and walk out.

On This Day:

In ancient Greece, the Day of the Nemesea was celebrated on this date. The festival honored the goddess Nemesis, who defended relics and the memory of the dead from insult and injury. In old Rome, this was the day of the Vertumnalia in honor of Vertumnus, the god of changing seasons and the transformation of flowers into fruits.

Born Today: Nicole Bobek (skater); Kobe Bryant (basketball player); Barbara Eden (actress); Gene Kelly (dancer/choreographer); Shelley Long (actress); Patricia McBride (dancer); Vera Miles (actress); River Phoenix (actor); Henry Pringle (journalist); Mark Russell (pianist/political satirist); Rick Springfield (singer/actor)

August 24

♍ Virgo, 6

The charming, sociable individuals whose birthdays fall on this date have been blessed with impeccable manners and a tendency to be more tactful and diplomatic than other members of their Sun sign. Although you may appear self-sufficient, you're a person who needs people. Peace loving and inherently agreeable, you do everything possible to avoid disagreements. Inherently civilized, cultured, and refined, you have delicate sensibilities and a great love for all things beautiful, artistic, and harmonious. You also have a practical, serious side that responds to any negative situation in typical Virgo fashion. First you worry about it, and then you try to fix it.

August 24th individuals are amiable, but they are definitely not pushovers. You may be helpful and considerate of others, but you won't do anything you don't really want to do. Your fascination with detail makes it difficult for you to arrive at concrete decisions, but once you decide what to do, you know exactly how it should be done. Career areas of particular interest to you may include music, art, writing, social work, medicine, law, politics, science, professional sports, and business.

You are someone who is likely to "fall in love with love." Your critical Virgo nature makes you seem rather cool and detached, but you crave romance and companionship and probably can't be truly happy without a partner to share your life.

On This Day:

Today is the first day of the Mania, the Roman festival of the Manes, or deified spirits of the ancestors. It is also the festival of Luna, the goddess of the Moon. In her temple, Luna Noctiluca (Moon that shines by night), the cover was removed from the Mundus Cereris, the labyrinthine passage to the underworld, to allow the spirits of the dead to roam free.

Born Today: Yasser Arafat (leader of the Palestine Liberation Organization); Dave Chappelle (comedian); Rupert Grint (actor); Steve Guttenberg (actor); Craig Kilborn (TV sportscaster/talk show host); Durward Kirby (TV co-host); Marlee Matlin (actress); Chad Michael Murray (actor); Cal Ripkin, Jr. (baseball player)

August 25

♍ Virgo, 7

Virgins born on this day are as much of a mystery to themselves as they are to others. While you genuinely want to help those who cannot help themselves, your preconceived notions of the right and wrong way to do things may lead you to believe that everything must be done your way or not at all. There is an intellectual side to your nature that requires constant mental stimulation and makes you something of an eternal student. At times you may feel the need to get involved in numerous physically and mentally challenging projects just to keep from getting bored.

You are a person with noble objectives. Once you've chosen a course of action, you pursue it with total commitment. You've been blessed with sound business judgment and regularly pick up on things that others tend to miss. You're quick thinking, but also exacting and meticulous in executing your plans and ideas. You could do well in almost any profession, but you're best suited to a career that calls for creative talent and good communication skills, such as writing, broadcasting, teaching, and politics.

In a close relationship, you're kindhearted and caring. Sentimental and romantic, yet apprehensive about expressing your true feelings, you prefer to demonstrate your love through actions rather than words. You can be hurt if your devotion is unappreciated.

On This Day:

On this day in ancient Rome, the Festival of Ops was held in honor of the goddess of abundance. Overseen by the Vestal Virgins, the festival honored the Earth goddess as the bringer of help. It was the custom for all who attended the rituals to sit on the ground in order to absorb some of the energy and earthy qualities of the goddess.

Born Today: Leonard Bernstein (composer/conductor); Tim Burton (director); Sean Connery (actor); Elvis Costello (singer); Rollie Fingers (baseball player); Monty Hall (TV game show host); Van Johnson (actor); Ruby Keeler (dancer/actress); Regis Philbin (TV talk show/game show host); Claudia Schiffer (supermodel)

August 26

♍ Virgo, 8

Focus and dedication are the keys to success for those celebrating birthdays on this day. A born executive, you are shrewd and skilled at getting the most from your associates. At times you can be rather controlling and demanding, but you are honest and straightforward in all your dealings. Your aim is to make sure the job at hand is done properly and completed on time. You scrutinize a situation carefully and consider all the options before making an important decision. Your efficiency and managerial abilities could prove extremely useful in business, industry, education, science, or government.

The hard-working August 26th individual possesses a down-to-earth practicality that virtually guarantees worldly achievement. Despite your ambitious nature, you are extremely patient and willing to wait for the best possible opportunity before making your move. You have a fine analytical mind and remarkable manual dexterity, along with a keen appreciation for art, music, dance, drama, and literature. Many born on this date also have considerable talent along these lines and go on to outstanding careers in the media, the arts, or athletics.

You may appear somewhat aloof on the surface, but at heart you're a true romantic and more passionate than most Virgo natives. Although you can be moody and difficult to live with, when you overcome your insecurities, you make a loving, caring, loyal, and totally dependable partner.

On This Day:

Today is the feast day of the Finnish goddess Ilmatar, or Luonnotar, the water mother who created the world out of chaos. The periodic rebirth of the Hindu god Krishna is celebrated by his faithful worshipers at midnight services. Images of the baby Krishna are paraded among the people, who welcome back the god on his return to Earth.

Born Today: Ben Bradlee (newspaper editor); Macaulay Culkin (actor); Geraldine Ferraro (U.S. congresswoman); Peggy Guggenheim (art patron/collector); Tommy Heinson (basketball player/coach); Christopher Isherwood (writer); Branford Marsalis (jazz musician/bandleader); Valerie Simpson (singer); Rufino Tamayo (artist)

August 27

♍ Virgo, 9

The kind, sympathetic nature of persons born on this day makes them eager to do what they can to help those in need. A natural healer and counselor, you have a strong desire to be of service to the community. Mentally perceptive, insightful, observant, and precise in your actions, you are particularly good at dealing with emergencies. Your indomitable strength of purpose makes it difficult for anyone to divert your attention from your goals. Your forceful personality and belief in your mission tend to sway others and win them over to your way of thinking.

There's an aura of prophetic wisdom about someone born on August 27. You listen carefully to what others have to say, and when you express an opinion, it usually cuts right to the heart of the matter. You refuse to tolerate bigotry or injustice of any kind. However, in your haste to do what's right, you often get carried away. When you give in to impractical ideas, your potential for doing good can become hopelessly lost in a haze of aimless dreaming.

Love is high on your list of priorities. Without it, you often feel the need to retreat into the fantasy world of your imagination. In an intimate relationship you provide warmth, tenderness, and tons of romance. You expect no less in return.

On This Day:

On this day in 1910, Mother Teresa was born in Skopje, Macedonia. At the age of eighteen, she left home to join the Sisters of Loreto and was sent to Calcutta, India. In 1950, Mother Teresa received permission to start her own order, the Missionaries of Charity. The missionaries primary task was to care for people nobody else was willing to look after.

Born Today: Daryl "The Captain" Dragon (singer); Theodore Dreiser (writer); Georg Hegel (philosopher); Lyndon B. Johnson (U.S. president); Ira Levin (writer); Man Ray (artist); Martha Raye (comedienne); Paul "Pee-wee Herman" Reubens (TV show host/actor); Alexa Vega (actress); Tuesday Weld (actress)

August 28
♍ Virgo, 1

T he fiercely independent individuals born on this day have strong personalities and a penchant for doing everything their own way. A genuine original, you are a unique combination of level-headedness and intuition. You have a crusading temperament with noble intentions and a desire to be of service to your community. However, you also crave personal success and recognition. An unremitting perfectionist, you throw yourself completely into every project. You're quick on the uptake, yet exacting and meticulous in the execution of your plans and ideas.

Once you are involved in a course of action, you pursue it with total commitment. Blessed with sound business judgment, you pick up on things that others tend to miss. With your sharp mind and quick wit, you're a master of the clever quip and swift comeback. You possess quite a devilish sense of humor that can send those around you into fits of hysterical laughter. You could do well in any profession, but you're best suited to a career that calls for creative talent and good communication skills, such as writing, acting, journalism, broadcasting, teaching, and politics.

Physically you're passionate, but emotionally you can blow hot and cold. A true meeting of the minds is probably more important to you than romance. When the impetuousness of the root number one makes you want to rush headlong into an intimate relationship, your cautious Virgo Sun gets you to think twice.

On This Day:

In ancient Egypt, the nativity of the funerary goddess Nephthys, the younger sister of Isis, Osiris, and Set, was celebrated on this date. In Norway on this day, the citizens celebrate an old pagan harvest festival. The ancient Norse goddesses and gods are invoked to protect the spirit of the harvest through the dark half of the year.

Born Today: Charles Boyer (actor); Ben Gazzara (actor); Scott Hamilton (skater); James Wong Howe (cinematographer); Donald O'Conner (singer/dancer/actor); Jason Priestley (actor); LeAnn Rimes (singer); David Soul (actor/singer); Leo Tolstoy (writer); Shania Twain (singer/songwriter); Johann von Goethe (writer)

August 29
♍ Virgo, 2

Virgins born on this day are team players. Naturally peace loving and tactful, you have impeccable manners, and you strive to avoid disagreements and discord whenever possible. Civilized, cultured, and refined, you have excellent taste and a deep-seated appreciation for art and beauty. Despite a practical, serious side to your character, you really do love your creature comforts. When you work, you work hard. But when it's time to play, you want to relax and enjoy yourself in the company of family and friends.

You could be considered fortunate, yet it's actually hard work, not luck, that makes it possible for you to succeed in life. Guided by good sense and a strong need for security, you're shrewd with money and material possessions. You expect value for every dollar you spend, but you also demand the best quality. You are self-restrained and like to take your time when making important decisions. Some people may get the impression that you are not overly ambitious, but that is definitely not the case. You just don't like starting anything, unless you're sure that you can finish it.

Individuals with August 29th birthdays are among those most likely to "fall in love with love." Although you appear self-sufficient, you're actually someone who craves companionship. You can be critical of others, but you need affection and probably can't be happy without a partner.

On This Day:

Today is the festival of Urda, the oldest of the three Norns, or Norse fates. Urda represents "that which was." On this day, the Egyptians celebrated the nativity of the cow-headed goddess Hathor. In Nigeria on this date, the Yoruba people celebrate the Gelede, an annual ritual of dancing and wearing masks to drive away evil sorceresses.

Born Today: Richard Attenborough (actor/director); Bob Beamon (long jumper); Ingrid Bergman (actress); William Friedkin (director); Elliott Gould (actor); Michael Jackson (singer); Robin Leach (TV host); John Locke (philosopher); Charlie "Bird" Parker (jazz musician/composer); Isabel Sanford (actress); Preston Sturges (director)

August 30

♍ Virgo, 3

ndividuals celebrating natal days today are quick witted and fast on their feet. Intellect and physical dexterity are among your great strengths. Naturally self-expressive and creative, you're exceptionally fluent in speech and writing. Shrewd and insightful, you are particularly good at detecting and understanding other people's underlying motivations. There is something of the eternal student about you that requires constant mental stimulation. You particularly enjoy exploring the physical world in which you live and the inner world of ideas and imagination.

The lively mind of the person born on August 30 functions as a constant source of innovative plans. You are inherently inquisitive, with a nervous temperament that requires repeated doses of variety and change to calm its restive nature. In business, you act in a straightforward manner that's honest and sincere, although at times you're a bit too outspoken. Career fields most likely to attract your attention include education, philosophy, law, science, religion, metaphysics, sports, and travel. In the creative area, you have a definite flair for drama, art, writing, and public speaking.

You are sociable and friendly and enjoy exchanging ideas with everyone you meet. In intimate relationships, you're romantic, sentimental, and idealistic. Your perfectionism, however, creates a gap between your dreams and everyday reality. You want to find true love, but few are able to live up to your high ideals.

On This Day:

Today is the first day of the month of Thoth, the New Year's Day of the fixed Greco-Egyptian calendar of Alexandria. On this day, the Roman festival of thanksgiving, the Charisteria, was celebrated. This date is also sacred to Saint Rose of Lima, the first Roman Catholic saint of the New World and patroness of Latin America and the Philippines.

Born Today: Elizabeth Ashley (actress); Shirley Booth (actress); Timothy Bottoms (actor); Cameron Diaz (actress); Jean-Claude Killy (skier); Peggy Lipton (actress); Fred MacMurray (actor); Frank "Tug" McGraw (baseball player); Robert Parrish (basketball player); Mary Wollstonecraft Shelley (writer); Ted Williams (baseball player)

August 31

♍ Virgo, 4

Virgins born on this day are down to earth, hard working, and efficient. Since, in your view, function is vastly more important than form, you expect practical results from your labors. You excel at bringing order out of chaos by organizing systems and streamlining procedures and techniques. New ideas come easily to you, and you have a knack for formulating them into workable plans. You usually know the best way to get a project up and running and keep it functioning properly. Your forte is your single-minded ability to focus your concentration on what you are doing, to the exclusion of everything else.

Whatever the business or profession of those celebrating birthdays on August 31, admiration is as important to them as financial compensation. You like knowing that your work is considered useful and your efforts appreciated. You can be rather critical and controlling of others, but you have an independent streak that causes you to resist any attempts to restrain your activities. Although the creative impulse may incline you toward an artistic career, your common sense and realistic take on life are particularly well suited to the world of business and finance.

In intimate relationships, you are tender and affectionate. You show how much you care by being helpful and dependable. Although some members of the zodiacal family may be more exciting than you, none are more trustworthy, or caring.

On This Day:

On this day in the Nigerian capital of Lagos, masqueraders known as Eyos perform an ancient custom. They walk through the streets dressed as demons in white robes and brandishing long sticks. This Ritual Walk of the Eyos symbolizes authority and represents individual families. Its original purpose was the purification of family spirits.

★★
★ **Born Today:** Eldridge Cleaver (political activist); James Coburn (actor); Richard Gere (actor); Arthur Godfrey (radio and TV host); Buddy Hackett (comedian); Alan Jay Lerner (lyricist); Maria Montessori (educator); Van Morrison (singer); Itzhak Perlman (violinist); Frank Robinson (baseball player); William Saroyan (writer)

September Birthdays

September 1

♍ Virgo, 1

Virgins born on this day are ambitious and career oriented, with an intense desire for success and recognition. A born professional, you combine a meticulous eye for detail with wholehearted enthusiasm for your projects. Considerably less patient than other Virgos, you're more likely to act now and think about it later. You forte is coming up with innovative ideas and making them work on a commercial level. Although you're more confident and self-motivated than many of your Sun sign counterparts, you are not nearly as certain of your own talents and abilities as you appear.

Those with birthdays on September 1 are perfectionists with clever minds and sharp tongues. Once involved in a course of action, you pursue it with total commitment. However, you do not suffer fools gladly and can be downright intolerant of anyone who is not as competent or dedicated as you. You've been blessed with sound business judgment and regularly pick up on things that others tend to miss. Full of good advice and well-intentioned criticism, you rarely hesitate before letting others know what you think of their efforts.

Whereas the impulsiveness of the number one's vibration can cause you to rush headlong into an intimate relationship, cautious solar Virgo makes you think twice. In love, you're affectionate and attentive, and you show how much you care by being helpful and dependable.

On This Day:

This day is sacred to Roman Catholic Saint Giles. Wounded in the leg by an arrow while protecting a stag that the king of Provence was preparing to shoot, Giles became the patron of the disabled, who pray to him for cures. On this date in ancient Rome, the people honored Jupiter the Thunderer, a sky and weather deity who also rules over the harvest.

Born Today: Edgar Rice Burroughs (writer); "Gentleman" Jim Corbett (boxer/actor); Yvonne DeCarlo (actress); Gloria Estefan (singer); Vittorio Gassman (actor); Barry Gibb (rock star); Rocky Marciano (boxer); Dr. Phil McGraw (psychologist/TV talk show host); Seiji Ozawa (conductor); Lily Tomlin (comedienne); Conway Twitty (singer)

September 2

♍ Virgo, 2

People celebrating birthdays today have charming, sociable, courteous natures that bring balance and harmony to all their interactions. Your impeccable manners make you less critical and more diplomatic than most Virgos. Although you seem less driven and more relaxed than other members of your Sun sign, you are as ambitious as any of them. Because of your ability to get people to like you, you succeed in life without taking aggressive action. In fact, you're living proof of that old saw about catching more flies with honey than vinegar.

Those born on this day are amiable without being pushovers. As a team player, you are prepared to compromise, but you won't do anything you don't really want to do. You have a way of appearing cooperative and conciliatory without letting others take advantage of you. Moreover, you have a decided knack for getting people to go along with your plans and ideas. When you feel your efforts are being thwarted, you mix a bit of cunning in with your charm to help turn things around. Career areas that may be of particular interest to you include the arts, the law, the sciences, and professional sports.

In matters of the heart, you're a person who needs to love and be loved. Yet you consider intellectual rapport, mutual respect, and a harmonious union as important to personal happiness as passion and romance.

On This Day:

On this date in ancient Greece, the annual Grape Vine Festival was held in honor of the god Dionysus and his consort Ariadne. Today is the first day of the Celtic tree month of Muin, which represents harvest time and releases prophetic powers. Muin is sacred to the intellect, spiritual illumination, and the Irish Sun deity, Lugh, god of light.

Born Today: Terry Bradshaw (football player); Marge Champion (dancer); Jimmy Conners (tennis player); Alan Drury (writer); Mark Harmon (actor); Salma Hayek (actress/producer); Clifford Jordan (jazz musician/composer); Lennox Lewis (boxer); Christa McAuliffe (teacher/civilian astronaut); Keanu Reeves (actor)

September 3

♍ Virgo, 3

Those born on this day are known for sharp intellects and their ability to communicate thoughts and ideas. Although you are self-expressive, talkative, and fluent in language, you are also prepared to listen to what others have to say. A deep thinker, you possess a superior memory that allows you to recall important information that you can later use to solve problems quickly and efficiently. On the one hand, you are expansive, philosophical, and eager for learning and adventure, but on the other, you're practical, analytical, and eminently sensible. Ultimately, the innate enthusiasm and optimism of your outer personality overcomes the inherent caution of your more serious inner self.

A hard worker, you can succeed in virtually any occupation. However, your idealism makes it important for you to find a career that arouses your passion and dedication. Although you can be critical of others, you are invariably hardest on yourself. You are eager to help people whenever you can, and many born on this day are drawn to occupations in medicine, law, science, social work, government, education, and journalism. Others may choose more creative career paths in the arts and entertainment.

In intimate relationships, you need freedom as well as love. You're something of a perfectionist, which can create a gap between your romantic dreams and everyday reality. You want to find true love, but few people are able to live up to your high ideals.

On This Day:

Every year on this date, the Maidens of the Four Directions are honored in a Hopi Indian women's healing ceremony known as the Lakon. The Akan people of Ghana, Africa, hold their annual Path Clearing Festival, called Akwambo, on this day each year to honor and receive the blessings of their ancient god of the sacred well.

Born Today: Carl D. Anderson (physicist); Eileen Brennan (actress); Loren Eiseley (anthropologist); Jeffrey Goldstone (physicist); Kitty Carlisle Hart (actress/singer/writer); Alan Ladd (actor); Valerie Perrine (actress); Geraldine Saunders (astrologer/writer); Charlie Sheen (actor); Louis H. Sullivan (architect)

September 4

♍ Virgo, 4

The diligent individual born on this day is intent on constructing a firm foundation for others to build upon. The need for stability in your own life plays a huge role in your desire to help establish order in the world around you. With your interesting mixture of practicality, personal ambition, and sensitivity to the problems of others, you want to be involved in work that helps advance society and promotes good will among its people. Despite your ambitious nature, however, you are patient enough to carefully analyze the various aspects of a situation before taking action.

September 4th individuals have faith in their own abilities. If you have misgivings or insecurities, you keep them well hidden beneath a mask of confidence. You believe that others don't truly understand or appreciate your capabilities, and you trust your own instincts more than anyone else's opinion. Your penetrating intellect and technical and mechanical abilities help you understand how things function and how to keep them performing at optimum levels. You could be successful in almost any occupation, but your idealism makes it important for you to find a vocation that engages your passions.

In a close union, you're extremely loyal. When you commit to a relationship, you stick with it through good times and bad. You can be critical and demanding, but when your demands are met, you're capable of giving your all for love.

On This Day:

At sunrise on this date each year, the Native American Apache tribe of Arizona begins its annual Changing Woman Ceremony. The rite, which lasts for four consecutive days, marks the coming of age of female members of the tribe. During the ceremony, the initiates are ritually transformed into the spirit goddess, Changing Woman.

Born Today: David H. Burnham (architect); Craig Claiborne (food writer); Dawn Frazier (swimmer); Mitzi Gaynor (dancer/singer); Liz Green (astrologer); Beyonce Knowles (singer); Darius Milhaud (composer); Mike Piazza (baseball player); Ione Skye (actress); Tom Watson (golfer); Richard Wright (writer)

September 5

♍ Virgo, 5

The virgin born on this day is a rebel with a cause. While other members of your Sun sign are striving to bring order out of chaos, you're a paradigm-buster attempting to inject the established order with some fresh, original ideas. You possess a paradoxical nature that is sensible and practical on the one hand, unconventional and avant-garde on the other. As a result, you're a one-of-a-kind visionary capable of materializing your dreams and ideas in the real world. Your ability to focus on what actually works allows you to use your creativity to produce ground-breaking innovations in art or science.

Those born on this date are independent, critical, and judgmental. Although you hate it when anyone tells you what to do, you readily advise other people how to live their lives. Yet you have a kind heart, and you're eager to help others whenever you can. Your notion of the right way to do things, however, may lead you to believe that everything must be done your way. Career fields likely to attract your interest include entertainment and the arts, the sciences, the law, education, medicine, sports, and politics.

In relationships, you need more freedom than the typical Virgo. You are idealistic, and your innate perfectionism may create a gap between your romantic dreams and everyday reality. You want to find true love, but few can live up to your high standards.

On This Day:

The neopagan goddess month of Hesperis ends on this day. Ganesh, the elephant-headed Hindu god of good luck and prosperity is honored on this day throughout India with parades and festivals of rejoicing. In ancient Rome, the Roman Games were held in honor of the god Jupiter. They began annually on this date and lasted until the thirteenth day of September.

Born Today: John Cage (composer); William DeVane (actor); Cathy Guisewite (cartoonist); Werner Herzog (director); Arthur Koestler (writer); Carol Lawrence (singer/actress); Freddy Mercury (rock star); Bob Newhart (comedian); Susumu Tonegawa (molecular biologist); Raquel Welch (actress); Dweezil Zapper (guitarist)

September 6

♍ Virgo, 6

Although the affable, sociable individuals celebrating birthdays today appear self-sufficient, they are "people who need people." With your tendency to seek advice and approval, you can be easily influenced by other people's opinions. You possess impeccable manners and are tactful and diplomatic with everyone you meet. With your delicate sensibilities and love of beauty and harmony, you find people or situations that are boorish, crude, or vulgar extremely distasteful. You have a knack for using your considerable charm to gain the upper hand and convince others to do your bidding.

Virgo natives born on September 6 are self-expressive, creative, imaginative, artistic, and musical. You love your home and derive great joy from being surrounded by family and friends. Although you come off as always upbeat and sunny, you have a hidden, serious side to your character. You enjoy nurturing and caring for people, especially those who aren't able to take care of themselves. Moreover, you refuse to give up on people and have helped many a grateful acquaintance stave off disaster. You could find your professional niche in one of the helping occupations or in a field requiring artistic or literary talent.

You are a good deal more affectionate and romantic than the typical Virgo native. Love matters to you, but so does friendship. When you find the security and contentment you're looking for, you make a caring, generous, considerate partner.

On This Day:

The Hindu Festival of Durga is held around this time each year. As the days grow short, the goddess Kali is invoked to protect goodness from the evils that dwell in the shadows. Today is also sacred to Temazcalteci, the Aztec goddess of cleanliness, who keeps demon spirits away from bathers. Her name means "grandmother of the baths."

Born Today: Jane Addams (social reformer/founder of Hull House); Jane Curtin (actress); Johnny Kelley (runner); Joseph P. Kennedy (financier/ambassador to the U.K.); Swoozie Kurtz (actress); Marquis de Lafayette (French general); Rosie Perez (actress); Billy Rose (entrepreneur/showman/songwriter); Page Smith (historian)

September 7

♍ Virgo, 7

The enigmatic individuals born on this day are deep thinkers who play their cards close to the chest. Others may regard you as secretive or mysterious because your somewhat solitary nature is much given to private contemplation. Capable and self-sufficient, you can't bear it when your plans are interfered with. You like working at your own pace, and when left to your own devices, you get the job done. Answers arrived at by other people rarely satisfy you because you prefer figuring things out for yourself.

Unlike other virgins, those born on September 7 think with their hearts and follow their instincts. Despite a tendency to be highly critical of everyone and everything, your own sensitivity and touchiness make it difficult for you to deal with criticism or disapproval that is aimed at you. This combination of the practicality, efficiency, and perfectionism of your intellectual Virgo Sun, along with the spirituality, creativity, and imagination of the number seven, produces an odd dichotomy of artistic temperament and scientific mentality. This mix bodes especially well for a career in medicine, scientific research, social services, education, the media, the arts, politics, or religion.

A loving union is high on your list of priorities, and without it you may retreat into the fantasy world of your imagination. In a close relationship, your emotional inner nature craves tenderness and warmth, but your cerebral, rational side prefers stimulating intellectual companionship.

On This Day:

This day is sacred to Asclepigenia of Athens, a pagan philosopher and priestess of the Greek Eleusinian mysteries. Asclepigenia applied her knowledge of Plato and Aristotle to metaphysical and religious questions. Daena, the maiden goddess of the Parsee community, is honored on this date each year with a religious festival in India.

Born Today: Corbin Bernsen (actor); Michael DeBakey (cardiac surgeon); Elizabeth I (queen of England); Gloria Gaynor (singer); Buddy Holly (singer); Julie Kavner (actress); Elia Kazan (director); Grandma Moses (artist); Sonny Rollins (jazz musician); James Van Allen (physicist)

September 8

♍ Virgo, 8

The highly responsible people celebrating birthdays today are willing workers always ready to lend a hand. Practical problems occupy your mind, and you know how to exclude extraneous thoughts from your psyche and concentrate on the plans you consider truly important. You make no apologies for your ambition and materialistic values. To your mind, public recognition and substantial financial rewards are fair compensation for a job well done. You may be eminently loyal to your company and respectful of those in authority, but you function even better when you're the one charge.

September 8th individuals are mentally sharp and meticulous in the execution of their ideas. Outwardly cool and calm, you're particularly good at solving problems and dealing with sudden emergencies. A born executive, your business sense and organizational skills are exceptionally sound. Although you may be considerably less sure of yourself on the inside, you never let it show. Your apparent confidence inspires confidence in others and encourages them to follow your lead. You could be successful in virtually any profession, but you're best suited to a career that calls for quick thinking, efficiency, and leadership.

You may seem somewhat aloof on the outside, but your inner self is both kindhearted and vulnerable. Once you overcome your fear of emotional involvement, you make a caring, loyal, totally dependable friend or lover.

On This Day:

The feast of the Birth of the Blessed Virgin Mary has been celebrated in the Catholic Church since the eighth century C.E. It was started in 695 when Pope Servius was told about a monk who heard a heavenly choir each year on this day. When the monk asked the angels why they were singing, they said it was because this was the Virgin Mary's birthday.

Born Today: Louis Barrault (actor/director); Sid Caesar (comedian/actor); Patsy Cline (singer); Antonin Dvorak (composer); Sam Nunn (U.S. senator); Claude Pepper (U.S. congressman); Richard I, "The Lionhearted" (king of England); Peter Sellers (actor); Robert Taft (U.S. senator); Henry Thomas (actor); Jonathan Taylor Thomas (actor)

September 9

♍ Virgo, 9

The typical virgin born on this day is a warrior with the heart of a poet. Virgo's intellect and practicality, combined with the intuition and imagination of the number nine's vibration, provide you with your scientific mind and artistic temperament. Like a prickly pear, you have a somewhat thorny outer skin, but you're a lot softer and sweeter on the inside. Your courage and adventurous spirit give you the wherewithal to confront any challenge or undertake any crusade. And your sensitive, sympathetic nature makes you charitable, caring, and willing to aid people and animals in need.

People whose birthdays fall on this day are sincerely devoted to their ideals. Your main focal point may be humanitarian, political, artistic, or spiritual; but no matter where your interest lies, you are prepared to sacrifice everything for your beliefs. The dreamy emotionality of your inner nature exerts a powerful influence that is essentially foreign to Virgo's cautious realism. As a result, you are considerably more impulsive and likely to go to extremes than most of your Sun sign counterparts. Sometimes you get so carried away by your impractical ideas that your potential for doing good gets lost in the shuffle.

In love, you crave total union with another soul. Yet you're rather touchy and inclined to reserve a part of yourself that you can't, or won't, share with anyone. You are romantic and passionate one moment, moody and enigmatic the next.

On This Day:

Around this time each year, people in China drink chrysanthemum wine and add chrysanthemum petals to their salads for longevity and wisdom. They honor Tao Yuan-Ming, a Chinese poet who was deified as god of the chrysanthemum. Traditionally, this day is considered a weather marker. Nice weather today means forty fine days lie ahead.

Born Today: Angela Cartwright (actress); Hugh Grant (actor); James Hilton (writer); Elvin Jones (jazz musician); Michael Keaton (actor); Billy Preston (keyboardist); Otis Redding (singer); Cliff Robertson (actor); Adam Sandler (comedian/actor); Roger Waters (rock star); Michelle Williams (actress)

September 10

♍ Virgo, 1

People born on this date are quick to spot opportunity, and they have the wherewithal to excel at almost anything that catches their fancy. Ambitious, strong-willed, persistent, and meticulous, you are considerably more self-confident than other natives of your Sun sign. Determined to rise to a position of power and prestige, you're prepared to work as hard and as long as necessary to achieve your personal goals. You know what you want, you're not afraid to pursue it, and you're not likely to stop until you get it.

Your desire to reach the top of your profession is enhanced by your knack for dealing with people and your ability to make helpful connections in your chosen field. Although you may seem acquiescent, you're not likely to be content in a subordinate position. You're a natural leader with a way of motivating others by making them feel that their contributions are useful and important. Exacting and sensitive, you're an idealist with high standards, and you demand the best from yourself and everyone else. Always honest and straightforward in your dealings, you expect nothing less in return.

Although physically you are ardent and loving, emotionally you tend to blow hot and cold. Since a true meeting of the minds is as important to you as romance, if you don't find it, you may prefer living life on your own.

On This Day:

Around this date each year, the village of Abbots Bromley in Staffordshire, England, hosts the Ceremony of the Deermen. Starting at dawn, horned dancers wearing reindeer antlers and carrying poles with antlers escort Robin Hood, Maid Marion, court jesters, and others dressed in medieval costumes and riding hobbyhorses in a fun-filled parade.

Born Today: Bernard Bailyn (historian); Jose Feliciano (singer); Stephen Jay Gould (paleontologist); Amy Irving (actress); Randy Johnson (baseball player); Charles Kuralt (TV journalist); Roger Maris (baseball player); Arnold Palmer (golfer); Ryan Phillippe (actor); Uma Sumac (singer); Franz Werfel (writer); Robert Wise (director)

September 11

♍ Virgo, 2

Virgins celebrating birthdays on this day are charming and sociable, with a gift for seeing all sides of a situation. You possess a magnetic personality, well-developed insight and intuition, and high ideals. Your contradictory nature is an unusual blend of humility and confidence. On one level, you yearn for independence, yet on another you truly enjoy being part of a couple, group, or team. When you're feeling inspired, you show amazing persistence in carrying out your plans and ideas. Otherwise, you may scatter your energies and have difficulty focusing on your goals.

The challenge of September 11 involves working toward self-mastery materially and/or spiritually. Your professional accomplishments depend on your ability to get the disparate sides of your character to perform together. As a practical thinker and capable doer, you can further your creativity by learning to trust your instincts. A career in the arts, literature, or the media would allow you to use the full range of your mental and creative talents. Since you display both the human touch and the ability to grasp technical details, you may be attracted to an occupation in science, medicine, education, law, or business.

You love intensely, yet matters of the heart can prove to be your undoing. You thrive on cheerful company, warmth, and affection, but your quest for the perfect love makes you especially vulnerable to hurt and disappointment.

On This Day:

Today is the anniversary of the devastating attack on the United States of America that killed more than 3,000 people and changed the world forever. In Egypt, a festival known as the Day of Queens is celebrated in honor of Queen Hatshepsut, Queen Nefertiti, and Queen Cleopatra, who were worshiped as goddesses in ancient times.

Born Today: Franz Beckenbauer (soccer player/coach); Paul "Bear" Bryant (football coach); Brian DePalma (director); Lola Falana (singer/dancer); Louis Joliet (explorer/priest); Tom Landry (football coach); D. H. Lawrence (writer); Herbert Lom (actor); Kristy McNichol (actress); O. Henry (writer); Arvo Part (composer)

September 12

The person born on this day is an unusual combination of broad philosophical idealism and detail-oriented practicality. You have an adaptable intellect that moves effortlessly from the general to the specific and back again. Your flexibility and capacity for critical analysis help you deal with the large concepts and small technical aspects of any problem or situation. Mentally alert and physically active, you're quick thinking, fast moving, straightforward, and sincere. As a skilled communicator, you possess the courage to speak your mind regardless of possible repercussions.

Those celebrating birthdays on September 12 are personable, intelligent, witty, and fun to be around. Your restlessness and nervous temperament make it difficult for you to stay cooped up for long periods. When you feel the tension building, you need to get some exercise or spend time outdoors where you can be close to nature. In business, you profit by tempering your frank, outspoken manner with a modicum common sense. Career fields likely to attract your interest include travel, education, law, science, and sports. In the creative area, you have a distinct flair for drama, writing, and public speaking.

You make friends easily and enjoy meeting new people and visiting new places. In a close relationship, you are loyal and responsible, but prone to bouts of boredom and discontent if life becomes dull or humdrum. You need a partner who is capable of providing mental stimulation along with love and affection.

On This Day:

In France on this day each year, people gather in the central produce markets to search for the Mother of all Pumpkins. Once found, the squash is decorated and enthroned at the annual Pumpkin Festival. At the conclusion of the festivities, the pumpkin is cut open, made into bread and soup, and shared among those attending the festival.

Born Today: Ben Blue (comedian); Maurice Chevalier (actor/singer); Linda Gray (actress); Henry Hudson (navigator/explorer); Benjamin McKenzie (actor); Yao Ming (basketball player); Maria Muldaur (singer); Jesse Owens (runner/jumper); Peter Scolari (actor); Rachel Ward (actress); Barry White (singer)

September 13

♍ Virgo, 4

The ambitious virgin born on this day has an infinite capacity for hard work. Structure and order are the touchstones of your existence. Leaving nothing to chance, you formulate your plans carefully and carry them out with precision and efficiency. Your realistic view of life gives you great respect for wealth, status, and other manifestations of worldly accomplishment. Yet despite your preoccupation with practical problems, humanitarian concerns loom large in your mind. You are charitable and caring, with a compelling need to serve society in some meaningful way.

Those celebrating birthdays on September 13 possess a strong sense of purpose and an indomitable will that keeps them going long after others have run out of steam. Although you may have to overcome many obstacles on your way to the top, the ultimate outcome is never really in doubt. Others may think that luck or magical powers are somehow responsible for your good fortune. However, it's actually your persistence and dedication, not luck, that is the basis of your success.

As a lover or friend, you're extremely loyal and totally dependable. Because of your workaholic tendencies, you may appear less interested in love and romance than you really are. When you let yourself relax and follow your emotions, you make an extremely thoughtful, kind, and considerate mate or partner.

On This Day:

In ancient Egypt, this day was dedicated to the Ceremony of Lighting the Fire, when lighted lamps were placed in front of the images of the gods. Today is the first day of the runic half-month of Ken, the rune that represents the forge of the creative fire, where natural materials are transmuted by human actions into mystical substances.

Born Today: Fiona Apple (singer/songwriter); Jacqueline Bissett (actress); Nell Carter (actress/singer); Claudette Colbert (actress); Roald Dahl (writer); Roger Howarth (actor); John H. Pershing (U.S. general); Walter Reed (bacteriologist/pathologist); Ben Savage (actor); Jean Smart (actress); David Clayton-Thomas (rock star); Mel Torme (singer)

September 14

♍ Virgo, 5

Those whose birthdays fall on this date are farseeing visionaries with innovative ideas and the unique ability to materialize them in the real world. You're charming and articulate when discussing your thoughts and plans, but you have considerably more difficulty sharing your feelings. You are actually more comfortable analyzing and categorizing your emotions than expressing them. Because you are independent, assertive, intelligent, and ambitious, when you find something you really believe in, you pursue it with a remarkable enthusiasm that virtually guarantees success.

People born on September 14 are among the most intriguing and enigmatic members of the solar Virgo group. Your Sun sign prefers tried and true traditional ways, but the root number five inclines toward the unconventional, avant-garde, and unusual. There is something of the eternal student about you that requires constant mental stimulation. Your inquiring mind wants to know why things are the way they are. Freewheeling and adventurous by nature, you may need repeated doses of variety and change to calm your restive temperament. Sometimes you need to get involved in a physically or mentally challenging project just to avoid boredom.

In an intimate relationship, your emotionally aloof nature can create a huge gap between your romantic dreams and everyday reality. Moreover, idealism tends to make you overly critical. Yet, with the right person, you are capable of giving your all for love.

On This Day:

In Rome, the Feast of the Holy Cross was celebrated on this day in honor of the supernatural vision of a cross in the sky and the ensuing victory in combat of Emperor Constantine I. On this date in 1814, the Battle of Fort McHenry inspired Francis Scott Key to pen "The Star Spangled Banner" while watching from aboard a ship in Baltimore harbor.

Born Today: Larry Brown (basketball player/coach); Larry Collins (writer); Joey Heatherton (actress); Alberto Pedro Calderon (mathematician); Charles Dana Gibson (illustrator); Clayton Moore (actor); Sam Neill (actor); Harve Presnell (actor/singer); Margaret Sanger (nurse/birth control pioneer); Nicol Williamson (actor)

September 15

♍ Virgo, 6

The sociable, charismatic individual celebrating a birthday on this day is happiest when everything runs smoothly, with a minimum of stress or discord. You are a compassionate idealist with a deep sense of responsibility toward family and friends. Moreover, you truly enjoy taking care of others, particularly those who cannot care for themselves. Even when your own life is peaceful, your empathy for those around you has a way of drawing you into their problems. You need to be careful, however, or your sympathy for other people may be taken too far, leaving you open to accusations of meddling in their affairs.

The unique combination of intelligence and charm that characterizes those born on September 15 favors popularity and attracts opportunity. You are rational and analytical on the one hand, creative and artistic on the other. You possess both the human touch and the ability to grasp technical details. A career in the arts or the media would allow you to use the full range of your intellect and creativity. In business and the professions, you could be attracted to occupations in architecture, fashion, design, catering, scientific research, medicine, law, social services, politics, or diplomacy.

In love, you're a genuine romantic, and partnership is extremely important to you. Although it may take you awhile to make a firm commitment, when you do, you expect to be in it for the long haul.

On This Day:

Chinese emperor Ming Wong was in his garden when he asked a priest what the Moon was made of. Instead of answering, the priest transported the emperor to the Moon. When he returned, the emperor spent his days showering his people with gold coins, explaining the miracle had happened because that day was the Moon's birthday.

Born Today: Robert Benchley (writer); Agatha Christie (writer); Jackie Cooper (actor); James Fenimore Cooper (writer); Tommy Lee Jones (actor); Dan Marino (football player); Merlin Olsen (football player/sportscaster/actor); Oliver Stone (director); William Howard Taft (U.S. president); Fay Wray (actress)

September 16

♍ Virgo, 7

The typical Virgo native born on this day is a thoughtful, contemplative, analytical truth seeker. Unable to accept a thing at surface value, you strive to discover its underlying reason or cause. Although not necessarily religious in the traditional sense, you have a deeply spiritual nature that could lead to the study of alternative or unorthodox belief systems. Your reserved manner and mystical aura sets you apart from other people and allows you to tune into life's subtler aspects. Musical, poetic, or artistic ability is quite common among those with this birth date, and you may be skilled in writing, dancing, drama, or painting.

The intriguing and enigmatic September 16th person is a critical intellectual who does not suffer fools gladly. Basically secretive and suspicious of other people's motives, you build trust slowly, and few are granted admittance to your private world. A born sleuth, you're constantly probing and prodding for the answers to life's mysteries. Moreover, the opinions and solutions arrived at by others do not satisfy you. You prefer figuring things out for yourself by researching a subject on your own. You'd make an excellent detective, researcher, psychologist, doctor, lawyer, systems analyst, or preacher.

In an intimate union, you are loving and loyal, but also critical and demanding. However, once you are committed to a relationship, you're inclined stick with it through good times and bad.

On This Day:

Mexican Independence Day commemorates this date in 1810 when Miguel Hidalgo, a parish priest, issued a declaration of Mexico's freedom from Spanish rule. The revolt that followed ended in victory in 1822. The holiday begins with Mexico's president voicing "El Grito" (the Cry for Freedom), followed by parades and fireworks.

Born Today: Marc Anthony (singer); Lauren Bacall (actress); Tina Barrett (golfer); Ed Begley, Jr. (actor); Dennis Connor (yachtsman); David Copperfield (illusionist); Peter Falk (actor); Allen Funt (TV host); Henry V (king of England); Mickey Rourke (actor/boxer); Jennifer Tilly (actress); Robin Yount (baseball player)

September 17

♍ Virgo, 8

Virgins born on this day are specialists who employ their talents and training in very specific ways. With your single-minded thoroughness, you fare particularly well in those endeavors that require persistence and strict attention to detail. You possess an indomitable strength of purpose that makes it extremely difficult for anyone to divert your attention from your goals. Success comes to you through you own ingenuity and through your knack for promoting yourself and your ideas in the world marketplace. Your unique combination of level-headedness and intuition allows you to come up with innovative ideas that work on a practical level.

People with birthdays on September 17 are friendly, compassionate, and kindhearted, but also serious and self-contained. Guided by good sense and a strong need for security, you have a natural shrewdness with money and material possessions. Inherently self-restrained, you like to take your time before making important decisions. You rarely start anything unless you're sure you can finish it. You put your faith in logic and reason and solve problems through careful analysis. With these traits, you're well suited to a career in business, science, research, technology, law, medicine, or education.

In an intimate relationship, you're sensual and affectionate. You show how much you care by being helpful and dependable. People born under some other Sun signs may be more exciting, but none is more loving, trustworthy, or responsible.

On This Day:

This is the first day of the Egyptian month of Hathor, the beloved sky goddess and patron of lovers. In ancient Greece, the goddess Demeter was honored annually on this date with a festival of secret women's rites. This is also the natal day of the German visionary nun Hildegard of Bingen, the abbess of Rupertsburg, who was called the "Sybil of the Rhine."

Born Today: Frederick Ashton (dancer/choreographer/director of the Royal Ballet); Ann Bancroft (actress); George Blanda (football player); Mark Brunell (football player); Ken Kesey (writer); Roddy McDowall (actor); Cassandra "Elvira" Peterson (actress/TV host); John Ritter (actor); Hank Williams (singer/songwriter)

September 18

♍ Virgo, 9

The individual celebrating his or her birthday today is self-sufficient, serious, and mysterious. Inherently secretive and suspicious of people's motives, you limit admittance to your private world to a small number of trusted associates. Ironically, the main obstacles to the privacy you covet are your prodigious talent and your ability to attain the type of worldly success that inevitably leads to celebrity status. Moreover, the harder you try to hide from the spotlight, the more public interest you seem to attract. You are considerably more emotional than others of your Sun sign. When your personal feelings come into play, your responses are usually more instinctive than logical.

Those born on September 18 are compassionate humanitarians with a tremendous capacity for understanding the joys and sorrows of the human condition. You're actually less self-confident than you appear, and your sensitive nature makes it difficult for you to deal with the criticism or disapproval of others. Despite your talent for overcoming difficult challenges in times of trouble, in those times when everything is going well, you may be plagued by self-doubt and nervous anxiety about the future.

Although you appear glamorous, illusive, and enigmatic on the surface, you are actually quite shy and unsure of yourself. Your public mask is little more than a ploy to hide private insecurities. It may take a great deal of tenderness, understanding, and acceptance on the other person's part to win your love and devotion.

On This Day:

The festival of Scouring the White Horse takes place on this date each year in Berkshire, England. People gather at the hillside to help clean the huge, centuries-old clay figure of the White Horse of Uffington, which is carved into the landscape. The festival, which lasts for two days, also includes various games and athletic competitions.

Born Today: Eddie "Rochester" Anderson (actor); Lance Armstrong (cyclist); Frankie Avalon (singer/actor); Robert Blake (actor); William Collins (artist); Agnes DeMille (dancer/choreographer); James Gandolfini (actor); Gretta Garbo (actress); Edwin McMillan (physicist); Jada Pinkett Smith (actress); Jack Warden (actor)

September 19
♍ Virgo, 1

People born on this day are ambitious and have an intense desire for success and recognition. While you tend to project more self-confidence than you actually feel, you are so fiercely independent that your insecurities are rarely noticeable. There are, however, certain inconsistencies in your makeup. You have big plans and noble ideas, but you may have trouble putting them into effect. You would accomplish more by acting first and talking about it later, instead of the other way around.

September 19th individuals like winning, and their naturally competitive temperaments encourage them to take risks that other Virgos would rather avoid. Innately sociable and friendly, you like people and enjoy exchanging ideas with everyone you meet. You are intuitive, sensitive to the thoughts and feelings around you, and easily influenced by conditions outside yourself. With your crusading nature and empathy for people's problems, you have a way for getting involved in everyone's troubles. Mentally alert and precise in your actions, you're particularly good at dealing with emergencies.

You're a good deal more emotional and romantic than the typical virgin, and your touchy feelings are easily hurt. However, when you find security and contentment in a relationship, you're an extremely caring, affectionate, loyal, and loving partner. Your inherent generosity makes you anxious to please your significant other. In return, you expect nothing less than his or her undying appreciation.

On This Day:

In the Alexandrian calendar, this date signified a day-long fast in honor of Thoth, the god of learning, wisdom, and magic. Thoth gave the Egyptians hieroglyphic writing and mathematics. On this day in ancient Babylonia, an annual festival of prayers and feasts was held in honor of Gula, the goddess of birth.

Born Today: Jim Abbott (baseball player); "Mama" Cass Elliott (singer); Jeremy Irons (actor); Leslie "Twiggy" Lawson (model); Joan Lunden (TV talk show host); Randolph Mantooth (actor); David McCallum (actor); Alison Sweeney (actress); Trisha Yearwood (singer); Adam West (actor); Paul Williams (singer/songwriter)

September 20
♍ Virgo, 2

Virgins born on this day are devoted to the welfare of others. You have a kind, sympathetic nature that makes you caring, considerate, and eager to help people in need. When your compassionate nature urges you to answer the call, you do so willingly. Moreover, you're prepared to give of yourself in every sense, including financially. An excellent organizer and manager, you work hard to insure the smooth, harmonious running of the projects and enterprises you're involved in.

Those with birthdays on September 20 may be agreeable, but they are not pushovers. Rarely will you do anything you don't want to do, but you have a way of getting others to go along with *your* plans and ideas. As a peacemaker, your capacity for understanding all sides of an argument helps you bring the bickering factions together. You can always be counted on in an emergency. Although you may worry before and after the fact, you rarely panic during a crisis. Career areas that could be of particular interest to you include social work, psychological counseling, human resources, medicine, education, and business.

On a personal level, you can find it rather difficult to relax and express your deepest feelings. However, partnership has a very high priority for you. It may take you awhile to make a commitment, but when you do, you're in it for the long term.

On This Day:

South of the equator, the spring equinox falls on or around this date. The Inca considered this day the Sun's birthday and honored their Sun god with feasting, sacrifices, and divinations. Festivals were held throughout South and Central America to celebrate the birthday of the god Quetzalcoatl, who was known as the Feathered Serpent.

Born Today: Red Auerbach (basketball coach); Dr. Joyce Brothers (psychologist); Sister Elizabeth Kenny (pioneer nurse); Anne Meara (comedienne/actress); Ferdinand "Jelly Roll" Morton (jazz musician/composer); Sophia Loren (actress); Fernando Rey (actor); Stevie Smith (writer); Upton Sinclair (writer/social activist); Vittorio Taviani (director)

September 21

♍ Virgo, 3

The skilled communicator born on this day is charming and sociable, with a quick wit and a terrific sense of humor. An original thinker, you have a unique approach to problem solving. With your ability to think outside the curve, you eliminate what is no longer useful and replace it with fresh, innovative ideas. Highly intelligent, creative, and analytical, you possess a special talent for uncovering new trends in thought. Although you're more of a fashion style-setter than a follower, you keep up with the prevailing tastes of the time. As a result, you always know what's hot and what's not.

With their exuberant personalities, excellent communication skills, creative talents, and physical dexterity, September 21st individuals are well suited to career fields that put them in the public eye, such as the arts, the media, professional sports, and politics. People consider you lucky, because even your problems and difficulties seem to have a way of working out for the best. However, it's not luck as much as hard work and good sense that allows you to achieve your dreams.

In relationships, you require more personal freedom than other Virgo natives. Sentimental and idealistic, your perfectionism may create a gap between your ideals and everyday reality. Since you value friendship and companionship as much as love and romance, you need a partner who challenges you intellectually.

On This Day:

The Egyptian Feast of Divine Life is dedicated to the three-fold goddess: the mother (the creator of all things), the daughter (the renewer), and the crone (the absolute), In ancient Greece, this date was celebrated as the birthday of Athena. In England, Saint Matthew's Day is a marker for predicting the weather and time for performing divinations.

Born Today: Leonard Cohen (singer/songwriter); Dave Coulier (actor); Henry Gibson (comedian); Cecil Fielder (baseball player); Larry Hagman (actor); Faith Hill (singer); Stephen King (writer); Ricki Lake (actress/TV talk show host); Joseph Mazzello (actor); Rob Morrow (actor); Bill Murray (comedian/actor); H. G. Wells (writer)

September 22

♍ Virgo, 4

Persons born on the Virgo/Libra cusp are extremely sensitive to their surroundings, and they require a harmonious environment in which to live and work. Focused and dedicated, you exhibit a practical, down-to-earth dynamic that often leads to material success and achievement. You have a sixth sense with regard to current developments, and you pride yourself on being up to date and aware of the latest trends in fashion, art, and technology. While your personal approach to change is inherently cautious, your intuitive understanding of what is worth keeping from the past and what should be discarded could prove particularly valuable in business and commerce.

Despite an ambitious nature, the September 22nd person is patient enough to wait for the best possible opportunity before making any important moves. Because of your ability to see all sides of a situation, you sometimes have difficulty coming to a concrete decision. There are actually two distinct sides to your personality. You can be charming and concerned on the one hand, yet critical and disapproving on the other.

You appear more self-sufficient than you actually are. Your critical Virgo nature makes you seem cool and detached, but your birth date on the Libra cusp means that you really want companionship. You may discover that you're not truly happy until you find someone to share your life.

On This Day:

In the northern hemisphere, the autumnal equinox falls on or around this date each year. During this time, darkness overtakes light, and the nights grow longer than the days. Today also marks the Druidic festival of Alban Elfed, or the light of the water (called Mabon by the Welsh), when the Sun begins to descend into the ocean of winter.

Born Today: Scott Baio (actor); Shari Belafonte-Harper (singer/actress); Andrea Bocelli (opera singer); Tai Babilonia (skater); Debbie Boone (singer); Tom Felton (actor); Joan Jett (rock star); Ingemar Johansson (boxer); Tommy Lasorda (baseball manager); Paul Muni (actor); Yang Chen Ning (physicist); Erich von Stroheim (director/actor)

September 23

♎ Libra, 5

Libra natives born on this day are charming, witty, and communicative. Typically, you possess an amiable personality and a sunny disposition that assures your popularity wherever you go. Although you are friendly toward everyone, you usually prefer the company of mentally stimulating individuals who share your cultural and artistic interests. Because of your open, friendly nature, you rarely seem down or depressed. Your knack for coping with the unexpected gives you the confidence to try different things and engage in unusual and exciting new ventures. A considerable amount of luck and good fortune follows you around and helps you bounce back from difficulties.

People celebrating birthdays on this date enjoy occupying center-stage, and they want to be accepted and well thought of by others. Self-expression is your great strength, and you are a superb conversationalist. Your eloquence and ability to present your ideas clearly and tactfully make you particularly well suited to a career in the media, education, law, politics, advertising, publicity, or sales. For many born today, artistic and dramatic talent goes hand in hand with literary fluency, and these Libras often go on to become artists, writers, actors, or musicians.

Solar Libra's tendency to think in terms of "we" and "us" is diminished to some extent by the freedom-loving vibration of the root number five. Although you are affectionate and caring, you project a certain airy detachment even in your most intimate relationships. Your ideal love combines romance with friendship and intellectual rapport.

On This Day:

Beginning on this day, the sacred festival of Greater Eleusinia was celebrated in honor of the goddess Demeter and her daughter Persephone. It was a secret observance, open only to initiates of the Eleusinian mysteries. The rite of Eleusinia commemorates the descent of Persephone into the underworld for the winter months.

Born Today: Jason Alexander (actor); Octavius Augustus Caesar (emperor of Rome); Ray Charles (singer/songwriter/pianist); John Coltrane (jazz musician/composer); Julio Iglesias (singer/songwriter); Tom Lester (actor); Walter Lippmann (writer); Mary Kay Place (actress); Mickey Rooney (actor); Bruce Springsteen (rock star)

September 24

Libra, 6

The quintessential Libra native celebrating a birthday on this date is imaginative and creative and has an innate love of music, art, and beauty. With your excellent taste, you value everything that is attractive and pleasing to the senses. You particularly enjoy being surrounded by lovely objects in a tranquil and luxurious environment. However, relationships mean more to you than material things, and you're devoted to your family and friends. Your amiable nature, genial disposition, and knack for understanding differing points of view make you extremely easy to live with.

As an idealist with an almost mystical faith people, you believe in the importance of teamwork, cooperation, and compromise in human relations. Although you thrive on debate and discussion, you dislike quarreling and rarely lose your temper. You have a strong sense of justice and will do everything possible to see that everyone enjoys an equal chance in life. You like working for good causes, and you're usually able to inspire others to join as well. Your fine intellect and judicial mind help you evaluate the world dispassionately, making you an excellent candidate for a career in law, education, politics, or diplomacy.

You thrive on the love, affection, and attention of your significant other. Courtship is your forte, and you will go the whole nine yards in order to provide a pleasant, romantic atmosphere for yourself and your partner.

On This Day:

In ancient Egypt, the death and rebirth of the god Osiris was celebrated annually on this date. A festival held in his honor consisted of songs, dances, and ceremonial plantings. In West Africa, this day is sacred to the hermaphrodite deity Obatala, who is believed to have given birth to all the Yoruban gods and goddesses.

Born Today: F. Scott Fitzgerald (writer); Phil Hartman (comedian/actor/artist/writer); Jim Henson (puppeteer/director/producer); Linda McCartney (singer/photographer); Jim McKay (sportscaster); Sheila McRae (singer/actress); Anthony Newley (actor); Charlotte M. Sitterly (astrophysicist); Nia Vardalos (writer/actress); John W. Young (astronaut)

September 25

♎ Libra, 7

People with the sign of the scales born on this day are friendly, witty, and charming. Essentially upbeat and outgoing, you adore parties and other social gatherings. However, you're subject to bouts of moodiness, during which you require time alone to engage in quiet contemplation and meditation. Your insight and intuition work in tandem with your agile, analytical mind to glean and disseminate data and information. Physically active and mentally alert, you possess deep reservoirs of wisdom, a decidedly philosophical outlook, and perceptive powers bordering on the psychic.

September 25th individuals have so many new interests and projects always in the works that they are rarely bored and never boring. Your restless nature is continually on the lookout for exciting adventures and challenging experiences. You particularly enjoy traveling, seeing fresh faces, and exploring exotic places. Your strong suit lies in your ability to grasp broad concepts and abstract ideas. The tendency to move from one thing, person, or place to the next keeps you from stagnating. However, too much spontaneity can turn into a liability, especially if it leaves a number of unresolved situations in its wake.

In relationships, you may feel as if you're being pulled in opposite directions. As a romantic, you yearn for companionship. Yet you are independent and hate being tied down. For the best of both worlds, you need to find a partner who loves you and respects your personal space.

On This Day:

Today is the birthday of Sedna, the Inuit goddess of the sea and the underworld. Sedna's natal day is celebrated annually in Greenland, Siberia, and the Arctic coastal regions of North America. On this date each year in ancient Greece, a feast of beans known as the Pyanopsia was held in honor of the great Olympian god Apollo.

Born Today: Michael Douglas (actor/producer); William Faulkner (writer); Mark Hamill (actor); Catherine Zeta-Jones (actress); Heather Locklear (actress); Christopher Reeve (actor/director); Phil Rizzuto (baseball player); Will Smith (actor); Cheryl Tiegs (supermodel); Aida Turturro (actress); Barbara Walters (TV journalist/talk show host)

September 26
♎ Libra, 8

The charm and diplomacy of those born on this date mask a fiercely competitive nature. Outwardly you seem calm and relaxed, yet a steely determination lurks beneath the surface of your easygoing personality. Shrewd and insightful, you're willing to work extra hard in pursuit of your goals. You crave material success and recognition for your accomplishments, and you will almost certainly find a way to get them. Concerned for the welfare of the less fortunate, you manage to be sympathetic and helpful without losing sight of your own agenda and objectives.

September 26th people are intuitive, persuasive, and understanding, as well as practical and clear thinking. You possess both the human touch and the ability to grasp technical details. Although you have a definite flair for business and commerce, your idealism and artistic temperament suggest that you may be better fulfilled in a creative career in the professions, athletics, or the arts. Fields usually associated with this birthday include music, acting, writing, filmmaking, architecture, teaching, psychological counseling, law, social services, diplomacy, and government service.

Your amiable nature, genial disposition, and willingness to compromise make you fairly easy to get along with. In a close relationship, you're capable of total loyalty and devotion to the right person. You may long for a permanent union, but you're so focused on personal goals that it could take quite awhile before you decide to settle down.

On This Day:

Theseus, the Athenian hero who slew the Minotaur and conquered the Amazons, was honored on this date in Greece with a yearly festival called the Theseia. In ancient times, a goat sacrifice was performed annually on this day to appease Azazel, a fallen Hebrew angel who seduced mankind. Azazel was associated with the planet Mars.

Born Today: T. S. Eliot (writer); George Gershwin (composer/pianist); Linda Hamilton (actress); Olivia Newton-John (singer/songwriter/actress); Jack LaLanne (fitness guru); Jack London (writer); Julie London (singer); Ivan Pavlov (physiologist/psychologist); George Raft (actor); Serena Williams (tennis player)

September 27

♎ Libra, 9

People celebrating birthdays on this day are ambitious, yet amiable and sensitive to the moods of others. Inherently tactful, you go out of your way to avoid arguments and unpleasant situations. However, you refuse to tolerate injustice and can usually be found in the forefront of any battle against inequity. As a born detective, you're a stealthy observer of the human condition. Your chameleon-like personality allows you to blend in no matter where you are. Yet your own complex character can be rather difficult for other people to read or understand.

The psychic-like intuition of those born on this day helps them anticipate other people's reactions. Anything you're unable to figure out intellectually, you pick up on intuitively. Genuinely concerned about the problems of others, you have a gift for making everyone feel comfortable and at ease in your presence. Your understanding of the public need bodes especially well for a career in business or the helping professions. Many actors, artists, writers, and musicians are also born on this day, and you may find the best outlet for your own creative talents in the arts or entertainment.

In an intimate relationship, you are romantic, idealistic, kindhearted, and generous. Moreover, you always seem to know exactly what your partner wants. Just remember that love is a partnership, and you are entitled to get as much out of it as you put into it.

On This Day:

In Hawaii, this date marks the beginning of the weeklong Aloha Festival, a celebration of local custom and history complete with dances, parades, and sports competitions. In China, the Moon Festival honors the Moon with rites of thanksgiving for an abundant harvest. Women conduct the rituals, because the Moon represents the yin.

Born Today: Marvin "Meat Loaf" Aday (singer); Louis Auchincloss (writer); Wilford Brimley (actor); Shaun Cassidy (actor); William Conrad (actor); Barbara Howar (TV journalist); Jane Meadows (actress); Greg Morris (actor); Arthur Penn (director); Mike Schmidt (baseball player); Heather Watts (dancer); Kathy Whitworth (golfer)

September 28

♎ Libra, 1

The intelligent, imaginative individual born on this day craves the spotlight and basks in the approval of others. The blend of Libra's inherent good manners with the impulsiveness and aggression of the root number one is a combination of polar opposites. You can be indecisive one moment and impulsive the next. Since you appear more reasonable than you actually are, people often get caught off guard by the iron will hidden beneath your serene exterior. Although your initial approach is tactful, when diplomacy doesn't get the job done, you mount a more direct assault.

The idealism and strong sense of justice common in people celebrating birthdays on this date make them dedicated crusaders for causes they believe in. Since you are usually better at soothing over other people's problems than solving your own, you could be perfectly suited to work as a negotiator, counselor, teacher, lawyer, politician, or diplomat. Creativity and ease of self-expression may draw you to fields connected to the media, art and entertainment, or professional sports. Your ambition and executive abilities bode well for success in the world of business and commerce.

Relationships are central to your life, and you enjoy everything about the rituals connected to romance. Despite your need for change and excitement, you want the companionship of a lasting union. But if the spark goes out of your love, you may begin to look elsewhere.

On This Day:

The first day of the runic half-month of Gyfu falls on this day. On this date in ancient Athens, an annual festival known as the Thesmophoria was celebrated in honor of the Greek goddess Demeter. This is also Michaelmas Eve, a time of preparation for the celebration of the feast of Michaelmas, which honors Michael the Archangel, Captain of the Heavenly Hosts.

Born Today: Brigitte Bardot (actress); Al Capp (cartoonist); Hillary Duff (actress/singer); Peter Finch (actor); Janeane Garofolo (comedienne/actress/radio talk show host); Steve Largent (football player); Gwyneth Paltrow (actress); Marcello Mastroianni (actor); John Sayles (director); Mira Sorvino (actress); Ed Sullivan (columnist/TV variety show host)

September 29

♎ Libra, 2

The September 29th individual is personable and cooperative rather than competitive. Particularly good at dealing with people, you can be counted on in a crisis because you rarely panic. You're a good listener, and your capacity for understanding all sides helps you win over bickering factions. Much of your negotiating success lies in your ability to avoid extreme positions. You respect each person's point of view without losing sight of what's fair and equitable for all concerned.

People born on this day are outgoing and friendly, with an amiable nature and genial disposition. Your willingness to compromise makes you especially easy to get along with. Imaginative and creative, you could probably be successful in any one of the occupations related to the arts and entertainment. Your love of harmony and beauty bodes well for success in fashion, cosmetics, interior design, landscaping, or architecture. Your fine intellect and judicial mind help you evaluate the world dispassionately, and these qualities make you a perfect candidate for a career in law, education, government service, or diplomacy.

Since you are the consummate romantic, other people often have difficulty living up to your idealistic expectations. Although a failed or broken relationship can upset you to the point of actually making you ill, if things get really unpleasant, you could be the one who decides to walk away.

On This Day:

This day is sacred to Gwyn ap Nudd, a Welsh warrior king of the Otherworld, whose sacred mountain is Glasonbury Tor. Today is the festival of the Norse god of light, Heimdall, who is the watcher of the gods and guardian of the Bifrost bridge between Asgard and Earth. His castle, called Himinbiorg, stands at the apex of the bridge.

Born Today: Michelangelo Antonioni (director); Miguel de Cervantes (writer); Sebastian Coe (runner); Anita Ekberg (actress); Enrico Fermi (nuclear physicist); Greer Garson (actress); Bryant Gumbel (TV talk show host); Madeline Kahn (actress); Stanley Kramer (director); Jerry Lee Lewis (rock and roll singer/pianist)

September 30
♎ Libra, 3

Individuals born on this day are enthusiastic, charming, witty, and communicative. A born raconteur and relentless networker, you thoroughly enjoy spending time in smart, interesting company. Thanks to your breezy, lighthearted manner, you are welcome in virtually in any group. You like occupying center-stage and want to be accepted and well thought of by your friends and acquaintances. Despite a reputation as something of a social butterfly, you have a decidedly serious side to your nature. Highly ambitious and conscientious, you possess an agile mind with a tremendous amount of creative potential.

People with September 30th birthdays are superb conversationalists. You're a quick study, and even if you know only a little bit about something, you manage to give the impression of being deeply knowledgeable. You have impeccable taste and a keen eye for beauty. As a gregarious and clever observer of the social scene, you should fare well in an occupation that involves dealing with the public. With self-expression and creativity as your great strengths, you could be successful in most any career area associated with writing, performing, or teaching.

You want a committed, loving relationship, yet you can be rather fickle in your attachments. Actually, friendship and intellectual companionship are as vital to you as love and romance. In an intimate union, you're tender and considerate, but it may take awhile before you decide to settle down with one person.

On This Day:

In India on this date, the annual festival of Lakshimi Puja honors Lakshimi, goddess of good fortune and vegetation. She is the daughter of Brahma-Prajapati and is the wife of Vishnu. As empress of the sea, she's the patroness of fishermen. The festival celebrates her goodness, as manifested in the abundance of the harvest.

Born Today: Monica Bellucci (actress); Truman Capote (writer); Lacey Chabert (actress); Kieran Culkin (actor); Angie Dickenson (actress); Fran Drescher (actress); Jenna Elfman (actress); Martina Hingis (tennis player); Deborah Kerr (actress); Marilyn McCoo (singer); Johnny Mathis (singer); Buddy Rich (jazz musician)

October Birthdays

October 1

♎ Libra, 1

In people born on this date, the assertiveness and individuality of the number one's vibration is often at odds with Libra's spirit of teamwork and cooperation. The result is a dichotomy of independence versus dependence. Your head often tells you one thing, your heart another. Consequently, you may be indecisive one moment and rash and impetuous the next. Although you enjoy the tranquility and harmony of peaceful surroundings, the driving force of your nature is ambition coupled with a desire for worldly success and recognition.

Since the October 1st person appears more reasonable than he or she actually is, others are likely to be caught off guard by the surprisingly strong will hidden beneath your charming exterior. Idealism and a strong sense of justice make you a crusader for those causes you believe in. Since your energy comes in spurts, your tendency is to alternate between periods of intense activity and peaceful relaxation. Creativity, ease of self-expression, and physical dexterity draw many with birthdays on this day to career fields connected to the media, arts and entertainment, the law, politics, or athletics.

Naturally affectionate, romantic, outgoing, and sociable, your relationships are central to your life. A desirable and rewarding partner, you enjoy everything about the rituals of love and romance. Despite your innate love of freedom, you want and need the companionship of a fulfilling, lasting union.

On This Day:

On or around this date each year, hundreds of thousands of Muslims make the pilgrimage to Mecca to touch the Black Stone and drink from the sacred Well of Ishmael. In old Rome, the festival of the goddess Fides was celebrated on this day. Fides is the personification of good faith. Her ancient cult dates back to the time of King Numa.

Born Today: Julie Andrews (actress/singer); Tom Bosley (actor); Jimmy Carter (U.S. president); Rod Carew (baseball player); Richard Harris (actor/singer); Vladimir Horowitz (pianist); Walter Matthau (actor); Mark McGwire (baseball player); George Peppard (actor); Randy Quaid (actor); James Whitmore (actor)

October 2

♎ Libra, 2

The sweet-natured individuals celebrating birthdays today are some of the nicest people in the zodiac. A natural optimist, you refuse to look on the dark side of any situation. Besides being gracious and charming, you're a good listener with the ability to see all sides of an argument. You avoid extreme positions and manage to show respect for everyone's point of view without losing sight of what is equitable for all concerned.

Libra natives born on October 2 are actually not as easygoing as they appear. In your search for the best of everything, you can be as much as of a perfectionist as any Virgo. Your desire for beauty impels you to seek only the finest and most luxurious, and you're always on the lookout for ways to improve life by making it more graceful and harmonious. With your creativity and excellent taste, you could do very well in any occupation related to music, art, literature, architecture, fashion, or interior design. Your judicial mind helps you evaluate the world dispassionately, making you the perfect candidate for a career in politics, law, education, or diplomacy.

As an idealist and admirer of culture and beauty, you naturally gravitate toward others who share your sophisticated tastes and refined interests. Whether searching for the perfect relationship, job, outfit, or decorating touch, you like to take your time and weigh all your options before coming to an irrevocable decision.

On This Day:

Guardian Angel's Day is a pre-Christian Roman holiday that is still celebrated in many parts of Europe. On this date, people give thanks to the guiding spirits that protect them throughout the year. It is considered the perfect time for communicating with spirit guides thorough prayer, meditation, the Ouija board, a trance state, or a dream.

Born Today: Bud Abbott (comedian); Lorraine Bracco (actress); Mahatma Gandhi (nonviolent social activist/religious leader); Donna Karan (designer); Groucho Marx (comedian); George "Spanky" McFarland (actor); Don McLean (singer/songwriter); Rex Reed (movie critic); Kelly Ripa (actress/TV talk show host); Sting (rock star)

October 3

♎ Libra, 3

The self-expressive, talkative person celebrating a birthday on this date is a born raconteur. Friendly, witty, and charming, your clever quips and entertaining stories hold your audience's attention while endearing you to everyone who's listening. Your reputation as a social butterfly is not entirely undeserved, since you adore parties, gatherings, and get-togethers. You like occupying center-stage and want to be well thought of by your friends and acquaintances. Your taste is impeccable, and you possess a keen eye for beauty and style. Nevertheless, despite your obvious social skills and fascination with the beautiful people, you're too cultured to allow yourself to be seduced by the indulgences of *la dolce vita*.

October 3rd persons are dynamic, versatile, intelligent, and imaginative. Physically active and mentally alert, you're constantly on the lookout for challenging new experiences. Naturally artistic and creative, you have a genuine gift for synthesizing your knowledge and ideas and conveying them to others. With your fine mind and interest in art and communication, you could garner success in any occupation associated with photography, television, filmmaking, acting, writing, painting, or music.

You make a loving partner, but friendship and intellectual companionship are as important to you as romance. You think you want a committed relationship, yet you can be rather fickle in your attachments. It may take quite awhile before you actually decide to settle down with one person.

On This Day:

October 3 is the Day of German Unity, a national holiday. It is the anniversary of the 1990 reunification of the East and West zones after forty-five years of division. Dionysus, god of wine, was honored on this date in ancient Greece. Wine from the previous year was mixed with the new wine to celebrate the end of the harvest season.

Born Today: Erik Bruhn (dancer/choreographer); Lindsey Buckingham (rock star); Neve Campbell (actress); Chubby Checker (singer); James Herriot (writer); Roy Horn (magician/animal trainer); Tommy Lee (rock star); Ashlee Simpson (singer); Stevie Ray Vaughan (guitarist); Gore Vidal (writer); Eric von Detton (actor)

October 4

♎ Libra, 4

Individuals born today are strong-minded, ambitious workaholics. Despite Libra's artistic temperament, you have a serious side to your character. Since you're so sweet natured and gracious on the outside, few people are aware of your steely inner resolve. You enjoy being recognized for your accomplishments, but you also need more tangible evidence of your success in the form of material rewards. If it comes down to a choice between fame and fortune, you may decide to take the cash and let the credit go to someone else.

People with birthdays on October 4 know what they want, and one way or another they get it. However, because you place a high value on fairness and justice, you care about doing the right thing. You may want the best for yourself, but you're also sympathetic to the desires of others. Your devotion to the principles of law and order make you well suited to work in law enforcement, social services, government service, or politics. You are imaginative and creative, yet sensible enough to turn your dreams into practical realities. Many prominent individuals in entertainment and the arts were born on this date.

Relating comes naturally to you, and you may feel incomplete without the companionship of a significant other. However, it takes more than just romance to hold your interest. You need someone who shares your goals and your strong sense of purpose.

On This Day:

Today is the feast day of one of the most revered of the Christian saints, Francis of Assisi. He was distinguished for his joyous piety and compassion for all living creatures. The son of a rich merchant, Francis renounced all rights to his inheritance after quarreling with his father about having taken items from the family business to help rebuild a church.

Born Today: Rachael Leigh Cook (actress); Rutherford B. Hayes (U.S. president); Charlton Heston (actor); Buster Keaton (actor/director); Jean-Francois Millet (artist); Lowell Nesbitt (artist); Anne Rice (writer); Damon Runyon (writer); Susan Sarandon (actress); Alicia Silverstone (actress); Alvin Toffler (futurist/writer)

October 5

♎ Libra, 5

The scales' tendency to think in terms of "we" and "us" is tempered by the autonomy of the number five, which represents freedom. While you can be as charming as any other Libra, your diplomatic inclinations tend to fray a bit around the edges when your ideas are challenged. You're a team player, but you want the team to do things your way. Although the conciliatory side of your nature prompts you to go along with the crowd on most things, you refuse to compromise your ideals. Moreover, you don't let your ideology or personal beliefs stand in the way of having a good time.

Despite a controversial streak and an inability to mince words on important issues, you are an extremely skilled negotiator. You're generally more decisive than other members of your Sun sign, and your knack for getting everyone to pull together makes you a strong leader. You have a flair for blending artistry, science, and practical considerations in a way that allows you to see possibilities others miss. A marvelous conversationalist, you are an equally good listener. Although ideas matter to you, people matter even more.

Your love life is a tug-of-war between the independence of your spirit and the desire to find a soul mate. Naturally funny, charming, clever, and stylish, you probably have little trouble attracting companionship. Your ideal union is a harmonious blend of romantic intimacy, friendship, and intellectual rapport.

On This Day:

The Mundus, or second day, of the Roman Festival of Mania was for remembering departed ancestors. The passage to the underworld was opened, and the shamans journeyed to the under-world and then back to the middle world. In Celtic tradition, the gate to the Otherworld opens to allow the spirits of the dead to return for the day.

Born Today: Karen Allen (actress); Chester Alan Arthur (U.S. president); Bob Geldorf (rock star); Richard Gordon (astronaut); Nicki Hilton (socialite); Glynis Johns (actress); Ray Kroc (business entrepreneur); Louis Lumiere (chemist/pioneer filmmaker); Bernie Mac (comedian); Steve Miller (rock star); Kate Winslet (actress)

October 6

♎ Libra, 6

Beauty, harmony, justice, and love are powerful motifs in the lives of those born on this date. You have high expectations and little tolerance for anything you perceive as unpleasant or unjust. Your affable nature is cooperative rather than competitive, and you are particularly good at dealing with people. Cooperation is one of your main assets, and persuasion is another. Your forte is your amazing ability to bring people together and mold a group of diverse individuals into a comprehensive whole.

People whose birthdays fall on October 6 are romantic idealists who prefer looking at the world through rose-colored glasses. Your appreciation of the good things in life includes pleasant, harmonious surroundings and the beauties of nature. You like socializing and attending parties. You love entertaining in your own home and derive great joy from spending time with family and friends. In a working environment, you seek balance and harmony. You can be successful in any career that allows you to combine your love of beauty with your sense of fair play and desire to please.

Since you don't like living or working alone, relationships are the main focus of your life. You just don't feel complete without a partner. In fact, love is so important that you may find yourself falling more in love with the "idea" of love than with the actual person who serves as the object of your affections.

On This Day:

On this date in Nepal, an annual nine-day religious festival begins in commemoration of the Hindu god Vishnu. Traditionally, secret offerings are made to the god and placed in unripe pumpkins. In northern England, cakes baked in honor of Saint Faith of Foi were used to divine the identities of the future husbands of young women.

Born Today: Paul Badura-Skoda (pianist); Britt Ekland (supermodel/actress); Thor Heyerdahl (adventurer/writer); Amy Jo Johnson (actress); Le Corbusier (architect/city planner); Carol Lombard (actress); Edwin Fischer (pianist); Elisabeth Shue (actress); Florence B. Seibert (biochemist); George Westinghouse (engineer/manufacturer)

October 7
♎ Libra, 7

Libra natives born on this date are intelligent, witty, charming, and philosophical. You possess both the human touch and the ability to grasp complex technical details. Your analytical mind, combined with an instinctive psychic ability, allows you to size up any situation quickly and accurately. Your tactful approach and your understanding of human nature make you a good manager. A professional career in the arts, the media, the sciences, education, law, or politics would put the full range of your mental and creative talents to good use.

October 7th individuals possess deep reservoirs of wisdom and spirituality. Whether you choose to follow a traditional religion or seek an alternative path, the paradoxes in your spiritual nature may be misunderstood. At times you come off as a compassionate, intuitive, idealistic humanitarian and, at others, a moody, analytical, rather self-absorbed intellectual. Because you spend time alone in meditation or private contemplation, people tend to regard you as enigmatic or mysterious. Since you're something of a visionary, you may find that you function best in an environment where you are the sole authority.

On a personal level, you are a romantic idealist. Partnership has a high priority for you, yet you can have difficulty expressing your deepest feelings to the object of your affection. It may take you awhile to make a commitment, but when you do, you're likely to stick around for the long term.

On This Day:

Today is sacred to the Greek goddess Pallas Athena. She was worshiped in Rome as the goddess Victoria, the divine personification of triumph. In fifteenth century Germany, the peasants celebrated a festival called Kermesse. An icon buried the previous year was unearthed. At the end of the festival week, a new icon was buried for the following year.

Born Today: June Allyson (actress); Shawn Ashmore (actor); Niels Bohr (nuclear physicist); Toni Braxton (singer); Andy Devine (actor); Yo-Yo Ma (cellist); John Mellencamp (singer/songwriter); Rachel McAdams (actress); Vaughan Monroe (singer/bandleader); Henry Wallace (U.S. vice president)

October 8

♎ Libra, 8

The individual born today is the prototypical example of the "iron fist in the velvet glove." Your knack for getting power and diplomacy to work together makes you a shrewd negotiator and a formidable adversary. Although outwardly courteous and conciliatory, you can be an unyielding force when you believe you are in the right (which is most of the time). Your personal ambition and agenda are only part of the story. As a passionate believer in justice and equity, you're willing to fight for your own interests and those of anyone who is not getting a fair shake.

The competitive side of an October 8th birth date is tempered by an uncanny ability to see all sides of an issue. You have what it takes to succeed in virtually any career field, and you are willing to work as hard as necessary to gain the recognition and material success you crave. In business, you would make an exceptional executive because you're a skillful organizer who is equally popular with superiors, co-workers, and clients.

In an intimate union, you're capable of total loyalty and devotion to the right person. Although part of you longs to be loved, there is another portion of your workaholic nature that may prefer the solitary life. In a love union, control could become an issue. You like being in charge and won't put up with a lover who wants to play boss.

On This Day:

On or around this date each year, Jews celebrate Simchat Torah, the rejoicing of the law. The holiday marks the ending and restarting of the year's cycle of readings from the Torah, the first five books of the Bible. After the last chapter is read, the scrolls of the Torah are removed from the Ark and paraded around the synagogue.

Born Today: Rona Barrett (gossip columnist); Chevy Chase (comedian/actor); Matt Damon (actor/screenwriter); Paul Hogan (actor); Jesse Jackson (social and political activist/Baptist minister); Juan Peron (president of Argentina); R. L. Stine (writer); Sigourney Weaver (actress); Stephanie Zimbalist (actress)

October 9

♎ Libra, 9

Many well-known actors, writers, and musicians celebrate their birthdays on this date. With your artistic temperament and magnetic personality, you could find your niche in the arts and entertainment. Your exceptional sensitivity to atmosphere, color, texture, sound, and music helps you relate to the world around you in a creative manner. At the same time, your inherent compassion and spirituality impel you to fight for worthy causes. As a true diplomat, you are adept at rallying people and bringing them together. Whether furthering your own work or helping to save the world, you know exactly how to put your literary talents and promotional abilities to the best possible use.

A natural born detective with a quick and penetrating mind, you are a stealthy observer of the human condition. Although your feelings of responsibility for others can cause you to proselytize for your principles and beliefs, you often refuse to go along with society's ideas of right and wrong. Nevertheless, you have a subtle way of inspiring people to do their best.

If your intense idealism is disappointed, you may retreat into a deep funk. However, your depressions don't last long, because you're a highly social person. All anyone needs to do to cheer you up is invite you to a party. Partnership is important to you. In an intimate relationship, you make an exceptionally giving mate or lover. As one of the last of the true romantics, you're generally inclined to put your partner's needs ahead of your own.

On This Day:

In Italy, the Festival of Felicitas, the Roman goddess of luck and good fortune, takes place on this date. It's a good time for making amulets that attract luck and ward off evil. Each year, the festival and birthday of the goddess A-Ma is held in the Macao region of China. A-Ma is the protector and patroness of fishermen and sailors.

Born Today: Scott Bakula (actor); Jackson Browne (singer); Steve Burns (actor/musician); Bruce Catton (historian); Miguel de Cervantes (writer); John Entwistle (rock star); John Lennon (rock star); Aimee Semple McPherson (evangelist); Sharon Osbourne (TV personality/host); Camille Saint-Saens (composer); Jacques Tati (actor/mime)

October 10

♎ Libra, 1

The dynamic individuals celebrating birthdays on this day are usually as amiable and agreeable as other Libras, yet they can be as assertive and aggressive as members of their opposite sign, Aries. As long as things go your way, you are polite and obliging. When they don't, you're not afraid to speak out and voice your displeasure. A born leader and crusader, you are driven by your ideals and convictions. Your belief in equity and fairness, combined with your mental and physical courage, may incline you toward the legal profession or a career in the military or law enforcement. You are particularly good at initiating projects and recruiting others to help you carry out your plans.

October 10th individuals are ambitious, determined, and geared toward accomplishment. However, your energy flow is erratic, and you may find yourself alternating between periods of intense activity and all-out laziness. Although you're essentially a team player, the impulsive, action-oriented side of your personality has a way of overcoming your desire to please everyone. You possess the type of vivid imagination and fine appreciation for culture and beauty that can lead to an artistic career.

You are affectionate, outgoing, and sociable. Emotionally, you tend to go back and forth between independence and dependence. Yet partnership inevitably wins out in the long run, because your need for love is stronger than your need for freedom.

On This Day:

Throughout Brazil, today is the first day of the annual two-week-long celebration of the Festival of Lights. It begins with a parade of penance that is followed by the lighting of torches, candles, hearth fires, and oil lamps to symbolically drive away the evil spirits of the darkness that create confusion and bring bad luck and misfortune.

Born Today: Charles Dance (actor); Dale Earnhardt, Jr. (racecar driver); Brett Favre (football player); Helen Hayes (actress); Richard Jaeckel (actor); Thelonius Monk (jazz musician/composer/arranger); David Lee Roth (rock star); Tanya Tucker (singer); Giuseppe Verdi (composer); Ben Vereen (dancer/actor); Ed Wood (director)

October 11

♎ Libra, 2

Those born on this day are society's genial peacemakers. You project a charming manner and a cooperative spirit that puts people at ease. Your gift for understanding all sides of an argument has a calming effect on warring factions. However, your amiable nature in no way implies a lack of strength. You actually have considerable grit and determination, but you realize that "more flies are caught with honey than vinegar." And you catch more flies than anyone.

The typical October 11th individual is imaginative, artistic, and intellectual, with a knack for communicating thoughts and ideas. With your creative talents, you may find personal fulfillment in an artistic or literary occupation. Your love of harmony and beauty bodes well for accomplishment in the worlds of fashion and interior design. Although essentially an idealist, you are able to evaluate the world dispassionately. This air of analytical detachment can make you seem emotionally cool, when you're actually quite warm and loving.

You thrive on the affection and attention of a partner. You don't like being alone, and intimate relationships are very important to you. However, you're the consummate romantic idealist, and few people are able to live up to your unrealistic expectations. A failed romance may upset you to the point of making you ill. If things get really unpleasant, you'll go off in search of more peaceful surroundings.

On This Day:

This is the day of the Roman Bacchanalian Festival of Vinalia, a harvest thanksgiving during which the new wine is tasted and tested. The Greek Festival of Thesmorphoria is a celebration of motherhood in honor of the goddess Demeter. In Denmark and Germany, people honor the Old Lady of the Elder Trees, a pagan spirit who watches over the trees.

Born Today: Joan Cusack (actress); Dawn French (actress/writer); Henry John Heinz (business entrepreneur); Darryl Hall (singer); Orlando Hernandez, "El Duque" (baseball player); Ron Leibman (actor); Elmore Leonard (writer); Luke Perry (actor); Jerome Robbins (choreographer); Eleanor Roosevelt (U.S. first lady); Michelle Wie (golfer)

October 12

♎ Libra, 3

Libras born today are bright, sociable, entertaining, and enthusiastic. A quick study with an agile mind, you absorb new information with surprising ease. Self-expression is your forte, and you're a superb conversationalist. Your breadth of knowledge makes it possible for you to field most questions with insightful responses and witty, off-the-cuff remarks. Your eloquence, humor, and ability to present your ideas tactfully make you a natural salesperson. You could probably get the Eskimos to buy tons of ice, but you wouldn't do it because your strong sense of values keeps you from exploiting others.

The self-confidence and optimism of the typical October 12th individual makes you to seek the best that life has to offer. Moreover, you usually find it. Adverse conditions don't get you down, because you have faith in yourself and in your ability to achieve your goals. Your charm and diplomacy combine to attract help and support in your chosen career. You are especially good at taking charge and coping with people and their problems. Many born on this date choose careers in the media, art and entertainment, business, teaching, law, government service, or politics.

The basic contradictions in your nature tend to surface in romantic relationships. You yearn for companionship, but you are independent and dislike being tied down. For the best of both worlds, you need a significant other who loves you and also respects your personal space.

On This Day:

In ancient Rome, this day was sacred to Fortuna Redux, the goddess of successful journeys and safe returns. It was also the festival of Meditrinali, an ancient celebration associated with Jupiter and the goddess Meditrina. Little is known about the Meditrinali, except that was associated in some way with the new vintage of wine.

Born Today: Susan Anton (supermodel/actress); Kirk Cameron (actor); Dick Gregory (comedian/activist/nutritionist); Hugh Jackman (actor); Marion Jones (track star); Tony Kubek (baseball player); Richard Alan Meier (architect); Luciano Pavarotti (opera singer); Chris Wallace (TV news correspondent)

October 13

♎ Libra, 4

The person whose birthday falls on this date is generally regarded as the tough cookie of the Libra group. You're a genuine survivor with the capacity to overcome whatever obstacles life throws in your path. An excellent strategist and careful planner, you set your sights on a goal and pursue it with total dedication. Driven by ambition, you're capable of remaining totally focused on the prize until the race is won.

The sweet, benevolent outer personality of individuals born on October 13 belies their pragmatic, fiercely competitive inner nature. Unlike some lazier Libras, you're perfectly willing to work extra hard in pursuit of your objectives. Invariably fair and equitable in your dealings with people, you're as sympathetic as any of your Sun sign counterparts when it comes to the needs and desires of others. Somehow you always manage to help people without losing sight of your own personal agenda. A natural leader, you would make an excellent business executive. Although many born on this day choose artistic careers, others prefer science and technology, education, the law, or politics.

Relationships may be difficult for you because you're a bit of a workaholic. When you do get involved with someone, you're capable of total loyalty and devotion. However, control may become an issue, because you need to be the one who is in charge.

On This Day:

On this day in old Rome, the people celebrated Fontinala, an ancient festival honoring the fresh water deity Fons, god of wells and springs. Flower garlands were thrown into the springs and placed around the tops of wells to appease Fons, petition for his continued blessing, and assure the water supply for the coming year.

Born Today: Ashanti (singer/songwriter); Lenny Bruce (comedian); Nancy Kerrigan (skater); Yves Montand (actor); Nana Mouskouri (singer); Marie Osmond (singer); Kelly Preston (actress); Jerry Rice (football player); Nipsey Russell (comedian); Paul Simon (singer/songwriter); Margaret Thatcher (British prime minister); Cornel Wilde (actor)

October 14

♎ Libra, 5

The major challenge for someone born on this day is to find a way of combining the root number five's freewheeling, independent lifestyle with Libra's constant need for companionship. Expressive, inquisitive, and articulate, you're a good conversationalist with an extremely persuasive manner. Since you live more in your mind than in your senses, you feel things mentally rather than emotionally. However, the affability, charm, and diplomacy of the people-oriented portion of your nature have a way of obscuring the cerebral intellectual who resides inside your head.

October 14th individuals believe that most problems can be resolved best through discussion and compromise. You are considerate and kindhearted, with a personal world view that is idealistic, altruistic, tolerant, and eclectic. Your keen insight into human nature makes you a good judge of character and motivation. You're very astute when it comes to getting your own ideas across in an inoffensive, yet convincing, manner. You should thrive in any professional arena that encourages you to make the most of your creativity, communication skills, and ability to help others, such as psychological counseling, the law, education, the sciences, the media, or the arts.

You are a true romantic, but your need for independence is constantly at odds with your belief that life is incomplete without a partner. When you find your soul mate, you expect an ideal relationship that includes both friendship and love. You are not likely to settle for anything less.

On This Day:

Winter's Day, or Vinternatsblot, marked the beginning of the winter season in the old northern European calendar. On this day, all summer activities were stopped and preparations for the coming winter given priority. In Bangladesh, a festival called Durga Puja is celebrated in honor of this great mother goddess and her triumph over evil.

Born Today: Harry Anderson (comedian/actor); ee cummings (poet); Dwight D. Eisenhower (U.S. president/U.S. Army general); Lillian Gish (actress); Stacy Keibler (wrestler); Ralph Lauren (designer); Roger Moore (actor); William Penn (Puritan leader/founder of Pennsylvania); Sir Cliff Richard (singer); Usher (rap star)

October 15

♎ Libra, 6

The sociable people born on this day don't relish solitude and actively seek the partnership and cooperation of others. You crave the attention and approval of others, and your charming manner and vivacious personality practically assure your popularity. You know how to play to an audience, even if you aren't in the entertainment business. Clever and well informed, you can talk to anyone about anything. You love debating and will jump into any discussion, from the latest movie or hairstyle to global warming. However, you hate quarrelling and rarely display your anger in an overt fashion.

The typical abode of the October 15th individual is graceful, harmonious, and furnished with lovely things. Your desire for beauty and luxury impels you to look for the very best. You adore entertaining and filling your home with music, laughter, and the lively conversation of interesting, intelligent people. You know how set a mood and bring diverse individuals together. To your way of thinking, good taste is more important than a balanced budget. You would rather stay at home than show up at a party wearing a tacky outfit or bearing a cheap gift.

In an intimate union, you're the quintessential romantic. Generous with compliments, you like being on the receiving end of flattering remarks as well. Since you believe in giving your all for love, you may not feel complete unless you're involved in a long-term, loving relationship.

On This Day:

Today is the feast day of Roman Catholic Saint Theresa of Avila. Theresa was born in northern Spain in 1515. When she was twelve, her mother died and her father placed her in the Carmelite Convent of the Incarnation near Avila. At age forty-three, Theresa set about founding a new convent that went back to the basics of a simple, contemplative order.

Born Today: Richard Carpenter (singer/songwriter); Sarah Ferguson (Duchess of York); Emeril Lagasse (TV chef/restaurateur); John Kennneth Galbraith (economist); Linda Lavin (actress); Vanessa Marcil (actress); Penny Marshall (director/actress); Jim Palmer (baseball player); Mario Puzo (writer); Arthur Schlesinger, Jr. (writer/historian)

October 16

Although Libras born on this day are as amiable and cooperative as their Sun sign counterparts, they have a deeper understanding of the dark side of human nature and fewer expectations concerning other people. While you're gentle on the outside, you're tough on the inside. An enthusiast in everything you do, you can be as passionate about the arts, politics, or religion as you are about love and romance. You prefer to avoid stepping on anyone's toes, but when challenged, you're capable of giving as good as you get.

October 16th individuals are magnetic, charismatic, and charming, with a knack for drawing people to them. Nevertheless, you possess a very un-Libra-like propensity for calling things as you see them and refusing to pussyfoot around the truth. Extremely curious and always searching for answers, you're not afraid to experiment with spiritual or political beliefs that fall outside the mainstream. You want to be liked and accepted, but you need time alone to recharge your batteries, so you'll occasionally retreat into solitude. As a result, you may garner a reputation for being mysterious, elusive, and rather difficult to get to know or understand.

Intimate relationships are very important to you, but you need to feel comfortable and in control before committing yourself. You're an exciting and generous lover. You seem to know exactly what your partner wants, and you're quite capable of providing it.

On This Day:

On this day each year, the Japanese Shinto ceremony of Kan-name-Sai, or Good Tasting Event, takes place. In Japan, rice is the symbol of abundance and divine provisions and represents immortality. The rice from the first harvest is offered to the Imperial Ancestors and the Imperial ancestral deity, the ancient Sun goddess Amaterasu.

Born Today: Dave DeBusschere (basketball player); Angela Lansbury (actress); Henry Lewis (conductor); Kellie Martin (actress); John Mayer (singer/songwriter); Eugene O'Neill (playwright); Tim Robbins (actor); Suzanne Somers (actress); Noah Webster (lexicographer/creator of the first American dictionary); Oscar Wilde (writer)

October 17

♎ Libra, 8

Persons celebrating their birthdays on this day are among the most industrious of the solar Libras. You possess a dynamic personality with marked executive ability, sound business judgment, and a knack for gaining the respect and cooperation of others. Success isn't likely to come to you overnight or as the result of a stroke of luck. When you make it big, in all likelihood it will be the result of your own efforts. There may be some formidable obstacles for you to overcome on your way to the top. Nevertheless, when you extend you best efforts, there is little you cannot accomplish.

Those born on October 17 are artistic and creative as well as logical and analytical. You take your responsibilities seriously, yet your tactful approach and keen understanding of human nature make you a good manager of people. You go out of your way to avoid arguments and unpleasant situations, yet you are usually able to get others to agree to your plans and do things your way. Occupational arenas associated with this date of birth include business and industry, the arts and entertainment, architecture, education, publishing, social services, government service, and politics.

Despite your tough outer shell, in personal relationships you have difficulty expressing your true feelings. You're capable of total loyalty and devotion to the right person, but you expect fidelity and a great deal of emotional reassurance in return.

On This Day:

In modern Asatru, today is the festival of Hengest, commemorating the Saxon general who, in the fifth century C.E., began the Germanic settlement of eastern Britain, which eventually became England. Throughout the world, the United Nations International Day for the Eradication of Poverty is observed each year on this date.

Born Today: Jean Arthur (actress); Spring Byington (actress); Jimmy Breslin (newspaper columnist); Nick Cannon (actor); Montgomery Clift (actor); Eminem (rap star); Alan Jackson (singer); Margot Kidder (actress); Evel Knievel (daredevil motorcyclist); Norm McDonald (comedian); Tom Poston (actor); Rita Hayworth (actress)

October 18

♎ Libra, 9

The visionary qualities and compelling personalities of Libra natives born on this day enable them to persuade others to join in their crusade to improve the human condition. Tact and cooperation come so naturally to you that you prefer accomplishing your purposes diplomatically. However, while you may be a poster child for passive resistance, you are not afraid of anything or anyone. When charm and statesmanship don't work, you're not above resorting to a more direct assault.

Those with birthdays on October 18 possess a complex, chameleon-like character that others may be unable to read or understand. Your air of mystery captivates people and prevents them from probing the depths of your psyche. Yet you are a born detective and a stealthy watcher and observer of those around you. You're less a talker and more a listener than most solar Libras, and your ability to tune into people's feelings intuitively provides you with insight into the public mind. Consequently, you often know what people want and need before they do. Occupations associated with this birthday include psychological counselor, teacher, business or salesperson, designer, writer, actor, and musician.

Because you are sentimental, idealistic, and romantic, you may have some unrealistic notions regarding love relationships. In an intimate union, you're an exceptionally giving partner. You are so kindhearted and self-sacrificing that you could get carried away and fall prey to an unscrupulous lover or friend.

On This Day:

In some parts of Britain, the Great Horn Faire has been held continuously since medieval times. It includes a parade of men wearing antlers to celebrate the power of the lord of the forests. The horned god has been known by many names, including Hu Gardern among the ancient Druids, Hern and Cernunnos among the Celts, and Atho among the Welsh.

Born Today: Chuck Berry (rock and roll star); Peter Boyle (actor); Pam Dawber (actress/ model); Mike Ditka (football player/coach); Lotte Lenya (singer/actress); Melina Mercouri (actress); Martina Navratilova (tennis player); Laura Nyro (singer/songwriter); Anita O'Day (jazz singer); George C. Scott (actor)

October 19

♎ Libra, 1

People born on this day are battlers, but their chosen weapon is persuasion, not intimidation. You charm, coax, and cajole until the other person either comes around to your point of view or tires of listening to your wheedling and gives in. When sweet-talk doesn't work, you follow up with a logical, well-thought-out presentation of your ideas. Your crusading spirit is driven by ideals and convictions rather than a desire for personal gain. Nevertheless, if an opportunity to feather your own nest happens to present itself, you won't turn it down.

People whose birthdays fall on October 19 are warm, outgoing, and sociable. You enjoy entertaining and bringing people together. No matter what the occasion or how large or small the gathering, you are a genial, thoughtful host. Your particular blend of creativity, tact, and authority gives you tremendous personal appeal. Professionally, your talents are most suited to a career that puts you in the public eye. An abundance of artistic talent, ease of self-expression, and physical dexterity draw many of those born on this date to occupations in the media, art and entertainment, fashion, sports, or politics.

Although your may start out as something of a social butterfly, Libra's need for partnership trumps your fascination with the freewheeling lifestyle. Eventually you will decide to find your soul mate and settle down.

On This Day:

On this day in Tokyo, Japan, an annual fair called Bettara-Ichi, or Sticky-Sticky Fair, is held near the sacred shrine of the god Ebisu. The children carry sticky pickled radishes tied to straw ropes through the streets in the hope of chasing away evil spirits and receiving the blessings of the seven Shinto gods of luck and good fortune.

Born Today: Jack Anderson (newspaper columnist); Marilyn Bell (swimmer); Eddie Daniels (jazz musician); Devine (female impersonator/actor); Chris Kattan (comedian/actor); Evander Holyfield (boxer); John Le Carre (writer); John Lithgow (actor); Peter Max (artist); Robert Reed (actor); Jeannie C. Riley (singer)

October 20

♎ Libra, 2

Libra is a sign of paradox, and two is a root number of duality. The result is someone with two distinctly different sides to his or her personality. One side is the quintessential diplomat spreading a harmonious message of collaboration and teamwork. However, Libra's symbol is the scales, and scales are not always in perfect balance—they tend to dip back and forth. Like the scales, you have your ups and downs. When you are down, you can become as sulky and quarrelsome as any Aires.

The individual whose birthday falls on this date likes everything that is beautiful, artistic, and pleasing to the senses. You are reasonable and persuasive, and along with your friendly personality, these traits provide you with the requisite assets for success in business or the professions. Your imagination and creative talents bode well for a career in art, music, or literature. You have both the human touch and the intellectual ability to grasp technical details. Moreover, you're able to put your intelligent, rational mind to good use communicating ideas and exchanging thoughts with like-minded individuals.

On a personal level, you're a romantic idealist. You look at the world through rose-colored lenses and dream of a grand passion with your one true love. When life fails to live up to your fantasy, you may be upset to the point of becoming physically ill.

On This Day:

Today is the feast day of Roman Catholic Saint Paul of the Cross. In his youth, his family planned for him to become a merchant, but Paul was granted a vision. While still a young layperson, Paul founded the Barefoot Clerks of the Cross and the Passion. At one point, all the brothers deserted him, but his order eventually received Pope Benedict's approval.

Born Today: Art Buchwald (political humorist); Sir James Chadwick (physicist); Snoop Dogg (rap star); Mischa Elman (violinist); Charles Ives (composer); Bela Lugosi (actor); Mickey Mantle (baseball player); Viggo Mortensen (actor); Fayard Nicholas (dancer); Jerry Orbach (actor); Tom Petty (rock star); Sir Christopher Wren (architect)

October 21

♎ Libra, 3

The skilled communicator born on this day is charming, intelligent, and versatile. You are a natural entertainer with many interests and an outgoing, magnetic personality that draws others to you. People are attracted to your breezy lightheartedness and easygoing nature. You like occupying center-stage and want to be accepted and well thought of by your friends and acquaintances. However, there is more to you than just the social butterfly. An inventive, original thinker, you have an inquisitive mind and a great love for learning. Your inherent understanding of people and their needs makes you a particularly good negotiator and advisor.

You have pizzazz and knack for ferreting out up-to-date information. A trendsetter rather than a follower, you know instinctively what is coming in and what is on the way out. Because you see things with your mind's eye, you understand cycles and patterns. The ability to visualize future possibilities lets you take advantage of important opportunities far in advance of the crowd. With your eloquence and tact, you're well suited to a career in business, the media, the arts, law, politics, or the diplomatic service.

In an intimate relationship you are loving, caring, and considerate. You want to be part of a committed union, but you can be somewhat fickle in your attachments. It may take awhile before you decide to settle down with one person.

On This Day:

This is the feast day of the legendary Roman Catholic Saint Ursula and her "11,000 virgins." Ursula, the daughter of a British king, fled her home with her maidens to avoid an arranged marriage. In Cologne, they were taken prisoner by the Huns. In 451 C.E., the Huns massacred all of the women when the Christian Ursula refused to marry their pagan chieftain.

★★
★ **Born Today:** Samuel Taylor Coleridge (poet/literary critic); Carrie Fisher (actress/writer); Dizzy Gillespie (jazz musician); Jeremy Miller (actor); Benjamin Netanyahu (Israeli prime minister); Alfred Nobel (chemist/engineer/founder-endower of the Nobel Prize); Joyce Randolph (actress); Judge Judy Sheindlin (New York Family Court judge/TV judge)

October 22

♎ Libra, 4

Scales born on the Libra/Scorpio cusp are more determined and have a stronger sense of purpose than other members of their Sun sign. Your particular brand of abstract reasoning and intuitive understanding provides you with a keen insight into people's motives. Sometimes you come off as emotional and quite mystical, while at other times you're surprisingly scientific and logical. The cusp position adds emotional power to Libra's talent for smoothing over disputes. And, despite your airy Libran detachment, Scorpio's influence activates your need to gain and maintain control.

Those celebrating birthdays today are proud and ambitious, with a deep-seated desire for praise and recognition. You are extremely hard working, and career plays an important part in your life. Your creativity and artistic talents are bolstered by your capacity for turning dreams of glory into practical realities. A born detective, your quick mind and penetrating curiosity incline to a broad range of occupational interests that may include the sciences, medical research, education, jurisprudence, law or law enforcement, politics, art, literature, and business.

The October 22nd individual is playful, passionate, and exceptionally attentive to his or her significant other. In a love union with the right person, you are capable of absolute devotion. Given Libra's romantic temperament and Scorpio's sensuality, an intense, intimate relationship is more or less a necessity for you.

On This Day:

Hi Matsuri is a Japanese purification festival of communion with the gods, who come to Earth on this night. Beginning in the evening, there are torchlight processions through the streets in honor of the revered ancient ones. The processions come to an end at the sacred shrine of Kurama, where the deities' return is expected to occur at midnight.

Born Today: Sarah Bernhardt (actress); Brian Boitano (skater); Catherine Deneuve (actress); Joan Fontaine (actress); Annette Funicello (actress); Jeff Goldblum (actor); Dr. Timothy Leary (LSD lifestyle guru); Jonathan Lipnicki (actor); Franz Liszt (composer); Christopher Lloyd (actor); Robert Rauschenberg (artist); Tony Roberts (actor)

October 23

♏ Scorpio, 5

The scorpion born on this day has a commanding personality and a magnetic intensity that rarely fails to attract attention and admiration. Your wit, charm, and aura of supreme self-confidence cast such a strong hypnotic spell that people may start believing you can do no wrong. Your unique mix of insight and humor helps you get along with all types of people. Capable and self-motivated, you have the enterprise to succeed in almost any venture. You decide what needs to be done, and then you do it. As a result, you have scant patience with those who must be pushed and prodded toward accomplishment.

October 23rd individuals have definite opinions on virtually every subject, and they enjoy engaging in spirited debates regarding their ideals and ideas. You want to know why things are the way they are, and you possess an uncanny ability to get to the root of any question. You'll keep poking and digging until you find your answer. A master of subtlety, you mask your true motives so completely that you're usually able to finesse information from other people without their even realizing it.

Emotionally, you blow hot and cold. At times you may feel torn between your love of freedom and a deep-seated desire for a stable, committed love relationship. When you are involved in an intimate union, you make a passionate, caring, demanding lover.

On This Day:

This is the first day of the Norse festival of Asatru, commemorating the changeover to the winter half of the year. In Thailand on this date, the people celebrate Chulalongkorn Day in honor of Chakri king Rama V, who modernized the government. During his forty-two-year reign, Rama V accomplished many fine things, including the abolishment of slavery.

Born Today: Johnny Carson (TV talk show host); Michael Crichton (writer); Diana Dors (actress); Gertrude Ederle (swimmer); Doug Flutie (football player); Ilya Frank (physicist); Philip Kaufman (director); Edward Kienholz (artist); Emily Kimbrough (writer); Al Leiter (baseball player); "Weird" Al Yankovic (singer/comedian)

October 24

♏ Scorpio, 6

hose celebrating birthdays on this day must be enthusiastic about what they're doing, or they'll stop doing it. Although as proud and determined as any of your Sun sign counterparts, you are more cooperative and willing to compromise than most other scorpions. When it comes to bringing people together in the pursuit of a common goal, you're capable of working wonders. You are idealistic, yet shrewdly aware of the darker side of human nature and not all that surprised when good does not triumph over evil.

The October 24th individual functions best in harmonious surroundings with a minimum of stress and discord. Your innate understanding of people and your ability to put them at ease make you a perfect fit for any business or profession that requires frequent dealings with the public. Your dramatic or musical talent could lead to an accomplished career in the performing arts. Creativity and an eye for beauty and glamour may take you in the direction of fashion or design. Your intellect and eloquence bode particularly well for success as a writer, teacher, or politician.

Love makes your world go 'round. Your capacity for solitude is not high, and you tend to do better with a partner than on your own. Despite your exceptional loyalty, jealousy or possessiveness can make your closest relationships rather difficult to sustain.

On This Day:

Today is the feast day of Roman Catholic Saint Anthony Mary Claret, the founder of the Missionary Sons of the Immaculate Heart of Mary. Isabella II named Anthony to the post of archbishop of Santiago, Cuba, where his preaching against slavery resulted in an attempt on his life. Later recalled to Spain, he served as Isabella's personal confessor.

Born Today: F. Murray Abraham (actor); Pierre-Giles de Gennes (physicist); Moss Hart (playwright/director); Kevin Kline (actor); Antonie von Leeuwenhoek (microbiologist/microscope inventor) J. P. "Big Bopper" Richardson (rock and roll star); Dame Sybil Thorndike (actress/writer); Y. A. Tittle (football player)

October 25

♏ Scorpio, 7

The intense individuals celebrating their birthdays today are strong-willed, complex, and hard to get to know. You are stubborn, passionate, loyal, and rarely indifferent or indecisive. Once you've made up your mind about something, it is virtually impossible to convince you to change it. No matter how difficult the challenge, it is a mistake to count you out, because you refuse to give up on your desires. When it appears that you're beaten, you rise phoenix-like from your own ashes and begin again.

The secretive October 25th person has his or her own agenda and way of doing things. Even those close to you may have problems understanding your true motivation. Your ambition, enthusiasm, and enterprising spirit propel you into action. However, it's your powerful emotional nature that serves as the driving force behind everything you do. You are proud and self-reliant, and your surface poise does not desert you even when you're deeply disturbed. You're an expert at concealing your feelings, and most people are unaware of what's actually going on beneath your composed façade. No matter how bad things get, you refuse to let others see your pain.

Relationships are important to you, yet you would rather be alone than subjugated to someone else's whims. In an intimate union, you're exceedingly loyal, sympathetic, and capable of pledging a deep, long-lasting affection, but only to one who is willing to play by your rules.

On This Day:

The festival of the Dioscuri, sacred to Castor and Pollux, twin sons of Zeus and protectors of sailors, takes place on this day. Shoemaker's Day is celebrated in honor of the twin French Catholic brothers, Saints Crispin and Crisinianus, patrons of shoemakers. According to legend, a new pair of shoes bought on this day will bring you good luck and prosperity.

Born Today: Billy Barty (actor); Georges Bizet (composer); Leo G. Carroll (actor); Dave Cowens (basketball player); Dan Gable (wrestler); Abel Gance (director); Jimmy Heath (jazz musician); Bobby Knight (basketball couch); Tracy Nelson (actress); Minnie Pearl (singer); Pablo Picasso (artist); Helen Reddy (singer/songwriter)

October 26

♏ Scorpio, 8

The goal-oriented scorpions born on this day are among the hardest-working individuals in the zodiac. You're ambitious and conscientious, and it's not surprising that you crave power, money, and success. Of the three, however, you value power most—and you know how to wield it. As a tough and tenacious leader, you can be either a loyal ally or a formidable opponent. Although you expect a great deal from people, you're prepared to work as hard as anyone in pursuit of your joint objectives.

Beneath the serious demeanor of the October 26th person lurks a caring soul who feels duty bound to do whatever is necessary for family and friends. You don't balk at the first sign of trouble, and anyone who depends on you can rest assured that you will be there when needed. You have a good head on your shoulders, and you reason things out carefully, planning your moves with exactitude. You can be successful in virtually any career that appeals to you. Whatever your chosen occupation, it should provide you with material security and the opportunity to ascend to a position of authority.

You may seem distant and mysterious, yet your deeply passionate nature attracts love like a magnet. A loyal and devoted partner, you feel things very deeply. However, lack of trust can cause you to hide your vulnerability under a mask of indifference.

On This Day:

According to the calculations of James Ussher, a seventeenth century Anglican archbishop, God created the Earth on October 26, 4004 B.C.E. Although this date is uncertain at best, it is a good excuse for a birthday party in honor of Earth's goddesses, such as Tellas Mater, Gaia, Rhea, Demeter, Ops, Pandora, and Frigg.

Born Today: Hillary Rodham Clinton (U.S. first lady/senator); Jackie Coogan (actor); Cary Elwes (actor); Sid Gillman (football coach); Bob Hoskins (actor); Mahalia Jackson (gospel singer); John S. Knight (newspaper publisher); Reza Pahlavi (Shah of Iran); Pat Sajak (TV game show host); Jaclyn Smith (actress); Lauren Tewes (actress)

October 27

♏ Scorpio, 9

T he intuitive scorpion born on this date is blessed with an eerie insight that borders on the psychic. A vivid imagination is your forte. Whether channeled into the arts, the sciences, or business, your gift for visualizing your dreams and ideas helps you materialize them. On one level you are a shrewd and ambitious go-getter determined to further your own interests. But on another level you're a compassionate crusader for the rights of others. The sensitivity and empathy associated with the nine's vibration tempers the power and intensity of your Scorpio Sun sign, but it doesn't prevent you from taking assertive action when you deem it necessary.

People whose birthdays fall on this date love all things romantic, mysterious, and melodramatic. If coupled with artistic talent, these interests could lead to a career as a musician or a writer of mystery fiction or poetry. You might find that your true calling is in acting, filmmaking, painting, sculpting, or photography. In business, you can shine in public relations, advertising, or sales. Your understanding of people's problems suits you for an occupation connected to medicine, psychology, education, law, or politics.

In a love relationship, you're inclined to idealize your partner and place him or her on a pedestal. But if the union turns sour, you could be forced to face up to a reality that leaves you feeling severely hurt and disappointed.

On This Day:

In Cornwall England, the love divination of Allen Apple Day was all the rage for unmarried men and women. Each individual would pick an Allen apple and place it under his or her pillow. Arising at dawn, the single man or woman would wait under a tree. The first eligible person to pass was destined to be his or her future spouse.

Born Today: John Cleese (comedian/actor/writer); Ruby Dee (actress); Nanette Fabray (actress); Ralph Kiner (baseball player); Roy Lichtenstein (artist); Peter Martins (dancer/choreographer); Kelly Osbourne (singer); Nicolo Paganini (composer); Sylvia Plath (poet); Theodore Roosevelt (U.S. president); Dylan Thomas (poet/playwright)

October 28

♏ Scorpio, 1

Those born on this day are considerably more direct than the majority of their Sun sign counterparts. A physically active, emotionally intense powerhouse, you have an overwhelming desire to leave your mark on the world. Your clever, insightful mind has a knack for filtering out the irrelevant and cutting directly to the heart of the matter. Your greatest strength lies in your capacity for combining the stealth and strategy of Scorpio with the assertive leadership capabilities of the root number one. Once you focus on a goal, no power on Earth can stop you from reaching it.

Despite having aggressive natures, people celebrating birthdays today are actually quite sensitive and feel things very deeply. Inherently proud and dignified, you patently refuse to compromise your principles and ideals. You ooze personal magnetism, and when you turn on the charm, people have a hard time saying no to you. Whether in business, art, science, or politics, you aim high and fully expect to reach the top of your profession. If you have any doubts about your ability to attain your goals, you keep them to yourself.

In love, you're passionate and demanding and, once you enter into a lasting union, totally loyal. You will pursue the object of your affections with unremitting zeal, yet you may refuse to commit until you're convinced the other person is truly trustworthy.

On This Day:

On or around this date in Consuegra, Spain, the annual Saffron Rose Festival is held in honor of saffron, the world's most expensive herb. Associated with love, the Sun, and Eos, the goddess of dawn, this delicate herb is added to love sachets and potions. When made into a tea, saffron is believed to promote clairvoyant abilities.

Born Today: Nicholas Culpeper (herbalist/astrologer); Charlie Daniels (singer/songwriter); Dennis Franz (actor); Bill Gates (computer operating system pioneer/founder of Microsoft); Bruce Jenner (decathlon athlete); Joaquin Phoenix (actor); Julia Roberts (actress); Jonas Salk (microbiologist/developer of the polio vaccine)

October 29

♏ Scorpio, 2

Those born on this date radiate a bewitching, magnetic appeal that other people find hard to resist. In fact, your charisma is such that you're able to influence others without their even realizing it. Few people know that you are as stubborn and determined on the inside as you are pleasant and charming on the outside. Even so, you're considerably more cooperative and willing to compromise than many of your Sun sign counterparts. You actually do your best work when you have partners, and you prefer sharing responsibility to going it alone.

Poise, sociability, and a courteous nature are the hallmarks of the October 29th individual. In the attempt to live your life in a grand manner, you approach work and play with equal intensity. Despite a tendency to equate material comfort with emotional security, your occupation must be something more than just a means of paying the bills. You are a good listener and a persuasive talker. With your natural gift for research and investigation, you would make a great detective, investigative reporter, mystery writer, scientist, or teacher. Should your creativity manifest as dramatic or musical talent, you might enjoy a successful career in the performing arts.

Relationships are all-important in your life. In love, you're partnership oriented, romantic, affectionate, and faithful, and you expect fidelity and devotion in return. Because you dislike disagreements, you're usually the first to make up after an argument.

On This Day:

On this date, Native American tribes of the Iroquois Nation celebrated the Feast of the Dead. Bodies were first buried in shallow graves and then exhumed afterward. The bones were then preserved by relatives and later brought to a central burial ground. Following the feast, the bones were reburied, accompanied by offerings for the spirits.

Born Today: James Boswell (writer/biographer); Fanny Brice (comedienne/actress); Richard Dreyfuss (actor); Edmund Halley (astronomer); Kate Jackson (actress); Cleo Laine (jazz singer); Bill Mauldin (political cartoonist); Melba Moore (singer); Dennis Potvin (hockey player); Zoot Sims (jazz musician); Winona Ryder (actress)

October 30

♏ Scorpio, 3

People born on this day are typically more approachable and outgoing than their fellow scorpions. A lively conversationalist with a mesmerizing talent for working a crowd, you enjoy engaging in spirited exchanges of thoughts and ideas. Despite a stubborn attachment to your own personal ideals, you possess an inquiring mind and are interested in exploring and discussing diverse points of view. Your unique mix of insight and humor increases your popularity and helps you get along with all types of people.

October 30th individuals have paradoxical personalities that run the gamut from serious to lighthearted and back again. Sometimes you come across as intriguingly mysterious, yet on other occasions you seem totally open, carefree, and relaxed. When you get both sides of your nature working together, the result is a witty, intelligent, articulate communicator. With versatility and intellectual curiosity added to your need to investigate and probe every issue, you refuse to give up until you get to the bottom a matter. As a result, you are well suited to occupations that call for research, detection, and critical analysis.

In intimate relationships you are ardent and demanding. You long for the emotional security of a permanent union, but you also love variety and change. Although you may not be as quick to settle down as other Scorpios, when you do make a commitment, you stick with it.

On This Day:

In Mexico, the Angelitos (little Angels) festival takes place each year on this date. Its main purpose is the blessing of the souls of deceased children. The festival is sacred to Xipe Totec, the ancient god of death, and Tonantzin, the Aztec mother goddess who is known as Tlakatelilis to the Nahua people and the Virgin of Guadalupe to the Christians.

Born Today: John Adams (U.S. president); Charles Atlas (bodybuilder); Fyodor Dostoevsky (writer); Ruth Gordon (actress); Harry Hamlin (actor); Claude Lalouch (director); Louis Malle (director); Diego Maradona (soccer player); Ezra Pound (poet); Grace Slick (rock star); Henry Winkler (actor/producer)

October 31
♏ Scorpio, 4

The ambitious scorpions born on this day are persistent workers with the requisite patience and stamina to see their projects through to the end. Your forte is your ability to plan your strategy carefully, with an eye toward the ultimate goal. Your analytical capabilities help you understand intricate technical details, while your creative intuition comes up with innovative new solutions to old problems. Your organizational skills may be your obvious strengths, but it's your shrewd handling of people that assures your ultimate success.

The October 31st individual has the rational intellect of a scientist with the emotional temperament of an artist. Your relentless drive toward achievement is motivated less by a desire for status and monetary reward than by a deep-seated need for respect and approval. Although you may not be consciously seeking popularity, your vibrant, dynamic personality tends to attract admirers. Whatever you may lack in flexibility and diplomacy as a boss or manager, you make up for by your willingness to work as hard, or harder, than anyone else.

You want love and affection as much as other scorpions, but discretion makes it harder for you to express your desires. You tend to be rather critical of your partner, but you are generous and caring and not likely to run off at the first sign of trouble.

On This Day:

Each year on this date, Samhain Eve, or Halloween, the most important of the eight witches' Sabbats, is celebrated around the world. In Celtic Britain, Samhain Eve was the beginning of the New Year, when the gates between this world and the next were opened to allow the spirits of the dead to roam free and communicate with the living.

Born Today: Barbara Bel Geddes (actress); John Candy (comedian/actor); Deidre Hall (actress); Dale Evans (actress); Peter Jackson (director); John Keats (poet); Michael Landon (actor/producer); Jane Pauley (TV news anchor/talk show host); Dan Rather (TV journalist/news anchor); David Ogden Stiers (actor); Ethel Waters (jazz singer/actress)

November Birthdays

November 1

ᴍ Scorpio, 1

The high-energy Scorpio native born on this day has a huge appetite for life. Driven by your restless, energetic spirit and intense, determined temperament, you are one of life's true warriors. However, there are two distinct sides to your proud, ambitious nature. You're sunny, gregarious, and outgoing one moment, yet subtle, shrewd, and moody the next. Your great strength lies in your ability to confront challenging situations with a mix of scorpionic strategy and the aggressive vitality of the number one's vibration.

November 1st people surround themselves with an aura of mystery that others find intriguing. Competent, capable, and extremely hard working, you believe in yourself and in your capacity to succeed in your endeavors. Once you latch onto a plan or idea, there is virtually no stopping you. Despite a fierce determination to get to the top, you are inherently sensitive and feel things very deeply. When life doesn't turn out as you'd hoped, you can be sorely disappointed. You're given to brooding over the slightest setback. Although you never get over the pain, you always manage to bounce back from it.

Your magnetic charm attracts love and makes you a much sought-after romantic partner. In an intimate relationship, you're ardent and passionate but not easily pleased. Although caring, devoted, and fiercely loyal, you can also be demanding and controlling.

On This Day:

In parts of Britain, Cailleach's Reign, a festival in honor of the ancient Celtic crone goddess, is still celebrated annually on this date. Cailleach is the hag aspect of the Triple Goddess. She returns each year on November 1 to bring the winter and its snows. The magical staff that she carries freezes the ground wherever she taps it.

Born Today: Al Arbour (hockey coach); Stephen Crane (writer); "Sweet Lou" Donaldson (jazz musician); Larry Flint (magazine publisher); Count Louis "Cheiro" Harmon (numerologist/ astrologer); Hannah Hoch (artist); Lyle Lovett (singer); Marcel Ophuls (director); Gary Player (golfer); Fernando Valenzuela (baseball player)

November 2

♏ Scorpio, 2

Those celebrating birthdays on this date are inherently gregarious individuals with a deep-seated need to be involved in all types of social activities. Your warm, courteous manner works wonders when it comes to bringing people together in pursuit of a common goal. Because you're a master of Scorpio's art of nonverbal communication, a look or subtle change in your attitude is usually all it takes for you to get your message across. One of your great strengths is your capacity for getting people to do your bidding, while letting them think that what they are doing is their own idea.

November 2nd people are loaded with charm and personal magnetism. In fact, you're so likeable that others often have a difficult time saying no to you. You are a true diplomat, yet your calm, conciliatory manner masks an emotionally intense inner nature. Despite being a team player, you won't allow anyone to control your actions or tell you what to do. Inherently proud and dignified, you usually function better when you're first among equals or in a position of authority.

While you are sociable and entertaining in a group situation, in a one-to-one relationship, you tend to be rather secretive and may have trouble expressing your true feelings. Nevertheless, intimacy is so important to you that you're usually willing to work with your partner to make the union a success.

On This Day:

On All Soul's Day in old England, small offerings known as soul cakes were set out for the dead. In Mexico, today is the Day of the Dead, when the departed souls are remembered, not with mourning, but with celebration, music, and good humor. People visit the cemeteries and share their food and drink with the spirits of their dead relatives.

Born Today: Marie Antoinette (queen of France); Daniel Boone (frontiersman/pioneer); Paul Ford (actor); Warren G. Harding (U.S. president); Leon Hart (football player); Burt Lancaster (actor); k.d. lang (singer/songwriter); James K. Polk (U.S. president); Stefanie Powers (actress); Luchino Visconti (director); Ray Walston (actor)

November 3

♏ Scorpio, 3

The intelligent, witty conversationalists born on this day are consummate networkers. You surround yourself with drama and excitement, and your exuberant, compelling personality rarely fails to attract attention. You can be rather opinionated and overly passionate with regard to your own ideas, yet you enjoy exchanging knowledge and information with others. Although your Scorpio Sun tends to favor running the show from the shadowy areas behind the scenes, the number three in your birth date impels you to seek the glare of the limelight.

People celebrating birthdays today sometimes feel as if they are being pulled in two opposite directions. However, when there is a conflict between your mind and your emotions, you're more apt to follow your heart than your head. A deep, penetrating insight is one of your great assets. The inclination to keep probing and prodding until you get to the root of a problem helps you understand people and evaluate their situations. Your intuition, insight, investigative skills, and fluency with language could lead to a successful career as a detective, journalist, mystery writer, or medical researcher.

In love relationships, you may be torn between the inclination toward loyalty and fidelity on the one hand and your naturally flirtatious, independent spirit on the other. You'll take your time before making a commitment, but once you do, you'll stick to it.

On This Day:

Today is the feast day of Roman Catholic Saint Martin de Porres, born in 1579 in Lima, Peru. His mother was Anna Velazquez, a free black woman, and his father was Juan de Porres, a Spanish nobleman. Prior to entering the religious life, Martin apprenticed with a barber-surgeon. At the Dominican Friary in Lima, he served as a barber and infirmarian.

Born Today: Ken Berry (actor); Charles Bronson (actor); Kate Capshaw (actress); Roy Emerson (tennis player); Bob Feller (baseball player); Larry Holmes (boxer); Andre Malraux (writer); Dennis Miller (comedian); Roseanne (comedienne/actress/producer); Martin Cruz Smith (writer); Dong Zeng (physician/research professor)

November 4

♏ Scorpio, 4

he hard-working scorpion born on this date is practical, down to earth, and thoroughly reliable. Despite your decidedly realistic world view, many of your actions are determined by your highly charged emotional nature. Endowed with considerable business acumen and financial savvy, you prefer focusing your skills and talents in areas that promise material rewards as well as creative satisfaction. Even so, your occupation must be something more than just a means of paying the bills. Inspired and idealistic, with an enterprising nature, you aim to make your mark in the world, and there is little doubt that you'll succeed.

November 4th individuals are so charismatic and self-confident that they are able to influence other people without their even realizing it. On the surface you may appear cooler and more intellectual than other Scorpio natives, but in personal matters your actions are usually based on instinct and emotion. You have a knack for research and investigation that could lead to a fulfilling career in science, the arts, or commerce. Whether your work is in acting, writing, medical research, psychology, or business, you'll approach it with total commitment and dedication.

On the surface you may appear cooler and more intellectual than other Scorpio natives, but in relationships you follow your instincts and emotions, rather than reason or logic. In love, you're sexy, ardent, affectionate, and more than a little possessive.

On This Day:

Every year in medieval England, a festival was held on this date (the Eve of Guy Fawkes Night) to propitiate the spirit of the Lord of Death. Remnants of this observance can still be seen in the mischievous pranks and bonfires associated with Mischief Night, which is still being celebrated in some parts of modern-day England.

★★
★ **Born Today:** Martin Balsam (actor); Art Carney (actor); Sean "P. Diddy" Combs (rap star); Walter Cronkite (TV news anchor); Ralph Macchio (actor); Matthew McConaughey (actor); Markie Post (actress); Jeff Probst (TV host); Doris Roberts (actress); Will Rogers (humorist); Loretta Swift (actress)

November 5

♏ Scorpio, 5

People celebrating birthdays on this date prefer doing things in their own inimitable way. A true visionary, your forte is the ability to spot cutting-edge trends long before anyone else does. Sometimes your mind seems to be focused in some other dimension. Yet, despite your dreamy, artistic temperament, you are doggedly determined and a real powerhouse when it comes to getting things accomplished. As a realist, you refuse to let your idealism get in the way of practical considerations.

Pride is the Achilles heel of the November 5th person. You thrive on praise and expect recognition and appreciation in return for your hard work. When it's not forthcoming, you may chose to suffer in silence, but you never forget your feelings of disappointment. In business or the professions, you're at your best when you are self-employed or in a position of authority with no one to tell you what you can or can't do. You love a mystery, and your relentless search for the truth may lead to a career as a philosopher, psychologist, archaeologist, doctor, lawyer, writer, actor, or politician.

In romantic situations you are passionate and devoted, but also controlling and possessive. The independence and relaxed attitude of the number five do not always mesh well with Scorpio's all-or-nothing approach to love and romance.

On This Day:

Guy Fawkes Night is a popular British holiday that was decreed by an act of Parliament. It commemorates the foiling of a 1605 plot by Guy Fawkes to blow up the Parliament building. Had it succeeded, the entire government would have been wiped out. Topping off the festivities, effigies of the would-be renegade are tossed into bonfires.

Born Today: Bryan Adams (singer/songwriter); Eugene V. Debs (labor leader); Art Garfunkel (singer); Vivian Leigh (actress); Javy Lopez (baseball player); Joel McCrea (actor); Tatum O'Neal (actress); Roy Rogers (actor); Elke Sommer (actress); Sam Shepard (actor); Ike Turner (rock and roll star); Bill Walton (basketball player)

November 6

♏ Scorpio, 6

The charming, gregarious, and seemingly easygoing outer façade of those celebrating birthdays today camouflages a tougher, more intense inner nature. You actually are all that you seem—idealistic, judicious, fair minded, and honorable. But there is a part of you that is shrewd, secretive, and mistrustful of the motives of others. Moreover, you refuse to settle for quick answers or superficial assessments. You want to believe in the goodness of humanity, so you optimistically hope for the best. However, you've seen too much of the dark side of human nature not to be prepared for the worst.

Charisma, poise, and sociability are the hallmarks of the November 6th person. Ambitious and determined, you're also something of a perfectionist. You know what you want to achieve and have a firm grasp on what you need to do to accomplish it. An insightful sounding board for the difficulties of others, you welcome the opportunity to help people find viable solutions to their problems. Although you offer assistance without ulterior motives, you won't object if your aid makes people feel obligated to you.

Your magnetic personality and overt sensuality fascinate perspective partners and draw them into your orbit. You have a lot to give, but you expect so much in return that your romantic partner may find your controlling nature a bit overwhelming.

On This Day:

In Babylonia, this date was celebrated as the birth of the goddess Tiamont, who, with her consort Apsu, created heaven and Earth and gave birth to all the gods and goddesses of the ancient world. This is also the feast day of Roman Catholic Saint Leonard, the patron of women in childbirth. With no one else available, he helped the queen through a difficult delivery.

Born Today: Sally Field (actress); Glen Frey (rock star); Ethan Hawke (actor); Walter Johnson (baseball player); Julian II, "The Apostate/The Blessed" (emperor of Rome); James Naismith (inventor of basketball); Mike Nichols (director); Maria Shriver (TV news correspondent); John Philip Sousa (composer); Pat Tillman (football player)

November 7

℠ Scorpio, 7

Scorpions born on this day have an illusive, paradoxical quality that surrounds them with an enchanting aura of mystery. Some people may think of you as aloof because you need time on your own for private contemplation. Your intuition provides you with an eerie, psychic-like insight into people and situations. As a born peacemaker, your serene, diplomatic manner helps you avoid confrontations and circumvent hostilities. However, despite your belief that contention is a waste of time, you patently refuse to compromise when it comes to your ideals and principles.

The typical November 7th person has an active and vivid imagination. When channeled into the arts, along with your love of all things romantic, mysterious, and melodramatic, it can lead to a successful career as an actor, musician, dancer, or writer of fiction or poetry. More than anything, you're a compassionate, empathetic crusader for the rights of the disenfranchised. Your sensitivity to people and their problems makes you well suited for any profession that is connected to medicine, psychology, education, social work, law, politics, or religion.

In a loving, intimate union, you're more likely than most other scorpions to idealize your partner and place him or her on a pedestal. If things should turn sour and you're forced to face up to reality, you could be severely hurt or disappointed.

On This Day:

In ancient Greece, a fire festival known as the Night of Hecate was held each year on this date to honor the crone of the waning Moon and the underworld and the guardian of the crossroads. Hecate's worship was performed at night. Wherever three roads crossed, food and drink were left as offerings to the venerable triple goddess.

Born Today: Albert Camus (philosopher/writer); Madame Marie Curie (physicist/chemist); Billy Graham (evangelist); Al Hirt (jazz musician); Dean Jagger (actor); Jim Kaat (baseball player); Keith Lockhart (conductor); Joni Mitchell (singer); Dana Plato (actress); Joan Sutherland (opera singer); Leon Trotsky (revolutionary)

November 8

♏ Scorpio, 8

The ambitious individuals whose birthdays fall on this day are instinctively drawn to the hub of power and prestige. With your sharp intellect and exceptional head for business and finance, you can go as far as you like in your chosen career. You are a tough, ambitious leader who can be either a loyal ally or a formidable opponent. As a boss or manager, you may be a bit over-bearing, but what you lack in diplomacy, you make up for in your willingness to work harder than anyone else.

November 8th individuals are natural born detectives. You probe and prod other people's psyches to find out what they're about, while keeping your own agenda top secret. Because of your guarded nature, you tend to build trust very slowly, and few people are admitted to your private world. You're intense and single-minded in the pursuit of your goals. No job is too difficult nor responsibility too great for you to undertake if it will help you achieve your objectives. It would be wise for you to learn to balance work with play, or you may burn yourself out in your effort to reach the top.

Close personal relationships can be more difficult for you to maintain than professional ones. You want the freedom to do as you please, yet you have great difficulty relinquishing control and extending the same independence to your mate or partner.

On This Day:

In Japan, Fuigo Matsuri, the Shinto Festival of Kitchen Gods, honors the god and goddess of kitchens, Oki-Tsu-Hiko-No-Kami and his wife Oki-Tsu-Hime-No-Kami. Their main duty is to look after the cauldron in which water is boiled. Another Japanese deity associated with the kitchen is Hettsui-No-Kami, the goddess of the kitchen range.

Born Today: Christian Bernard (cardiac surgeon/heart transplant pioneer); Milton Bradley (game manufacturer); Angel Cordero, Jr. (jockey); Alain Delon (actor); Christie Lee Hefner (magazine publisher); Kazuo Ishiguro (writer); Margaret Mitchell (writer); Patti Page (singer); Bonnie Raitt (singer/songwriter); Morley Safer (TV journalist)

November 9

♏ Scorpio, 9

The scorpion born on this day is an imaginative dreamer who is fascinated by all things strange, mysterious, unknown, or unknowable. Your psychic-like intuition is the touchstone of your existence. In fact, you're so receptive to the unseen vibrations that surround you that you easily pick up on things others are not even aware of. However, neither sensitivity nor inherent spirituality can keep you from taking assertive action when you deem it necessary.

On some level the November 9th individual is a shrewd go-getter with an extraordinary knack for turning dreams into profitable realities. You function at such a deep level of consciousness that the mundane details of everyday life sometimes escape your notice altogether. As a confirmed idealist with strong convictions, you can be very persuasive when trying to get others to see things from your point of view. With your creative talent, you may find your true calling in the arts or the sciences. Your sensitivity to people and their problems makes you well suited to an occupation connected to medicine, psychology, education, law, or religion.

Your passionate, caring nature may give some people the mistaken idea that you would be an easy target for an unscrupulous lover. What they don't realize is that your inner scorpion possesses the uncanny ability to spot a lie or a con game a mile away.

On This Day:

This day is sacred to Helena, deified wife of the Roman Emperor Julian II, known as "The Apostate" to Christians and "The Blessed" to pagans. Today's Feast of the Four Crowned Martyrs is held in great regard by Freemasons. In Thailand, this day is Loy Krathog, a wish-magic festival when people launch their little boats along with a wish.

Born Today: Lou Ferrigno (body builder/actor); Tom Fogerty (rock star); Bob Gibson (baseball player); Chris Jericho (wrestler); Nick Lachey (rock star); Hedy Lamarr (actress); Carl Sagan (astronomer/writer); Sisqo (rap star); Mary Travers (singer); Ivan Turgenev (writer); Tom Weiskopf (golfer); Sanford White (architect)

November 10

♏ Scorpio, 1

The individual whose birthday falls on this date is independent, assertive, and extremely persuasive. Quick mentally as well as physically, you're a dynamic, adventurous visionary with inspired, cutting-edge ideas. You have a competitive nature that relishes any opportunity to confront and overcome challenges. Driven by your fiery courage and steely determination, you just keep going until you've reached your goal. Inherently proud and dignified, you patently refuse to compromise your principles and ideals. As one of life's warriors, you rally to the call without a moment's hesitation. You are prepared to fight for any cause that you deem just and honorable.

Those born on this day like to surround themselves with drama and excitement, and their exuberant, magnetic personalities rarely fail to attract admiration and attention. However hard you might try, you're not much of a team player. You function best when you're the one in authority, because you can't stand having anyone else control your actions. Many well-known, creative individuals from various walks of life were born under the powerful influence of the November 10th vibration.

In close relationships you are ardent, loyal, loving, and passionate. Although you have a great deal to give, you expect as much or more in return. Your intense sensuality and obsessive, all-or-nothing approach to love fascinate some and repel others. Potential partners may find your spurts of jealousy and possessiveness a bit overwhelming.

On This Day:

In olden times, the pagan festival of Nincnevin, or Old November Eve (later Martinmas Eve), was celebrated throughout the Scottish countryside on this date. It honored an aspect of the goddess Diana with feasts and prayers. It was thought that the goddess made herself visible to mortals and rode through the air during the night hours.

★★★
★ Born Today: Richard Burton (actor); Donna Fargo (singer); William Hogarth (artist); MacKenzie Phillips (actress); John Northrup (aeronautical engineer); Mike Powell (long jumper); John Marquand (writer); Mabel Normand (actress/comedienne); Claude Rains (actor); Roy Scheider (actor); Friedrich Schiller (poet/playwright)

November 11

♏ Scorpio, 2

The intense scorpions born on this day are emotional powerhouses who are determined to maintain control of their own destinies. Extremely proud and self-reliant, you remain poised on the surface even when you are seriously distressed or disappointed. In fact, you are so good at concealing your true feelings that most people haven't a clue to what is really going on beneath your composed façade. As a lover, relative, friend, or business associate, you're loyal and supportive, but exceedingly demanding. However, you're so charismatic and intriguing that few are able to resist your magnetic allure.

The person whose birthday falls on November 11 is naturally defensive and suspicious of other people's intentions. You erect emotional barriers that few can cross. A born detective, you're adept at uncovering everyone else's secrets, but you prefer keeping your own safely locked away in the deepest recesses of your psyche. Despite your sensitivity to what others think, you're inclined to rely on yourself and your own ideas. You are strongly opinionated, and you defend your position with convoluted arguments that tend to leave your more straightforward opponents feeling totally frustrated and confused.

Deeply devoted to your family, you may be relied upon to take care of them, provide for them, and protect them from harm. Although you want love and support in return, you're hesitant when it comes to exposing your own emotional vulnerability.

On This Day:

Veterans Day in the United States is celebrated in honor of members of the armed forces who fought in any war that involved U.S. servicemen. Armistice Day is the holiday in Belgium, France, and other European countries that commemorates the 1918 end to World War I. In Ireland, today is the festival of the Lunantishees, the spirits that guard the holy blackthorn trees.

Born Today: Bibi Anderson (actress); Leonardo DiCaprio (actor); Calista Flockhart (actress); Demi Moore (actress); Pat O'Brien (actor); George Patton (U.S. Army general); Marc Summers (TV host); Kurt Vonnegut, Jr. (writer); Peta Wilson (actress); Jonathon Winters (comedian/actor)

November 12

♏ Scorpio, 3

The self-reliant individuals whose birthdays take place on this day know what they want from life and have a very good idea how to go about getting it. You are considerably more lighthearted and fun loving than many of your darker, more serious Sun sign counterparts. Your deep, penetrating mind and extraordinary depth of vision provide you with a tremendous potential for success in virtually any career field you find appealing. Although you can be quite stubborn with regard to your personal beliefs and values, your inquiring mind is always open to differing points of view.

The essential nature of the November 12th person may be likened to that of a sports champion. Your physical and mental stamina and the desire to win carry you to victory. Your attraction to danger may lead to a career in covert activities with an organization such as the CIA, FBI, law enforcement SWAT, or Military Special Forces. Whether in sports, the arts, politics, business, or the helping professions, you shine whenever you're able to put your energy, dedication, and idealism to practical use.

In a close relationship, you may find yourself torn between your need for personal freedom and a tendency to be possessive of those you love. Naturally flirtatious, you enjoy playing the field and may have great difficulty settling down with one person. However, when you do, you expect unquestioning loyalty and fidelity from your partner.

On This Day:

In ancient Rome, an annual festival, the Epulum Jovis in honor of the goddesses Juno and Minerva and the god Jupiter, was celebrated on Capitoline Hill, where all three were enshrined. Animal sacrifices were made at the temples in the city, and in the evening there were blazing bonfires and an impressive torchlight processional.

Born Today: Nadia Comaneci (gymnast); Tanya Harding (skater); Grace Kelly (actress/princess of Monoco); Auguste Rodin (sculptor); Wallace Shawn (actor); Sammy Sosa (baseball player); David Schwimmer (actor); Jo Stafford (singer); Elizabeth Cady Stanton (feminist/social reformer); Neal Young (rock star)

November 13

♏ Scorpio, 4

Scorpions born on this day are endowed with prudence, patience, perseverance, endurance, and determination. You are as prudent and cautious in your dealings with others as you are secretive and reticent about your own affairs. Strategy is your forte. You're skilled at organizing and working out all the details of a plan or project. Your hard-working, focused intensity makes you a natural leader and an extremely effective administrator. A born detective, you probe and prod until you get to root of things, and then you scrupulously analyze the results of your investigations.

The actions of the November 13th individual, although they seem cool and controlled, are more likely to be based on instinct and emotion than logic and reason. You think with your heart and feel with your head. Bright, clever, and creative, you possess an artist's temperament with a scientist's mentality. Your analytical capabilities help you understand intricate technical details in business, scientific research, law, and medicine. Your critical faculties and intuition alert you to the wants and needs of the public and to the best ways of providing them.

You are a loyal and devoted lover who feels things very deeply. Yet at times you appear distant and mysterious. This is particularly true when lack of trust causes you to hide your emotional vulnerability beneath an impenetrable mask of disinterest and nonchalance. Even so, your deeply passionate nature attracts suitors like a magnet.

On This Day:

The Roman Festival of Feronia honored the goddess of thermal springs, orchards, woodlands, volcanoes, flowers, and fire. Great fairs were held at Feronia's November festivals, where offerings of the first fruits were given to the goddess. Slaves were set free, and men walked barefoot across hot coals to the cheering of the crowds.

Born Today: Nathaniel Benchley (writer); Rachel Bilson (actress); Edwin Booth (actor); Louis Brandeis (U.S. Supreme Court justice); Whoopi Goldberg (comedienne); Garry Marshall (actor/director/producer); Chris Noth (actor); Jean Seaberg (actress); Robert Louis Stevenson (writer); Oskar Werner (actor); Charles Frederick Worth (designer)

November 14

♏ Scorpio, 5

T he person born on this day is torn between the role of dispassionate, intellectual observer and intense, in-your-face redeemer of humanity. You're a visionary idealist and a strongly independent thinker. It doesn't matter whether you are liberal or conservative, your lofty idealism prompts you to pursue the truth (or your version of the truth) with passionate determination. If you get the disparate sides of your nature to work in tandem, you can become a powerful force in the arts, science, philosophy, or politics.

The November 14th individual brings a distinctly personal world view to each challenge he or she confronts. In addition, you possess the requisite intelligence and stamina to succeed in any venture that interests you. If you have an Achilles heel, it's your pride. You expect recognition and praise in return for all your hard work. If it's not forthcoming, you prefer suffering in silence to admitting your disappointment, but you feel hurt and slighted nonetheless. You're a natural for a career as a writer, psychologist, educator, lawyer, actor, politician, or preacher.

In intimate relationships, you are passionate, possessive, and controlling. Your physically ardent nature does not mesh all that well with your intellectual temperament. Emotionally, you tend to blow hot and cold. Although you long for sexual fulfillment as much as other scorpions, you also need a lover you can talk to.

On This Day:

In ancient times, the Feast of the Musicians, a Druidic festival dedicated to bards and musicians, took place on this date. It's celebrated today by some neo-pagans with offerings to the Celtic gods of music. It is customary to gather around a bonfire for an evening of songs and storytelling, ending with everyone tossing a wish into the flames.

Born Today: Charles (Prince of Wales); Aaron Copland (composer); Robert Fulton (steamboat inventor); Brian Keith (actor); Veronica Lake (actress); Joseph McCarthy (U.S. senator); Claude Monet (artist); Jawaharal Nehru (prime minister of India); Dick Powell (actor); Condoleezza Rice (U.S. secretary of state); McLean Stevenson (actor)

November 15

♏ Scorpio, 6

Scorpions born on this day are gracious, charming, and fun loving on the outside, but within, they are much tougher and more intense than anyone realizes. When challenged, you marshal all your considerable forces to combat the opposition, and then you give as good as you get. Despite your humanitarianism and desire to be of help to the community, you have a deep-seated understanding of the dark side of human nature and hold few expectations where other people are concerned.

Those celebrating November 15th birthdays tell it like it is. Inherently proud and dignified, you refuse to compromise your principles and ideals. As a result, you're less likely than most of your Sun sign counterparts to pussyfoot around the truth. Your natural instincts incline toward culture and refinement. You enjoy the arts in any form and may have creative talent yourself. No matter what your calling in life, you patently refuse to settle for easy knowledge or easy answers of any kind. You keep on digging and probing until you unearth what you need in order to outdo and outshine the competition. Many notable actors, musicians, artists, writers, scientists, and politicians were born on this date.

In romantic relationships, your all-or-nothing attitude makes you somewhat demanding and possessive. Love is important to you, and you long to belong to someone. But you need to feel comfortable and in control before you'll commit yourself.

On This Day:

In Japan, Shichi-go-San, a centuries-old Shinto festival, is performed annually on this date. Also known as the Seven-Five-Three, it is a huge birthday celebration for children who have reached these ages. Parents take their youngsters to local shrines for the blessings of the gods and goddesses and candy decorated with symbols of good fortune.

Born Today: Ed Asner (actor); Petula Clark (singer/actress); W. Averill Harriman (financier/New York governor/diplomat); Sir William Herschel (astronomer); Curtis Le May (U.S. Air Force general); Mantovani (conductor/arranger); Georgia O'Keeffe (painter); Irwin Rommel, "The Desert Fox" (German field marshal); Sam Waterston (actor)

November 16

♏ Scorpio, 7

The enigmatic individual celebrating a birthday on this date is a studious intellectual on the one hand and a psychic intuitive on the other. The story of your life is one that flips back and forth between your rational mind and mystical imagination. Through your feelings and emotions, you can sense things that other people aren't even aware of. A lively conversationalist, you have a mesmerizing gift for gaining and holding the attention of a crowd. You have strong, definite opinions and particularly enjoy participating in lively discussions about ideas and ideals.

The keen perceptions and acute powers of observation of those born on November 16 allow them to see through other people's façades. However, where your own life is concerned, you're a private person who much prefers keeping personal business hidden under a cloak of secrecy. Mystery, melodrama, whimsy, humor, and romance are all part and parcel of your basic makeup, and your thoughts tend to move from the sublime to the ridiculous and back again. You would make a fine actor, writer, dancer, musician, athlete, artist, publicist, politician, or preacher.

Love plays a major role in your life. However, your emotional nature is so deep and complex that your romantic life can be as turbulent as it is passionate and intense. You can display a poignant vulnerability one moment and then become possessive, jealous, and demanding the next.

On This Day:

In India on or near this date each year, which is the beginning of the Hindu New Year, the people celebrate Dewali, the Festival of Lights. Candles are lit to honor Dharani, the wealth-giving, luck-bringing, abundance aspect of the Hindu goddess Lakshmi. Homes are decorated with ancient good-fortune ritual designs called kolams.

Born Today: Chinua Achebe (writer); Oksana Baiul (skater); Lisa Bonet (actress); Frank Bruno (boxer); Antonio Gades (dancer); Dwight Gooden (baseball player); W. C. "Father of the Blues" Handy (pianist/composer/arranger); George S. Kaufman (playwright); Burgess Meredith (actor); Shigeru Miyamoto (video game designer)

November 17

♏ Scorpio, 8

Ambition is the middle name of the hard-working scorpion celebrating a birthday today. You've known from an early age that you wanted do something special with your life. Consequently, you focus on your long-term goals with a passionate intensity and single-minded determination. You present your plans and ideas to the world marketplace in such a way as to virtually guarantee your future success. Moreover, anything you're unable to accomplish with toughness and tenacity, you can usually finesse through clever strategy and gentle persuasion.

November 17th individuals refuse to compromise their ideals and principles. With courage and conviction, you'll step up to help anyone you believe has been wronged or mistreated. You resonate with the suffering and injustices in the world, and your desire to do something about them may lead to a career in medicine, psychology, education, social reform, law, law enforcement, politics, or religion. Creatively, you could find your means of self-expression as a writer, actor, comedian, musician, or dancer. No matter what you decide to do with your prodigious talents and abilities, you won't rest until you've gained the praise and recognition of your peers.

In an intimate relationship, you make a sensual and passionate lover. However, you have a private side to your personality that makes its hard for you to reveal your deepest feelings. When you do commit to another person, you're loyal, generous, and devoted, but a lack of trust can cause you to act in a controlling and possessive manner.

On This Day:

This is the feast day of Roman Catholic Saint Hilda, the daughter of a king of Northumbria. At the age of thirty-three, Hilda entered the Chelles Monastery in France. Later, she returned to Northumbria to become abbess of Hartlepool. In time, Hilda was named head of the double monastery of Streaneschalch, at Whitby. Saint Hilda is regarded as one of England's greatest women.

Born Today: Danny DeVito (actor/director); Daisy Fuentes (actress/TV host); Rock Hudson (actor); Lauren Hutton (supermodel/actress); Gordon Lightfoot (singer/songwriter); Lorne Michaels (producer); Martin Scorsese (director); Tom Seaver (baseball player); Lee Strasberg (actor/director/founder of the Actor's Studio)

November 18

♏ Scorpio, 9

Those born on this day combine the spiritual, the creative, and the material in their natures in a way that makes them seem to be "all things to all people." This chameleon-like quality allows you fit in anywhere, with anyone. You're so perceptive and intuitive that it's downright spooky. You pick up on things, like unspoken words and repressed feelings, that elude most people. On one level you come off as a sensitive, poetic dreamer and, on another, as a shrewd, ambitious, super-achiever who appears to thrive on hard work and challenges.

People whose birthdays fall on November 18 understand the human condition, and in their interactions with others they're selfless and courageous. A born crusader, you're not afraid of anything or anyone. Since you refuse to tolerate injustices, you can usually be found in the forefront of any battle against inequity. You possess an active imagination that, when channeled into the arts, science, or business, can help you materialize your plans in phenomenal ways. Your interest in the romantic, mysterious, and melodramatic could lead to a successful career as an actor, artist, musician, filmmaker, or writer.

Your innate emotional vulnerability is protected to some extent by an uncanny ability to discern the truth. Nevertheless, in a love relationship you're inclined to place your lover on a pedestal and willingly sacrifice your own interests in favor your partner's. If disappointment ever forces you to face up to reality, your heart will surely be broken.

On This Day:

In southwestern Asia, Ardvi Sura, the goddess of heavenly waters, who is an aspect of the Persian goddess Anahita, mother of the stars, is honored on or around this date each year with a sacred festival called the Day of Ardvi. The festival, which has been celebrated by the faithful since ancient times, takes place under the nighttime stars.

Born Today: Imogene Coca (comedienne); Louis Daguerre (painter/inventor of daguerreotype); Linda Evans (actress); George Gallop (pollster); Eugene Ormandy (violinist/conductor); Ignace Paderewski (pianist/president of Poland); Elizabeth Perkins (actress); Alan Shepard (astronaut); Brenda Vaccaro (actress); Owen Wilson (actor)

November 19

♏ Scorpio, 1

Scorpions born on this day are determined to be great and leave an indelible mark on the world. Driven by fiery courage, steely determination, and raw ambition, you relish any opportunity to confront difficult and challenging situations. Once you get going on something, there's no stopping you. Since patience is not your strong suit, you often plunge ahead without considering all the consequences. As a leader who can usually be found in the forefront of an enterprise, you have little or no sympathy for shirkers or stragglers.

The confident people celebrating birthdays today know exactly where they stand and what they want. Once you decide to do something, you waste neither time nor energy on doubt or hesitation. You apply your hard-driving power to your work, and you expect the same kind of application and energy from others. You are also highly emotional and sensitive. Despite your strength of character, you need the approbation and good opinion of other people. If you don't receive the praise and appreciation you consider your due, you hide your disappointment behind a smile. However, you never forget or forgive the slight.

In love, you're ardent, but demanding. You pursue the object of your affection with unremitting zeal. You may refuse to commit until you're convinced that the other person is trustworthy. But once you enter into a romantic union, you're completely devoted and dependable.

On This Day:

Today, the Hawaiian festival of Makahiki marks the beginning of the harvest season, when the Pleiades constellation becomes visible in the night sky. It honors Lono, the Hawaiian god of agriculture, peace, and fertility. The celebration includes chanting, hula dances, cleansing rituals, awa-drinking ceremonies, and a feast with laulau, fish, and poi.

Born Today: Hiram Bingham (archaeologist/U.S senator); Dick Cavett (TV talk show host); Tommy Dorsey (bandleader); Jodi Foster (actress); Indira Gandhi (prime minister of India); Larry King (TV and radio talk show host); Calvin Klein (designer); Meg Ryan (actress); Billy Sunday (evangelist); Ted Turner (TV media mogul)

November 20

♏ Scorpio, 2

The gracious surface personality of the Scorpio native celebrating a birthday today hides an intense, emotionally demanding inner nature. Despite your stubborn pride, you are actually a good deal more cooperative and willing to compromise than many of your Sun sign counterparts. You're an idealist, but one who is shrewdly aware of the shortcomings of human nature. When smoothing out disputes, you try to be as diplomatic and tactful as you possibly can without playing havoc with the truth.

Although seemingly cool and detached, the November 20th person needs to be in control of every situation. Career plays an important role in your life, and any old job won't do. To be fulfilled, you need to feel emotionally involved in your work. Your quick mind and penetrating curiosity can lead you to a broad range of interests. Whatever you choose to pursue, you prefer relying on your intelligence, talent, and charm to win the day. However, if that doesn't work, you're not above turning up the pressure and making the proverbial offer that can't be refused.

When you are romantically involved with the right person, you're a generous lover who knows intuitively what your partner wants and is more than capable of providing it. However, if your need to merge with another person can't be met on your terms, you may choose to sublimate your passion and divert it into creative projects.

On This Day:

This is the feast day of the Greek proconsul Praetextatus and his wife Paulina, who were guardians of the Eleusinian mysteries. In 364 C.E., they resisted the order of Roman Christian Emperor Valentinian to suppress the very ancient, sacred Greek pagan rites. Praetextatus allowed the mysteries to be performed as if the emperor's edict wasn't valid.

Born Today: Duane Allman (rock star); Kaye Ballard (actress/singer); Alistair Cooke (TV host/writer); Richard Dawson (actor/TV host); Bo Derek (actress); Edwin Hubble (astronomer); Richard Masur (actor); Robert F. Kennedy (U.S. senator); Estelle Parsons (actress); Dick Smothers (comedian/musician); Sean Young (actress)

November 21

♏ Scorpio, 3

The person born on the Scorpio/Sagittarius cusp is typically more outgoing than most of his or her Sun sign counterparts. Sagittarius contributes humor, optimism, and lightheartedness to Scorpio's darker, more serious nature. The sign of the archer also adds a philosophical turn of mind that is sometimes absent from the obsessive Scorpio mentality. While others of your sign are busily probing and prodding people's psyches, you're seeking knowledge and wisdom in the hope of uncovering the meaning of life.

November 21st individuals are much too complex and secretive to be easily understood, and even the people who know them best may have a hard time divining their true motivations. You seem flexible and progressive until someone tries to get you to change your mind about one of your pet theories. Once you have settled on a firm opinion, you can be stubborn to the point of intractability. An intelligent and witty conversationalist, you enjoy exchanging thoughts and information with others. Inherently adventurous and courageous, you love traveling, especially to dangerous, unusual, and exotic places. Your temperament is that of a sports champion whose stamina and competitive instincts are invariably focused on overcoming challenges and defeating the competition.

In an intimate relationship, you may be torn between Scorpio's inclination toward loyalty and fidelity and the archer's naturally flirtatious, independent spirit. However, when you make a firm commitment to someone you love, you stick by it.

On This Day:

On this date in Mesoamerica, the ancient Mayan people held a joyous festival honoring Kukulcan, "the feathered snake whose path is the waters." Later merged with Quetzalcoatl, "the plumed serpent," and identified with the planet Venus, Kukulcan was a god of wisdom and fertility and the inventor of agriculture and the Mayan calendar.

Born Today: Troy Aikman (football player); Bjork (singer/songwriter); Joseph Campanella (actor); Ken Griffey, Jr. (baseball player); Goldie Hawn (actress); Sid Luckman (football player); Rene Margritte (artist); Juliet Mills (actress); Stan Musial (baseball player); Harold Ramis (actor/director); Marlo Thomas (actress); Voltaire (writer/philosopher)

November 22

✗ Sagittarius, 4

Archers born on this day are ambitious leaders with multifaceted personalities and tremendous potential for material and social success. The dynamic power of the root number four's vibration combines with your Sagittarian spirit of freedom to make you a practical dreamer. You see life in terms of the large philosophical picture as well as the nitty-gritty everyday details. You may be something of a maverick, but you're generally more comfortable implementing your innovative ideas within an established framework.

Driven by ambition and the desire to succeed, there is virtually nothing those born on November 22 can't do when they put their minds to it. Moreover, you want to accomplish something useful that will make an impact on the world. Along with the realization of your dreams, you expect to reap the prestige and financial rewards due someone who is a master at his or her profession. Enormously persuasive, you're able to talk anyone into anything. Consequently, you would make a fine salesperson, preacher, politician, or teacher. Creative occupations appeal to you, and you would derive great personal satisfaction from a career in writing, drama, music, or art.

In love, you're steadfast and sincere. You have less of a roving eye, and you're more willing to commit than many of your Sagittarian Sun sign counterparts. Even so, you need to retain a certain amount of independence in all your relationships.

On This Day:

In Norse tradition, today is the festival of Ydalir, the Valley of the Yews, and falls under the rule of Ullr, whose name means "brilliant one." Ullr is the god of legal disputes, sacred oaths, hunting, skiing, and winter. Stepson of the god Thor and son of the Earth mother Sif and an unknown father, Ullr is thought to have giant blood.

Born Today: Abigail Adams (U.S. first lady); Hoagy Carmichael (pianist/songwriter); Jamie Lee Curtis (actress); Rodney Dangerfield (comedian); Mariel Hemmingway (actress); Charles de Gaulle (president of France/WWII symbol of French resistance); Billie Jean King (tennis player); Robert Vaughn (actor)

November 23

↗ Sagittarius, 5

For those individuals celebrating birthdays on this date, experiencing life is more important than stability or security. You aim to broaden your vision through study and travel, and you see your existence as an exciting, ongoing adventure. Innovation is your forte, and you're not afraid to defy conventional wisdom in an attempt make the world a better place. However, your free-wheeling nature and determination to flout convention sometimes blind you to the practical necessities of daily life.

People born on November 23 are mentally and physically alert and quick on the uptake. You love learning new things and sharing your knowledge with others in ways that would make you an excellent teacher. You have a flair for organization and promotion, along with a jovial nature that can garner success in business, especially in sales or advertising. With your musical talent and artistic creativity, you may be prompted to try for a career as a musician, composer, actor, or filmmaker. As a natural athlete who loves the outdoors, you may discover your niche in professional sports. Your keen sense of justice and ability to discuss ideas and ideals could make you a fine lawyer, journalist, broadcaster, writer, or politician.

Emotionally you're a bit of a paradox. You enjoy partying and flirting, and you might find a romantic escapade a lot more appealing than a long-term, serious union. You regard love as a glorious experience, but your need for personal freedom makes loyalty rather difficult to sustain.

On This Day:

Today is sacred to the Norse wizard Wayland the Smith, a Saxon god and patron of blacksmiths and metal workers. In Japan, a rice harvest celebration called the Shinjosai Festival for Sakuya Konohana-Hime is held annually on this date. The holiday is dedicated to the goddess who is a granddaughter of the ancient solar deity Amaterasu.

Born Today: William "Billy the Kid" Bonney (outlaw); Otis Chandler (newspaper publisher); Shane Gould (swimmer); Boris Karloff (actor); Harpo Marx (mime/comic actor); Jose Orozco (artist); Franklin Pierce (U.S. president); Alexander Rodschenko (artist/photographer); Helen Rogers Reid (newspaper publisher)

November 24

✒ Sagittarius, 6

Somehow, the friendly, warm-hearted person whose birthday falls on this day manages to be honest and tactful at the same time. You tell it like it is, but you do it in a way that doesn't offend anyone. Your charming manner and aura of youthful exuberance attracts others to you. Extreme action is not your style, and your response to most situations and problems is decidedly calm and harmonious. However, despite your willingness to compromise and cooperate, you are much more likely to rely on your own judgment than on someone else's.

November 24th individuals are good natured and cheerful, with a sincere concern for others. People seek you out because they like being around you. Although you are easygoing, your independent spirit keeps you from being overly influenced by outside forces. You are a born salesperson with an instinctive understanding of what's in and what's on the way out. On the creative side, you may find that you prefer working in the arts or the professions to pursuing a career in business. Many born on this date make a splash as writers or entertainers, and others find rewarding opportunities for success in law, education, or politics.

In your intimate relationships, you are romantic, affectionate, refined, and caring. Since you truly need a loving companion to share your life's journey, you're probably more willing to commit to a long-term partnership than the typical solar Sagittarian.

On This Day:

On or around this date each year, the holiday of Thanksgiving is celebrated throughout the United States. The tradition of the Thanksgiving feast began in Plymouth Colony in 1621 with the Pilgrims' celebration of their first year's harvest. In modern times, the festivities generally include bountiful meals, big parades, and football games.

Born Today: William F. Buckley, Jr. (magazine publisher/columnist); Scott Joplin (pianist/composer); Bat Masterson (U.S. marshal); Oscar Robertson (basketball player); Father Juniper Sierra (Spanish California missionary); Baruch Spinoza (philosopher); Zachary Taylor (U.S. president); Henri Toulouse-Lautrec (artist)

November 25

↗ Sagittarius, 7

The visionary individuals born on this day lead intense inner lives of sentimental dreams and crusading ideals. Your makeup is a unique mix of a philosopher's mentality, an artist's temperament, and a mystic's spirituality. You possess a deep reservoir of wisdom, a vivid imagination, and possibly clairvoyant or psychic abilities. A concerned humanitarian, you are very sensitive to people's needs. With the missionary spirit so strong inside you, your ultimate aim is to help guide others along a path of higher values.

November 25th people typically see themselves as truth seekers on a quest for the grail of honesty, sincerity, and loyalty. Although you sometimes give the impression of being a bit of a loner, you're actually searching for meaningful ways to connect with other people. You could satisfy your creative muse and establish a forum for your ideas as a writer, journalist, publisher, artist, musician, or actor. As a natural athlete with a genuine love of the outdoors, you might garner great success in the world of professional sports.

In love, you have so much affection to give that your partner may not be able to share the depths of emotion that you feel. You are very romantic and prone to falling hopelessly in love with an ideal. Should the flesh and blood person fail to live up to your dreams, you could be devastated.

On This Day:

On or near this date each year, the Chinese celebrate their Harvest Moon Festival. Small cakes are made in the shape of the Moon. Along with these Moon cakes, cookies are baked in the shape of small rabbits. The rabbit is important, because in Chinese mythology a rabbit that lives in the Moon is busy pounding out the elixir of life.

Born Today: Christina Applegate (actress); Andrew Carnegie (industrialist); Paul Desmond (jazz musician/composer); Joe DiMaggio (baseball player); Donovan McNabb (football player); John F. Kennedy, Jr. (magazine publisher); John Larroquette (actor); Ricardo Montalban (actor); Carrie Nation (temperance activist)

November 26

↗ Sagittarius, 8

The high-achieving archers born on this day are hard working, accomplishment oriented, and determined to do things their own way. Your forte is a knack for using practical means to accomplish seemingly impractical or improbable goals. You are willing to travel far and wide in order to fulfill your career aspirations. Moreover, your restless nature and enthusiasm for roaming and exploring is exacerbated by a nervous temperament that can make it difficult for you to remain in one place for long periods of time. When you feel the tension building, you might try spending time outdoors where you can be close to the natural world you love.

If those celebrating birthdays on November 26 have a fault, it is a propensity for saying exactly what they are thinking. Nevertheless, you are charming, capable, and enormously persuasive. In fact, you could talk anyone into anything, from taking a flyer on an innovative new invention to switching political loyalties. Consequently, you would make an excellent salesperson, publicist, preacher, politician, or teacher. Creative occupations also appeal to you, and you could derive great personal satisfaction from a life dedicated to acting, writing, music, or art.

In intimate relationships, you tend to blow hot and cold. You are romantic, warmhearted, and idealistic, but you're also critical of anyone who doesn't measure up to your high standards. Although you like the excitement and variety of an independent existence, you need the affection, devotion, and emotional security of a permanent union.

On This Day:

Around this time every year in the Basari villages of Senegal, the young men are initiated into manhood with elaborate rituals, competitions, dancing, and feasting. On this date in Nepal, the goddess Gujeswari Jatra is honored by Hindus and Buddhists. The day's activities include prayers, music, and songs of praise to Gujeswari.

Born Today: Cyril Cusack (actor/poet); Frances Dee (actress); Robert Goulet (singer); Eugene Ionesco (absurdist playwright); Rich Little (comedian/impersonator); Samuel Reshevsky (chess player); Charles Schultz (cartoonist); Eric Sevareid (TV news anchor); Tina Turner (singer); Norbert Wiener (mathematician)

November 27

The compassionate, concerned archer born on this day is deeply sensitive to the needs and desires of other people. Intellectually, you are clever and astute, but on an emotional level you can be rather impatient and impulsive. The dreamer in you yearns for an idyllic, utopian reality where everyone has whatever he or she needs. However, when you allow your sympathetic heart to totally rule your rational mind, you may become so embroiled in the problems of others that your potential for helping them resolve their difficulties becomes lost in aimless dreaming.

November 27th individuals are forward-looking innovators who are naturally drawn to progressive enterprises. You have a gift for zeroing in on new possibilities that others often miss. Mentally alert and physically active, you enjoy traveling and exploring the material world just as much as the inner world of ideas and imagination. Likeable, sincere, and outgoing, you radiate a friendly personality that makes you popular socially and professionally. Your honest, outspoken manner suits you to a career in the helping professions. Your keen sense of justice and ability to talk endlessly about your ideals and beliefs could help you become a fine lawyer, teacher, writer, broadcaster, or politician.

You are a caring, generous, devoted lover. Physically, you're ardent and passionate, but emotionally, you're so idealistic and impressionable that your intimate unions can be rather difficult to sustain.

On This Day:

On this day, the Greek feast of Aphrodite and Hermes honored the divine feminine and masculine in harmony. On this date each year, a religious festival called the Parvati-Devi takes place in India. It reveres the triple goddess known as the Mother of the Universe in her three forms: Sarasvati (maiden), Lakshmi (mother), and Parvati (crone).

Born Today: James Agee (writer/film critic); Jimi Hendrix (rock star); Robin Givins (actress); Caroline Kennedy (writer/co-founder of the Profile in Courage Awards); Brooke Langdon (actress); Bruce Lee (martial arts expert/actor); Eddie Rabbit (singer); "Buffalo" Bob Smith (children's TV show host); Jaleel White (actor)

November 28

♐ Sagittarius, 1

The fiery archers born on this day are fearless pioneers continuously on the lookout for action and excitement. You believe that challenge is the name of the game, and you don't expect things to come easily. Nevertheless, wherever you go, luck and good fortune seem to follow. Sagittarius is a dual sign and as much the home of philosophers and truth seekers as of athletes and adventurers. Consequently, you're just as likely to be found defending your intellectual ideas as competing for sports awards and trophies.

November 28th individuals have both depth of vision and the ability to swiftly grasp the essentials of any situation. You may have some difficulty coping with small details, but you can usually pass the grunt-work along to someone else. Driven to explore, create, and then act on what you've created, you are restless and in need of the type of stimulation that's best provided by new faces and places. Once a pet project is well underway, you may decide to leave it to others to finish what you started.

In intimate relationships you are passionate, affectionate, and generous. Despite being something of a romantic idealist, you probably don't take love all that seriously. You are devoted and attentive for as long as you stick around. But once your wonder-lust kicks in, you are quite capable of taking off with few regrets and no backward glances.

On This Day:

This is the first day of the runic half-month of Is, meaning ice. Ice represents a static period of enforced rest. Last Chance Day was considered to be the last chance to marry before Advent. It was believed that the groom would not have to assume his new wife's debts if he took her, dressed only in her undergarments, from the hands of the priest.

Born Today: Brooks Atkinson (theater critic); Joe Dante (director); Alexander Godunov (dancer); Gigi Gryce (jazz musician); Ed Harris (actor); Morris Louis (writer); Judd Nelson (actor); Randy Newman (singer/songwriter); Scarlett Pomers (actress); Paul Shaffer (musician/bandleader); Jon Stewart (comedian/TV show host/writer)

November 29

↗ Sagittarius, 2

The refined, high-minded individuals celebrating their birthdays today are more inclined toward aspiration than ambition. Your strength lies in your unique ability to achieve worldly success without compromising your personal ideals and principles. You possess a deep love for art, beauty, and music and a sharp intellect that is attracted to literature, mathematics, and the sciences. Essentially a visionary, you are not afraid to take enormous risks with regard to your art, philosophy, or ideology. More than anything, you're a crusading idealist with innovative, imaginative ideas that are often on the cutting edge of the artistic, academic, social, or political scene.

Those born on November 29 have a romantic streak that manifests on a creative level rather than a personal one. No matter what type of work you do, you'll channel your artistry into it in an interesting and imaginative manner. Nothing is too difficult for you once you set your mind to it. With your understanding of broad abstractions and small details, you can be successful in business or the professions. You always seem to know exactly what it is that the public wants and what the best way is to provide it.

In relationships, you're a true romantic. You go back and forth between wanting the independence to roam the world and needing the safety of a secure, committed union. Once you reconcile your conflicting impulses, you make a loyal and loving partner.

On This Day:

Sophia, the ancient Greek goddess of wisdom and inner truth, is honored and invoked annually on this date with chants, libations, and secret rituals performed by those who wish to acquire arcane knowledge. The Roman festival of the Sons of Saturn relates to the ancient god who was dethroned by his sons Jupiter, Neptune, and Pluto.

Born Today: Louisa May Alcott (writer); Kim Delany (actress); C. S. Lewis (writer); Chuck Mangione (jazz musician); Cathy Moriarty (actress); Adam Clayton Powell, Jr. (U.S. congressman/civil rights leader); Vin Scully (Los Angeles Dodgers radio broadcaster); Gary Shandling (comedian); Sir Philip Sidney (Elizabethan poet/courtier)

November 30

✗ Sagittarius, 3

The multifaceted Sagittarian born on this date has been blessed with intelligence, eloquence, wit, charm, and enthusiasm. The sky's the limit as far as your creative potential is concerned. Your restless temperament abhors a vacuum, and it is standard operating procedure for you to do two things at the same time. Inherently inquisitive and eminently sociable, you adore traveling, meeting new people, and learning new things. You view your life as a series of experiences consisting of as many exciting adventures and stimulating conversations as possible.

November 30th individuals have engaging personalities and the amazing ability to talk their way into or out of any situation. You enjoy the spotlight, and popularity and acceptance come easily to you. In business, you can make your mark in sales, advertising, promotion, or travel. However, your true calling may be in the media, the law, politics, or religion. With your quick, active mind and fluent, dramatic way of expressing yourself, you might garner great acclaim as an actor, singer, writer, publisher, or teacher.

You are freedom oriented and have a relaxed attitude toward love. Relationships work best for you when you're able to establish a strong intellectual rapport. You're a kind and generous lover, but there is something of the romantic gypsy in your makeup. You might decide to stick around for a lifetime, or you could be gone tomorrow.

On This Day:

Today is the Festival of Andros. An aspect of the god Dionysus, Andros was the personification of manhood and the principle of virility. Saint Andrew's Day honors the patron saint of fishers and fishmongers and of Scotland, where, during the fourth century, some of his bones were brought to what is now Saint Andrew's in Fife.

Born Today: Shirley Chisholm (U.S. congresswoman); Winston Churchill (prime minister of England); Dick Clark (TV host/producer); Richard Crenna (actor); Robert Guillaume (actor); Abbie Hoffman (radical political activist); Billy Idol (punk rock star); David Mamet (playwright/director); Mandy Patinkin (actor/singer); Ben Stiller (actor)

December Birthdays

December 1

↗ Sagittarius, 1

Archers born on this day are outspoken and idealistic, yet practical and flexible enough to get along in the world without surrendering their personal theories and beliefs. Although you like having things your own way, you're willing to compromise when you deem it necessary. Even so, your high-minded principles won't allow you to compromise with the truth. Still, your optimism, vitality, and enthusiasm impress people, and you're able to win them over with a combination of eloquence, charm, and humor.

The fearless trailblazers born on this day are innovative, courageous, and perpetually on the lookout for action and excitement. Your lively, adventurous spirit may take you on a journey to the ends of the earth—or beyond it into the far reaches of outer space. Despite a tendency to scatter your energies, you have little trouble achieving your goals. Change and variety are the spices that make your life worth living, and experience is vastly more important to you than security or stability. Your inherent restlessness is appeased by a continuing array of new faces and places.

Despite a streak of romantic idealism, you tend not to take intimate relationships very seriously. You are loving and attentive for as long as you stick around. However, once your wonder-lust kicks in, you're perfectly capable of leaving without so much as a backward glance.

On This Day:

Today is the ancient Greek festival of Poseidon, god of the sea and rebirth. On this date in some parts of the world, young girls perform the art of cromniomancy (divination by onion sprouts) to find out the names of their future husbands. This day is sacred to the Roman goddess Pieta, a deity of respectful duty.

Born Today: Woody Allen (comedian/actor/writer/director); John Densmore (rock star); Dame Alicia Markova (dancer); Mary Martin (actress/singer); Bette Midler (actress/singer); Richard Pryor (comedian); Lou Rawls (singer); Cyril Ritchard (actor); Eric Rohmer (director); Carl Schmidt-Rottluf (artist); Lee Trevino (golfer)

December 2

↗ Sagittarius, 2

The sociable individuals celebrating birthdays today are warm-hearted people pleasers bent on bringing conflicting parties together. The fiery, outspoken personality of Sagittarius is tempered by the helpfulness and consideration supplied by the number two in your birth date. Extreme action is not your style; your response to difficult situations is usually calm and harmonious. Although you are easygoing and cooperative, you're no pushover. Your independent spirit keeps you from being overly influenced by outside forces.

Those born on December 2 are flexible and are not afraid to make changes in order to ensure success. Ever determined to achieve your goals, you approach work and play with enthusiasm and wholehearted involvement. No matter what you decide to do in life, you should leave plenty of room for originality and creative self-expression. In business, you have a flair for sales and promotion, with an intuitive sense of which trends are new and hot and which ones are kaput and on the way out. Many born on this date find that they prefer the arts or the professions to a career in trade or commerce.

Love and friendship are extremely important to you. In intimate relationships you're romantic and affectionate, but rather less emotional than most other archers. You want a loving companion to share your journey, and you could be quicker to commit to a long-term partnership than others of your Sun sign.

On This Day:

On this day, Tibetan Buddhists make their annual pilgrimage to the world's oldest tree in the place that is now known as Bodh Gaya, India. The sacred tree, planted in 282 B.C.E., is honored with prayers, chants, and flags. It is believed to be an offshoot of the same Bodhi (or Bo) tree that the Buddha sat under when he attained enlightenment.

Born Today: Maria Callas (opera singer); Nelly Furtado (singer/songwriter); Lucy Liu (actress); Michael McDonald (singer/songwriter); Stone Phillips (TV news anchor); Charles Ringling (circus showman); Monica Seles (tennis player); Georges Seurat (artist); Brittany Spears (singer); Gianni Versace (designer)

December 3

↗ Sagittarius, 3

The most obvious assets of those born on this day are enthusiasm, intelligence, and charm. You view your life as an ongoing search for knowledge, experience, and adventure. You like learning interesting new things and then sharing what you've learned with others. You especially enjoy traveling and meeting exotic people. You possess a wide range of interests and a philosophical turn of mind; consequently, you're as fascinated with mental journeys as you are with physical ones. Sagittarius is about initiating things. You're driven by an insatiable curiosity and the need to seek out and explore innovative projects and fresh ideas.

Your warmth and friendliness are evident in everything you do. You are creative and versatile, and your willingness to compromise often leads to successful joint ventures. Nevertheless, you have a will of iron that helps you overcome adversity and stand up for yourself in a controversy. You are an ambitious, hard-working "idea person" and a dynamic leader. Your interests are many and varied, and it's important for you to learn to focus on significant things and not scatter your energies in too many directions.

With your sociable nature and ceaseless interest in people, you probably have lots of pals and confidants. In romantic love, you thrive on challenge and excitement, yet despite your freedom-loving, freewheeling soul, you are devoted to family and friends.

On This Day:

During the ancient Roman festival of Bona Dea, the Good Goddess, the Vestal Virgins conducted the woman's rites, secret ceremonies from which all males were barred. Hungarians celebrate the mother and guardian goddess Boldogasszony, who watches diligently over children, and many wedding festivals take place on this day.

Born Today: Brian Bonsall (actor); Anna Chlumsky (actress); Holly Marie Combs (actress); Joseph Conrad (writer); Anna Freud (psychoanalyst); Jean-Luc Goddard (director); Daryl Hannah (actress); Bucky Lasek (skateboard champion); Ozzy Osbourne (rock star); Gilbert Stuart (artist); Andy Williams (singer); Katarina Witt (figure skater)

December 4

↗ Sagittarius, 4

Archers born on this day appear relaxed and easygoing on the outside, but within they are exceedingly ambitious and determined to succeed. Like others of your Sun sign, you consider the journey important. However, your real goal is the prize at the end of the line. You're a dynamo of activity, but it's not the aimless activity of rushing around just to keep moving. You know exactly where you are going, and you have a good idea of how to get there. Your ability to plan and strategize and your resolute attitude and personable demeanor attract opportunities and people willing to support your efforts.

Although December 4th individuals possess the restlessness common to all Sagittarians, their passionate enthusiasm for roaming and exploring is tempered significantly by the level-headedness of the number four's vibration. Your winning personality and responsible approach are your ticket to success and happiness. Although you sometimes feel as if you are in a tug-of-war between work and play, work invariably wins out. Nevertheless, it is important for you to take a break from time to time to regenerate your energies.

You live your life with gusto, enjoying the company of all kinds of people and adapting easily to a variety of situations. In a romantic relationship, you're steadfast and likely to commit to a long-term union as long as you can retain a measure of your former freedom and independence.

On This Day:

In West Africa, this day is sacred to the Yoruban god Chango. The embodiment of passion, virility, and raw power, Chango, the son of the deities Yemaya and Orungan, is a god of lightning bolts. Today is the festival of the Greek goddess of wisdom and the useful arts, Pallas Athena, counterpart of the Roman goddess Minerva.

Born Today: Tyra Banks (supermodel); Jeff Bridges (actor); Sergei Bubka (pole vaulter); Francisco Franco (Spanish dictator); Jay-Z (rap star); Lew Jenkins (boxer); Lila McCann (singer); Rainer Maria Rilke (poet); Lillian Russell (actress); Jozef Sabovcik (skater); Marisa Tomei (actress); Dennis Wilson (rock star)

December 5

✈ Sagittarius, 5

Innovation is the key word for the farseeing archer born on this day. Naturally drawn to innovative ventures and progressive enterprises, you have a talent for picking up on possibilities that others usually miss. The creative urge is strong in you, and your artistry is as likely to utilize the medium of words and ideas as that of paint and clay. You excel at tackling difficult problems and resolving them through a combination of brainstorming and tangible action. Strongly opinionated, you know how to present your case, and you're particularly eloquent in the defense of your personal beliefs.

People celebrating birthdays today are adventurous and generally willing to try anything new and unusual. Whether you are an intuitive thinker or an eccentric genius, the touch of rebelliousness in your nature assures that you're never dull or boring. Your distaste for sham and deception prompts you to say exactly what you're thinking, letting the chips fall where they may. However, your warm, friendly manner and wonderful sense of humor make you so much fun to be with that most people are willing to overlook your no-holds-barred frankness and the forthright way in which you express your opinions.

In an intimate relationship, you're generous and passionate but wary of any commitment that impinges on your ability to move about freely. Although no one will ever own you, an understanding partner may win your loyalty and affection.

On This Day:

For small children in the Netherlands, Sinterklaasavond (Saint Nicholas Evening) is more important than Christmas. Sinterklaas brings presents to every child who has been good during the year. The children leave hay and carrots for Saint Nicholas' horses, and Saint Nicholas and his helpers put fruit, nuts, and coins in the children's wooden shoes.

Born Today: Gary Allan (singer); Morgan Brittany (actress); George Armstrong Custer (U.S. Army general); Walt Disney (animator/producer/founder of the Disney empire); Jim Messina (rock star); Otto Preminger (director); Little Richard (singer); Strom Thurmond (U.S. senator); Martin Van Buren (U.S. president)

December 6

↗ Sagittarius, 6

Those celebrating birthdays today are cheerful and well mannered, with a sincere concern for others that makes them excellent mediators. Your innate understanding of the art of gentle persuasion helps you win over bickering factions and make peace between them. People enjoy your company because of your genial disposition, optimistic outlook, and engaging, fun-loving personality. Your quick, active mind and the ability to talk your way out of difficult situations could prove helpful both personally and professionally.

December 6th archers are among the luckiest of the solar Sagittarians. You expect good things to happen, and they usually do. A "people person" with a wonderful zest for living, you derive great joy from parties and other social gatherings. The entrepreneurial spirit is strong in your nature and, in combination with your innovative ideas, virtually guarantees your success in any career that appeals to you. It is natural for you to express your creativity in the arts as a writer or entertainer. You may also find particularly rewarding opportunities in business, law, education, or politics.

An old-fashioned romantic, you love companionship and dream of finding your perfect mate. As a result, you're prone to falling hopelessly in love with an ideal. If the flesh and blood person fails to live up to your dreams, you could be devastated, and it might take you quite awhile to put your life back together.

On This Day:

Today, Advent begins on the fourth Sunday before Christmas, but in olden times it began on Saint Nicholas' Day. In northern Europe, Saint Nicholas absorbed pagan attributes from Odin, chief of the hunt, who rides through the sky with his reindeer. After the reformation, Saint Nicholas merged with Father Christmas to become the modern-day Santa Claus.

Born Today: Dave Brubeck (jazz musician); Pearl Buck (writer); Wally Cox (actor); Lynn Fontanne (actress); Ira Gershwin (lyricist); Charles Martin Hall (chemist); William S. Hart (actor); Tom Hulce (actor); Joyce Kilmer (poet); Agnes Moorehead (actress); John Singleton "The Grey Ghost" Mosby (Civil War Confederate colonel)

December 7

The intellectually independent archer born on this day possesses an insatiable curiosity. A plethora of nervous energy fuels your relentless pursuit of new ideas, places, and people. As a humanitarian crusader on a mission to save the world, you're truly interested in the many causes you advocate. Moreover, you don't just talk the talk; you also walk the walk. You're very clear about your principles; if they are challenged, you will fight tooth and nail to defend them.

December 7th people are spiritually oriented with a deep faith and a great deal of insight into themselves and others. You may be deeply religious in a traditional sense, or you may be drawn to various aspects of mysticism and the occult. Your intellect and intuition work hand in hand with your analytical mind to tie everything together. You have a great deal to say and the ability to put your ideas across with relative ease. Although you can make a success of just about any career you choose, you're best suited to an occupational field that allows you to help people, such as education, law, social services, politics, or religion.

In a romantic relationship, you're ardent and generous. Although you regard love as a glorious experience, your somewhat solitary nature requires time alone for private contemplation. Consequently, you may have difficulty finding a partner who is tuned to your wavelength and willing to adjust to your mood swings.

On This Day:

In the U.S., this is National Pearl Harbor Remembrance Day. On this day in 1941, Japanese aircraft carried out a surprise attack on the U.S. Pacific Fleet anchored at Pearl Harbor, Hawaii. There were nearly 3,000 deaths, and few U.S. ships escaped damage on the "date that will live in infamy." The next day, the United States declared war on the Empire of Japan.

Born Today: Larry Bird (basketball player); Johnny Bench (baseball player); Ellen Burstyn (actress); Aaron Carter (singer); Harry Chapin (singer/songwriter); Ed Hall (TV announcer); Ted Knight (actor); Tino Martinez (baseball player); Louis Prima (singer/bandleader); Tom Waits (singer/songwriter); Eli Wallach (actor)

December 8

♐ Sagittarius, 8

Those whose birthdays fall on this day lead an active lifestyle fueled by tons of nervous energy. You have big dreams and a huge appetite for living. There are, however, two distinct aspects to your basic nature. Enthusiastic and philosophical on the one hand, you are ambitious and determined on the other. Although your expansive, impulsive side longs to travel and socialize, the worker bee within thinks only of success.

The December 8th individual has a wonderful, acerbic wit and a dry sense of humor. When you are willing to take time out to play, you're the life of the party. Much of the time you are torn between a quest for meaning and a burning desire to accomplish something concrete and useful. With a multiplicity of interests and so many irons in the fire, you're constantly on the go. If you don't learn how to slow down and relax, you risk burning yourself out. You possess the wherewithal to be successful in any type of endeavor. However, in a creative or intellectual career, you can take advantage of your natural talent for teaching, writing, acting, music, athletics, or the law.

In love and romance, you blow hot and cold. You are warm-hearted and idealistic, but also critical of those who don't meet your high standards. You like excitement, variety, and independence, but you also want the emotional security of a permanent union.

On This Day:

At this time each year, the most ancient of the Shinto divinities, the solar goddess Amaterasu, is honored in temples throughout Japan. This day is also sacred to Astraea, the star maiden, a Greek goddess of justice who chose to live among humans. After Pandora's box was opened, Astraea was the last of the gods to abandon the Earth.

Born Today: Gregg Allman (rock star); Kim Basinger (actress); David Carradine (actor); Lee J. Cobb (actor); Sammy Davis, Jr. (singer/dancer/actor); Teri Hatcher (actress); Mary Stuart (Queen of Scots); Jim Morrison (rock star); Diego Rivera (artist); Maximilian Schell (actor); James Thurber (cartoonist/writer); Flip Wilson (comedian)

December 9

↗ Sagittarius, 9

The archer born on this day leads an intense inner life of romantic dreams and crusading ideals. The hallmark of your being is a strong missionary spirit. Your innate compassion and brooding sense of society's spiritual and material needs motivates you to help people improve their lives. In your humanitarian work, you are dedicated, selfless, and courageous. As a born fighter, you are not afraid of anything or anyone. Moreover, you absolutely refuse to tolerate injustice, discrimination, or inequity of any type.

The unification of intuition and imagination in December 9th individuals fuels their yearning to explore both the material universe and the internal world of fantasy and ideas. Mentally, you are clever and quick witted, yet also thoughtful and philosophical. Although you may not be quite as confident and secure as you appear, you know your own worth. Since you are inherently restless, your attention is easily diverted from your objectives. You function better when you're involved in several different projects at once. If your vocation lacks variety, you'll either lose interest and move on to something new or find ways to supplement your job with hobbies or volunteer work.

In a love relationship, you are passionate and caring. Inherently sociable, warm, and generous, you enjoy the intimacy of a committed union. Nevertheless, you do need occasional time on your own for contemplative withdrawal or worldly exploration.

On This Day:

Before the Spanish conquest of Mexico, the first day of the twenty-day festival known as the Descent of Rain (Atemozli), in honor of the Aztec mother goddess Tonantzin, was celebrated on this date. Tonantzin is the Lunar Lady and Queen of the Waters whose temple stood atop Tepeyac Hill, the current site of the shrine of the Virgin of Guadalupe.

Born Today: Beau Bridges (actor); Dick Butkus (football player/actor); Judy Dench (actress); Douglas Fairbanks, Jr. (actor); Kirk Douglas (actor/producer); Redd Foxx (comedian); Margaret Hamilton (actress); Buck Henry (screenwriter/actor); Emmett Kelly (clown); John Malkovich (actor); John Milton (poet); Dick Van Patten (actor)

December 10

♐ Sagittarius, 1

There aren't many couch potatoes celebrating birthdays on this date. Since going and doing are what you're about, you always seem to be on your way to or from somewhere else. You're constantly on the lookout for fresh, innovative ways to implement your many plans and ideas. You set such a fast pace that others often have to struggle just to keep up. With your impatient, impulsive nature, you tend to act first and think about it later. You live life on the edge, and you love every exciting minute.

The typical sociable, fun-loving person born on December 10 has numerous friends and admirers. Active both mentally and physically, you're as likely to be found defending your intellectual ideas and personal values as competing for athletic trophies and awards. You're a natural leader with a depth of vision and a swift grasp of the essentials of any situation. However, you are extremely restless and require a type of inspiration that is best provided by new faces and places. Once a project is up and running, you may decide to take off and leave it to others to finish what you've started.

In a romantic relationship, you're a passionate and inventive lover. But you have a way of falling in love with the idea of being in love. Your capacity for tolerating boredom is low, and you'll stick around only as long as your partner holds your interest.

On This Day:

On or around this date each year, Inuit hunters of the Arctic coastal regions of North America perform the centuries-old December Moon Ceremony. The observance begins with a series of purification rites, followed by a full-moon propitiation ritual for the souls of the animals that the participants have hunted and killed during the prior year.

Born Today: Dan Blocker (actor); Kenneth Branagh (actor/director); Susan Dey (actress); Emily Dickinson (poet); Cesar Franck (composer); William Lloyd Garrison (journalist/abolitionist); Chet Huntley (newscaster/TV co-anchor); Dorothy Lamour (actress); Dennis Morgan (actor); Ray Nance (jazz musician)

December 11

↗ Sagittarius, 2

The optimistic archer born on this day is not afraid to take chances when the rewards seem worth the risks. Inherently friendly and magnanimous, you like people and they like you. You're a kindhearted diplomat with a sparkling wit and a fiery spirit. Honest to the core, you still manage to tell it like it is without hurting anyone's feelings. You may sometimes feel uncertain about what you want to do in life. However, once you find a truly exciting project, your enthusiasm won't quit until your goal has been reached.

December 11th people, with their cheerful temperament and sincere concern for others, rarely fail to make a good impression. Blessed with a capacity for understanding all sides of an issue, you have a knack for combining intellectual reasoning with intuition, which accounts for many of your wise decisions. Your response to most problems and difficulties is calm and harmonious. While you may be easygoing, however, your Sagittarian independence keeps you from being overly influenced by other people's opinions. Although you listen to what everyone has to say, in the end you make your own decisions.

In an intimate relationship, you long for the emotional security of a committed partnership. But you also need freedom and independence. You get bored and restless if you stick close to home for too long. Your ideal mate is someone who understands the duality of your nature and supports or shares your love of travel and adventure.

On This Day:

The Netherlands festival of the Blowing of the Midwinter Horn, which takes place on this day, dates back more than two thousand years. Farmers around the country take out their birch-wood horns and blow them to scare away evil influences and announce the presence of Skadi, fur-clad goddess of winter and spirit of the north wind.

Born Today: Hector Berlioz (composer); Terri Garr (actress); John Kerry (U.S. senator); Fiorello LaGuardia (New York mayor/U.S. congressman); Brenda Lee (singer); Donna Mills (actress); Rita Moreno (actress/singer); Carlo Ponti (director); Gilbert Roland (actor); Susan Seidelman (director); Alexander Solzhenitsyn (writer)

December 12

↗ Sagittarius, 3

The freewheeling individuals whose birthdays fall on this date dislike feeling boxed in or tied down. Dull situations or boring company won't hold your attention for long. Your ultimate aim is to broaden your vision through study and travel. Physically as well as mentally alert and agile, you enjoy traveling as well as various outdoor activities, sports, and athletics. Your tendency to move from one place to another and from experience to experience is part and parcel of your continuous search for variety and change.

Those born on December 12 are quick witted, with exceptional communicative abilities that allow them get their ideas across swiftly and convincingly. You like learning new things and then sharing your newly acquired knowledge with others. Your flair for organization and promotion and your friendly, outgoing personality practically guarantee your success in advertising, marketing, or sales. Creativity, a keen sense of justice, and the ability to talk endlessly about your ideas and ideals could make you a fine lawyer, teacher, novelist, journalist, broadcaster, lecturer, actor, or politician.

In a romantic relationship, you are passionate, generous, and eager for love. However, it takes both intellectual and physical stimulation to keep you interested. Too much emotion scares you off. If an intimate union becomes cloying, you may go in search of greener, less restrictive pastures.

On This Day:

This is the feast day of Our Lady of Guadalupe. In 1531, on Tepeyac Hill north of Mexico City, an Indian named Juan Diego encountered the apparition of a beautiful lady. She told him to go to the bishop with her request that a shrine be built to her on that site. After the lady's image miraculously appeared on Juan Diego's cloak, the bishop agreed.

Born Today: Tracy Austin (tennis player); Bob Barker (TV game show host); Mayim Bialik (actress); Jennifer Connelly (actress); Sheila E. (singer); Connie Francis (singer); Cathy Rigby (gymnast); Edward G. Robinson (actor); Frank Sinatra (singer/actor); Dianne Warwick (singer); Joe Williams (jazz and blues singer)

December 13

Sagittarius, 4

Archers born on this day are practical idealists who see the large philosophical picture as well as the fundamental details. You're no nerdy academic, yet you are a perennial student who's always interested in learning new things. Your reputation is that of an obsessive planner and dedicated workaholic. Despite a low threshold for boredom, once you start something, you stick with it to the end. Consequently, you work quickly and efficiently to turn projects around as fast as possible.

December 13th individuals are excellent communicators. You have lots to say, and you're able to put your ideas across with relative ease. Although life is not all fun and games to you, you do have a lively and sometimes bawdy sense of humor. Your forte is the ability to bounce back from any setback. There's no obstacle that you can't surmount. When you get knocked down, you bounce back up more determined than ever. You yearn to do something useful for society, and in return you expect appreciation and significant financial compensation.

In love, you're steadfast and sincere and have less of a roving eye than many of your Sagittarian Sun sign counterparts. But your romantic dreams tend to create a gap between your idealism and everyday reality. You want to find true love, but few potential partners are able to live up to your high ideals.

On This Day:

This date is the Ides of December. It is also the beginning of the runic half-month of Jara. The rune Jara represents the union between the spiritual and temporal. This is also Saint Lucy's Day, or Little Yule. On this date, a candlelight festival is celebrated throughout Sweden. One daughter in each family wears a white dress with a red sash and a crown of candles on her head.

Born Today: Steve Buscemi (actor); Christie Clark (actress); John Davidson (singer/ TV game show host); Gustave Flaubert (writer); Jamie Foxx (actor); Ferguson Jenkins (baseball player); Carlos Montoya (flamenco guitarist); Archie Moore (boxer); Kenneth Patchen (poet); Christopher Plummer (actor); Dick Van Dyke (actor/comedian)

December 14

✐ Sagittarius, 5

The December 14th individual is a risk taker who plunges into life without a safety net. You think of existence as an adventure in which experience is more important than stability or security. Action oriented and concerned about the big picture, your go-go nature has little patience for small details. You're a doer, not a planner. When you come across an idea that feels good, helps someone, or adds beauty to the world, your adrenaline starts pumping, and you want to jump right in and get the ball rolling.

Optimism, enthusiasm, and exuberance are the hallmarks of your nature. You make a great cheerleader for your own goals and for the ambitions of others because you remain upbeat no matter what the circumstance. You have an open, jovial nature, a flair for organization, and a talent for advertising and promotion. December 14th people are sometimes referred to as the "traveling salespersons of the zodiac." However, life is not all fun and games to you. As a Sagittarian philosopher and truth seeker, you genuinely want to make the world a better place for everyone.

Emotionally, you're something of a paradox. Your relationships, even the romantic ones, are firmly grounded in friendship. You regard love as a glorious experience, yet your need for freedom can cause you to shy away from commitment. If you do decide to settle down, your depth of feeling for your loved ones may surprise you.

On This Day:

This is the feast day of Roman Catholic Saint John of the Cross. Despite a life of poverty and persecution, John was a compassionate mystic who lived by the belief that "where there is no love, put love—and you will find love." The Hopi Soyal Festival takes place on this day to honor the Blue Corn Maiden, Sakwa Mana, who participates in the festival carrying a tray of corn and spruce.

Born Today: Morey Amsterdam (comic); Jimmy Doolittle (aeronautical engineer/pilot/Air Force general); Patty Duke (actress); George VI (king of England); Michael Owen (soccer player); Nostradamus (seer/prophet), Cecil Payne (jazz musician); Lee Remick (actress); Charlie Rich (country singer); Margaret Chase Smith (U.S. congresswoman)

December 15

Archers celebrating birthdays on this date thrive on social interaction. Despite being ambitious and hard working, you value friendship and companionship more than either success or material possessions. Moreover, you do your best work when teamed with others. A born explorer, you particularly enjoy sharing the wonders of your journeys with those you love. Diplomacy is your forte, and you excel in negotiation. No matter what the problem, you'll come up with a compromise that pleases all concerned.

December 15th individuals are the archetypal Good Samaritans who refuse to give up on people. Your intellectual curiosity is insatiable, but when its focus turns to personal matters, you are sometimes accused of meddling in the affairs of others. You are not a long-term planner and prefer to "go with the flow." If something seems like a good idea at the moment, you jump in without thinking too much about where it may lead. You're probably best suited to an artistic or creative occupation that calms your restless spirit by capturing your imagination and challenging your intellect.

You love to party, and in all likelihood you enjoy an active social life. In an intimate relationship, you make a charming, sexy lover who is straightforward, affectionate, and sincere. You're also an extraordinarily romantic for a Sagittarian native. Since you tend to think in pairs, you may not feel complete without a partner at your side.

On This Day:

This is the first of seven Halcyon Days prior to the winter solstice when, according to legend, the halcyon bird creates a time of tranquility by calming the wind and waves. During this peaceful period, the kingfisher was able to lay her eggs in peace. A magical bird, the kingfisher is a symbol of the Greek goddess Alcyon, daughter of the wind king.

Born Today: Maxwell Anderson (playwright); Jeff Chandler (actor); Tim Conway (comedian); Barry Harris (jazz musician); Friedenstreich Hundertwasser (artist/architect); Don Johnson (actor); Nero (Roman emperor); Danny Richmond (jazz musician); Betty Smith (writer); Maurice H. F. Wilkins (molecular biologist)

December 16

♐ Sagittarius, 7

The extraordinary individuals born on this day have little use for established paradigms and conventional methods. Drawn to innovative ventures and progressive enterprises, you excel at tackling tricky problems and resolving them in previously untried ways. By using a combination of brainstorming, intuition, and imagination, you're able to pinpoint new possibilities that others miss. Aware that other people lack your insight, you feel compelled to share your philosophy with them, either verbally or indirectly through your art.

The scientific mentality of the person celebrating his or her birthday on December 16 is complemented by a truly artistic temperament. You're an unashamedly idealistic humanitarian and an eloquent, world-class communicator. Likeable, sincere, and outgoing, you know how to get your beliefs and ideals across to an audience. Your restless spirit abhors a vacuum, and you prefer excitement and adventure to security and stability. You're a typical Sagittarian in that you are fond of travel, change, and amusement. You tend to measure your successes in terms of creative accomplishments, not material gains. Nevertheless, between your pride in your work and your good luck, you're likely to garner both fame and fortune.

In relationships, you are passionate and loving, yet wary of making commitments that curb your ability to move around freely. Although no one will ever own you, a genuinely understanding partner may win your love and loyalty.

On This Day:

This day is sacred to the Sophia, goddess of wisdom. The ancient Jews revered her in the form of the Wise Bride of Solomon. The Greeks knew her as Athena, the goddess of wisdom and war. She was also Sapientia, Roman goddess of wisdom. In the Christian tradition, the veneration of Sophia continues in the Eastern Orthodox Church.

Born Today: Jane Austen (writer); Ludwig van Beethoven (composer); Benjamin Bratt (actor); Arthur C. Clark (writer); Noel Coward (playwright); Wassily Kandinsky (artist); Margaret Mead (cultural anthropologist); William "Refrigerator" Perry (football player); Leslie Stahl (TV news correspondent); Liv Ullmann (actress)

December 17

Archers celebrating birthdays on this date are an intriguing blend of the optimism, directness, and foresight of Sagittarius and the ambition, shrewdness, and practicality common to the number seventeen. Success comes to you though your own ideas and your ability to convince others of their viability. Your intuition gives you a sense of how things are likely to turn out, thus allowing you to chart the future course of events. Personal integrity is your strong point and helps you build a reputation for honesty and hard work. As a practical realist, you garner a good deal of responsibility. However, your shoulders are broad and more than capable of bearing the burden.

December 17th individuals have the courage and vitality to achieve any goal they set for themselves. You're both a doer and a thinker. A traveler at heart, your restless nature impels you to be either physically or mentally on the go at all times. With your boundless enthusiasm and inner fortitude, you have what it takes to succeed over the long haul. However, the reckless expenditure of energy can become a problem. You risk burning yourself out unless you learn how to kick back and relax.

Love and companionship are truly important to you, but you place intellectual rapport ahead of romance and sentiment. You enjoy your independence, but you'll remain loyal and committed to a partner who understands your need for personal freedom.

On This Day:

On this date in ancient times, the Roman god Saturn was honored with a one-week festival known as the Saturnalia. All the shops and schools were closed during this week of feasting, merriment, gambling, charades, and gift giving. The ceremonies started off with a sacrifice at the Temple of Saturn, followed by a huge public banquet.

Born Today: Erskine Caldwell (writer); Arthur Fiedler (conductor); Bob Guccione (magazine publisher); Mila Jovovich (supermodel); John Landau (artist); Mike Mills (rock star); Paracelsus (chemist/physician/alchemist); Bill Pullman (actor); William Safire (journalist); John Greenleaf Whittier (poet); Vanessa Zima (actress)

December 18

↗ Sagittarius, 9

L ike the brave knights that frequented King Arthur's Round Table, those born on this day are dedicated to fulfilling their life's mission with honor and high ideals. Your approach to both work and play is one of wholehearted involvement. Your strong point is your ability to see the big picture without overlooking the small details. Like other archers, those born on December 18 are courageous risk takers. Your eye for quality and lofty goals prompts you to stand up for the things you believe in. Investigative curiosity triggers your ventures into uncharted waters, and you're not afraid to go out on a limb in defense of an untried idea or project.

When you avoid scattering your energies, you're able to move mountains. Your understanding is exceptionally wide-ranging, because the root number nine includes the qualities of all the other numbers. With a basic nature that's a combination of intellectual, creative, and spiritual qualities, you sometimes try to be all things to all people. You care a great deal about your work, and it should give you the opportunity to express your creativity and originality.

You're a sociable, charismatic, sensitive Sagittarian with a chivalrous heart. You'd relish the chance to ride in and rescue your beloved from a desperately unhappy situation. However, once the dragon has been vanquished and you settle down into a humdrum daily routine, your interest may fade along with your enthusiasm.

On This Day:

The ancient Roman feast of Eponalia, a celebration of the Celtic goddess Epona, fell on this day, as does the Latvian Winter Festival in honor of the god Diev and the rebirth of the Sun. In the Philippines, the annual festival of Mesa de Gallo begins at sunrise. Parades of people take to the streets with all kinds of noisemakers that they use to frighten away evil spirits.

Born Today: Christina Aguilera (singer); Ty Cobb (baseball player); Ossie Davis (actor); Christopher Fry (playwright); Betty Grable (actress); Katie Holmes (actress); Paul Klee (artist); Brad Pitt (actor); Keith Richards (rock star); Roger Smith (actor); Steven Spielberg (producer/director); George Stevens (director)

December 19

The innovative, independent archer born on this day represents the quintessential pioneering spirit. Excitement, adventure, and advancement are what you seek. You're a born leader, and things always move ahead rapidly when you are in charge. As a natural executive, you like to be in the forefront of every action. Even when you're not in charge, you assume responsibility and take over wherever you can. Sometimes your aggressive temperament can get in your way. However, you're so self-confident and handle people with such ease that others automatically accept your authority.

December 19th individuals are often impulsive or precipitant in their actions. Your intense, gung-ho approach to getting things accomplished can limit your awareness of what other people are feeling. In your single-minded pursuit of a goal, idea, or ideal, your inclination is to rush full speed ahead. Human frailties are not something you understand well, and your totally open and frank approach does not always mesh well with the dispositions of more sensitive souls. Nevertheless, your dynamic personality and wide-ranging intellect hold a certain popular appeal that garners people's admiration and affection.

In a romantic relationship you are ardent, attentive, and loving for as long as you happen to be around. However, you are something of a romantic gypsy. You may be here today, but if your wonder-lust kicks in tomorrow, you could be gone in a flash.

On This Day:

The festival of Ophelia, in honor of Ops, goddess of the abundant harvest, was celebrated on this day in ancient Rome. On or around this date in India, the Hindu goddess Maranka Sankranti is venerated with sacred cleansing, blessing rituals, and offerings of sweet rice that take place during the three-day solstice and harvest festival known as Pongol.

Born Today: Jennifer Beals (actress); Marcel Cerdan (boxer); Bronislav Huberman (violinist); Al Kaline (baseball player); Richard Leakey (paleontologist); Alyssa Milano (actress); Tim Reed (actor); Fritz Reiner (conductor); Sir Ralph Richardson (actor); David Suskind (producer); Cicely Tyson (actress); Robert Urich (actor)

December 20

↗ Sagittarius, 2

The happy-go-lucky person born on this day has a cheerful nature and a sincere concern for friends and family. You excel at avoiding arguments, and when others disagree, you step up and assume the role of mediator. Your temperament is that of an artist, and you possess an incurably romantic streak that is likely to manifest creatively rather than personally. You're more intellectual than emotional, and you're able to take most annoyances with a grain of salt. An active social life is extremely important to you, and the good impression you make often proves an important asset in professional matters.

Those who celebrate birthdays on December 20 are inherently open hearted and open handed. Consequently, you set yourself up for many a disappointment. Yet you find consolation in your unshakable optimism and belief that everything usually works out for the best. Success comes to you in business or the professions through your sound reasoning abilities, accurate perceptions, strong powers of comparison, and balanced judgment. In the arts and entertainment, you weave a poetic spell that captivates your audience.

In an intimate relationship, you make an ardent, affectionate, generous partner. Despite being exciting and fun loving, you are also reliable and dependable. Although your freewheeling Sagittarian Sun sign yearns for adventure, your inner self prefers the security of a committed union.

On This Day:

In northern traditions, this night denotes the Eve of the Winter Solstice, a time to honor the Disir, a group of female divinities known as the Divine Grandmothers. Tonight is the Norse midwinter festival of Mother Night, or Modresnach, when dreams are thought to be prophetic and when people decorate pine trees to represent the tree of life.

Born Today: Jenny Agutter (actress); Billy Bragg (singer/songwriter); Peter Crisscoula (rock star); Irene Dunne (actress); Uri Geller (psychic); George Roy Hill (director); John Hillerman (actor); JoJo (singer); Max Lerner (political science writer); John Spencer (actor); Mitsuko Uchida (pianist); Robert Van der Graaf (nuclear physicist)

December 21

Those born on the Sagittarius/Capricorn cusp are the scholars of the zodiac. In your ongoing quest for truth and the meaning of life, you explore the physical world and the world of books, dreams, and imagination. You set out with no particular bias and take new experiences and ideas as they come. You are about action and leadership, yet have more patience and persistence than the typical archer. Since your goal is broadening your vision, you view existence as an ongoing adventure to be enjoyed and not hurried.

Life is not all fun and games to those born on December 21. Your gaze may be fixed on the far horizon, but you genuinely want to make the world a better place for yourself and others. In business and finance, you're naturally lucky and know how to sell yourself and your ideas. Despite your high spirits, you have a good grasp of reality. Everything you do is above board and rendered in an honorable manner. You aim for the top and will probably to get there aided by a mixture of idealism, faith in yourself, and practical good sense.

In love relationships, you're ardent and rather flirtatious. However, you are also open hearted in your affections and loyal in your attachments. Although you may be slow to make promises, when you do, you keep them.

On This Day:

Today is the Druidic festival of Alban Arthuan, or Arthur's Light. It's the traditional birthday of King Arthur, and money and gifts are bestowed on the poor. The Winter Solstice, or first day of winter (also known as Yule, Winter Rite, and Midwinter), is the time of new beginnings when pagans reflect on the past and formulate future plans.

Born Today: Andy Dick (comedian/actor); Phil Donahue (TV talk show host); Chris Evert (tennis player); Jane Fonda (actress); Samuel L. Jackson (actor); Kiefer Sutherland (actor); Florence Griffith Joyner (sprinter); Joe Paterno (football coach); Ray Romano (comedian/actor); Joseph Stalin (Russian dictator); Frank Zappa (rock star)

December 22

♑ Capricorn, 4

People born on the Sagittarius/Capricorn cusp are ambitious, determined, and dedicated to achieving their goals. More of a scholar than other Capricorns, you use your knowledge to help you understand the world. Although you seek the true meaning of life, you're also practical, realistic, and careful not to get carried away by your ideals. As a doer, thinker, and worker, you lead an active lifestyle driven by huge amounts of nervous energy. If you cannot learn to relax, you may risk burning yourself out. You have a wonderful, acerbic wit, and when you take time out to play, you can be the life of the party.

Those celebrating birthdays on this date have a multiplicity of interests that can help them gain success and acclaim in materialistic and humanitarian endeavors. While the path is not always smooth, your intense desire to triumph fuels your perseverance. You are enormously persuasive and are pragmatic enough to make your mark as an entrepreneur in the business world, particularly in those areas related to management, advertising, promotion, publishing, sales, or travel. Creatively, you may have the requisite talent for writing, broadcasting, art, acting, or music.

In your personal relationships you're passionate and loving, but rather more freewheeling and adventurous than the average Capricorn. Your best bet for remaining committed and devoted is in a union with a partner who is understanding and provides genuine intellectual rapport.

On This Day:

On or near this date, Jews begin the annual celebration of Chanukah, the Festival of Lights. In 162 B.C.E., Syrians profaned the altar of the temple in Jerusalem, provoking a rebellion. A new altar was constructed, but there was not enough ritual oil to consecrate it. Miraculously, the small amount of oil left in the lamp burned for eight days.

Born Today: Dame Peggy Ashcroft (actress); Barbara Billingsley (actress); Hector Elizondo (actor); Steve Garvey (baseball player); Maurice Gibb (rock star/songwriter); Robin Gibb (rock star/songwriter); Lady Bird Johnson (U.S. first lady); Gene Rayburn (actor); Diane Sawyer (TV journalist/talk show host)

December 23

VS Capricorn, 5

Those celebrating birthdays today have the uncanny ability to foresee impending possibilities without losing sight of tried and tested principles. Although you hold yourself to traditional standards of conduct, you recognize the inherent value in innovative ideas. Your fluency with language and ease of self-expression assure that you're never at a loss for words. You assimilate knowledge quickly and use what you've learned to convince others of the validity of your arguments.

On an emotional level, December 23rd individuals tend to be changeable and contradictory. You can be high spirited one moment and then suddenly shift gears and become solemn the next. Nevertheless, you know how to reach people and draw them to you. Moreover, you like being involved with the public, and your sincerity and genuine interest in others make you a much sought-after companion. Clever, shrewd, and ambitious, you are well suited to just about any intellectual, scientific, or athletic occupation. With your wonderful imagination and talent as a speaker and writer, you could find your niche working in the media or the arts.

In a romantic union, you yearn for love, yet appear cool and aloof until you feel secure in the other person's company. You might put off commitment until you're certain that a relationship is right for you, but when you do make a promise, you stick to it.

On This Day:

Today is the "missing," or intercalary, day in the Celtic Tree Calendar. Known as The Nameless Day, it is referred to as the "Secret of the Unhewn Stone." Since it falls outside the thirteen-month Celtic year, its symbolism is the unshaped potential in all things. Although not ruled by any tree, the Druids linked The Nameless Day to mistletoe.

Born Today: Chet Baker (jazz musician/singer); Robert Bly (poet); Jose Greco (dancer); Cory Haim (actor); Paul Hornung (football player); Bob Kurland (basketball player); Susan Lucci (actress); Connie Mack (baseball manager/owner); Joseph Smith (founder of the Mormon religion); Eddie Vedder (rock star); Dick Webber (bowler)

December 24

♑ Capricorn, 6

The individual born on this day is as purposeful and aware of personal goals as other goats. Nevertheless, the competitive side of your nature is considerably softened by your tact and spirit of cooperation. Essentially a positive person, you have an almost inspirational faith in your own infallibility. You may be a bit eccentric at times, but you're always amiable and sympathetic to the needs of others. Despite your busy-busy lifestyle, you somehow manage to find time to engage in social pleasantries and pursue cultural and artistic interests.

Those celebrating birthdays today dislike direct conflict or hostile situations. Capable of exercising sound and impartial judgment, you instinctively do whatever is necessary to preserve peace and order. Moreover, you have a knack for spotting the flaws in a plan before it's implemented, thereby avoiding serious problems. Your fondest desire is to get ahead in the world and assume responsibility, especially in a professional or business setting. Career interests are considerably enhanced by your ability to bring others around to your point of view through persuasiveness and outright charm.

You are an affectionate, warm, sensual lover and a generous, reliable mate. Relating comes naturally to you, and you probably don't feel complete without the companionship of a loving partner. However, it takes more than love and romance to hold your interest. You want someone who shares your life's goals and your strong sense of purpose.

On This Day:

In old England, the Yule log was lit on Christmas Eve. Although the holiday is less popular in modern England, throughout the rest of Europe its significance is greater in many places than that of Christmas Day. In some lands, Christmas gifts are exchanged. In others, the most important of the holiday meals takes place on this night.

Born Today: Kit Carson (frontiersman/scout/U.S. Army general); Mary Higgins Clark (writer); Michael Curtiz (director); Ava Gardner (actress); Howard R. Hughes (industrialist/ aviator/producer); Jan Ramon Jiminez (poet); Emanuel Lasker (chess player); Ricky Martin (singer/actor); Ryan Seacrest (actor/TV show host)

December 25

♑ Capricorn, 7

The standard of behavior among goats born on Christmas Day is very high, and they patently refuse to compromise on principle. Even so, you're usually able to find a way around a sticky situation that satisfies all concerned. Despite being a private person and a good listener, you thoroughly enjoy an interesting conversation. However, you clam up when asked about your own life. You tend to express yourself in quiet ways, yet you somehow manage to communicate approval or disapproval without saying word.

December 25th people need to be emotionally involved in their work, or they begin to lose interest and their energy stagnates. Whatever you do, you do with total commitment. Your personality is a unique blend of practicality, seriousness, and ambition on the one hand, and moody restlessness on the other. You have a rather solitary character that is much given to private contemplation. When you feel misunderstood or unappreciated, you tend to go off by yourself to nurse your wounds. Although people may think of you as a reasonable person, it's hard for them to persuade you that you're wrong about anything.

Your deepest desire is to love and be loved, but you are extremely cautious where your emotions are involved. You prefer holding back to appearing needy or vulnerable. When you decide to trust another person enough to let down your guard, you make a caring, sensuous, dependable partner.

On This Day:

The name of the Christmas holiday comes from the words "Cristes Maesse," or Christ's Mass. For Christians around the world, this day commemorates the birth of Jesus Christ. Historians date the first celebration of this holiday to Rome in 336 C.E. In America, today is a major holy day as well as one of the merriest days of the entire year.

Born Today: Clara Barton (nurse/founder of the American Red Cross); Humphrey Bogart (actor); Jimmy Buffet (singer/songwriter); Cab Calloway (bandleader); Carlos Castaneda (anthropologist/writer); Annie Lennox (singer/songwriter); Sir Isaac Newton (mathematician); Rod Serling (screenwriter/director); Sissy Spacek (actress)

December 26

♑ Capricorn, 8

Goats born on this day are motivated by a deep sense of obligation to society. Despite your inherent respect for law and tradition, the spirit of defiance and rebellion is strong in you. Courageous enough to confront issues others shy away from, you are an outspoken critic of deceit and deception. Your inner nature is rather rigid and unbending. You demand truth and decency and reject anything you consider unjust or unethical.

December 26th individuals have unlimited potential for success as long as they're engaged in work that they love. While you long to make the world a better place, you are also ambitious for yourself and single-minded in your desire to achieve your personal goals. Beneath your serious outer demeanor, you have an incongruous, offbeat sense of humor that takes people by surprise. When your sharp wit surfaces, it often sends those around you into fits of uncontrollable laughter. Reliability is the key to your sterling character, and people can depend on you to do exactly what you say you are going to do.

In love, you are naturally reserved and can be slow to warm up to someone. However, when you do, you are passionate, generous, loyal, and demanding. You have a great deal of pride and a rather fragile ego that requires constant reassurance in the form of admiration, respect, and appreciation. Your standards are exceptionally high, and you insist that your mate or partner live up to them.

On This Day:

Boxing Day is observed in Canada, the United Kingdom, and many other countries. The name comes from the old custom of servants and other functionaries carrying boxes for Christmas gratuities or bonuses. Kwanzaa, or "first fruit," a modern, seven-day-long celebration by African-American families of their heritage and ancestry, begins today.

Born Today: Steve Allen (comedian/TV host/composer/writer); Carlton Fisk (baseball player); Alan King (comedian/actor); Henry Miller (writer); Ozzie Smith (baseball player); Phil Spector (music producer); Mao Tse-tung (Chinese Communist Party leader/dictator); John Walsh (TV host/victims' advocate); Richard Widmark (actor)

December 27

♑ Capricorn, 9

The demeanor of those celebrating birthdays on this day can give the impression of great forcefulness. However, you actually have two distinct sides to your personality. You're a great deal more intuitive and receptive to outside influences than the average goat, and you're less likely to be driven by a desire for power, money, or status. The practical, ambitious side of your nature is tempered by humanitarian concerns and compassion for the problems of others. You refuse to tolerate injustice and can usually be found in the front lines of any crusade against discrimination and inequity.

The highly intuitive goat born on this date has a feel for the truth about people and situations. Your logical mind makes it easy for you to assimilate theoretical knowledge, and your artistic temperament gives you your strong creative impulse. A knack for understanding the public mind keeps you from trying to sell people things they aren't buying. Your wide-ranging capabilities are a mixture of intellect and creativity, and your willingness to work hard means that you can succeed in various career areas, including education, science, politics, the media, literature, art, drama, and music.

You are tender-hearted and something of a romantic. In love, you're loyal and devoted, with a humorous, whimsical side that makes you fun to be with. You may be less serious than the typical Capricorn native, but you're just as reliable and protective.

On This Day:

The birthday of Freya, the Norse goddess of fertility, love, and beauty, falls on this day. Also Saint John's Day, this is the feast day of Roman Catholic Saint John the Apostle. John was called by Jesus to be an apostle in the first year of the ministry. He is known as the "beloved disciple" because he was the only one who did not forsake Christ at the moment of the crucifixion.

Born Today: John Amos (actor); Marlene Dietrich (actress/singer); Gerard Depardieu (actor); Sydney Greenstreet (actor); Bunk Johnson (jazz musician); Oscar Levant (pianist/composer); William Masters (sex therapist/researcher); Louis Pasteur (chemist/bacteriologist); Cokie Roberts (TV news anchor/journalist)

December 28

♑ Capricorn, 1

The purposeful goat born on this day has a strong drive to succeed and is willing to work very hard to insure that it happens. An extremely vital, self-sufficient person with a dynamic personality, you believe in yourself and in your ability to accomplish your goals. There is a shrewd quality in your nature that suggests you're cognizant of the ways of the world and can deal with them effectively. No matter what the situation, you may be counted upon to be tactfully agreeable. You understand when it pays to be assertive and when it is better to hold your peace.

In business, December 28th people have a knack for combining the shrewd, practical mentality and organizational ability of a tycoon with the enterprising spirit and innovative ideas of an entrepreneur. Your forte is the ability to get a project off the ground quickly and efficiently. You like being in charge of an undertaking because you usually believe that you're the one most qualified to run the show. Your idea of a diplomatic approach to problems is to speak softly and carry a big stick, and it usually works.

Although you appear controlled on the surface, at heart you're a genuine romantic who is warmer and more passionate than other goats. You are loyal and dependable, but you can be so moody and demanding that your mate may find you difficult to live with.

On This Day:

During the Middle Ages, the Feast of Fools was a very popular holiday that captured the light-hearted spirit of the Roman Saturnalia. On that day, normal roles were often reversed, with masters waiting on their servants. The usually puritanical style of reverence for the Christmas season was replaced with frolicking, frivolity, and pleasure.

Born Today: Lew Ayres (actor); Arthur Eddington (astronomer); Earl "Fatha" Hines (jazz musician/composer); Nigel Kennedy (violinist); Hildergarde Knef (actress/writer); Manuel Puig (writer); Dame Maggie Smith (actress); Steve Van Buren (football player); Denzel Washington (actor); Woodrow Wilson (U.S. president)

December 29

♑ Capricorn, 2

Those born on this date are sociable and like having people around them. Although you seem more laid back than other Capricorns, you're just as willing to work hard for what you want. Despite your active, busy life, you manage to make time for your social, cultural, and artistic interests. You dislike conflict and hostile situations, and your ability to preserve the peace and smooth ruffled feathers is appreciated by everyone. Your forte is your facility for controlling people and situations without appearing domineering.

December 29th individuals have a tendency to think in pairs. Friendship and companionship are among your top priorities, and a loving union is your ultimate goal. Self-dramatizing and communicative, you win people over to your way of thinking because they can't resist your charm and charisma. Blessed with intelligence and the gift of gab, you enjoy holding court and expounding on your latest ideas and inspirations. Naturally artistic, you love the limelight, a fondness that is equaled only by your desire for material success. Your creative talents are particularly well suited to fields in the arts and entertainment.

You may be looking for the ideal love, but in the meantime you enjoy the company of intelligent, creative, successful people. If and when you find your soul mate, you'll expect him or her to fulfill all your romantic dreams. You have a lot to give, and you expect no less in return.

On This Day:

On this date, the ancient Greeks celebrated the Day of the Nymphs in honor of Andromeda, Ariadne, and Artemis, as well as the Haloa, a winter fertility festival to venerate Demeter, Dionysus, and the Eleusinian mysteries. In some parts of China, offerings are made to the gods at an annual festival of peace and spiritual renewal.

Born Today: Pablo Casals (cellist/conductor); Ted Danson (actor); Marianne Faithfull (singer/songwriter); Fred Hanson (pole vaulter); Andrew Johnson (U.S. president); Gelsey Kirkland (dancer); Jude Law (actor); Viveca Lindfors (actress); Mary Tyler Moore (actress); Laffit Pincay, Jr. (jockey); Jon Voight (actor)

December 30

♑ Capricorn, 3

People born on this day exude a type of youthful exuberance not typically associated with Capricorn natives. A bubbling fountain of energy and vitality, you communicate your enthusiasm to others with ease. Mental curiosity stimulates your interest in learning and provides you with a great deal of fascinating and useful information. A good planner and organizer, you're capable of swiftly assimilating visionary ideas and turning them to practical uses.

Considering the outwardly glib, witty personalities of those born on December 30, it's rather surprising that these Capricorns are actually quite serious and ambitious underneath. Sometimes you come off as if you didn't have a care in the world. On other occasions, you worry too much and allow your anxieties to assume undue proportions. Yet, no matter what happens, you are never at a loss for words. Your intense curiosity, facility of expression, and talent as a speaker and writer can lead to a successful career in the media, the arts, education, or science. In business, you could shine in sales, advertising, promotion, or product development. Many well-known sports champions were born on this date as well.

With others, you are very companionable and relish the company of creative, intelligent people. In love, you seek a stable, lasting relationship. Although you want freedom of movement for yourself, you expect absolute loyalty and devotion from your mate.

On This Day:

At the end of the Christmas season, a few English villages still put on mumming plays, a form of drama developed in seventeenth century England and based on the legend of Saint George and the dragon. The plays are closely associated with the medieval sword dance, which symbolizes the reawakening of the earth from the death of winter.

Born Today: Bo Diddley (rock and roll singer/songwriter); Rudyard Kipling (writer); LeBron James (basketball player); Sandy Koufax (baseball player); Matt Lauer (TV talk show host); Jack Lord (actor); Bert Parks (TV game show host); Patti Smith (singer/songwriter); Tracey Ullman (comedienne/actress); Tiger Woods (golfer)

December 31

♍ Capricorn, 4

Beneath the serious, yet charismatic, demeanor of the goat celebrating a birthday today, there is a protective, caring soul who feels duty bound to do whatever is necessary to aid those in need. Known for your ability to hang in and see things through to the end, you are extremely persistent in pursuit of your objectives. Once committed to an idea, project, or cause, you apply yourself with total dedication. There are no quitters born on this date, and you can be counted on not to balk or run off at the first sign of trouble.

The dramatic December 31st individual seeks attention and basks in the warmth of the spotlight. Despite your vibrant personality, there are actually two distinct sides to your nature. On the one hand, you're often plagued by pessimism and melancholy. On the other, you're known for your audacious charm and the delicious, offbeat sense of humor that keeps everyone around you in stitches. You want it all: wealth, fame, and status. You will almost certainly get it too, because you have the grit and determination to make it big in just about any profession that interests you.

You need security and stability in a love relationship. You are passionate, generous, and loyal, but you're also demanding. Your fragile ego requires constant reassurance in the form of admiration and appreciation. Although you have a lot to give, you expect as least as much in return.

On This Day:

New Year's Eve celebrations begin on this day. Hogmanay, or "First Footing," is still celebrated in many parts of England and Scotland, where revelers hold parties, set off fireworks, ring bells, and make New Year's resolutions. At the stroke of midnight, the front doors of all the homes are opened to permit the entry of good luck in the new year.

Born Today: Barbara Carrera (actress); John Denver (singer/songwriter); Sir Anthony Hopkins (actor); Val Kilmer (actor); Ben Kingsley (actor); George C. Marshall (U.S. Army general/initiator of the Marshall Plan); Henri Matisse (artist); Sarah Miles (actress); Bebe Neuwirth (actress); Odetta (singer); Donna Summer (singer)

Acknowledgments

A special thanks to my incomparable agent, Al Zuckerman, who makes it all possible, and, at Fair Winds Press, to my publisher, Holly Schmidt, for her faith in this project from the very beginning, and my editor, Ellen Phillips, for her patience, encouragement, and unremitting support.

About the Author

Phyllis Vega is an astrologer, numerologist, and tarot reader and has been a New Age counselor for more than three decades. She is the author of *Power Tarot* and *Sydney Omarr's Astrology, Love, Sex, and You*, as well as four other books on divination. She lives in Miami, Florida.

Index

H

Halcyon Days, 451
Halloween, 399
Hara Ke Day, 141
Harvest Moon Festival, 427
Hathor Day, 329
Hecate Festival, 313
Heimdall Festival, 363
Hemera Festivals, 260
Hengest Festival, 385
Hera and Zeus Celebration, 140
Heraclia Festival, 321
Hercules Invictus Festival, 312
Hi Matsuri Festival, 390
Hiketeria, 180
Hilaria, 155
Hildegard of Bingen Day, 351
Hindu Festival of Durga, 340
Hocktide Festival, 173
Hogmanay, 467
Holi Festival, 146
Horus Day, 280
Hukuli Dance, 93
Husband's Day, 83

I

Ice Saint Days, 209
Ides of December, 449
Ides of March, 145
Iduna Day, 150
Ilmatar Feast Day, 326
Imbolic Festival, 99
Incan Festival of the Sun, 248
Inti Raymi, 256
Ishtar Festival, 186

J

Jana Festival, 73
January birthdays, 63–95
Janus Festival, 65, 73, 160
John Barleycorn Celebration, 294
July birthdays, 265–297

June birthdays, 231–262
Junonalia, 137
Jupiter the Thunderer Day, 335

K

Kachina Dances, 293
Kalends of January, 65
Kalends of March, 131
Kalevala Day, 126
Kallyntaria Festival, 218
Kan-name-Sai, 384
Kermesse Festival, 375
King Frost Day, 102
Knut Day, 276
Kronia Festival, 277
Kukulcan Day, 423
Kwan Yin Festival, 95, 158, 169
Kwanzaa, 462

L

Lady Godiva Day, 302
Lady of Fatima, 211
Laghnasadh Feast, 301
Lagu Day, 193
Lakon, 337
Lakshimi Puja Festival, 364
Lammas Festival, 301
Last Chance Day, 430
Latvian Winter Festival, 454
Leap Year's Day, 127
Lemuria, 207
Lenaia, 67
Leo
  birthdays, 289–322
  character/personality, 29
  color, 29
  elements, 19
  gemstone, 29
  metal, 29
  myth, 30
  planetary ruler, 29
  qualities, 19
  relationships, 29–30

  Sun Sign Chart, 18
  symbol, 29
Lesser Eleusinian Mysteries, 99
Lesser Panathenaea, 149
Li Ch'un, 105
Liberalia, 157
Libertas Festival, 177
Libra
  birthdays, 357–390
  character/personality, 33
  color, 33
  elements, 19
  gemstone, 33
  metal, 33
  myth, 34
  planetary ruler, 33
  qualities, 19
  relationships, 33–34
  Sun Sign Chart, 18
  symbol, 33
Litha Festival, 253
Little Yule Day, 449
Loch-mo-Naire Day, 304
Loch Ness Monster Day, 288
Loki Day, 297
Loy Krathog Day, 411
Luckiest Day of the Year, 278
Luna Festival, 161
Lunantishees Festival, 413
Lupercalia Feast, 113
Lychnapsia, 312

M

Maat Day, 271
Mabon ap Modron Day, 156
Magalesia Mater, 168
Maia Day, 199
Maidens of the Four Directions, 337
Makahiki Festival, 421
Makara-Sankranti, 76
Manes Festival, 324
Maranka Sankranti Festival, 455
March birthdays, 129–161